HERMAN HOLLERITH

HERMAN HOLLERITH

Forgotten Giant of Information Processing

Geoffrey D. Austrian

COLUMBIA UNIVERSITY PRESS
NEW YORK   1982

204950

Library of Congress Cataloging in Publication Data

Austrian, Geoffrey.
  Herman Hollerith, forgotten giant of information processing.

  Includes bibliographical references and index.
  1. Hollerith, Herman.   2. Electronic data
processing—Biography.   I. Title.
QA76.2.H64A97   001.6′092′4   [B]   81-7752
ISBN 0-231-05146-8   AACR2

Columbia University Press
New York   Guildford, Surrey

Copyright © 1982 Columbia University Press
All rights reserved
Printed in the United States of America

Printed on permanent and durable acid-free paper.

Book designed by Ken Venezio.

To my mother, Beryl S. Austrian,
who also broke the mold.

Contents

Preface

The use of computers is taken so much for granted today that it would be difficult to envision our modern society without them. They are used to simulate the actions of our economy, make long-range weather forecasts, land planes at busy airports, and monitor the heartbeat, blood pressure, and other vital signs of patients in hospital intensive care units. We carry pocket calculators, costing a few dollars, that employ the circuitry that computers use. Advances in the microelectronic technology computers use are so rapid that the cost of computing has fallen by some 15 to 20 percent a year, leading to a hypergrowth industry, composed of hundreds of firms, that tends to render its own products obsolete within a handful of years. The velocity of progress is such that it allows little time for introspection, for a recognition that many of the ideas behind modern data processing systems date back to earlier times, to inventors such as British mathematician Charles Babbage, who tried unsuccessfully to build calculating machines organized very much like today's computers.

Standing like a giant among these pioneers, but almost totally unknown, is the American inventor Herman Hollerith, the subject of this book.

Where does an industry's fledgling technology come from? What needs does it seek to fill? How do its customs and practices evolve? Who are its first customers? What determines the early uses for its products? By what means is its equipment developed? How is it sold, installed, and serviced? More fundamentally, what must take place for a major new industry to be born?

Working in the electromechanical technology of his day, Herman Hollerith answered many of these questions for the early data processing industry, just as surely as did Henry Ford, Alexander Graham Bell, and Thomas Alva Edison for their respective fields. Hollerith's pioneering punched card tabulating machines made it possible for the first time for government and business to process large amounts of information in an efficient, economic, and timely way—to act on the basis of current facts, as one of his associates put it, before they became ancient history.

Hollerith's basic equipment—his punches, tabulators, and sorters—are as crude, compared to modern computers, as the first "cats-whisker" radio receivers are to today's radio and television sets. In retrospect, his inventions may be different in *kind*, as well as in degree, from today's computers. Yet, born while Lincoln was President, Hollerith left behind a profitable business embodying a viable technology. Refined, added to, and improved by others over the years, it became part of the sure stream that flowed into the development of the first electronic computers. Similarly, the uses he established for his machines, such as inventory control and sales analysis, became the bread-and-butter jobs for the new electronic machines when they came along. In the course of his business, Hollerith set down the beginnings of an industry not only in the United States but in many countries overseas. And many of the customers that he convinced to try his equipment remain among the most innovative users of data processing equipment today. The familiar punched card that Hollerith settled on as a practical medium for holding information nearly a hundred years ago—but never claimed to invent—is becoming increasingly obsolete today. But when cultural anthropologists are sifting through the remnants of our civilization a thousand years from now, they may well fasten upon it as a hallmark of our age.

Why is Hollerith virtually unknown, even in his own country? Part of the answer lies in the character of the man. He was devoted to his work, his family, and little else. Intensely private, he eschewed the use of advertising, and even of salesmen, to promote his machines. Like Babbage, he was also embittered by his unfortunate experiences with his own government and, possibly for this reason, withdrew further into his private world. Finally, he sold his business in 1911 to a small company, later to be renamed IBM. Under the forceful leadership of Thomas J. Watson, it would

soon become celebrated throughout the world, and, without in-
tending to, it would eclipse its early beginnings.

Hollerith's life raises questions that go beyond the scope of this
book. Is there still a place for highly individualistic, strong-willed,
and even eccentric individuals in a society that appears to em-
phasize "getting along" and functioning as "a member of the
team"? Would his career, and those of other inventive go-getters,
still be possible in a closely regulated society that seems to value
short-term security as much as risk taking and the chance for
material gain? In today's science-based technologies, where the
development and manufacture of new products often calls for the
joint efforts of hundreds of engineers and technologists, is there
still a place for the old-fashioned inventor-entrepreneur? Or are
such characters to be relegated to the movies and the depths of
the national psyche?

The author holds the optimistic view that many creative, in-
dependent-minded individuals are, in fact, at work today in both
large and small organizations. But in a world replete with problems
that cry out more than ever for innovation, there is an urgent
need for a new social and organizational climate that gives greater
scope and reward to creative effort. If Herman Hollerith's example
and career are obsolete in modern terms, the question may still
be asked: what kinds of individuals will take his place?

Acknowledgments

Like many other things in life, this book came about through a happy combination of circumstances. Several years after joining IBM, I was asked to gather background materials for the New York City Mayor's Office in connection with an appearance by Mayor Robert F. Wagner at IBM Day at the 1964 New York World's Fair. In the course of this research, I looked into the city's use of IBM machines over the years. I discovered that in the 1920s and before, the devices were called Hollerith machines. Who was Herman Hollerith? And was the modern-day emergence of the computer industry foreshadowed, in part, by what this little-known figure had done many years before?

The question was filed away until 1968, when, again by chance, I met theatrical producer Charles Hollerith, Jr. Was he related to Herman Hollerith? The answer was "yes," and this grandson of the inventor generously provided introductions to his family.

This book would not have been possible without the thoughtful and generous help of the Hollerith family. I am indebted to Charles Hollerith, a successful inventor-entrepreneur of the old school. After two lengthy interviews, this charming gentleman asked why the book was not being written about him. A good question—one should have been. Herman Hollerith, Jr., also an engineer, was rumored to have his father's ferocious temper. When I visited him in Oxford, Maryland, however, he turned out to be an interested participant and generous host. The impression left by this family member who most closely resembled his father convinced me that Herman Hollerith was a more complex and many-sided character than I at first believed.

I owe a special debt to Virginia Hollerith, who handled with skill, patience, and responsiveness the onerous chores of family historian. With her sisters Lucia and Nan, she made my many visits to the inventor's Washington home, and a trip to his Virginia farm, both rewarding and pleasurable. Virginia and Nan answered countless questions over the years, turned up new leads, and caught blunders in the final manuscript.

Thanks are due to other members of the family. Lucia Lefferts provided information on the family's roots in Germany and some unusual photographs of her grandfather. Richard Hollerith supplied articles I would otherwise have missed. Hermann Brunn, a retired designer with the Ford Motor Company, furnished background on Hollerith's mother's family. Otto and Joachim Hollerith, members of the German branch of the family, sent little-known information. An unusual perspective was given by Madeline and J. George Hollerith, niece and nephew of the inventor. They never knew their famous uncle, but their description of their father, George Hollerith, revealed that the brothers shared many traits and characteristics thought to belong uniquely to their uncle.

While the family deserves much of the credit for providing me with insights on Herman Hollerith, they are in no way responsible for any errors and misinterpretations, which are my own. I deeply regret that a number of the family members mentioned have passed away and will not be able to see the book to which they so amply contributed.

A second major debt is owed to IBM. In 1972, the company became interested in encouraging the writing of a book on Herman Hollerith. Recognizing that I had such a project already under way, they arranged for a generous six-month leave and granted access to major portions of the company archives. Without this help, the required research could never have been done and many valuable sources would have remained beyond my reach. Special thanks go to Dean R. McKay, Jane Cahill Pfeiffer, Chester B. Hansen, and Arnold Lerner, who helped arrange the author's leave, and to James B. O'Connell, who followed the project through its various stages. It is not often that any company will give an author, much less one of its own employees, a virtually free hand in delving into its early history. Yet, IBM did just that—

without trying to influence the final product. I appreciate the measure of trust, as well as the fact that IBM continued to furnish me with a livelihood while I worked over many years to complete the book on my own time.

Retired IBM employees made invaluable contributions. Harold C. Christensen and John C. McPherson shed light on the early Watson years. Eugene Saber wrote of marketing to the Russians in the 1930s. Joseph Langley, who went to work for Hollerith at age thirteen, provided the first-hand recollections of one who was there. IBM Fellow Dr. Herman Goldstine, one of the real computer pioneers, pointed to fascinating parallels between Hollerith and Charles Babbage, the noted British mathematician.

I spent an especially rewarding day with F. Steele Blackall, III, president of Taft-Peirce, which manufactured Hollerith's equipment for many years. Mrs. Alexander D. Shaw described her father, Otto Braitmeyer. Dr. Uta Merzbach, curator of the mathematical instruments at the Smithsonian, enlarged my understanding of Hollerith's inventions.

Skilled librarians, who will never be replaced by computer, were a *sine qua non.* Oliver W. Holmes guided me through the National Archives. Young H. Quick of Western Electric and Harley Holden of Harvard helped to turn up previously undiscovered materials. Don Kenney of the IBM Archiver was unfailingly helpful. Thanks also go to former Columbia students Richard Ericson and John Bleinaier for their fine translations.

John D. Moore, director of Columbia University Press, immediately recognized the historical value of the project. However, he made me toe the mark by responding to several tough-minded critiques before accepting the manuscript for publication. Especially valuable were knowledgeable comments by Thomas M. Smith, professor of the history of science at the University of Oklahoma. I am also grateful to my copy editor, Mimi Koren, for improving the final manuscript. In addition, Albert Z. Carr offered expert editorial advice at the outset of the project. Adrian Murphy drew on extensive business and professional knowledge to improve the manuscript. John C. McPherson and Claire Stegmann also caught lapses in the final product.

Any long-term project such as this exacts a toll on those close to it. I thank my wife, Sonia. Only she and I can appreciate the extent of her many contributions. Thanks also to Susan and Sarah, who probably cannot remember when their father was not working on this book.

*Many ingenious minds labour in the throes of invention, until at length
the master mind, the strong practical man, steps forward, and straightway
delivers them of their idea, applies the principle successfully, and the thing
is done.*

Samuel Smiles, Self-Help, *pp. 28–29*

*. . . if we could get together all of the clippings . . . letters, etc., and have a
good writer go over the proposition with you . . . he could write a very
interesting story about the tabulating machine and the man who invented
it.*

*Thomas J. Watson
to Herman Hollerith, February 7,
1918 (IBM Archives)*

The final test of a going economy is the creativeness *it evokes. Few systems
in history have attracted so much talent and put it to use.*

Max Lerner
America as a Civilization, *p. 273*

1

Discovering the Census Problem

"There ought to be a machine."

Arriving in Washington, D.C., in the fall of 1879 to work as a special agent in the U.S. Census of 1880, nineteen-year-old Herman Hollerith went through a personal transformation. Gone was the boyish look and sparse mustache of the senior class photo from Columbia College School of Mines. A formal portrait, taken within a year, captures a dashing figure in tight black leather gloves, handsome frock coat and top hat, sporting the confident handlebar mustache of a man about town. Not only did he plunge eagerly into his work at the Census Office—at the end of the year his $600 annual salary was raised by a third for superior efficiency. Soon, word of his unsuspected facility for leading the German, a form of square dance, spread through Georgetown parlors.

The Census that he had come to work on would be different, its superintendent General Francis Amasa Walker had assured the Congress. Following the recommendations of a commission, Congress had for the first time removed the special inquiries, such as Hollerith was assigned to, from the hands of politically picked enumerators. Walker had informed the Congress that previous statistics relating to mining, fisheries, agriculture, manufactures, and many other matters of social and industrial interest had often been discreditable and even disgraceful. According to Walker, a journalist, lawyer, economist, and son of a leading economist, the new census would be different. It would be the lively pulse-taking of a nation.

Hollerith's post as special agent was described as one requiring "not only technical knowledge, but high scientific training and wide observation." This was an impressive standard for a pupil whose early education had gotten off to a less than auspicious start. At nine, he had bolted public school when time for spelling drill arrived and had adamantly refused to return. But other than a life-long sensitivity to a supposed weakness in spelling, he more than made up for the deficit under tutoring by a Methodist minister. At fifteen, he stood fourteenth in a class of 108 students at the College of the City of New York, a school for bright but penurious young men. And at barely nineteen, he was graduated with distinction from Columbia School of Mines.

If the school, housed in a former broom factory at 50th Street and Fourth Avenue, was rickety, its curriculum was not. Besides such specialized courses as assaying, where ore samples in duplicate were analyzed under the eye of the instructor, Hollerith took such broad-based subjects as physics and chemistry. In a day when engineering had not yet fully emerged from the cut and try practices of the mechanic and metal worker, the emphasis was on practical experience as well as on classroom work. Students visited machine shops and metallurgical establishments of the city while school was in session. And they were required to show, "from reports of works visited" over the summer, that they had digested the practical aspects of the subjects they had taken before being allowed to resume their studies in the fall. Such training may have been ideal for collecting census statistics on manufacturing establishments. But it seemed to foretell little in Hollerith's future.

Although he would easily, and almost naturally, apply electricity in his inventions, despite purely mechanical solutions readily at hand, Hollerith took no course in electricity. It was not yet given. Neither did he take statistics, although he would someday be called the first statistical engineer. Moreover, although he would build rugged and highly reliable machines, he received a barely passing grade of 6.0 in the subject. However, as at City College, where he was seventh in a class of 108 in drawing, Hollerith displayed a strong visual sense that perhaps was the key to his inventive ability. At Columbia, he received perfect grades of 10.0 in descriptive geometry, graphics, surveying, and in a memoir in mechanical engineering in which equal weight in grading was given to drawings and text. Like the camera that he carried almost everywhere, his mind was decidedly visual, with the added gift of almost total recall. It could, as time would prove, soak up jigsaw pieces of detail, store them away, and later fit them together in eclectic fashion in a way that often astonished himself most of all.

In his background, too, and perhaps in his genes, were elements that would later emerge. His father, who died in an accident when Hollerith was only seven, had been a loner and a freethinker, a teacher of Latin and Greek who put down his schoolbooks to fight for a free Germany in the Revolution of 1848. "Paddle your own canoe," he often told his sons. In contrast, his mother's family, the Brunns, were solid, down-to-earth, and highly industrious folk. For generations, they had been locksmiths in the Old World, a craft second in precision only to clockmaking. At Buffalo, New York, where Hollerith was born, they took up a new trade, and Brunn's Carriage Manufactury soon expanded to cover an ample tree-shaded site at the corner of Main and Summer streets. Uncle Henry Brunn, it was said, not only knew every detail of the carriage business, he also "produced many novel and beautiful designs in carriages and sleighs, he being not only a skilled workman but a designer as well."

Little is known of Hollerith's early years. In college, he sought out close relationships with his professors, perhaps to make up for the father he could hardly have known. In turn, the older men responded, sounding out his interests, assuring him of his abilities, and helping him to establish an identity of his own. "A teacher," Henry Adams would write, "affects eternity. He can never tell where his influence stops." In Hollerith's career, the relationships with his professors were pivotal. Before he became engaged, Hollerith brought his future fiancée to New York to gain the blessing of School of Mines Dean Thomas Egleston, Jr., fondly called "Tommy Rocks" by the students. An even closer tie was that with Professor William P. Trowbridge. An ample and cheerful man, the head of the school's Engineering Department made time to know his students, although he had eight children of his own. "Each student," it was said, "felt he could rely upon an affectionate personal interest if he wanted advice or help."

Considering Hollerith's solid record at the school, there was probably nothing unusual in Professor Trowbridge's asking him to join him in working on the Census, where Trowbridge was a chief special agent. Another student and several instructors were taking part as well. Nevertheless, the approval of Hollerith's appointment by Secretary of the Interior Carl Schurz, the Civil War hero and friend of Lincoln, raises an interesting speculation. Did Schurz recall Hollerith's father, with whom he became acquainted when both were fighting for a free Germany and with whom he was imprisoned at the fortress at Rastatt following the unsuccessful uprising? The answer will probably never be known. The government at Washington was a lot smaller then, and Schurz, as head of the Interior Department, closely controlled the purse-strings and appointments to the Census Office, not yet a permanent department. Most likely, his approval of the appointment was a mere formality. Then, as now, the Census provided ample employment, and Hollerith was well qualified for the post. His particular assignment—to collect statistics on steam and water power used in iron and steelmaking—also posed an interesting opportunity for a young man to learn about the steel industry, in which he was probably intent on making a career.

In Hollerith's report, submitted and published under his own name, he probed such equations as the relation between power and product and the number of hands employed. He found that, while the use of water power had stayed almost even over the decade, there had been an astonishing gain of 336 percent in the application of steam power to steelmaking, due to the new Bessemer and open-hearth steelworks coming into operation. In the future, Hollerith's own machines would pose some equally startling equations, relating the mechanization of information to the productivity of men and machines.

Despite his activity, which included some travel outside of Washington, Hollerith found time to enjoy himself. He organized barge parties, pulled lazily by mule up the Chesapeake & Ohio Canal, and joined the Potomac Boat Club. Ostensibly, it was to row on the river. But judging from Hollerith's later attitude toward exercise—he once bought a bicycle but never rode it—the affiliation was probably more social than athletic. Although organized for aquatic exercise and pleasure, the club had, in recent years, become equally the home of the cotillionist. Its well-appointed clubhouse at the foot of 31st Street boasted the largest assembly rooms in the city. Outside of his own work, Hollerith also found time to compute a lot of life tables "as an amusement or at least a diversion" for Dr. John Shaw Billings, head of the division of Vital Statistics at the Census. The older man was grateful. "I am also indebted to Mr. Herman Hollerith," he wrote in the letter transmitting his report on vital statistics, "for valuable assistance in the compilation of the life table and the diagrams illustrating them." As it turned out, both the boat club and Dr. Billings would have a lasting association.

There are varying accounts of how Hollerith happened to invent his punched card tabulating machine. When asked in later years how it came about, the inventor would smile and invariably quip, "Chicken salad." When this teasing reply failed to satisfy, he would then recount one special entertainment at the boat club.

On a humid August evening in the summer of 1881, Hollerith, whose squared-off shoulders and close-cropped hair gave him a somewhat military bearing, escorted his partner from the dancing to a bunting-trimmed booth. In a gesture calculated to impress the young lady, he bought up all the unsold chances in a raffle for a beer mug—except for one. The unsold ticket won the prize.

Making up for his misfortune, Hollerith suggested, "Let's spend the money left on something we might enjoy," and moved on to a plentiful buffet. There, he attacked the chicken salad with such gusto that the young lady, impressed by the onslaught, asked her mother to invite him to a Sunday night supper to enjoy some more. Any romantic intimations of the evening came to naught, for the young lady, Kate Sherman Billings, would soon marry someone else. But the Sunday supper led to some shoptalk with her father, Dr. Billings, whom Hollerith had aided at the Census. On a later occasion, Hollerith took a photograph of the room. And forty years later he would recall:

I have been cleaning up old negatives and only the other day I ran across the negative of the diningroom in which I had the chat with Dr. Billings which started me on the problem and was the beginning of tabulating machines. At first, my impulse was to scrap it with the rest, but somehow I could not do it and laid it aside for the present.

Just what was said at the historic meeting is unfortunately unknown. In fact, one account places the meeting at Dr. Billings's tea table while another has it in the Census Office as the two men are strolling by clerks who are laboriously engaged in copying information from schedules by hand. Both accounts, and others, may be essentially correct, since the two men undoubtedly discussed building a machine to do census calculations on more than one occasion. And all accounts, including Hollerith's, give Dr. Billings full credit for providing the inspiration. In a letter dated August 7, 1919, Hollerith would recall:

He said to me there ought to be a machine for doing the purely mechanical work of tabulating population and similar statistics. . . . his idea was something like a type distributing machine. He thought of using cards with the description of the individual shown by notches punched in the edge. . . .

The second principal account, by Dr. Walter F. Willcox, for many years a Cornell professor who worked in the Census Office in 1900, quotes Dr. Billings as saying: "There ought to be some mechanical way of doing this job, something on the principle of the Jacquard loom whereby holes in a card regulate the pattern to be woven."

What Dr. Billings actually proposed and how specific his suggestions were are questions that will probably never be settled. Following Dr. Willcox's remarks made at a meeting in New York City on April 9, 1926, he received a letter from Mrs. K. B. Wilson, the same Kate Sherman Billings of the chicken salad episode. She wrote:

I do not remember hearing of Father's remarks to Herman Hollerith about those machines being applied to census tabulation, but I do remember the first little wooden model which Herman Hollerith brought to our library many evenings while they were puzzling their brains over its adaptation. Father had no mechanical gifts—so the entire credit is Mr. Hollerith's.

Dr. Willcox forwarded a copy of the letter and of his address to Hollerith and added:

It [the paper] is based on my memory of a conversation which I had with you many years ago and very probably my memory has played me a trick. The paper is likely to be published and . . . I would be glad to have this passage corrected by you.

Hollerith evidently did not take the trouble to reply, further clouding what has become a matter of controversy. However, a look at Dr. Billings's career can help clarify the relationship between the two men and place the event in proper context.

Twice Hollerith's age when they met, Dr. Billings, at forty, had already earned a formidable reputation for compendious knowledge, energy, and dispatch. A tall rangy man with piercing blue eyes, he was constantly in motion. As medical inspector for the Army of the Potomac during the Civil War, he had always been on horseback collecting medical statistics, arranging for ambulances and supplies, drawing up orders, collecting specimens, and operating in difficult cases. Following the war, the hospitals turned in some $85,000 in savings to the Surgeon-General's Office. Dr. Billings was allowed to use the money to build its library. And under his care, it grew from 600 to more than 50,000 volumes. More imposing than the collection was its *Index Catalog*. Prepared by Dr. Billings with the help of Dr. Robert Fletcher, it was recognized at once as a world-renowned guide to all of medical literature.

When the Baltimore merchant Johns Hopkins left an unprecedented sum in 1876 for the building of a hospital, Dr. Billings entered a competition for its design and organization. His essay won over five others. Late in life, when most men think of retiring, he would organize the New York Public Library with its unique branch system. The architectural firm of Carrier and Hastings would draw the design for the interior of its main building at 42d Street—with its easy access to special libraries—from Billings's postcard sketch.

The best description of the doctor's *modus operandi* comes from Dr. William Osler, hand-picked for the staff of Johns Hopkins

Medical School by Dr. Billings. Later Regius Professor of Medicine at Oxford, Dr. Osler recalled a visit by Dr. Billings in 1889:

He came to my rooms. . . . Without sitting down, he asked me abruptly, "Will you take charge of the Medical Department of the Johns Hopkins Hospital?" Without a moment's hesitation, I answered, "Yes." "See Welch about the details; we are to open very soon. I am very busy today, good-morning," and he was off, having been in my room not more than a couple of minutes.

Clearly, one of Dr. Billings's greatest talents was his power of judging not merely performance but promise in young men, and choosing them for purposes that *he* wanted accomplished. A colleague would give the key:

He was a member of the executive profession whose members—it may be a great banker, a great merchant, a great manufacturer . . .—are always leaders, commanders of men and affairs. He did many things well; he could have done almost anything well.

Following his famous chat with Billings, Hollerith went to Mr. Leland, the head of the Population Division, and asked to be taken on as a clerk to see what the job was. "After studying the problem," he later recalled, "I went back to Dr. Billings and said I thought I could work out a solution for the problem and asked him to go in with me." The recollection is revealing. Not only did Hollerith believe he could solve the problem, he was also intent on building a business around its solution. In typical fashion, the doctor turned the offer down, as he did many other opportunities for material gain. "He was not interested any further," Hollerith would remember, "than to see some solution worked out."

One critic has hinted that Hollerith made a nuisance of himself and possibly traded on Dr. Billings's considerable reputation for his personal benefit. The assertion is difficult to support in view of Dr. Billings's continued interest in Hollerith's invention. To pave the way for trials of the system by the Baltimore and New Jersey health departments, Billings would describe the forms of cards to be used, and for a trial in New York, he would include instructions for punching and handling of the cards as well. He also personally demonstrated the system on several occasions. When the Census of 1890 came along, it was Dr. Billings's division that ordered the first machines.

Undoubtedly, Dr. Billings was the most important of the older men who took a fatherly interest in the young engineer and helped to further his career. Without his specific suggestion, it is unlikely that Hollerith would have invented the tabulating machine. But it was also widely acknowledged that the art of census taking had changed scarcely at all since the ancient Babylonians had carved their tallies on clay tablets. "It was a wonder," as one writer put it, "that many of the clerks did not go blind or crazy." In view of the state of the art—the 1880 Census was barely completed within the decade decreed by Congress—it would have been surprising if others besides Dr. Billings had not been intent on improving census methods and in finding talented people to do the job.

On taking office ten years before, Superintendent Walker had "sought promptly to encourage the inventive ability of those who had the requisite acquaintance of the problems to be solved." So far, the net result of his efforts was the development by Charles W. Seaton, the chief clerk of the Census, of the Seaton Tabulating Machine. Built of wood and operated by hand, the box-shaped device contained a series of rollers over which blank paper was unwound. A slot in the box, facing the operator, presented a surface of paper upon which the operator entered in adjacent columns figures relating to six or eight related classes of information from the Census schedules, and then advanced the rollers to present another parallel surface of blank paper. Despite its simplicity, the device saved considerable time and eyestrain by bringing together into close proximity positions to record information that had formerly to be entered on separate forms. Following recording, the roll was removed from the device and cut into sections for counting and consolidation.

During the summer of 1882, Hollerith moved to a desk in Colonel Seaton's private office in the Second National Bank Building on 7th Street. The office, it appears, was the closest thing approximating a development laboratory. Hollerith's impressions of the Seaton device are not recorded, although he probably noted that Congress had belatedly granted the colonel the sum of

$25,000 for his protracted efforts. Hollerith was much more impressed with the working model of a small adding machine designed by an inventor-attorney named Tolbert Lanston and personally funded by Seaton. He liked the positive action and sure feel of the well-designed device as he tried adding columns of figures on the machine, which had the unusual capability of accepting numbers as they were written in a column from left to right. Two years later, Hollerith, while drawing up the first patents for his own census machine, negotiated with Lanston (who was then preoccupied with launching his own successful monotype typesetting machine) "with regard to manufacturing and placing the [Lanston] machine on the market." In recognizing its importance, Hollerith showed commendable foresight, for adding machines would not generally be introduced to the business world for another decade.

The philosopher Jeremy Bentham once noted that business talent for promoting an invention seemed to occur in men "in inverse proportion to the talent for creating inventions." Yet the glimpse of Hollerith in Colonel Seaton's office dispels the picture of a studious young man taken in hand by Dr. Billings to solve the census problem. The young engineer had a strong entrepreneurial bent of his own.

Hollerith's activity in Colonel Seaton's office raises an interesting speculation. Was he asked to come to Washington solely to help his teacher collect statistics for a report on manufacturers? Or was he hired for other abilities as well?

In an unpublished report on machine tabulation in the Census Office, Robert H. Holley—who knew Hollerith at a later period—writes:

The . . . inability of the office to produce little more than the total population returns, the encouragement of Superintendent Walker and . . . of Dr. Billings stimulated Mr. Hollerith to a consideration of the problems involved and prompted him to devote his inventive talent in search of a solution. . . . It is probable that prior to this time, Mr. Hollerith had demonstrated inventive ability and that he accepted the appointment for the specific purpose of acquainting himself with these problems and of making a concerted attack upon them. He was hardly just another one of the 1,500 employees of the office at this time.

Instructor at M.I.T.

". . . miles of paper to count a few Chinamen."

In the fall of 1882, Hollerith left Washington to become an instructor of mechanical engineering at the Massachusetts Institute of Technology. As early as the spring of the previous year, Census Superintendent Walker had reported that the investigations of the 1880 Census, the most extensive ever, had caused a more rapid exhaustion of appropriated funds than had been contemplated. By the following fall, Walker himself had resigned from the office to assume the presidency of M.I.T., returning to Washington every third week to supervise without charge what was left of the Census activity. With the Census winding down and sorely in need of funds, Hollerith in all probability quite simply needed a job. He may also have viewed going to Boston, a center for the development of electrical machinery, as an opportunity to continue his experiments on a machine to solve the census problem.

George F. Swain, whose statistics on water power Hollerith had used in his own report, had also returned to his post as an instructor of civil engineering at M.I.T.; but not before he and Hollerith had become fast friends. On January 24, 1882, Swain wrote to Hollerith "to consult you informally and provisionally concerning your future plans." The letter disclosed that the Mechanical Engineering Department might decide to appoint an instructor, depending largely "on whether a good man is in sight." "The question I would now like to ask," wrote Swain, "is whether you would feel disposed to take into consideration such an invitation."

The prospect of teaching students several years his senior might reasonably appear flattering to a young man not yet turned twenty-two. But Hollerith needed to be convinced. He was apparently reluctant to take a $100 cut in pay, despite Swain's assurances that his $800 annual salary from the Institute might be supplemented by "some commercial outside employment at good hiring rates." As he often did, Hollerith turned to a former teacher for advice. On March 8, Professor Trowbridge, lured to Columbia by a salary two and a half times as great as the new Sheffield Scientific School at New Haven could afford, responded to a letter from his former pupil. "The amount of the salary is not a measure of the compliment nor of your usefulness," he wrote. "Some of our institutions can't afford to pay well and yet they must have well."

General Walker, who penned his correspondence in longhand to avoid the cost of a secretary and supplemented his salary as president with outside work, also sought to overcome Hollerith's reservations. He would, he wrote, personally recommend his appointment to the corporation, and added: "We are very poor, but we are also very prosperous numerically, and such a school ought to have a great future. I think it would be worthwhile to come to us and stay."

Hollerith accepted. By the start of classes, he was placed in entire charge of the seniors in the mechanical engineering course. Their first term alone took in hydraulic motors, machine design, steam engineering, descriptive geometry, blacksmithing, strength of materials, and metallurgy, among other subjects. Conditions at the overcrowded school were less than ideal. "The drawing room," it was reported, "is at present a near approach to the famous black hole of Calcutta in point of crowding and lack of ventilation." Whatever his previous reservations, the young instructor jumped right in. "Mr. Hollerith," the student publication, *The Tech*, reported by October 11, "is beginning his work in an energetic and practical way which bids fair to win for him the respect and esteem of the students." Besides his classes, Hollerith led field trips, one to nearby Watertown to examine a testing machine. The young instructor also found time to present a formal paper to the Society of Arts. In it, he compared two types of dynamometers, instruments for measuring the power transmitted to machines. Despite a lack of teaching experience, he was to achieve "a marked success as a teacher and director of laboratory practice." Somehow, working after hours, he also managed to make progress on his census machine. "While at Boston," he would later recall, "I made my first crude experiments."

During his stint in Colonel Seaton's office at the Census, Hollerith had studied past methods of census taking. These included the recording of information about each person across a strip of paper or on individual cards, a method employed in the Massachusetts Census. The near-at-hand Seaton device, in which blank paper was advanced over a series of rollers, may have suggested Hollerith's first approach. At first, he tried punching holes in long strips of paper, as he recalled many years later.

My idea was to use a strip of paper and punch the record for each individual in a line across the strip. Then I ran this strip over a drum and made [electrical] contacts through the hole to operate the counters. This, you see, gave me the idea of an ideal automatic feed.

The concept was not new—although Hollerith's application of it might have been. The automatic telegraph, developed the decade before, employed a moving paper tape with perforations corresponding to dots and dashes. Electrical contacts made or broken through perforations in the tape, which ran over a metal cylinder, relayed the information far faster than could be done by hand. Only, instead of transmitting the information, Hollerith counted it. He would describe his first design in a patent applied for in 1884.

Items to be counted were represented by a double row of holes punched across the width of the paper. "Various statistical items for a given person," Hollerith explained, "are recorded by punching suitable holes in a line across the strip, being guided by letters on the guide plate" (a template superimposed over the tape). The position of the hole indicated whether a person was male or female, native or foreign-born, and white or colored, in addition to his or her age category.

Once the record was made, the strip was advanced over rollers to repeat the operation. Hollerith verified the individual portraits by placing a lettered template, similar to the guide plate, across the paper strip. Small seals of paper were used to cover wrongly punched holes.

Hollerith then fed the roll of punched paper into his counting machine, which advanced the paper over a metal drum. Metal pins, positioned according to the holes in the plate, were pressed against the drum by a spring. Each time they encountered a hole in the paper strip, they made contact with the drum, completing an electric circuit. The impulse activated an electromagnet whose action registered a "one" on a counter provided for that hole.

The idea of counting by the use of a punched hole was simple. Yet the notion of having the presence or absence of a hole stand for a numerical quantity or a specific item of information would be absolutely fundamental to computing in the years ahead. It is interesting to note that many years later, it would be reinvented by Hollerith's two oldest sons. Hearing of a puzzle contest in a Washington newspaper in which the prize went to the person who came closest to counting the number of dots printed on a donkey, Herman, Jr., and Charles hooked up a steel plate to one terminal of a battery. From the other, they ran a wire to one of their father's counters and from the counter to an icepick. When the icepick was pushed through a dot, coming into contact with the metal plate, the operation was registered on the counter. "You could tell where you put the icepick through," Charles explained, "since there was a hole where the dot had been." Despite their ingenuity, however, the boys failed to win the prize.

Hollerith's first approach in using a continuous strip of paper worked well when all records were to be read. But he soon found the strip cumbersome for locating particular information that might be recorded anywhere along its length, as he later recalled: "The trouble was that if, for example, you wanted any statistics regarding Chinamen, you would have to run miles of paper to count a few Chinamen." Was there any way of isolating units of information that could be plucked from a continuous record and perhaps rearranged for further counting? Ironically, later computer designers would face a similar problem in the 1950s, when information was stored on long reels of magnetic tape and it was necessary to search hundreds of feet of tape to locate particular records. Their search would spur IBM engineers to develop a "random access" storage system, in which a specific record could be located anywhere on a spinning disk resembling a phonograph record by means of an arm descending on it.

One can imagine Hollerith pondering the question late at night in the rooms that he shared with Swain or, perhaps, turning it over in his mind as he walked along the snow-covered streets breathing in the sharp winter air. Reaching back in his memory, he recalled an experience on a train years before, perhaps during the summer he spent in Michigan.

I was traveling in the West and I had a ticket with what I think was called a punch photograph. . . .the conductor . . . punched out a description of the individual, as light hair, dark eyes, large nose, etc. So you see, I only made a punch photograph of each person.

The resulting punch card, based on his recollection of the punch photograph, solved Hollerith's problem by furnishing a standardized and easily interchangeable unit for the recording of information. That Hollerith's first punched card, employed a few years later in Baltimore, clearly resembles the railroad tickets of the time tends also to confirm his later recollection. A complementary piece of evidence is a small conductor's punch tucked away in a bureau drawer of his Washington home today. The punch, which his daughters say was also employed in Baltimore, replaced the awl-like instrument that he used to make holes in the paper tape. Stamped on it are the words "Warren Hill, Boston, No. 3, Patented July 20, 1880," indicating that he may have purchased it in Boston after that time.

Because of the punch's short jaws, Hollerith's first punched cards contain punching positions around the edge. The center of the card remains blank, since the instrument could not reach far beyond the edge of the card.

Hollerith's allusion to the "punch photograph" reveals an eclectic mind with a remarkable ability to sort through seemingly incidental experience for the solution to an immediate problem. A confirmed photography buff since boyhood, he often applied the analogy of photography to census taking itself. The enumeration, he would write, corresponded to the exposure of the photographic plate, while the compilation of the census was equated with its development.

As the first flow of the developer brings out the prominent points of our photographic picture, so, in the case of a census, the first [census] tabulations will show the main features of our population. As the development is continued, a multitude of detail appears in every part while at the same time, the prominent features are strengthened and sharpened in definition, giving, finally, a picture full of life and vigor.

The punched card unit was the key. It supplied the means by which units of information could be processed once, rearranged in new combinations, and processed again, until every bit of useful information was extracted. In abandoning the continuous paper strip for the punched card, Hollerith had taken the critical step in the development of his tabulating system.

Hollerith is often credited with the invention of the punched card, called the Hollerith card for many years and later more familiarly known as the IBM card. Yet, significantly, he never claimed it for himself. His basic patents always encompassed the use of punched cards *in combination with* his machines. Does this mean that he was aware of and influenced by the use of earlier punched cards?

More than a century before Hollerith was at work, Joseph Marie Jacquard had employed a chain of punched cards to guide his mechanical loom. Employing as many as 50,000 cards, the looms—still very much in use today—could weave incredibly complex patterns. An admirer of the Frenchman, British mathematician Charles Babbage proposed the use of Jacquard cards in his projected Analytical Engine. Babbage planned to use the cards, not just to direct his machine through a set series of operations; he also envisioned a second set of cards containing variables on which the first set of cards was to operate. The storing of both data and instructions on punched cards was well known to scores of punched card machine inventors, well before the electronic computer came along. For example, IBM inventors borrowed from Babbage in carrying information from one counter position to another and in early mechanisms for reading counters for printing.

However, Babbage's basic idea of storing instructions in punched cards seems to have been overlooked and had to be reinvented, in the form of programming, when modern electronic computers emerged.

Did Hollerith also have to reinvent what had gone before? In gathering materials for an informal history by C. A. Everard Greene, general manager and director of The British Tabulating Machine, Ltd., the inventor's youngest daughter Virginia Hollerith writes: "His brother [George Hollerith] said the Jacquard loom suggested the punched card idea. His brother-in-law Albert Meyer was in the silk-weaving business, so was familiar with the loom."

Between his first and second years at Columbia, Hollerith had moved from East 58th Street to 161 East 61st Street. The new address was the home of Albert Meyer, an importer with offices at 460 Broome Street in the heart of Manhattan's textile district. Recalled by the family as a large and friendly man, Meyer took an interest in the promising young man, which went beyond his older sister Bertha, whom Meyer was to marry. For Meyer became an early backer of Hollerith's census machine. Hollerith apparently reciprocated by showing an interest in textile machinery, which perhaps was part of the reason for the older man's solicitude.

In a letter describing Hollerith to a relative, Theodosia Talcott wrote of her future son-in-law: "I think one of his sisters is engaged or interested in a silk manufacturer, for Hollerith has recently made some inventions in looms and speaks of being interested in these silk looms." The letter, written in 1888, links Hollerith directly with looms. However, a search of patents under his name and Albert Meyer's fails to tie him to any weaving inventions. Perhaps out of self-interest, Meyer had tried to steer Hollerith's inventive talents toward the textile field. He apparently failed— but the merchant may have indirectly supplied the spark of inspiration via the widely known textile technology for Hollerith's modern punched card. For what Hollerith had done was to apply electricity to the principle of the Jacquard loom.

Regardless, Hollerith left his teaching post at M.I.T. after only one year. His reason, the family says, was that he balked at repeating the course material for a second time. But a more compelling reason is that, having found the key to his census machine,

Hollerith was eager to perfect and exploit it to maximum advantage. The young man's next port of call seems to bear this out. In May 1883, even before the close of the academic year, he received an appointment as an assistant examiner in the U.S. Patent Office at the not inconsiderable salary of $1,200 a year. That he knew little or nothing about patent law deterred him not in the least. He realized its importance to any inventor—and the painful experiences that come to those who fail to master its essential elements. Eager to learn, Hollerith would soon turn his newly acquired expertise to full advantage.

Along with the usual recommendations for the new position, depicting him as a young man of the highest moral character and of temperate and industrious habits, came one from Charles W. Seaton, the inventor of the Seaton machine whose office Hollerith had shared before leaving for M.I.T. Seaton wrote: "he has been admirably trained, has a robust, vigorous mind, excellent judgment, immense capacity for work, is fertile in expedience, conscientious."

And Seaton added: "While I have not a very definite knowledge of the duties of an examiner in your office, I have no doubt you will find him exceptionally well qualified to discharge them, whatever they may be."

Grounding as a Patent Expert

"I Herman Hollerith have invented . . ."

On returning to Washington in the spring of 1883, Herman Hollerith had ready access to the whole spectrum of American invention. Claims for inventions of every sort poured into the Greek Revival Patent Office building downtown at F and 8th streets. More than 21,000 of the claims would be recognized as inventions that year, belying the fears of Henry L. Ellsworth, who as patent commissioner, thirty-nine years earlier, had forewarned that "the advancement of the arts, from year to year, taxes our credulity and seems to presage the arrival of that period when human improvement must end."

Even if such skeptics might still be found, the newly appointed assistant patent examiner was doubtless too preoccupied to listen to them. Moreover, the previous decade, as the young man was aware, had seen Edison's invention of the incandescent electric lamp and the phonograph; Bell's patent on "telegraphy," which turned out to be the telephone; and an improvement in fences known as "barbed wire," which made possible the cheap and efficient fencing of vast areas of western farmland. In just ten years, the annual rate of inventions had doubled.

Although Hollerith's duties centered on examining the claims of other inventors, it may safely be said that he was eager to probe through the layers of claims and counterclaims relating to his own particular interests. His likely objectives? To secure the base for a future business and, perhaps, find out what, besides the census machine, needed to be invented. By mastering the intricacies of patent law along the way, he was also equipping himself with the means of earning a livelihood.

That Hollerith had this last goal in mind came out a short time later. On March 31, 1884, less than a year after returning to Washington, he resigned his position at the Patent Office and quickly hung out his own shingle nearby as an "Expert and Solicitor of Patents." Despite the security of the government job, Hollerith chafed at the notion of working for others. He was intent on being his own man.

Within sixteen months of leaving M.I.T., he was also confident that he could secure the broad patent protection he needed to start his own business. In taking this next step, he acted with impressive sureness of what he was about.

On September 19, he started a letter to "Dear Albert." The intended recipient was the same Albert Meyer who had encouraged his "inventions with looms." Hollerith began by recalling a conversation of a few days before in which the silk merchant had "felt disposed" toward helping him financially with his census machine.

In those days, it was not enough for an inventor to have a promising idea and sell it or assign it to a large company that could help him exploit it or leave him free to pursue other ideas. Ideas, even good ones, were plentiful commodities, as much so as the ribbon and broad goods that the merchant sold. The inventor had to convince someone else that his idea was practical; he had to figure out how much it would cost to prove it; how his invention could be built and financed; who would try it; and, finally, how he could repay the money needed to get it off the ground.

With characteristic thoroughness, Hollerith had plotted every inch of ground. "As regards patent rights," he began, "as I am the first in the field of invention, I can secure what is technically known as a 'foundation patent' covering the ground broadly and, therefore, all subsequent improvements would be subject to my broad patent." Not only could he obtain basic patent protection in his own country, Hollerith continued, "I could also, of course, secure patents in foreign countries (England, Germany, France, etc., all of which countries compile elaborate statistics)."

From the first, Hollerith was thinking broadly, in terms of exploiting his invention abroad if not explicitly of an international business. His inventions, he continued, were applicable to the work of almost any statistical bureau. In his own country, for example, if he took out his patent January 1, 1885, it would run until the start of 1902, covering the censuses of 1890 and 1900.

But what assurance was there that his invention would actually be used? Was a census machine, in fact, needed? After all, thousands of invention models were currently gathering dust on Patent Office shelves without any assurance of ever being put to use in final form.

Hollerith's letter went on in a half humorous vein. "I am aware of the fact regarding inventions," he wrote, "which is well expressed by Dr. Raymond when he said, 'My dear boy, half the art of invention consists in knowing what needs to be invented.'" Dr. Billings, he informed the merchant, had told him of the expense of present census methods and of the necessity of some mechanical devices for doing the work. Both Superintendent Seaton and Chief Clerk Richards had expressed the same idea. "It is therefore that I feel confident," he concluded, "that something is needed."

How far along was he? Had the invention taken tangible form? "I wish to impress you," Hollerith continued, "that my invention is no longer a 'crude idea,' but that I have pretty well considered the ground and have practically demonstrated some parts. I am confident that it will work."

So, too, was Colonel Seaton, who had gone over the plans. But a machine would have to be built on a small scale so that it could be tried. There also had to be a means of demonstrating it, beyond workshop experiments.

As it turned out, there were plenty of statistics gathered in the last Census but not processed, simply because of lack of money. If Hollerith could apply his new invention to these statistics—records of people reported as single, married, widowed, and divorced—and classify them into categories of age, his machines would be doing actual work.

Before writing to Meyer, Hollerith had walked from his own office on 7th Street to the nearby Census building to make a somewhat forward suggestion. If he furnished the machines for such work, would Superintendent Richards detail the clerks to carry it out? In effect, he was asking to prove out his invention at government expense.

Richards agreed, and Hollerith could write to Meyer: "This offer on the part of Mr. Richards is a very liberal one, and is, I think, indication of his faith in my method of compiling statistics."

Finally, after fully setting the stage, Hollerith brought up the matter of financing.

You asked me [he wrote] how much money I should want to carry out my project. I . . . would estimate it as follows. An experimental machine for trial in the census office as described about $1500. This machine would serve as a model to illustrate it to any persons interested in such matters. To secure patents in this country (first patents) $175. Patents in foreign countries, $500. Printing and advertising, $200.

His brief experience in the Patent Office had given him the business knowhow to proceed. His letter continued:

This money need not all be invested at once. I can try the machine on a small scale first at an expense of about $200. If this succeeds, I can then go ahead again. I need not take out any patents until I have proved the practicability of the machine. Likewise, I need not do any advertising until the machine has been tried. On the other hand, it might be found desirable after trial, if successful, to elaborate some parts even more than this.

In all, about $2,500 would cover expenses. In a footnote to the letter, Hollerith detailed what the merchant might expect in return. He would pay him one half of net profits up to $12,000 plus 6 percent interest on the money loaned. Despite Meyer's status as a close friend of the family and prospective brother-in-law, it was a strictly businesslike proposition.

Something should be done soon about this matter [Hollerith concluded]
I think I have a good thing . . . let me know as soon as possible because, should you not care to go into it, I must try to secure money from some other source.
I am determined to make a desperate effort.

The reply was swift, perhaps faster than the mails nearly a century later would have carried it. For, on September 23, 1884, only four days after writing, Hollerith, apparently assured of backing, was confident enough to move ahead. He filed the first patent application for his census machine. "I Herman Hollerith," the application began, "have invented certain new and useful improvements in the Art of Compiling Statistics." The claim describes Hollerith's early design approach to the census machine. Holes punched in a strip of paper were sensed by pins or pointers making contact through the holes to a drum. The completion of an electric circuit through a hole advanced a counter on a dial.

In filing his early patents, Hollerith clearly knew what he was about. He divided the initial application a year later and renewed it twice—steps that extended the life of the patents. He would file another patent for his census machine in June 1887. When a trio of patents was issued on January 8, 1889, Hollerith would receive full protection for his census machine for another seventeen years. Significantly, the package of pioneering patents would supply the generic concepts upon which all of his later data processing refinements would be based.

4

Experiments with Air Brakes

*"Whether electricity was a
sufficiently reliable element . . ."*

On April 30, 1885, Herman Hollerith filed three patents for
electrically actuated railway car brakes. He must have been perfecting the devices at the same time that he was busy with his
census machine. Although he had actually filed for his trio of
pioneering data processing patents seven months earlier, the railway brake patents, issued on January 12, 1886, were the first of
any kind to bear his name.

His sudden branching out into another line of invention seems
strange in retrospect, since his name, in only a handful of years,
would be tied inseparably to tabulating machines. But to the
twenty-five-year-old inventor, looking ahead at the start of his
career, there was no certainty where his main chance might lie.
If the gamble on his census machine paid off at all, and there was
no assurance that it would, the opportunity still lay five years
ahead in the taking of the next decennial census.

As a patent examiner he could not help but have noticed that
more than half the claims for new inventions that came across his
desk were for improved couplings, signaling devices, and other
railroad equipment. Since the close of the Civil War, the railroads
had more than quadrupled their operating mileage. As anyone
was aware, they were the country's largest and most important
industry—and something more. They carried people, raw materials, and finished goods to every corner of the land, creating
insatiable demands for better methods and improvements of every
kind.

The particular need that Hollerith now saw as an opportunity might never have arisen had it not been for another inventor's inspiration. In 1869, when Hollerith was only nine years old, another upstate New Yorker, twenty-two-year-old George Westinghouse, had patented a railway car brake and started up a company to manufacture it. Locomotive brakes had been around for more than a quarter of a century, since Englishman Robert Stephenson had patented a steam-driven brake applied to the engine's driving wheels in 1833. But until Westinghouse, railway car brakes, with small exception, had been crude, hand-operated affairs. His radically new design was actuated by compressed air stored in a tank in the locomotive. To stop the train, the engineer opened a valve on the tank, sending air, compressed to seventy pounds to the square inch, hissing back through the train via a pipeline and rubber hoses that made connections between the cars. As the air reached each car, it pressed against a piston in a brake cyclinder under the car, which in turn caused the brake shoes to press against the car wheels.

Devising a better braking system was one thing; getting it accepted, quite another. Before the time of regulation, the railroads operated pretty much as they pleased. They had at first virtually ignored the Westinghouse brake as they had another significant safety device—Eli Hamilton Janney's automatic coupler, patented only the year before the Westinghouse brake. Hand brakes, operated from the tops of rolling and bucking cars and link and pin couplers appeared to do the job. For the railroads were undeniably safer than other forms of transportation, at least as far as shippers and passengers were concerned. Less noticed were the thousands of railroad workers killed or maimed each year because of accidents with hand brakes and coupling pins. In mild weather and while crossing level country the top of a freight train could be a scenic and even pleasant place to be. But the brakeman's lot could change suddenly on a freight careening down a mountain grade or in winter when he was called upon to jump between ice-coated car roofs to do his job. The safety devices were there, but most railways appeared reluctant to install them. "The radical cause of their neglect," the Rev. Lyman Abbott wrote in *Harper's New*

Monthly Magazine, "is probably the fact that the lives of railroad workers are inexpensive."

By the mid-1880s, growing public pressure had encouraged most railroads to adopt the Westinghouse brakes on the relatively short passenger trains. By now, Westinghouse had also substantially improved his braking system through the development of a device called the triple valve. Installed in air reservoirs under each car and on the locomotive air tank, this ingenious device enabled the engineer to stop the train by *reducing* rather than increasing air pressure. The advantage: when a train broke in two or the braking system otherwise failed, the resulting loss in pressure automatically applied the brakes, bringing all cars to a halt. Still, the new system was not yet considered practical for freight trains, which, with increased locomotive power, now often ranged up to fifty cars in length. The reason: the effect of the engineer's action in reducing air pressure took time to travel all the way through the train pipe and hoses to the rear of the train. The undesirable side effect of a fast stop was that the still unbraked cars at the rear of the train jolted into the already braked cars in front of them.

Here is where Hollerith saw his chance to improve on Westinghouse. When Hollerith took out his patents in the spring of 1885, no more than 4 percent of the freight cars in service in the United States were equipped with power brakes. If he could improve such systems with a device for releasing air pressure quickly and uniformly in all of the cars, from front to back, even long freight trains could be brought to a smooth and rapid stop. There was a huge market waiting for such a device.

In approaching the problem, Hollerith turned instinctively to electricity at a time when Edison had barely perfected the incandescent lamp and few people had lighting systems in their homes. He drew from the same strain of development he was following in his census machine—with one important difference. Instead of employing electromagnets to open electrical relay switches in order to register different data on counters, he now employed electromagnets to open and close the valves that admitted or exhausted air from brake cyclinders.

The essential advantage that Hollerith grasped in applying electricity to the air brake problem was its speed. It could activate or release the air brakes on any car of a train at virtually the same moment—regardless of whether the car was the first or the fiftieth in line from the locomotive. The basic concept was broad enough in scope so that it could be applied to several types of braking systems.

Besides speed and uniformity of action, Hollerith's brake design offered a second fundamental advantage. In the Westinghouse triple-valve system, the opening of the inlet valve closed the exhaust valve and vice versa, leaving the brakes either fully on or fully off. In contrast, Hollerith designed his system so that the valves could be operated independently of each other. This meant that the engineer could apply the brakes with as little or as much force as needed. The design also lessened the danger that vacuum pressure in the system might be exhausted. "In descending long grades," Hollerith wrote,

it is desirable to be able to apply the brakes continuously under only a part of the pressure obtainable when the brakes are fully on, and also to be able to increase or diminish the [air] pressure at will; and, while the variations of pressure in the brake cylinders are taking place, it is desirable that the maximum pressure should be maintained in the auxiliary reservoir or power chamber, so that the full pressure of air may, at any time, be instantly availed of in case of an emergency.

Hollerith's solution to the problem was impressive in its simplicity.

The opportunity to test the new braking system was provided by what has been described, with only little exaggeration, as an epochal event in railroad history: the brake trials conducted at Burlington, Iowa, in 1886 and 1887 by the Master Car Builders' Association. Their objective was plain: to determine whether there was any power brake fit for a freight train. But preparations for the contest were anything but simple. Each competing company was required to show up with a fifty-car train, complete with crew, equipped with its braking system.

Considering the importance of the Burlington trials, and the probable fortune awaiting the winner, it is strange that Hollerith's family knows little about this period of his life. He may have been too busy to keep them informed. But there is also another possible explanation.

In mid-1885, when his brake patents list him as a resident of St. Louis, some 150 miles south of Burlington, Hollerith received a letter from Albert Meyer. Only ten months before, the silk merchant had promised financial support for Hollerith's census machine. Now he had apparently lost interest. Although Meyer's letter has been lost, Hollerith's reaction to its contents is one of stunned disbelief. "I personally have perfect confidence in the scheme of electrical tallying," he replied, "else I should not have spent time and money which I have already spent in this matter." Hollerith explained the need for trying the machine on a more extended scale. Then he urged the merchant to "send someone skilled in such matters to examine my plans and then base your decision on such person's opinion and not on mine." He concluded on a note that reflects growing discouragement and a hint of anger.

I have not only spent money which you advanced, but . . . every cent over and above what living has cost me. It is not much to be sure, but if I had more, I would not now be applying to you.

Hollerith's letter, dated July 14, is the last recorded one to the merchant, who apparently did not respond. Meyer lost interest, the family says, because he felt the idea was not a profitable one. At about the same time, according to a niece, the inventor asked his brother George to back his invention and was turned down. "Father was newly married at the time and struggling along on a professor's salary," the niece recalls. "He was in no position to put money into an invention." Hollerith probably went to other family members for help. If so, he was unsuccessful. According to one account, when he showed the machine to his family, they laughed at him. Whatever the reasons, the inventor broke off completely from his family at this time, and his own children would grow up almost completely unaware that they had a family on their father's side.

The break with his family makes it difficult to account for Hollerith's activity in St. Louis. *Gould's St. Louis Directory* for the year ending April 1, 1886, identifies him as a manager of the Mallinckrodt Brake Company at 404 Market Street. And a pamphlet, dated 1884, describes that company as being formed for the purpose of introducing a brake invented by John F. Mallinckrodt, a one-time repairman of Westinghouse air brakes for the Denver and Rio Grande Railroad. The booklet lists other patents that the company had a right to use. Among them were seven patents for electromagnetic devices for operating air brakes issued in 1884 to Colonel Henry Flad of St. Louis, the president of the company of which Hollerith was manager.

Who was Henry Flad? And what was his possible connection with the young engineer? As it turns out, Colonel Flad, then president of the Board of Public Improvements with offices on the third floor of City Hall, was a rather extraordinary individual. As chief assistant engineer to James B. Eads, who built the famous bridge bearing his name across the Mississippi, Colonel Flad was credited with some of the boldest features of this great enterprise. To avoid blocking river traffic during construction, Flad had designed a cantilever system that no one had ever tried before. Instead of propping up the arch of the bridge with temporary "false work" that could be torn out once the bridge was finished, Flad supported the great arching jaws of the bridge as they were extended toward each other from *above*, a feat he performed by hanging them from overhead cables attached to temporary towers built on top of the bridge's stone piers. It was feared by many that the highly unorthodox technique would fail, plunging the steelwork into the muddy waters far below. It didn't. Obviously Flad was a highly-skilled and inspired engineer who knew what he was about. The year after Hollerith became associated with him, he was elected president of the American Society of Civil Engineers.

Earlier in his career, Colonel Flad, now sixty-two years old, had helped build railways in the East and the Middle West. During the Civil War, he had maintained railroad construction and built defensive works, rising from private to colonel in the Union forces. In the distant past, he had once commanded a company of engineers in making improvements along the Rhine River—until the Revolution of 1848, when the young man, who had graduated from Munich University with highest honors, was caught destroying an important span across the same river. Imprisoned and sentenced to death, he escaped as Carl Schurz had done. Like Schurz, and Hollerith's father, he was one of the industrious and highly independent '48ers who quickly made their own way in a new land. In fact, his mother, like Hollerith's own mother and grandmother, was named Franciska Brunn and similarly hailed from the small town of Speyer. Doubtless, the already famous engineer and the young inventor were cousins. Possibly Colonel Flad had asked his cousin to come to St. Louis to work on railway car brakes.

In the course of his career, the Colonel had taken out numerous patents, most drawn from his experience in improving waterways. He is also credited with having much to do with the introduction of the block signal system, a system of signals intended to keep fixed intervals of space between trains running on the same track. His own brake patents were acquired, in 1884, by the American Electro-Magnetic Brake Company of East St. Louis.

Significantly, the Colonel, known as a liberal-minded and approachable man, had no interest in the commercial exploitation of his inventions. ". . . although he took out new and numerous patents for new and useful inventions," it would be written, "to their introduction and utility he gave no thought. It was the work rather than its rewards for which he cared." His role in Hollerith's life may have been similar to that of the public-spirited Dr. Billings who had sparked the young engineer's interest in census machines without any thought of personal gain. Hollerith was apparently not averse to refining and extending what his talented cousin had begun.

Be that as it may, Hollerith's own interest in braking systems was intense. The first round of tests began July 15, 1886, on eight miles of track belonging to the Chicago, Burlington & Quincy Railroad west of Burlington. "The morning was hot but clear," reported *Railway Age*. Seated in the grandstand erected along the course and wearing a guest's purple ribbon was Iowa Railroad Commissioner L. C. Coffin. His long crusade for safety was largely responsible for bringing the occasion about. Four companies had entered the competition, among them, Westinghouse, American, and Eames. The final entrant suddenly withdrew on the morning of the trials after unsatisfactory private tests. It is not known whether Hollerith was present or participated.

The vast array of equipment drawn up on the prairie was impressive to the eye and the ear as the engines built up a full head of steam and men ran along the length of the fifty-car trains checking the braking apparatus beneath the cars. But despite the careful preparations, the first round of tests proved little short of disastrous. Men in the rear cars were thrown down and injured as the trains tried to halt as quickly and smoothly as possible at markers along the course. The slamming of metal and splintering of wood rent the air. After nineteen days of mechanical mayhem, the Master Car Builders sent the competing companies back to work for another year. None of the electrically actuated brakes had been tried.

By May 9, 1887, the major brake companies were ready to try again. This time, Hollerith was very much on the scene, sending back notes "taken in the field" to the *Quarterly* of the Columbia School of Mines, with the promise of a more complete and studious article at a later date. "The results," he predicted, "cannot help but be of great value to the railway service of the country and . . . must prove interesting to engineers." Although eight companies had entered the competition, only four of them appeared in readiness for the trial. They were Westinghouse, American (which owned the Flad patents), Carpenter, and Card. All had electrical attachments to help activate their brakes. The Westinghouse Company also fielded a purely pneumatic system as well.

In which of the competing systems was Hollerith's invention employed? According to notes made by the inventor's oldest daughter of a conversation with Edmund Talcott, who worked for Hollerith for many years, it was "Carpenter" who "financed the air brake experiments." Supporting evidence is supplied by *Railway Age*. Noting the attendance of persons interested in these tests during the first three days, the journal includes J. F. Carpenter, inventor of the "electro air brake," and "H. Holleraith who accompanies Mr. Carpenter." The Carpenter brake, the publication observed, "strongly resembles the Westinghouse air brake, but it has an automatic valve operated by electricity." (In the new Westinghouse system, the brake valve itself was not operated by electricity; but an electrical appliance placed between the cars supplemented the triple-valve break mechanism by making the escape of air "almost instantaneous.")

As the tests progressed, Westinghouse withdrew its purely pneumatic system. Equipped with a larger diameter train pipe and faster-acting triple action valves, the system operated with twice the speed of the purely pneumatic system fielded by the company the year before. Only five to six seconds were required to transmit the vacuum power to the last car on a fifty-car train. Even so, the shock experienced in the rear car was considerable. The withdrawal of the system narrowed the competition to the electrically operated brakes. "When electricity is not used to apply the brakes," commented *Railway Age*, "the shocks of an emergency stop appear to be very severe in proportion to the shortness of the stop . . ." The publication forecast that electricity and air combined presaged entirely new methods of handling freight trains.

Watching from the grandstand as the trains thundered down the nine-mile section of the Chicago, Burlington & Quincy main line, Hollerith felt his hopes rise with each passing day. While the Westinghouse and Carpenter systems ran neck and neck through most of the trials, it gradually became clear that the Carpenter system, in which the brake valves were controlled directly by electricity, had a slight edge.

In its preliminary report, the committee decided that the best brake for long freight trains "is the one operated by air in which the valves are actuated by electricity." Favoring Hollerith's design, the committee stated that the Carpenter brake "stops the train in the shortest possible distance; abolishes shocks and attendant damage to equipment, can be released instantly, and can be graduated perfectly." The evidence was plain. But the committee balked at making a final judgment. Whether electricity was a sufficiently reliable element, it observed, can only be determined by experiment. However, the benefits are so manifest, it added, "that the experiment is well worth trying."

In his promised studious article in the *Quarterly*, Hollerith urged such experiments. If others had doubts about the efficacy of the new element of electricity, he had none. ". . . it would seem strange," he wrote, "in view of the extended use of electricity at the present day, if, with a little attention and study of the requirements, such devices could not be rendered perfectly reliable." Besides, he pointed out, the electrical control of the brake was *in addition to* pneumatic control; "in the event of any failure, the brakes could still be operated by air until such electrical defects were remedied."

However, Hollerith was contending not only with technical considerations, which, in his view, were minor. He was also facing the innate conservatism of a wealthy and established industry. Diplomatically, he observed that "electricity in this connection is a new element, and it is but natural and proper that the men in charge of the motive power of our railroads should treat this subject with considerable conservatism." But he found it impossible to tolerate the ignorance that often accompanied such a set of mind. No doubt his temper rose to a rapid boil when reading the comment in a leading railroad journal, which editorialized, "whether the electrical appliances will remain efficient during a thunder storm is extremely doubtful."

Surprisingly, Hollerith encountered more strident opposition from another source. Without the constant harping of Iowa Railroad Commissioner Coffin, the trials would not have been held in the first place. But now the Populist gadfly, busy writing the nation's first railway appliance safety law, did not want technical refinements to stand in the way of his long-sought goal. Commissioner Coffin, the *Railway Review* reported, "thinks the time has come for the adoption of freight train brakes, and that the introduction of electricity will tend to occasion delay." While the journal felt that Coffin "was hardly just in dealing with the claims made for electrical application," the damage had already been done.

Hollerith's own stubbornness and a certain casualness in handling his business affairs might also have played a role. According to family accounts, the inventor was offered some money for his invention by Westinghouse, who may have felt his company's technical progress blocked by the young engineer's patents. Hollerith pointedly, and perhaps unwisely, ignored the offer. As he later wrote to a friend, he had been granted patents for his electrically actuated brakes only a week after the Burlington trials, and he felt certain they would cover the application of electricity to the Westinghouse brakes. Whether Hollerith actually had the patents, or had merely applied for applications that blocked Westinghouse, is uncertain. According to a daughter, "they threw out Daddy's brakes because they were not dated. So after that, Daddy got a big ledger and said, 'Edmund, everything we do, make a sketch and you write it down in this book and date it and have it witnessed.' He was not going to be caught again."

Regardless, Westinghouse acted on the threat. Immediately following the tests, he hurried back to his shops and again modified the triple-valve system to make it still faster-acting. By September 10—only four months after the start of the second round of trials—*Railway Age* could report:

Still further experiments are being made with the Westinghouse brake at Burlington. . . . the time now required [to activate the brakes at the rear of a fifty-car train] is less than two seconds, and our informant states that the brake action now strongly resembles that seen when electricity is employed.

The system is now almost as far ahead of what it was at the time of entering the last series of tests.

Leaving little to chance, Westinghouse, by October, had equipped a fifty-car train with the system and started a 3,000-mile journey, stopping at cities far and wide to demonstrate its superiority. "The journey," as a contemporary railroad writer put it, "was a splendid and conclusive demonstration that the air brake is now a thoroughly efficient and reliable contrivance for freight as well as passenger service."

Like a terrier tugging at a bone, Hollerith was not about to give up. He wrote:

It is hard to conceive of a condition when a second or a fraction of a second is of more consequence than in the case of an emergency on a railroad. With a train moving with a velocity of 60 miles per hour, the loss of two seconds is equivalent to a distance of 176 feet. With another train approaching under the same conditions, this would mean a loss of 352 feet, and, while this might not be sufficient to avoid a collision, still, the resulting damages would be considerably mitigated, by an amount, in fact, which would be represented by the work done by the friction of the brake shoes through a distance of 352 feet.

Such stops, Hollerith added, are required very rarely, "but when one considers the value of life and property often depending on such emergency stops, their relative importance becomes apparent."

Hollerith was right, of course. But as the years went by, he quickly saw himself foreclosed from the market for railroad brakes, as did scores of other inventors. The main reason was the need for standardization. Since the railroads frequently exchanged cars from one line to another, as they do today, their cars had to have compatible coupling and braking systems. By 1891, more than 100,000 freight cars were equipped with Westinghouse brakes.

Long after Hollerith's punched card machines had been proved out in censuses on both sides of the Atlantic, he was still waging his battle against "that scoundrel" Westinghouse, whose name was barred from use in the Hollerith household. "Hollerith is in New York on business of his brake patents," his mother-in-law wrote in 1892. "He is making arrangements to have it used in some of the railroads of this country and thinks he can make something out of it which he has not yet done." The following year, however, Congress passed the National Railway Appliance Act, requiring air brakes on all railway cars. The new law made Westinghouse's victory virtually complete.

It is not known if Hollerith's devices were ever put into service. George Hollerith, a nephew, thinks they were. And since the Carpenter brake was widely accepted in Europe, it is probable that they were tried there. However, in 1906, Hollerith's company wired instructions to his foreign correspondents to abandon both the Austrian and Italian railroad patents "upon which patents workings are shortly due." This meant letting the patents expire. Yet Hollerith's interest in railway safety would persist. In December 1905 he wrote to a friend after reading of an elevated railway accident in New York City:

The engineer deliberately went by signals . . . . how long will it be before railroads will arrange some device so that when a danger signal is passed, automatic brakes will be applied to the train . . . whether the engineer is asleep or not?

"Every once in a while," he concluded, "I get to thinking about brakes and the possibilities in that direction, but, of course, I cannot afford to give this matter any serious thought."

Hollerith's ideas for braking systems were many years ahead of their time. In the 1930s, the railroads would, indeed, start introducing electropneumatic brakes on passenger trains, although purely pneumatic systems are still employed on freight trains. On its seventy-fifth anniversary in 1944, the Westinghouse Air Brake Company would describe electropneumatic brakes as if they were an entirely new development.

Today, many high-speed passenger trains have a dual feature of brake control—one for electro-pneumatic, the other . . . pneumatic. The former . . . permits the instantaneous application of the brakes throughout the train and thereby materially shortens the stopping distance. At the same time, it removes any slack action between the cars . . . the locomotive engineer can [now] increase and decrease the brake pressure as accurately . . . as can be done by a driver in his automobile.

The typical streamliner, the account continues, takes four and a half seconds to begin building up braking pressure on the rear car with a purely pneumatic system. But the electrical elements "completely eliminate this lag. If 4½ seconds seems insignificant," the writer concludes, "they represent the time required by a train traveling at 100 miles per hour to go ⅛th of a mile." The sentence could have been taken almost verbatim from Hollerith's *Quarterly* article published more than half a century before.

Were Hollerith's experiments with railroad technology largely wasted? As far as immediate, profitable results are concerned, the answer is probably yes. In 1894, he patented a punched card system in which pneumatic pressure took the place of electricity and airtubes running to the counters replaced electric wires. Never built, it was more of an oddity than anything else. But it can also be strongly argued that his schooling in the pervasive railroad technology of the day had a far greater influence on his development of tabulating machines than the more obvious example of other calculating and adding mechanisms.

For one thing, the railroad itself was a complex system in which many elements had to work together, rather than a single invention. The same may be said of Hollerith's tabulating machines, in which punches, tabulators, and sorters all had to be designed to work in combination with each other as a system, rather than as separate units. Still more important, the concepts of precise timing, automatic control, and safeguarding against error—important to the development of railway braking and signaling systems coming into use—became equally critical considerations in Hollerith's later machines, in which feeding, sensing, and sorting all had to occur at precise intervals. Instead of a speeding train of closely coupled cars, imagine a carefully controlled procession of punched cards speeding through a machine, and the analogy becomes clearer. Hollerith's automatic control feature—in which a machine shuts down at the end of one run of cards, records the totals, and then starts up automatically when another batch comes along— closely parallels the railroad block signaling system, which prevents a second train from entering a section of track until it is cleared by the train ahead of it.

Look under the covers of his automatic sorter. It's a railway freight yard. Only instead of railway cars being switched from a single track onto separate spurs to make up new trains for further destinations, you have cards with common designations being sorted into separate pockets of the machine, arranged for further processing. For Hollerith, whose eclectic mind could soak up ideas from almost anywhere and later apply them with seeming ease in ways that he was not fully aware of, his exposure to railroad technology was a critical, if not central, consideration. But this is getting ahead of our story.

In 1902, the British publication *Engineering* took a look back at his tabulator employed in the 1890 Census and recognized the railway signal system in it.

The idea is similar to that exemplified in railway practice in the 'electric slot.' Sometimes a signal is under the control of several signalmen and can only be pulled off by the combined action of them all. Each may pull over his lever, but nothing occurs until all the levers are over when the signal falls . . .

Similarly, when a dial [on a tabulator] is set up to represent three, four, or more qualities or circumstances . . . that dial will only record when all these qualities or circumstances are noted on the card.

While it is interesting to speculate on what the future of punched card technology might have been if Hollerith had won his battle with Westinghouse and devoted all his energies to the railroads, it is equally fascinating to speculate on the subconscious debt Hollerith owed to his immersion in railroad technology. But these observations are made looking backward in time. For the young engineer who had journeyed west, the defeat of his apparently superior technology by forces beyond his control could only have been a harsh and disillusioning experience. It was an even more trying time in his personal life.

Some time earlier, Hollerith had fallen in love. The darkly handsome young lady was named Flora Fergusson. As determined in courtship as in other matters, Hollerith soon won her hand. But a year after the engagement was announced, Flora died of typhoid. Shortly after, on July 30, 1886, the inventor received his fiancée's Bible from a mutual friend, who had inscribed on a foreleaf, "I know how much you will prize the little Bible—Flora loved both you and it. Some day, it may be the means of reuniting you in that land where there is no parting and no tears."

Hollerith locked the Bible, along with some other momentos, in a black metal box. The effects of the tragedy could not be so readily put away. In the years to come, Hollerith would be over-solicitous of his own family's health. At his insistence, drinking water in the household was always boiled. And, when he went abroad, he used a special cable code to make frequent checks on the health of each member of his family and of the servants. "He was very protective," a daughter recalls. "If someone would scream or yell, he would come rushing in, alarmed that something had happened to us." Never highly favored by Hollerith, schools would henceforth become "places to catch other people's diseases."

Through most of his early career, Hollerith had plotted his future with the compulsive tidiness and precision of his German forebears. He had worked hard, been fortunate in his choice of friends and associates, and made the most of his opportunities. Now the world no longer seemed compliant to his wishes.

5

Trials for a Census System

"He has staked everything—all his money, his time and his thoughts—upon this invention . . ."

In appealing for financial backing for his census machine in 1884, Hollerith had spoken of the need for trying it on an extended scale. "I was at the office of Registration for the City of Baltimore," he wrote in his plea to Albert Meyer, "and if I cannot secure the use of returns of Massachusetts for purposes of the experiment, I can have access to those of the City of Baltimore."

Two years later—before the completion of the air brake trials—Hollerith returned to Baltimore to record vital statistics for the City's Department of Health. The trial was, most likely, arranged by Dr. Billings, and it marked an important occasion. It was the first use of a punched card for actual work in a data processing machine.

"I compiled the vital statistics by punching a card for each death with a conductor's punch," Hollerith recalled many years later. "I punched down one side, across the bottom and then up the other side." The 3¼ by 8⅝-inch card closely resembled the railway ticket that Hollerith claimed as his inspiration. For making holes, he used the small conductor's punch that fits easily inside the hand. When tried, the instrument penetrates ordinary paper with a minimum of pressure. But continuous punching of heavier card stock, as Hollerith discovered, could be quite punishing. The work at Baltimore may have continued for some time. Several years later, the inventor's mother-in-law reported:

Mr. Hollerith came over from Baltimore Friday. He is completely tired out. He has been punching cards at the rate of 1,000 per day—and each card has at least a dozen holes. He has done it all with a hand punch and his arm was aching and paining dreadfully. He really looked quite badly.

Clearly, punching devices would have to be improved. But the work at Baltimore demonstrated the distinct advantages of substituting cards for the continuous strip of paper used for recording in the inventor's earlier version of his system. In Patent No. 395,781, filed on June 8, 1887, Hollerith described the new methods and modified system used at Baltimore. The continuous strip, he pointed out, may be advantageous where a few statistical items and records could be prepared according to a prearranged plan:

but where the individual records embrace a great variety of characteristics and compilations are to be made from time to time covering different periods and embracing a wide range of statistical matter . . . the continuous record-strip is not well adapted for the purpose, as it does not afford the means for conveniently classifying and reclassifying the individual records.

Cards could be prepared at any time. They could easily be filed away—to take advantage of existing storage compartments, the thrifty inventor made his first cards the size of the dollar bills of the time. Once prepared, the cards could be used over and over. Moreover, the cards were easier to correct or replace than a continuous tape. Recording could even be done by an unskilled individual.

However the use of cards called for changes in the construction of the system. Hollerith replaced the drum of the earlier model with a press in which a top section was pulled down against a base with a wooden handle. To record the information on the card, the operator placed it between the two halves of the press, like the ham in a sandwich. The upper half of the press, equipped with an array of yielding pins, was then pulled down upon the bottom half of the press, which was stationary. Pins that met with the card telescoped back into the lid of the press. Pins aligned with holes passed through them into cups partly filled with mercury. Below the cups was a wire or binding post. As a pin entered the mercury, electricity passed through it, completing a circuit and actuating a counter.

For recording mortality statistics, each of the cards represented the record of an individual person. Hole positions along one side of the card stood for occupations, from blacksmith and clergyman through seaman and shoemaker. The hole positions on the other side left room to record place of birth and cause of death, from apoplexy and Bright's disease to premature birth and typhoid fever. While the processing of one batch of cards through the circuit-closing press could record a great deal of information, Hollerith expanded the flexibility and capacity of his system by the addition of another ingenious feature.

Next to the system stood a large wooden box, divided into numerous compartments. On top of each was a lid held fast by a catch and spring. The lid of a particular box popped open when a card with certain characteristics—say, white females—was sensed by the circuit-closing press. This "sorting box" enabled the operator to presort the cards for the next run with one hand while operating the press with the other. "As will be readily understood," Hollerith wrote,

The number and diversity of statistical items that can be compiled in this way is almost unlimited, as each item or combination of two or more items occurring in the various individual records can be made the basis of a new statistical compilation."

In a paper written in 1887, Dr. Billings looked over Hollerith's shoulder and liked what he saw. Recalling that he had urged the young man to develop and perfect such a machine only seven years before, the fatherly statistician now gave his approval. "I think that he has succeeded," commented Billings, "and that compilers of demographical data will be glad to know of the system." The health departments of New Jersey and New York City were eager to use the system. To help them, Billings accompanied his paper with a set of instructions for the punching and handling of the cards. Soon the *New York Post* would herald the arrival of the new device in that city. The Board of Health, it would note,

has introduced a machine which it is claimed will do automatically and by electricity, with correctness and dispatch, the arduous work of tabulating a vast amount of statistical information. . . . it is a most ingenious device, designed . . . with a special view . . . for use in the . . . exhaustive statistics of the 11th Census.

New Jersey adopted the system shortly after Baltimore, and New York City had it by mid-1889. On his part, Hollerith would always feel grateful to Baltimore as the first city willing to gamble on his untried device. Later, he would donate the machine to that city. Somewhat less imbued with a sense of history, the Baltimore city fathers ultimately lost track of the machine, although it may be the same model on display at the Smithsonian Institution today.

Things were clearly looking up. Hollerith could now put behind him his bitterness toward the silk merchant for the withdrawal of support and his disappointment over the railway brake trials, although he would continue to curse at the mention of Westinghouse in later years. As his business prospects improved, his personal life brightened as well.

One evening, he was attending the Georgetown Assemblies at Lithicum Hall, a mansion on O Street. Among the young ladies in white dresses, he spotted a strikingly handsome girl with jet-black hair, dark sparkling eyes, and finely drawn features set in a long face. Like Flora Fergusson, she wore a black velvet ribbon around her neck. Because she reminded him of Flora, he asked to be introduced. The young lady's name was Lucia Talcott, called Lu to distinguish her from an aunt for whom she was named.

He could have met her before in the tightly knit community, although she had recently returned from a postgraduation year visiting an aunt in Austria. Like most young women of the time, she was considerably more sheltered than young women are today. From Alt Ausse, where she had summered, she had written of washing her dog Flock "much to his disgust," and of rowing across a lake to the woods "where we wandered about and found lots of flowers." Some of them were Alpine roses, and she had picked a bunch.

Despite her innocence, however, the young lady also kept a tidy store of common sense. After being introduced to an army lieutenant in Vienna, Lu had written to her brother Ned:

I hear you are quite worried about the lieutenant. You need not worry at all. He is not good looking and he is poor and he will not be able to make anything for three or four years longer . . . . I am so glad we live in America . . . . the young can't do anything here to support themselves and half of them go into the army as there is nothing else for them to do.

In courting Lu, Hollerith sought a close relationship with her mother, as well. His strategy, at a time when young women were closely chaperoned, could have been intended to make headway in winning the young lady's hand. However, Hollerith also felt a strong affection for the strong, practical woman whose role in raising her children was not too different from that of his own mother. Hollerith's mother Franciska had kept a millinery shop in Buffalo, making hats to order for socially prominent women. She did so as an outlet for her talents, for hats in those days were considered artistic fabrications. But following the death of her husband, the widow refused to turn to her family for help. And her business, previously a hobby, became a necessity in raising her five children. Similarly, Theodosia Talcott had helped support four sons and a daughter, following her husband's death, by picking up letters at the Patent Office and copying them at home. Although most stenographers of the day were men, Hollerith's future mother-in-law persuaded the Office to hire her as one of its first women employees, taking the horse car on P Street to work in the city. Hollerith, it appeared, transferred his strong feelings for his own mother to the industrious widow.

On her part, Mrs. Talcott enjoyed the attention. "His devotion to me is very funny," she remarked. "When he is here [at Normanstone, the family home], he meets me and we ride over to the office together. Or, if anything prevents him doing that, he comes in the office and makes me a visit."

While recognizing "that he is fattening the cow to catch the calf," the widow, whose husband, Charles Gratiot Talcott, had been a distinguished engineer, quickly sized up the young man. "He has a fine education," she wrote, "and more than average ability and no end of perseverence."

He has staked everything—all his money, his time and his thoughts—upon this invention, and it would be a terrible disappointment to him if it failed. But should it fail, he can easily make a living with his patent practice. He can have as much or as little of that as he cares to undertake.

Hollerith's courtship took a strong technological bent. Returning from a business trip to New York, he brought with him a complete photographer's outfit, including separate lenses for landscapes and portraits. Soon, the main parlor at Normanstone was filled with blinding flashes of magnesium light. When the smoke of Hollerith's assaults lifted, Lu's elderly aunts sat blinking in surprise. The resulting portraits impressed the family, as intended. But Hollerith was far from satisfied. Believing a mistake had been made in blending the developer, he wrote an indignant letter to the Eastman Kodak Company, one of many such rebukes to manufacturers. His relationship to any machine—his own or someone else's—was personal and highly charged. He expected perfection from it and felt betrayed when he experienced anything less. A daughter recalls his throwing a coffee percolator out the window after it failed to perform to expectation. On another occasion, he is said to have abandoned a car after it expired in downtown Washington, refusing to have anything further to do with it. His daughters say the story is not strictly true, since he hired a man to recover recalcitrant vehicles. If he was temporarily frustrated with photography during his courtship, he nevertheless kept at it until he obtained a striking portrait of Lu seated in a field of daisies. His persistence won results. "She appears to like him," the mother wrote, "always going off and sitting alone with him and appearing very happy and contented. He has been very persevering, and would not take any rebuffs, for she certainly has, at times, been very rude to him."

While his own family had reportedly laughed at his machine, Hollerith found a sympathetic and interested audience in his newly adopted family. Usually tight-lipped, he confided his business plans freely to Mrs. Talcott. "He wants us to come to his office soon to see his census machine," Mrs. Talcott wrote, While Hollerith was rigidly precise and demanding as an engineer, his penchant for neatness extended more to others than to himself. He worked from two desks in his office. When one got piled too high with papers, he simply covered it with a cloth and moved to the other. For this occasion, he made a special effort. "Hollerith has been at work cleaning out his office," Mrs. Talcott reported, "and even swept it out himself." After giving Lu and her mother a personal demonstration of his machine, he treated them to oysters roasted over a fire.

In mid-April 1888, Hollerith disclosed to Mrs. Talcott that the Surgeon General's Office of the War Department planned to install one of his machines. The department would rent the system for $1,000 a year. If it was successful, the Navy Department might follow suit. The Department's Records and Pension Division would use the system for compiling monthly health statistics on individual soldiers. Most of the data were similar to those required in vital statistics or ordinary census work. That is, each card represented an individual, and each hole position stood for single items of information, such as the type of disease, whether it had been contracted in the line of duty, and whether the soldier had been admitted to sick report. But there was one important difference.

The problem, Hollerith later recalled, was "determining the number of days sick for the soldiers. The reports were made monthly and any case may have been sick from 1 to 31 days so I had to develop a machine for this."

While the census machine that he used in Baltimore merely was required to count single units of information, the new machine had to be able to handle aggregates. In other words, one hole position could stand for more than a single unit of information. When the press was closed, the machine now had to pause long enough to register one hole over and over again at the same time it registered other information. To perform this chore, Hollerith designed a special integrating machine. In doing so, he allotted a counter for each number position and a carrying device for moving totals from one counter to successive counters.

A contract for the machine was signed September 3, 1888, but not before Captain Fred C. Ainsworth, the head of the Division, insisted that Hollerith provide for the contingency of its failure, since the system "is to a certain extent still in an experimental state." The early integrating device would be used in the New York City Health Department machine and may also have been employed in agricultural and manufacturing statistics, where large numbers were involved, in the 1890 Census.

In October, Hollerith entrained for Boston to visit the Western Electric Shop where the War Department machine was taking shape. Just six years before, Western Electric had taken over the Court Street quarters from Charles Williams, Jr. Although Hollerith had little sense of history, they were the same premises at which Alexander Graham Bell had holed up to work on the "speaking telegraph" and Thomas Edison had installed himself while working on the repeating telegraph. (It is interesting to speculate on whether Hollerith frequented the shop while he was at M.I.T., since his earlier system resembled the repeating telegraph.) Hollerith returned to Washington after only a few days, evidently satisfied with the work. Soon he was busy preparing for the system's arrival.

Then, as now, the success of a data processing installation depends on advanced preparation. And Hollerith evidently was leaving little to chance. By October 23, Mrs. Talcott could report, "He is very busy just now as his new machine will soon be here and will be put in the War Department. He is now arranging for it and teaching the clerks there how to use it." By November 26, the machine had arrived at Hollerith's shop in Washington. It was moved to the War Department by December 9, when Hollerith took his new family there to see it. The preparations paid off when the machine went in on schedule by the first of the year. Nine days later, Captain Ainsworth could inform his superiors that the apparatus had been furnished and was in satisfactory working order.

In November, Hollerith had gone to New York to vote in the presidential election. With an eye to foreign business, he was firmly committed to the low tariff policy that Grover Cleveland espoused. After voting, he came straight back to Washington and retired, confident of victory for his man. However, he woke up in the morning surprised to find that Benjamin Harrison was far in the lead. Election of the fifty-five-year-old Harrison had serious consequences. Hollerith had been counting on the appointment of Carroll D. Wright, head of the Massachusetts Bureau of Statistics and Labor, as Superintendent of the Census. A close associate of General Walker, Wright had become the first commissioner of the newly created U.S. Bureau of Labor in 1885 while also holding down the Massachusetts post. Firmly committed to the gathering and publishing of official statistics, with an eye to their full and frank exposition, Wright, whom Hollerith knew, would almost certainly make use of a large number of census machines. The election of the Republicans, Hollerith feared, might even endanger the pending census bill.

The political reversal also affected Hollerith's personal plans. After driving Lu and her mother home from church, he asked for a word with Mrs. Talcott. He had previously asked her consent to an engagement. Now, because of the setback to his business plans, the engagement might have to be a long one. He could set no time to be married. At Lu's suggestion, it was decided not to disclose the engagement to anyone outside of the immediate family. "I am very sorry for his disappointments with his machines," the widow wrote, "but I am not in a hurry to part with my daughter."

In the meanwhile, despite the cost of transportation, Hollerith had applied for a permit to show his machine at the Paris Universal Exposition of 1889. Because the system would be practically a duplicate of his War Department system, Hollerith asked the Department for "some statement, in the nature of a certificate, regarding the operation and use of this system . . . so that I could use the same in connection with my exhibit at Paris."

The request, dated April 8, 1889, was addressed to the Secretary of War. That official, in turn, referred it to the Surgeon General's Office. From there, it found its way to Captain Fred C. Ainsworth of the Record and Pension Division, who reported to his superiors "that the machine in question has thus far given satisfaction, but it has not been in use sufficiently long to enable him to certify other than that." Finally, Hollerith received a reply from Major Charles R. Greenleaf, Surgeon, U.S. Army:

Sir, I am directed . . . to inform you that the Secretary of War . . . states that it is not the custom of the War Department to give certificates of the character you asked for.

If the twenty-nine-year-old inventor had been presumptuous in his request, he would soon gain a measure of revenge. As of July 1, the start of the government's fiscal year, the lease for

Hollerith's machine was up for renewal. Not only did Captain Ainsworth, the officer in charge of the machine since its installation, feel compelled to report his "entire satisfaction with its work," but in a letter to the acting Secretary of War, dated July 9, U.S. Surgeon General John Moore reported an awkward situation. Major Charles Smart, who would be taking charge of the work, he explained, "reports that some 50,000 cards are already prepared, and that it will be necessary to have this machine to make them available." Within six months, the War Department found itself dependent on the new device.

Meanwhile, Hollerith in mid-April had left for Paris. He stopped first in Berlin to exhibit his machine and see about the issuance of a German patent. He arrived in the French capital in mid-May, shortly after the exhibition opened, setting up his machine in the Instruments of Precision Section of the Liberal Arts Building. There, his system was placed among the "Machines à Calcul." In his *Rapport Général* on the exhibit, the French engineer Alfred Picard traced the development of calculating machines from Pascal to Leibnitz, then described the machines on display. Picard devoted primary attention to a machine "d'un type absolument nouveau," by Léon Bollée. It could, he pointed out, perform direct multiplication and division without going through successive addition or subtraction as required by previous machines. Then he described the Hollerith system.

"M. Hollerith de Washington," he noted, "exposait un compteur pour recensement de la population . . ." After observing that the census machine could provide totals indicating age, civil condition, number of children, etc., Picard stated that such an apparatus was currently being employed by the New York City Health Department. Apparently, the City's Health Department, although it would not install the machine until July, was less starchy about letting its name be used, if Picard had asked, than the War Department.

Pressed by business affairs, Hollerith was home again only two weeks after arriving in Paris. Whether he was impressed by any of the other exhibits, or by Alexandre Gustave Eiffel's tower put up for the event, is unrecorded. However, although he was awarded one of five gold medals given to Americans, his brief exposure to the French left him less than enthusiastic. "He did not like Paris at all and certainly did not like the French people," Mrs. Talcott reported. "He says that it was like a big lunatic asylum let loose."

On his return, Hollerith was welcomed by favorable and unexpected news. President Harrison had appointed Robert P. Porter as superintendent for the forthcoming U.S. Census of 1890. Not only was Porter a personal friend, but the versatile English-born journalist, who had served as an expert on wealth, debt, and taxation in the previous Census, was an enthusiastic booster of Hollerith's electric tabulating machines. Immediately, Porter sounded out Hollerith on heading the Division of Vital Statistics for the 1890 Census. The offer to follow in the footsteps of the distinguished Dr. Billings was, indeed, a flattering one. But seeing a potential conflict between working for the government and having it use his machines, Hollerith declined. "He wants to wait until he can make a contract," Mrs. Talcott wrote on May 24, "and he fears his having charge of any of the work might interfere with that."

In July, the start of the population count was nearly a year away. But if Hollerith's machines were going to be used, a large number would have to be built, tested, and installed. And a small army of clerks would have to be trained to operate them. With commendable foresight, Porter wrote to the Secretary of the Interior, to whom he reported, urging an immediate test of "what is known as the Hollerith Electrical Tabulating Machine." The system, he reported, was in use by the Surgeon General's Office and "is also favorably regarded by statisticians throughout this country and in England and Germany." The returns, he asserted, could be tabulated much more rapidly than before. At the same time, "the facts could be presented in a greater variety of ways."

Before he had taken office, Porter, as editor of the *New York Press*, had taken up Hollerith's cause. Noting that "this is an age of progress," he had predicted that "it is not unlikely that the next census will be tabulated by electricity." If the Hollerith system proved practical on a large scale, as it had already on a small scale in the Surgeon General's Office, Porter forecast that "the tabulation of all future censuses the world over will be made by electricity." Now that he was in office, however, Porter was ensuring that the Hollerith system be considered on a strictly impartial and businesslike basis.

Taking up Porter's suggestion, the Secretary of the Interior soon organized a committee of foremost statisticians "to thoroughly investigate the several systems of tabulation." To it he named Dr. Billings, whose reputation for scientific attainment throughout the civilized world placed him above any hint of partisanship; Mr. Henry Gannett, the Geographer of the Census and "a gentleman of national reputation as a scientist"; and Mr. William C. Hunt, the statistician of the Population Division, who had made a recent reputation in tabulating the returns of the Massachusetts Census of 1885. The commission's work was temporarily delayed when Mr. Hunt resigned to place his own method of tabulation in the running. His place was taken by Mr. L. M. E. Cooke, an expert on the mechanical questions involved in the test.

The tests were scheduled to begin in late September. In the meanwhile, Hollerith was making his own preparations. Where he had previously given his address as "Solicitor of Patents, 617 Seventh Street," he now had some new stationery printed, which carried the words "The Hollerith Electric Tabulating System" and the address "H. Hollerith, Room 48, Atlantic Building." Besides changing his profession, the inventor had rented quarters in a building in which the Census Office had recently taken space. To the Secretary of the Interior, Porter wrote, "Mr. Herman Hollerith, the inventor and owner of the machines, is willing to put one of them in a room in the Atlantic Building for which he pays the rent." The test, Porter added, would cost the Office nothing "except the detail of a few clerks."

In the tests, Hollerith's electrical system was staked against the "slip" system of Mr. Hunt and the "chip" system of Mr. Charles F. Pidgin. The slip system called for the transcription of census data onto slips of paper in various color inks. The slips were then counted and sorted by hand. The largely similar chip system entailed transcribing information onto cards of various colors, standing for different classes of data. The color-coded cards were then hand-sorted into significant groups before counting. The grist for the battle was actual population data, collected for the 1880 Census, from four enumeration districts of St. Louis. The outcome of the trial depended on two factors: the time required to *transcribe* and then to *process* the data on the 10,491 inhabitants.

Writing in April, Hollerith had stated that "holes may be punched with any ordinary ticket punch." And, indeed, he had employed a conductor's punch for transcribing data onto cards at Baltimore. But for the War Department system, he supplied a more efficient keyboard or "pantograph" punch, fashioned with the help of George M. Bond, the well-known expert of the Pratt & Whitney Company of Hartford. It was an ingenious device. The operator swung a handle over a metal plate pierced with labeled holes corresponding to hole positions in the card. By depressing the handle into the proper hole, the operator punched a corresponding hole in the card.

The new device enabled Hollerith to record the test data in 72 hours, 27 minutes, compared with 110 hours, 56 minutes for the Pidgin method and 144 hours, 25 minutes for the Hunt method. The performance of his tabulator, once the cards were prepared, was still more impressive. It ran through the cards in 5 hours, 28 minutes, compared with 44 hours, 41 minutes for the Pidgin method and 55 hours, 22 minutes for the Hunt method.

On November 1, a month before the commission report on the tests was published, Porter wrote:

While the final report in relation to the tabulation of population statistics has not yet been made, enough has been seen of the working of the Hollerith machine to recommend that this system be employed for tabulating the statistics of death for the forthcoming census.

Hollerith received an order for six machines, to be used in the vital statistics division, even before the official results of the population trials were in. Mrs. Talcott, as usual, was on hand to report the news. "Already," she wrote on October 27, "he has given Hollerith an order for six machines for one division. But for the whole census, it will take about 100 more." The inventor's own reaction is not recorded. But the prospect of $106,000 in annual rentals—about half of which would be profit—was overwhelming.

"Just at this time, the family is in very bad condition," Mrs. Talcott wrote. "So many accounts to settle and so little to do it with."

While the tests demonstrated the efficiency of the machines, they indicated nothing about their overall effect. Now Porter predicted that his friend's system would not so much dispense with the labor of the clerks so much as "render the same more efficient and more available for the intellectual work of the census." The Office could now make valuable compilations that had previously been neglected because of time and expense. In addition, little thought had been given to how the machines would actually be used. Who, for example, would supply the electricity required to run the devices? And who would be responsible for keeping them in working order? While Porter had apparently indicated that more than 100 tabulators were needed, would that many actually be required if they were kept running night and day? After all, mechanical devices did not get tired.

Porter told the Secretary of the Interior that nothing had been said about how long the machines could actually be used. He suggested that the right be reserved to use the machines night or day, "provided Hollerith has allowed the necessary time to keep them in order."

It will be an advantage for us to put on a night force and so we would not then have to get so many machines. My idea is that we should claim the right to use them at all times and that they will finally agree . . . that we can use them for two shifts each of eight hours duration.

Friendship or not, Porter was driving a hard bargain, If he had his way, it would mean that only about half as many machines would be used. As the lease for the first six machines, dated December 13, indicates, the Superintendent prevailed. The machines could be used "at all times either during the night or the day as the Superintendent may determine," provided sufficient time was given to make repairs. Hollerith agreed to keep the machines in good condition and complete working order at his own expense. This meant that he would also have to keep them properly connected. For, to tabulate different combinations of data, the wires leading from the press, where the holes on the cards were sensed, to the counters had to be resoldered between jobs.

What was more, Hollerith was required to keep extra machines in readiness for "instant connection." Porter further insisted that Hollerith be required to forfeit $10 a day for every day a machine was out of order. The inventor worried about the fair application of this penalty clause. On a draft of the lease he carefully wrote in ink, "no such forfeit shall be inforced . . . unless said party of the first part shall within reasonable time, such time not to exceed 24 hours after notice of such disablement, fail to repair such a machine or machines, or to substitute other machine or machines in good working order."

Hollerith was also responsible for furnishing the electric power. As Porter knew, this uncertain commodity had to be drawn from the new Edison lighting circuits to charge the batteries that actually ran the machines. There was some doubt about how reliable such utilities could be.

Perhaps the most important provision of the initial contract, which would serve as a model for others, was that the tabulating units were to be rented to the Office rather than sold. In inexperienced hands, Hollerith was aware, the machines could easily be put out of order. And any such failures would, doubtless, be attributed to him, impeding the future acceptance of his machines. In contrast to the tabulating machines and accompanying sorting boxes, the pantograph punches, which were less likely to get out of order, would be sold to the Office outright.

Porter was satisfied. "With these machines, and such precautions as would ensure the Office absolutely against fire," he wrote, "nothing can prevent the 11th Census from being out on time."

The first contract for six tabulating machines, at $1,000 each a year, was followed on January 4 by a similar agreement for fifty additional machines. Soon Hollerith placed the orders for the tabulating equipment into the hands of Harry Bates Thayer, manager of the Western Electric Company's shop in New York. A laconic Vermonter, Thayer, who was two years younger than Hollerith, had already earned a reputation for getting things done. Once asked how he managed it with so little wasted motion,

Thayer replied that his work philosophy came from an old Yankee carpenter, whose advice was "to measure twice and cut once." Personally plucked from Western Electric's Chicago shop by crusty old Enos Barton at age twenty-six to head the New York operation, the young man made it a practice to get out into the shop to see how jobs were done. It was a time when Western Electric had ceased being a supplier of telegraph equipment for Western Union and did not yet have enough business from the Bell companies to keep fully occupied. Eager for business, Thayer took a personal interest in the final development of Hollerith's system. The following April he would report: "We are making for Mr. Hollerith twenty-five or thirty thousand dollars worth of apparatus to be used in tabulating the census which is to be taken this year."

Dr. Billings had already ordered a dozen pantograph punches for preparing the death statistics. On December 4, he needed another six. Pratt & Whitney could ship them within thirty days. The first pantograph punches, fashioned under the personal supervision of George M. Bond, were rather elegant devices that came with enameled bases and cost $41.67 each. For the 650 more the Office now wanted, painted bases would have to do. They could have the larger quantity at $24.60 apiece.

A year before, Hollerith had said that he would be glad to have Lu's younger brother Edmund Talcott with him when things were a little more settled. Now he hired Ned as his first employee. Although census clerks would operate the machines, Hollerith needed help in assembling and testing them when they arrived, rewiring the counters between runs, and removing the systems for repair. The inventor also took on a fifteen-year-old office boy with the unlikely name of Otto Braitmeyer. Impressed that the Youngster's recently widowed mother cared enough to accompany him to the interview, Hollerith may have seen something of himself in the earnest young man. Although Otto was the son of a Georgetown-born engraver, his precise Germanic ways often resulted in his being mistaken for a native of that country—a conjecture also made about Hollerith himself.

The inventor's sons would later recall Otto, pad in hand, trotting rapidly to keep pace with their fast-striding father as he barked out orders. An efficient assistant who quickly grasped the details of the business, Braitmeyer would ultimately retire as an executive vice president of IBM.

The world was opening up for Hollerith. Not yet thirty, he was succeeding in the detailed plans disclosed to his silk merchant brother-in-law some five years before. The previous April, he had described his system in the *Quarterly* of the Columbia School of Mines. "Now that an account of his machine has been published," Mrs. Talcott noted, "he is paying the penalty of becoming famous. I have numbers of persons calling to see him and his machine. It takes up so much time that he can't accomplish any work." Never able to separate entirely the roles of public official and journalist, Porter had written glowingly of the system in *Leslie's Weekly*, which carried detailed illustrations. Announcement of the contracts brought further acclaim. Noting that electricity would be called in for the computation of the census, the *New York Mail & Express* exclaimed, "How our sedate great grandfathers would have opened their eyes in amazement could they have foreseen the pace at which work is done in these rushing days of ours!"

Such popular acclaim meant little to Hollerith, who sought recognition of a different kind. With money in his pocket, he contributed to the purchase of an Emery testing machine for the School of Mines. The machine, which could test for tensile compressive and transverse strains up to 151,000 pounds, would be erected in the school's new mechanical and electrical building, where Hollerith's name would appear with those of other contributors, including Thomas Alva Edison.

With the census job still before him, Hollerith took time out on February 2 to be honored by the prestigious Franklin Institute. Hearing of the tests, the Institute's Committee on Science and the Arts had journeyed from Philadelphia to see the system in operation. On January 2, its four members not only approved it for the Census, but, in deciding to award Hollerith the Elliot Cresson Medal, observed that "it is invaluable wherever large numbers of individual facts are to be summed and tabulated."

Was Hollerith satisfied? He had both the acclaim of the public and the affection of his newly adopted family. But approval that meant anything to the young man who could barely have remembered his own father would still have to come from older men of authority, such as the kindly Professor Trowbridge, who had encouraged him earlier in his career.

It now seemed only fitting that the school to which he owed so much, and to which he was a credit, should award him an honorary degree. And, indeed, Columbia's records show that at the school's June commencement he did, in fact, become Dr. Hollerith. The honor, however, did not arrive in a wholly conventional manner. The School of Mines faculty minutes for April 3 note that "a communication was received from H. Hollerith asking that he be awarded the degree of doctor of philosophy for the studies in which he has been engaged since he graduated, in connection with the tabulating system which has been adopted by the U.S. Government . . ." The unusual request did not comply with the school's bylaws for the degree. They demanded study at the school for at least two academic years and presentation of a thesis on a subject previously approved by the faculty. In special cases, however, the student might be allowed to perform work away from the school, "providing that such students matriculate at the school as graduate students and pay the same fees required of resident candidates for the degree." Hollerith did not qualify on either count.

However, Professor Trowbridge and Dean Egleston himself spoke up strongly in favor of the application. "Owing to the fact that Mr. Hollerith had neglected to make application to be recorded as pursuing a course of study leading to the degree . . . before he began his work," it was resolved that the board of trustees be requested to waive this requirement.

Four days later, Columbia's trustees acted in Hollerith's favor. It is not known whether he submitted a thesis on his subject. Most likely, his article, "An Electric Tabulating System," published by *The Quarterly* in April 1889, took its place. However, in granting the degree, the Columbia trustees did not waive another requirement, and on June 4, Hollerith paid a $5 matriculation fee and a $35 tuition fee for the courses he never took. It is not known whether the inventor actually showed up to collect the degree.

But, although he never approved of being called "Dr. Hollerith," the honor meant more to him than any he had received.

By the start of the U.S. Census, Hollerith had succeeded to a remarkable degree. Hard work, careful preparation, friends in the Census Office, and stubborn persistence had all worked in his favor. But in some ways Hollerith's clear-cut victory over older manual methods appears almost too easy. For the history of technology is replete with instances of parallel discovery and development. If Hollerith had stumbled, was another figure waiting in the wings?

A curious footnote is supplied by Robert V. Bruce in a biography of a noted teacher of the deaf who had taken a close interest in census work. In 1888, this expert on the mechanics of speech had, at the urging of a Senate committee, submitted forty-two specific questions for making the 1890 Census on the deaf more useful and accurate. But the interests of Alexander Graham Bell went further than that, as Bruce observes:

In 1889, Bell devised a sorting machine for punch-coded census cards "based upon the principle of turning the cards around an axis by the motion of a rod in a slot punched out of the card at different angles," only to find that the Census Bureau had decided to use Herman Hollerith's new electrical punch-card tabulating system (the Adam of modern data processing machines).

Bell accepted the decision with good grace. The Hollerith system "seems to be an ingenious and practical method," he wrote; "I do not propose to push my own method."

Was Hollerith aware of Bell's interest in a punched-card census machine? Asked the question, Virginia Hollerith, the inventor's youngest daughter and family historian, replied, "Father did have a good opinion of him, but I do not know why."

6

1890: Beating the Mills of the Gods

"An engineer might indeed . . . calculate the horsepower developed by this clerical force."

The Census Office sprang up overnight like a giant mushroom. "Within a few weeks," the *Philadelphia Ledger* of March 13 reported, "it will have 2,000 employees in its offices and 45,000 men in the field not counting thousands of special agents . . ." The Eleventh Decennial Census of the United States would be different, nearly everyone agreed. For eight of the nine decades before 1880, the nation's population had leaped upward by 30 to 36 percent. Only the decimating Civil War had interrupted the burgeoning growth.

With the country booming again, citizens expected a resumption of the strong upward thrust. Not only that. Fascinated by unparalleled material advances, citizens wanted to gauge achievements of every kind—to feel their nation's muscle. So the scope of the Census had been enlarged: from a scant five subjects of inquiry in 1870, to 215 in 1880, to 235 in 1890. Ownership of homes and farms; the amount of mortgages secured by real estate; the number of children born and living; questions on aliens and naturalization and the ability to speak the English tongue (was the tide of immigrants being absorbed?)—these inquiries had been included for the first time. The spirit of things to come was best captured by *The New York Times*:

Our males of arms-bearing age will make every civilized nation bear to us a pigmy relation, and our wealth will have grown by millions to more millions than purse-proud Britain can boast. These are faint foreshadowings of what the eleventh census will disclose during the coming months.

Census Superintendent Robert Porter, the man in charge of it all, was aware of the enormity of the undertaking. More than three months remained until the door-to-door or "dwelling house" count on June 1 signaled the official start of the census. Yet he had already rounded up what appeared to be every square foot of empty office and loft space in downtown Washington.

The scene was one of mild confusion at the newly constructed Inter-Ocean Building on 9th Street, where the main population count would take place. Workmen were still hammering away and adding coats of paint while Hollerith's machines were being hoisted up the outside of the building and swung in at the third floor. As quickly as they were uncrated and set in place, Ned Talcott, Hollerith's first employee, connected them to the wires that ran up the stairwell from the basement. Down below, the wires were secured to the terminals of two-foot-high white porcelain jugs filled with strong-smelling sal amoniac—the storage batteries needed to run the machines. Ned charged them once daily from the Edison circuits coming into the building.

Others had long ago shed their jackets. But Hollerith kept his on despite the warmness of the day. With his short-clipped hair, squared shoulders, and harsh voice barking out orders, he was the general keeping above the fray. He paused to lecture a group of census clerks on the workings of his system, supervised the testing of soldered wires on the backs of the machines to assure that connections were solid, and oversaw countless other chores. Little if anything escaped his attention.

Although front-to-back rooms and high windows allowed for circulation of air, Hollerith was dissatisfied. He insisted that electric fans be installed. When one broke down, he asked Ned to take it to his shop on 7th Street for repairs. Ned was tinkering with it there when the fan blade swung around, slashing the palm of his hand. Supported by Hollerith's black servant Andrew, Ned, who said he was going to faint, made his way to a druggist and from there to the hospital. Hearing of the accident, Hollerith dropped everything at the office, raced to the hospital, and drove Ned home in his buggy, seeing that the wound was properly dressed by Dr. Peters, the family physician. Ned was back at work the next day.

Things had settled down considerably by June 26, with the third floor of the building taking on the appearance of a factory or machine shop. "It is a very tidy and airy machineshop, however," a visitor reported, "where nice-looking girls in cool white dresses are at work at the long rows of counting machines. At first glance," he noted, "the machines remind one of upright pianos." The machine count would not begin in earnest until July 1, a month after the enumerators had visited households throughout the land. But already, the schedules, filled in with particulars on the nation's citizenry, were pouring into McDowell's Mill, a low brick building within a stone's throw of the main Census Office. There, the wooden crates, resembling dry goods boxes, were unpacked and the portfolios of schedules from all over the country checked off against bills of lading.

From the busy mill, where piles of empty crates already reached toward the ceiling, the schedules were hauled by wagon to the Inter-Ocean Building, where the long-skirted young ladies seated at the "statistical pianos" had already begun totaling up the population of the United States. "It is curious to stand in the long room on the third floor and watch the delicate flying fingers which are operating on these electrical machines," a reporter from the *Saginaw* (Michigan) *Weekly* noted. "Upon first entering the room, the whizzing of the electric fans and the ringing of bells, which are attached to each machine and respond to every touch upon the keys, are confusing." Soon, the scribe from Michigan found himself caught up in the rhythmic swing of "that maddest of all creations in the poet's brain, 'The Bells,' by Edgar Allen Poe."

Hear the Census with its bells
Electric bells!
What a world of work
Their wild confusion tells,
How they klingle, klangle, klingle
In that Inter-Ocean room
Till your tympanums all tingle

At the jingle, jangle, jingle
And you wish you were at home
Keeping time, time, time,
To some other sort of rhyme
Than the tin, tin tabulation of those bells!

To take the first count of the population, Hollerith had designed
a small keyboard unit about the size of a modern portable typewriter that did not punch holes in cards. It was simply a counter.
The device was set on the work surface of the tabulator unit. The
first row of keys was numbered from one to ten, the second from
eleven to twenty. "With a schedule before her, the lady strikes
a key indicating the number of persons in the household . . . If
a man lives alone, the operator strikes key one . . . Say the next
family is eight persons, the operator strikes the key numbered
eight." Opposite the operator and set into the upright portion of
the tabulator, twenty counters, set into two rows corresponding
to the keyboard, kept track of the count. By pressing the "eight"
key, for example, the operator moved a dial forward one position
in the counter reserved for families having eight members. A
twenty-first counter, positioned below the others, kept track of
the total number of families that were counted in an area, providing information for cross-checking.

"The machines cannot make mistakes," the *Chicago Tribune*
soon observed. "The girls who run them, however, are not so
thorough." It was a simple procedure. All the operator had to do
was to note the number of persons copied by the enumerator at
the top of each family schedule and press the corresponding key.
To verify the figure, the second young lady performed the same
operation on a second machine. Where totals did not agree, rec-
tifiers, in a room upstairs, ascertained the errors and corrected
them with skill and rapidity.

As the days went by, the operatives progressed in dexterity. By
August 8, the *Chicago Tribune* could say that "With the aid of one
of these machines, a young lady has counted 50,000 persons in
a day." Such astronomical feats, it was observed, demanded not
only dexterity but also a steadfast and industrious nature. Unfor-

tunately, not all of those who had clamored for the appointments proved cut out for the work. Clerks who could not become accustomed to the machines were dismissed and replaced by others. "The indolent girls have been weeded out," the *Tribune* assured its readers, "and none but the industrious are left."

Despite its novelty, the work turned out to be anything but a lark. After spending only four days at her machine, one female operative vented her irritation directly on the Superintendent of the Census. "Mr. Porter, I'm going home," she announced. "It is no fun here. No summer vacation about this!"

As they made the rough count of the country's population, the Hollerith machines at the Inter-Ocean Building were being put through a sort of preliminary canter. Much more strenuous and exacting was the next operation of recording the details from each schedule onto punched cards and then throwing this mass of detail about individual citizens into the meaningful combinations that would comprise the portrait of a nation. The problem, as one writer put it, was "how to extract the honey from the lion's jaw."

For the major part of the work, the schedules were hauled to the main Census Office Building on D Street, where other machines were waiting. ". . . machines invented by a former employee of the bureau are used," the *Tribune* reported. "The system is very ingenious. The young lady sits at a little table upon which there is a metal plate containing 240 holes." The metal plate was the keyboard of Hollerith's newly invented pantograph or keyboard punch. Over it swung a sharp index finger. The operator directed the index finger into any of the lettered or numbered holes, each standing for a different inquiry of the census taker—"male," "female," "single," "married," "widowed," "divorced," "place of birth," "occupation," etc. "When the index finger is pressed down into any of these holes," the newspaper commented, "the punch at the back says 'ditto' by stamping out a hole in a manila [punched] card."

A leading journal called the symbols to be read by the operators "refinements of torture." But the clerks who punched an average of 500 cards a day in the preliminary test were soon averaging 700 in actual use. "These innocent combinations," a visitor observed, "are no more burdensome on the memory than the details of a typewriter keyboard. On the contrary, they were found to be vastly interesting. Punching, it was discovered became as easy as any other task requiring ordinary intelligence."

In the next step, the operator identified the cards by the district in which the enumerator worked. For this part of the job, Hollerith had designed another punch. He called it a "gang punch," because it could punch through a "gang" of five or six cards at once. An area along the card's left end contained a field of forty-eight hole positions for this purpose. For each district, the cutters in the punch were set to represent a code number for that district. There were some 40,000 districts in all. In designing the pantograph punch and the simpler gang punch Hollerith had come a long way from the ordinary conductor's punch that had made his arm ache while recording the health statistics in Baltimore a few years before.

Unlike his earlier punched cards, Hollerith had left the cards for the 1890 Census unprinted, almost certainly to save the expense. As a result, the records were more intelligible to the machines than to their operators, although an experienced operator could decipher the documents from a glance at the hole positions. For the less experienced, Hollerith supplied a printed template. Placed over the card, it quickly revealed the mysterious meanings of the holes. A hole in one place might mean a white person; a hole in another place, a black. A combination of holes in another part of the card indicated a profession. Not only the twenty six inquiries that characterized an individual were recorded, but also the state, county, city, and enumeration district where he lived. The machine-made punched card records, which told about each of 62 million individuals, now took the place of the cumbersome hand-written family schedules. Each card was also stamped with a serial number so that it could be compared with the original return, should the need arise.

Hollerith had come up with a simple but comprehensive scheme for the electric sensing of hole positions standing for different types or quantities of information. Yet, rather than being pleased with his solution, he appeared vaguely dissatisfied, even apologetic. The idea, he may have felt, fell far short of one of his cameras, which recorded a host of details all at once on a plate that could be printed for the eye to see. In a speech shortly after the completion of the Census, he appeared to dismiss his system as "the mechanical equivalent of the well-known method of compiling statistics by means of individual cards, upon which the characteristics are indicated by writing." And he added:

As it would be difficult to construct a machine to *read* such written cards, I prepare cards by punching holes in them, the relative positions of such holes describing the individual. In the United States Census we used cards 3¼ inches by 6⅝ inches, the surface of which was divided into 288 imaginary squares ¼ inch square. To each of these spaces some particular meaning or value is assigned.

Once the cards were prepared, the tabulating machine came into play to elicit facts on the population from the mass of data on individual citizens. Perched on the work surface of the tabulating unit was the hand-operated press, or circuit-closing device, described earlier. Retractable pins on the upper or movable portion of the press were aligned above all the positions where holes could possibly be punched in the card. Where they found a hole in a card, when the press was closed upon it, they completed a circuit by passing through it, moving an indicator forward one position on a corresponding counter dial. Each of the tabulators held forty counters, which could register up to 9,999 and readily be reset to zero.

The machine set up in this manner could easily tally the single facts recorded in any group of cards for example, the number of males or females. But Hollerith wanted to know facts in combination. For example, how many males or females were there in each age group? To accomplish this, the inventor had inserted relays, or electrical switches, in the circuits of his machines. He explained: "By a simple use of the well-known electrical relay, we can secure any possible combination. It must not be understood that only two items can be combined. We are only limited by the numbers of counters and relays."

Without the use of relays, Hollerith would have obtained only forty categories of data in running the cards through his machines.

Instead, the first run produced seventy possible combinations of data regarding general population; six relating to naturalization for foreign white and foreign colored; seven to color for the native and foreign colored; and six to ownership of homes and farms, which concerned all householders.

But there was a limit. "It would be manifestly impractical," the *Scientific American* pointed out, "to make a single machine of sufficient capacity to include all combinations possible . . ." To further extend the range of the tabulator, Hollerith supplied each machine with a sorting box. "A box divided into compartments may be noticed at the side of the operator," the publication observed.

This has lids to its many compartments which are opened by electricity. As the operator presses the handle [of the press], one of the electrical connections . . . referring to race or any other desired particular, causes a special compartment of the box to open for the reception of the card just tabulated. Thus the cards are classified for transmission to other machines.

While one batch of cards was being put through the tabulator, they were at the same time being placed into new combinations by means of the sorting box, for a subsequent run through another tabulator. All told, there would be some seven runs of cards through the machines.

The important concepts of sorting and tabulating came close together in Hollerith's mind. The operations could be performed separately. But they were clearly intended to complement each other. While the operator was removing a card from the press of the tabulator with her right hand to be placed in an open sorting box to the right of the machine, she could, at the same time, place a new card into the press with her left hand.

Soon after the population count was under way, Superintendent Porter organized a night force to speed the work. "The work of enumeration goes on night and day," it was reported on August 8. "At dead of night, the tinkling of little bells is heard on the street outside." While the daytime work had been entrusted mainly to young ladies, the newly organized night force was made up of males from all classes of society. "Some are law students earning the wherewithal to climb the ladder of fame," it was observed, "others government clerks who apparently are never tired of depleting the exchequer of Uncle Sam." On arrival at the Inter-Ocean Building, each squad of new clerks was led to a remote part of the operating room by instructors expert in the business. At least some of the instructors, it seems, had become inordinately enthusiastic over their achievements and knowledge of the odd invention. But as with young lady operators, not all of the males took readily to the new devices. "Newcomers reporting for work the first night," it was observed, "are likely to become discouraged at the ever increasing intricacies of the machines and some have been known to resign after being in the office no more than an hour." Those who remained worked incessantly from 5:30 P.M., when they reported, until 11:30 P.M., "with an intermission of 15 minutes to refresh the inner man."

Arriving in the morning, the young ladies encountered unexpected difficulties. They found it troublesome to determine where the night shift had left off its work and where they were to begin. Another source of delay may have been the need to adjust and rewire the tabulators to count new combinations of facts. Porter's plan to keep the machines busy day and night was not working well. Also impeding a businesslike transition between shifts was a seemingly innocent feature of the machine itself. The highly logical Hollerith had provided each tabulator desk with a drawer where the operator, on completing a shift, was meant to leave a brief report on the status of the work. On occasion, however, this medium of exchange served a purpose not envisioned by the inventor. "In many cases," it was reported, "notes are exchanged between male and female (entirely unknown to each other) . . . which are, as a rule, answered in the same strain."

Romance, it appeared, would find a way in the new era of machine tabulation. But love, as it is wont to do, did not always run smoothly, as it was soon reported. "One young fellow . . . assigned to a machine for a week, having been cruelly removed and detailed to another, the party who succeeded him, on opening the drawer of the desk, found no less than half a dozen epistles of the character described!"

It was not surprising that Porter soon informed the Secretary of the Interior that the results "were not of sufficient advantage to continue the night force." Hollerith might have smiled inwardly at his friend's dilemma. If Porter had stuck to his original plan to order fifty additional machines, all of the work could have been done during the daytime, without any problem. However, Hollerith and Ned were too tired from keeping the machines in adjustment over two shifts and setting them up for the next day's work for self-congratulation. Both Hollerith's and Porter's reputation rode on the speedy and successful completion of the work.

To relieve the situation, Hollerith now offered to lease the government forty additional tabulating machines at $500 a year—half the rental he was charging for the fifty six already in use. It was a risky proposition. The lower rates might set a precedent Hollerith was unwilling to accept in the future. To guard against this, the inventor stipulated that all of the machines, including those already in use, could be employed only during regular office hours, between 9:00 A.M. and 4:00 P.M. Because the machines already installed had been working well, Hollerith offered a further inducement. He would guarantee that each of his tabulators would handle a monthly average of at least 10,000 cards, with three readings per machine each working day.

Porter quickly agreed. "The amount of work done based upon Mr. Hollerith's guaranteed average," he reported, "will more than cover any possible advantage that might be gained by running the machines at night." The additional machines, built by the following July, would be used for the last year's work. For Hollerith, it was a chance to build forty additional machines at government expense for future use.

By August 16, the rough population count of the nation's citizens had been completed. Barely six weeks had passed since the sleigh like tinkling of bells on Hollerith's machines had announced the beginning of the machine count. From 2,000 to 3,000 families a day, comprising 10,000 to 15,000 individuals, the white-aproned young ladies had progressed in dexterity until, on a recent day, forty three of them had counted 10,000 families totaling 50,000 people, with one young lady reaching the astonishing total of 16,071 families, or about 80,000 persons. On that singular day, no less than 1,342,318 families, or 6,711,590 people, had fallen prey to the statistical pianos. While scattered enumerators were yet to be heard from—the last card punched would be received by Porter on September 2—the *Washington Post* could report that "the rush and a great deal of the work incidental to taking the census of population is over . . ."

Free from worry and strain for the first time in months, Hollerith gave a dinner for chiefs of the Tabulating Section of the Population Division. He loved good food and the pleasure of sharing it with friends. With typically careful preparation, he saw to it that the dinner at Glen Echo Heights, overlooking the Potomac, was a splendid affair. Menus specially printed for the occasion detailed each of numerous courses. After the sumptuous meal, the celebration continued, with rounds of toasts and light-hearted banter running into the early hours.

Hollerith expressed appreciation for the energy and skill of the chief of the division, his assistants, and his clerks. It was due to them, he modestly declared, that the results were obtained. "While I devised the machines which were used," he commented, "you have made them a success." Never straying from the accustomed role of scientist and engineer, he cited the day when the division counted over one-tenth the population of the United States, and pondered the energy released in processing fifteen tons of schedules.

An engineer might indeed stop to calculate the number of horse power of physical energy developed by this clerical force. Or, if they do not appreciate what this means, let me ask them to consider a stack of schedules of thin paper higher than the Washington Monument. Let them imagine the work required in turning over such a pile of schedules page by page, and recording the number of persons reported on each schedule. This is what was done in *one day* by the population division of the Census Office.

Ever the journalist, Porter felt little constraint in celebrating "a great event." "For the first time in the history of the world," he commented, "the count of the population of a great nation has been made with the help of electricity." Noting that the population had actually been counted twice over, the Superintendent estimated that "with the work force that left work this afternoon . . . we could, with these electrical machines, count the entire population of the United States in 10 days of seven working hours each." Then Porter extrapolated on a still grander scale.

The bright young women and the sturdy young men of our Population Division could run through the entire population of the earth which, including Asiatics and savages, is estimated at 1,300,000,000 in less than 200 days, providing places could be found to store the schedules.

Picking up the theme of its founder and publisher, Porter's own paper, the *New York Press*, took heed of the event that transpired in Washington City. "Superintendent Porter," it editorialized, "is to be congratulated upon his grand showing and quick accounting. Like Alexander, who wept because he had no more worlds to conquer, Porter is said to be sad and tearful because he has no more nation to count."

Though the official count, setting the nation's population at 62,622,250, would not be issued until December 12, and another two years would be required to refine and publish all the data of the Eleventh Census, Hollerith's goal was clearly in sight. Before the Census, the Commission conducting the competitive test had projected that the tabulating machines would save $597,125 over previous methods. The expert statisticians—as experts have a way of doing—proved how wrong they could be. In actual use, the strange-looking statistical pianos would save more than two years' time over the previous census and $5 million in taxpayers' money. More important, in contrast to the 1880 Census, it had for the first time been possible to draw every desirable combination of fact from the schedules. "With the machines," Porter reported in a paper, "the most complicated tables can be reproduced at no more expense than the simpler ones." And the punched card system, he concluded, gave a far better check against error than the old system of tallying by hand. "The apparatus works as unerringly as the mills of the Gods," one expert reported, "but beats them hollow as to speed."

Unknown to any of the guests, the first large-scale application of the machines had set some enduring precedents for an industry yet to be born. Hollerith had rented his machines to the government rather than selling them outright, because he knew they could be put out of order by improper handling. As a result, for years, the vast majority of such equipment would be leased rather than purchased.

Keeping the machines in adjustment and setting them up for succeeding phases of the work required expert skill and knowledge. Timely and expert service, Hollerith was aware, was as important as furnishing the machines in the first instance.

Hollerith decided that the furnishing of punched cards for his machines was too important to be entrusted to others. Two months before the Census, the *New York Sun* had reported that a Mr. Al Daggett of Brooklyn had submitted the lowest bid of 31.7 cents per thousand for the 100 million tabulating cards to be used. "The 100 million cards desired," the *Sun* pronounced, "can be made of almost any material without destroying the usefulness of the tabulating machinery." The newspaper proved mistaken. During the early part of the Census, the poor-quality paper flaked off and clogged the mercury cups through which contact was made to the counters, causing some problems with the machines. Thirty-one years later, the British Government experienced similar difficulties when its Government Stationery Office insisted, against the advice of Hollerith's representatives, on employing paper of British manufacture for that country's census. Because they became warped, a million and a half cards had to be rejected.

Besides helping to establish new procedures, Hollerith's system had an underlying effect on the way work was done—and on the people who were doing it. Shortly after the Civil War, Christopher Latham Sholes had invented the first workable writing machine. But for many years the female mind had been considered too flighty to master typing and the female body too frail to operate the heavy machines. YWCA classes throughout the country had changed all that. Now "typewriters," as the girls were called, were invading offices previously held to be male sanctuaries. "I feel that I have done something for the women who have always had to work so hard," Sholes had said. "This will enable them more easily to earn a living."

The 1890 Census, started the year Sholes died, picked up where he left off. During the family count, the *Sun* had pointed out, women had averaged nearly one half more than men on the little machines.

It is worth noting that of the 43 who counted more than 10,000, 38 were women and only five men . . . . women are better adapted for this particular work than men. They are more exact in touch, more expeditious in handling the schedules, more at home in adjusting the delicate mechanism of the machine and apparently more ambitious to make a good record.

Porter commended the women workers for superior efficiency, and the *New York Herald* took up the refrain:

The field of women's employment . . . is steadily extending. Occupations once closed are now open to her. . . . in how many of these new spheres . . . would it appear, as in . . . census work, that women are superiors of men?

Another issue was raised by Hollerith's machines. Before the Census, Porter had assured his superiors that the machines would elevate the level of work rather than throw people out of it. Afterward, he would affirm that his friend's invention had, indeed, dispensed with drudgery. But he appears to have modified his views on its labor-saving potential. Comparing the Hollerith system to "the tedious and trying Seaton slips of paper on which the tally was made by pencil marks," he commented: "It saves the eyes of the tallyist, reduces the number of tally clerks required and relieves them of the difficult task of actual counting and avoids the possibility of error arising from their weariness or inattention." What reaction came from the machine operators themselves? Apparently, no one bothered to record what the typical census worker had to say. The only surviving description of the permanently altered relation between people and machine is quite possibly apocryphal and, no doubt, has been embellished over the years. Yet it wistfully signifies that, after the 1890 Census, things would never be the same. More than half a century later, Charles W. Springer of Bellerose, New York, who operated a tabulator at the Inter-Ocean building, wrote to Thomas J. Watson, Jr., who headed the business that Hollerith began. As the ninety-two-year-old recounted

Mechanics were there frequently . . . to get the ailing machines back in operation. The trouble was usually that somebody had extracted the mercury (which made the necessary electrical contacts) from one of the little cups with an eye-dropper and squirted it into a spittoon, just to get some un-needed rest.

My immediate superior was a Mr. Shaw, and it was a saying in the office that 'Shaw does nothing and Springer helps him.' This was not true . . . Much of the time I didn't help him at all . . .

Continuing in a humorous vein, Springer takes his superior's part against the onslaughts of the machine.

Shaw was a remarkable man. With a drink or two, he could add three columns of figures simultaneously and get the right answer faster than any machine before or since. If he could have been kept in just the right amount of liquor, Hollerith's machines might now be no more of a memory than the Inter-Ocean Building (and what would you, Mr. Watson, be doing now?).

Hollerith himself was characteristically reticent in evaluating the first large-scale application of his machines. In a speech shortly after the completion of the Census, he cited the importance to Government of complete and current statistics.

We . . . pay about $35 million annually in pensions. How long this will continue is . . . an interesting question. In . . . legislation relating to pensions, we will now know how many survivors of the late war there are at each age period, also . . . the age of widows of soldiers. In other words, we now have data upon which to base our calculations.

The nation, as President Van Buren had pointed out sixty years before, was not apt to legislate more intelligently until the census provided better statistics. Still unforeseen was that the machines and techniques that Hollerith had developed could not only pin-point the personal and economic well-being of the citizen, they would also make possible the mounting of large-scale programs to address the problems they uncovered. Forty-five years after the 1890 Census, refined versions of Hollerith's punched card machines would make possible the launching of the Social Security program during the Great Depression, in which an identifying number for each eligible citizen was punched in one of the inventor's punched cards. With new information-processing techniques at its disposal, the nation could begin to apply its resources more precisely and humanely to the life of the ordinary citizen.

Following the Census, the inventor's personal reaction to his accomplishment was one of relief more than anything else. He had carefully planned the application of his machines and developed them with painstaking thoroughness, yet he somehow found himself unable to believe that *he* was principally responsible for their success. His curious air of detachment is reflected in a letter composed forty years after the 1890 Census. "In due time, along came the census," Hollerith wrote, "and it was, indeed, a brave act on the part of Mr. Porter to award me a contract for the use of the machines in compiling the census.

"Where would he have been if I had failed?"

Hollerith clipped an article from an unidentified newspaper and pasted it in his scrapbook. The skeptical assessment by the unknown writer may have been summed up the ordinary citizen's view of the first large-scale use of punched card data processing machines, if, indeed, he thought about the subject at all. "The machine is patented," the writer observed, "but as no one will ever use it but governments, the inventor will not likely get very rich."

7

Taking the Census Abroad

"The instrument is not lazy. It is not made heedless by the state of the atmosphere."

Hollerith had driven himself through the unrelenting heat of a Washington summer since the Census had begun in June. Porter's insistence on keeping the machines going night and day had been especially punishing. Getting them ready for successive shifts had kept him constantly on call. He had gotten little sleep and had had to manage everything himself. Despite a lull following the completion of the population count in September, he began complaining of blinding headaches. He could not sleep and was unable to work. "He could not control his temper," Mrs. Talcott recorded, "and suffered all the time with his head."

Reluctantly, he visited Dr. Peters. He must go away at once, the doctor told him, have a complete rest, and forget completely about business. The inventor was dumbfounded. Who else would look after affairs at the Census Office? If he went away, he told the doctor, he would only worry about all the things he had left undone. But Hollerith also realized that he had little choice. He felt completely helpless and completely alone.

Over the summer, he had seen little of Lu. Now his thoughts swirled about her. It would do him no good to go away, he informed Dr. Peters, if Lu could not come with him. He would not leave without her.

From the doctor's office in Georgetown, Hollerith drove straight out to Normanstone. It was Saturday. Lu was away visiting a friend in Oxford, Maryland, until Monday, and there was no way of reaching her. Nevertheless, Hollerith announced to his fiancée's mother that they would be married on Monday afternoon.

Mrs. Talcott protested her daughter did not even have a dress to be married in. The one she was wearing would do, Hollerith insisted. There were dozens of other reasons given for delay. But he refused to listen to any of them. Realizing that Hollerith could not be reasoned with, the widow could do nothing but agree.

His mustache freshly trimmed and short brown hair neatly brushed, Hollerith drove his favorite horse Jack briskly to the station Monday morning. A lightly falling rain failed to dampen his spirits. As Lu stepped off the 7:30 train, he subjected her to a similar onslaught. What about their friends, she objected. And how could all the arrangements possibly be made?

They were to be married anyway, Hollerith persisted. Why not now? While the inventor usually kept his emotions carefully in balance, once they were loosed, he was virtually uncontrollable. Sizing up the situation, Lu realized she could not argue. Finally, she too had to agree.

As if in assent, the sun came out as the couple drove to Normanstone. Hollerith dropped off Lu and picked up her mother. First they called on the minister, Dr. Stuart. He could perform the service. Then they stopped at Dr. Peters's and invited him. Then it was off to Demonet's bakery where, as if they had placed their order days before, the baker had just taken a wedding cake from the oven. Finally, Mrs. Talcott and a friend went off to buy a white India silk dress for Lu. It turned out to be too large, but Lu's aunts went to work immediately taking it in. In early afternoon, with preparations still under way, Hollerith arrived at Normanstone with his best man, Holdsworth Gordon. Since there was nothing for them to do but get in the way, they were dispatched on a tour of the neighborhood. But Hollerith refused to go. Decked out uncomfortably in cutaway and striped trousers, he nervously paced the floor.

The ceremony started promptly at 4:30 as planned. Tall and willowy in the India silk dress, Lu made an aristocratic and lovely bride. Hollerith, though grown somewhat heavier in recent years, nevertheless made an impressive figure as he stood erect and proud at her side. His thoughts at this important moment are unknown. But shedding his customary reserve, he kept beaming and going up to Lu and gazing fondly into her face. "It was a very sweet, solemn and quiet wedding," the mother-in-law, who had assembled it in record time, reported.

Often abrupt and harsh with others, Hollerith would prove a gentle, adoring, and highly protective husband. In the Victorian manner of the day, he would appear to treat his wife almost as a child. Feminine and seemingly pliant, Lu would prove a source of quiet strength and an emotional counterbalance to her temperamental husband.

The whirlwind wedding on September 15, 1890, had left no time for honeymoon plans. With no set itinerary, the couple left for West Point, New York, to stay at Cranston's. If time allowed, they would continue north to Saratoga, Lake George, and the Adirondacks, winding up in Montreal. Within a week, Hollerith's headaches had almost disappeared. However, throughout his life, the inventor tended to be overly concerned about his own health. Before taking a bath, for example, he would carefully measure the water temperature to make sure that it matched the temperature of his body, to avoid any undue shock to his system. Now, with his attention focused elsewhere, he, for once, appeared relaxed and happy. "He writes Lu's letters for her for fear she will fatigue herself," Mrs. Talcott reported. "Perhaps it is as well that he should think her delicate and wait on her, as it gives him something to think about besides his own affairs and his own health."

Back in Washington, Census Superintendent Porter suddenly decided to sail to Europe because of his own health. Returning in early October, he summoned Hollerith home, cutting short the honeymoon. In an article headlined "Useless Machines," the *Boston Herald* had roasted both Porter and Hollerith, charging that hundreds of the devices for tabulating the census had proved useless. The machines, it claimed, had been invented by a cousin of Mr. Porter's under a contract with a company in which the inventor was foremost. The matter, the paper said, has been called to the attention of several Congressmen and an investigation would shortly be ordered.

Joining in the fun, the local *National Democrat* would soon question whether Porter's "sudden trip" was really due to overwork or ill health. "His boon companions," the paper charged, "looked upon him as a very healthy and vigorous man two days before he left and all who have knowledge of his methods and the conduct

of his office are surprised to learn that he overtaxed his brain."
What was more, positions in the Office had been farmed out, the
paper said, and hundreds of electrical machines contracted for at
$6 a day with a relative. Not one of the machines, the newspaper
added, had fulfilled the conditions of the contract. "With the
exception of adding, they were total failures," it reported, "and
the entire work must be done over." Taking direct aim at Hollerith, the paper added, "one noted supper for a favored few
recently cost the favorite contractor of the electric machines a
very large sum of money."

Interior Secretary John Noble immediately denied the charges
and asserted that Porter had indeed been ill. Stepping off the boat
from England on October 23, Porter branded the accusations
ridiculous. "The electric machines," he told the *New York Herald,*
"were chosen by a board." And the statement "that any relative
of mine was concerned . . . is a simple falsehood." But most surprising was Hollerith's reaction to the partisan uproar. Ordinarily
thin-skinned to criticism, the inventor simply let the accusations
roll off his back. "The newspapers are pitching into Mr. Porter
and incidentally into Mr. Hollerith," his mother-in-law reported.
"But he is so happy that he does not allow it to cause him much
annoy."

While Hollerith and Lu were honeymooning, Mrs. Talcott had
rented a three-story brick house for them at 3126 Dumbarton
Avenue in the heart of Georgetown. Hollerith, who had been
living in boarding houses since moving to Washington, could
hardly wait to move in. Well before the November 1 moving date,
he purchased furniture for the living and dining rooms, which was
now waiting to be put in place. Like his tabulating machines, it
was built of rugged oak and meant to last. With each new purchase,
the inventor announced that he would "go to the poorhouse." The
Census Office, in fact, was using only half the machines he anticipated, lowering his expected income, and he still had payments
to make to manufacturers on the equipment that was in use. Yet
he seemingly did not care. "Herman is disposed to be extravagant,"
his mother-in-law observed. Yet he went on spending as if there
were no tomorrow. For his new bride and himself, he would have
nothing but the best.

On moving day, Lu and her mother scrubbed the house from

top to bottom. They had just reached the kitchen, when Hollerith walked in. Spotting water bugs, he immediately rushed off to get a large bottle of turpentine and a sprayer, ripped out the shelves, and sprayed every crevice where the insects might hide. In matters of health and cleanliness, he laid down the law.

While some men fear entrapment in domesticity, Hollerith appeared to relish it. During the fall, a delegation of business executives from England and Germany descended on Washington to attend the Iron and Steel Institutes. They visited public buildings, including a stop at the Inter-Ocean Building, where Hollerith demonstrated his machines. Then there was a reception at the Executive Mansion at 3:00 P.M. to meet President Harrison. Although Hollerith was on the committee, he balked at attending the final event of the day when he discovered full-dress was required. Instead, he sent Ned to hear the Marine Band hold forth under its conductor John Phillip Sousa. It might have been advantageous, and good business, to mingle socially with the prominent businessmen from abroad. But he preferred a quiet evening at home with his bride.

In fact, everyone was enjoying the new home, except Bismarck, the inventor's large black and white cat. Although the backyard was encircled by a fence to protect Bismarck's preserve, the hardy neighborhood cats scaled the high wooden wall to feast on Bismarck's dinner. Hollerith boiled over at the intrusion. Rimming the fencetop with a wire leading back to batteries and a switch in a third-floor room, the inventor sat watchfully puffing a cigar. When a feline trespasser reached the top of the fence, Hollerith threw the switch, sending a jolt through the predator and making it jump off in surprise. Hearing of the electrical circus of screeching cats, Hollerith's friends from the Census Office soon stopped off with him to witness another novel application of electricity.

While preparing for the U.S. Census the previous spring, Hollerith had received inquiries from European countries eager to use his machines in their population counts. "The inventor," the *New York Sun* of March 24, 1890, had reported, "introduced his machines abroad, and the governments of various countries, including Austria and Italy, have adopted them and will use them in statistical work." Hollerith's plan, evidently couched to satisfy European patent laws, was to have at least some of his equipment built abroad. Harry Thayer, Western Electric's manager in New York, wrote to F. R. Welles, the firm's manager in Antwerp: "In order for him to hold his Belgian patent, it is necessary for him to commence manufacturing, which is the occasion of the order . . . to make up a machine." Far too busy with the U.S. Census and, most likely, unable to pay for the additional machines, Hollerith was not anxious to have the work rushed, as Thayer also explained.

He is not anxious to have the work particularly pushed, and if you can get a man to work, say making tools to make the counter of which we sent you a sample, and let him keep at it until you have a bill against Mr. Hollerith of not more than one hundred dollars, he thinks that will satisfy all the requirements.

The requirement to manufacture abroad probably explains why the inquiry from Austria's Central Bureau of Statistics was made to the inventor indirectly through the Vienna manufacturing firm of Otto Schaefler. On receiving his Austrian patents, Hollerith signed a contract with the company. It specified that he would furnish the plans for his system, while the Austrian firm would build a specified number of machines for that country's Census. Hollerith obligingly agreed to ship a tabulator abroad to make the job of copying it easier. "Ned has been very busy arranging and packing a census machine to go to Austria," Mrs. Talcott wrote on November 16, "and quite wishes he were going with it." The consequences of Hollerith's action were unexpected, as he later recalled:

I had the unfortunate experience with the Austrians which shows the ridiculousness of their patent laws. They were anxious to use the machines and ordered a number. I applied for an Austrian patent, but as it was impossible to have the machines made in Austria within the time allowed me, I had some sent over from America, simply as a matter of accommodation. When they arrived, the government promptly annulled my patents because the machines were not made in Austria.

The matter was worse than a technical abridgement of his patents, as the inventor discovered shortly before Christmas. "Hollerith has just seen a Vienna paper," his mother-in-law reported, "in which some man claims to have invented Hollerith's machines, gives excellent description and sketches, and then [says] he's going to take the Austrian census with it. In other words, he has stolen the whole thing." The blame was laid not on the manufacturer, but directly at the feet of "a prominent government official in Vienna."

Hollerith literally bristled. Although less than six feet in height, his square shoulders, square-set neck, short mustache, and closely cropped hair could, on occasion, give him a warlike mien not unlike that of the German statesman after whom he named his cat. Rapidly translating hurt to anger, he relished the prospect of a fight. If it meant taking on the whole Austro-Hungarian Empire, so much the better! He fired off a cable instructing his agent in Berlin to enforce his Austrian patent rights and planned to follow it abroad in person. Lu enthusiastically joined the campaign. Porter's summons had cut short their honeymoon. Now, a second honeymoon to Europe might be among the spoils.

The letter that arrived in early January could only have caused disappointment in the Hollerith household. The Austrians had agreed to compromise to avoid a lawsuit. But Hollerith would have none of it. Still smarting at the effrontery of the foreign officials, he was convinced he could obtain better terms than his agent. So Hollerith booked passage on the North German Lloyd liner *Eider*. He and Lu had made their first trips to Europe on that steamship. Now they would enjoy the crossing together. The only drawback was Ned.

Lu's younger brother had also been feeling the strain of long hours at the Census Office. If he got sick, Hollerith would have to come rushing home from abroad. So the inventor marched his first employee off to Dr. Peters to exact a promise of special care. But ordinary medical ministrations would not suffice. The inventor decreed that Mrs. Talcott should move with her son to the house on Dumbarton Avenue to be closer to the office. More important, Ned was to be served steak or chops for breakfast, a warm lunch in the city, and dinner with ale at Miss Woodward's boarding house on his return to Georgetown—all at Hollerith's expense. In Hollerith's view, food was often the solution to other problems. Whatever the medical merits of his regimen, it soon began to work. Almost immediately, Ned felt very much better. In fact, he told his mother that he was getting fat. "I tell him it's something in this house," Mrs. Talcott chided her son. Since his marriage, Hollerith too had been steadily adding weight. Only recently, he had given three outgrown suits and an overcoat to Ned.

On February 7, Hollerith cabled that he had reached a satisfactory compromise with the Austrians. Under a newly drawn contract, he would build a dozen tabulating machines for their Census, which had already been taken in December 1890 but would not be processed until the following October. The Hollerith devices, in slightly modified form, would be applied with an excruciating Germanic thoroughness that would not have been tolerated in Hollerith's own country.

The Austrian must give a full account of himself and his family, their ages, religions, languages, occupations, secondary occupations, indebtedness, income, expenditures, number of domestic animals including dogs, cats, and birds, character of clothing worn, size of rooms occupied particularly specifying height of ceilings, and he must produce a certified copy of his birth certificate.

Failure to provide this information could result in a fine of twenty florins or four days in jail. The machines would do their work with expected efficiency. Instead of costing the Austrians 87,700 florins—the amount for compiling the previous Census by hand—the job would cost the Austrians 22,300 florins, or slightly more than a quarter as much. But what should by all rights have been a personal success for Hollerith was turned, instead, into a single-handed triumph for the director of the Austrian Census Bureau, Dr. K. T. von Inama-Sternegg, who made his application of the devices sound like the breathless scaling of an unclimbed Alp:

Step by step we advanced, aided by an eminent technical expert; small experiments were followed by larger ones, all resulting to our satisfaction. . . . At last, we applied this unfamiliar device to our work, not without some hesitancy, and prepared for many surprises in its application on a large scale.

The Austrian Census head was rewarded for his vision by a visit to the Bureau by His Imperial Highness, the illustrious Archduke Karl Ludwig, and his Royal Highness, Prince Regent Luitpold of Bavaria. "The ministers, dignitaries, and officials of all classes, and the representatives of the press," the *Wiener Zeitung* reported, "were invited to see the performance of the experimental machine."

Before the Austrian Census was complete, Hollerith would see his machines successfully applied to the censuses of Canada and Norway. But he would continue to be hurt by the Austrian's practice of never giving him credit for his invention. Attending the International Institute of Statistics four years later, he would write: "Whatever interest the Austrians can arouse is simply that of an imitation. The credit certainly comes to me. All, except the Austrians, say the Hollerith machines. The Austrians say, 'Machine Electrique.'"

Returning home in March 1891, the couple brought with them a first cousin of Lu's. The young man, Henri Bolesslowski, had earlier contracted tuberculosis and, evidently, did not have long to live. The inventor's treatment of his wife's relative revealed an unsuspected side to the often brusk-mannered inventor. Soon it was reported that the bathroom of the house had been converted to a darkroom and that the young man and Hollerith were shooting pictures of everything in sight. Finding herself in the bathtub "surrounded by floating photographs," Lu complained good-naturedly at the innocent fun. Although Hollerith would soon have children of his own, he would continue to treat Henri in a generous and gentle manner until Henri died four years later.

Barely arrived home, Hollerith left for Newark, New Jersey, with Ned on March 9. "Hollerith will not stay more than two days," his mother-in-law reported, "but Ned may be there longer than that." The foundations for the trip had been laid some time earlier. While visiting New York the year before to check on the building of his machines at Western Electric for the forthcoming Census, Hollerith had gone out of his way to bring them to the attention of the insurance industry. The *New York Tribune* took note of the development in reporting on the meeting of the Actuarial Society held on April 25, 1890:

Any labor-saving device that can be used in the preparation of tabular statements is of interest to actuaries. The members of the society accepted the invitation of Mr. Herman Hollerith to inspect his electrical tabulating apparatus yesterday afternoon at the factory of the Western Electric Company at Greenwich and Thomas Streets. Among them were J. P. Lunger of the Prudential of Newark whose company expects to use the machine.

Hollerith had interested his first commercial customer *before* the first large-scale use of his machines in the U.S. Census. Now, a year after his meeting with the actuaries, he was installing two of the systems. A month after the trip to Newark, the perpetual "bugs" that plague many new installations appeared. "Ned has been home but one week and is going back tonight," Mrs. Talcott reported on April 11. "A couple of the machines at the Prudential Life Insurance Company need some attention so he is going to see about it." A few days later, after installing a new machine at the New York City Health Department, Ned looked in at the Prudential machines on his way back to Washington. "The ones put up in Newark," he was able to report, "are running fine."

Hollerith's interest in his insurance customer is surprising only if one accepts at face value the later assertion that he showed no interest in commercial business until losing the census as a customer some fifteen years later. However, it would have been perhaps more surprising if the alert young man who had computed some "life tables" for Dr. Billings, had bought up the Lanston adding machine to exploit it, and had heard the Franklin Institute tell him that his system "is invaluable wherever large numbers of facts are to be summed and tabulated," had been unaware of commercial possibilities. In broadening his patents a few years later, Hollerith would write: "my invention is not limited to such a system [for the census] but may be applied in effecting compilations of any desired series or system of items representing characteristics of persons, subjects, or objects."

Shortly after the machines went in at Prudential, Hollerith received a visit from the head of the Canadian Census Bureau.

"The Superintendent of the Canadian Census has been here," Mrs. Talcott wrote, "and is very anxious to make an arrangement with Hollerith to use some of his machines . . ." After inspecting the machines in use at the Census Office, the Canadian official ordered five tabulators to process his country's Census. The order, the *New York Post* noted, "was based . . . upon the theory that the population of Canada was about one-tenth that of the United States since, as we have had 50 tabulators at use on the 11th Census, Canada will use five."

Hollerith was proud that the order had arrived unsolicited, as had the one from Austria. If his machines were properly applied, he would often say, they would sell themselves. A conservative engineer, he abhorred the advertising and sales practices of the day, which he believed often tended toward dishonesty. Over the years, he would comment that he did not want his "machines to go anywhere where they were not a distinct benefit." And he would often add that he "did not want to leave any false impressions."

Ned looked forward to traveling to Canada to install the machines and was disappointed when Hollerith decided to make the trip himself. However, the Canadian officials were evidently pleased at their first use of data processing devices for population statistics, in the Census of 1891.

One of the advantages . . . is the accuracy with which the statistics are compiled. The instrument is not lazy. It is not made heedless by the state of the atmosphere in the room. It is not dishonest. It is absolutely impartial.

Hollerith's experience in taking the Canadian Census made up in part for his bitter disappointment with the Austrians, but he was unsuccessful in getting the staid British to change their ways. Referring to Great Britain's Tenth Census taken April 5, 1891, the *New York Times* had predicted that

The only thing American that is likely to be employed . . . will be the ingenious machine for tabulating the data received invented by Mr. Herman Hollerith of Washington, D.C. It seems to have stood the tests imposed upon it in a manner that has fully justified the inventor's claims . . . and there appears to be every prospect for its being officially adopted after the usual amount of circumlocution which is customary in British official circles.

But Britain, which had invented the steam engine and, indeed, the industrial revolution itself, was not to be hurried. Despite the setback, Hollerith was building his business and a worldwide reputation by taking the census at home and abroad. He was following, to the letter the strategy confided to his brother-in-law seven years before when pleading for backing for his census machine. In another four years, he would uncharacteristically boast to the *New York Sun*:

Not less than 100,000,000 cards have been passed through the machines. The last census here used 65,000,000, the Canadian Census took between 4,000,000 and 5,000,000 amd the other 30,000,000 are accounted for in Germany and in various individual states."

His only regret was that the census did not come around more often. "In December, the regular German Census will be taken," he declared to the *Sun*. "They have a census every five years as we should have here."

Considering their novelty, it seems incredible that the new systems were employed so easily and proved so reliable. But if the governments that used them were satisfied, what did the public think? "The decades ending 1890–1891 have been ominous ones for officials in charge of census work," Superintendent Porter said in an appearance before the American Statistical Society. Far from being pleased at the round of head counts, citizens at home and abroad were little less than outraged, as Porter also told the society.

The Canadian Parliament is trying to overthrow the government because the population increase was only 11.66%. Englishmen are grumbling because the population fell a million short of expectations. Frenchmen were alarmed because its census showed the population was short of their desires.

The anguish in Hollerith's own country was especially acute. While the *New York Times* had predicted that the population would resume its strong upward thrust, the results were clearly disappointing. Porter's official population count of 62,622,250, issued in December, set off a virtual explosion. As one writer noted, "It sent into spasms of indignation a great many people who had made up their minds that the dignity of the Republic could only be supported on a total of 75 million."

Part of the dissatisfaction could be traced to local boosterism. Vying with St. Paul for the larger population total, the twin city of Minneapolis persuaded enumerators there to accept the more robust count of the Businessmen's Union in place of its own. Arrested and brought to St. Paul, where they could hardly expect a fair hearing, the offending enumerators escaped what appeared to be certain conviction only because the U.S. District Attorney— a loyal resident of Minneapolis—refused to prosecute! Also coming under fire was the competence of the politically chosen enumerators. Urging adoption of the merit system for the next decennial census, Carl Schurz complained: "They cannot spell and they cannot do ordinary arithmetic. Fifty percent fail, and they fail because they cannot divide 100,000 by 4,038; that is, they cannot make the correct result."

Although most of the volleys were directed at Porter and his census workers, it was inevitable that some of the stray shots should be aimed at Hollerith and his machines. "Slipshod Work Has Spoiled the Census," headlined the *New York Herald*, adding, "Chances of Error largely Increased by the Mechanical Devices Employed . . ." Dr. Billings came to Hollerith's defense before the prestigious American Association for the Advancement of Science, detailing the successful implementation of the idea he had planted in the inventor's mind. "A complete set of the tabulating machines was operated to illustrate Dr. Billings' explanation," the *New York Independent*, reported, "and the room looked temporarily like a section of the Census Office." So, too, T. Commerford Martin, the friend and biographer of Edison, sprang to Hollerith's defense, following an investigation of the machines at work in the Census Office. The scientific journalist read an enthusiastic paper on the devices before the Electrical Club of New York while Hollerith, also a member of the organization at 17 East 22d Street, explained and operated the system. But even if the 1890 Census was marred by flaws, they could not, if taken on their face value, explain the sharp decline in population growth, as General Walker himself pointed out.

Although Hollerith himself was no demographer, he appeared before the American Statistical Association armed with the newly refined data from his machines. "Dr. Herman Hollerith has presented a very interesting paper," the *New Orleans Times Democrat* noted, "which proves that the number of marriages per thousand had dropped to 17 in the past decade from 20 in the period 1855 to 1874, despite there being more persons of marriageable age." There had also been "a decrease in the number of children," the inventor pointed out, "not only in regard to the total population, but in relation to each marriage."

"Dr. Hollerith's figures," the newspaper concluded, "confirm the theory that we have already announced, that the tendency of all civilized countries toward the slower increase of population would be entirely so but for immigration. No Malthus will ever be needed in this world, unless conditions greatly change."

Corroborating evidence a decade later would show that, despite its flaws, the Eleventh Census had come within 1 percent of gauging the population of the United States. The inventor might not have been unduly surprised to read an article published in the *Scientific American* more than three-quarters of a century later. Noting that there were already more deaths than births per year in Austria, Britain, East and West Germany, and Luxembourg, and that declines in fertility suggest that the population would begin to decline in Belgium, Denmark, Czechoslovakia, Hungary, Norway, and Sweden, the publication would conclude: "If the current trend toward reduced fertility continues, most of the world's developed countries are heading for an era of negative population growth."

If the stir had caused Hollerith any discomfort, he was too preoccupied to show it. On the previous July 1—exactly nine and a half months after his marriage to Lu—Hollerith had celebrated a growth in the population of his own household with the birth of Lucia, named for her mother. Hollerith was fascinated with the baby. "He sits and looks at her and can hardly tear himself away," his mother-in-law recorded. In typically Victorian fashion, the inventor regarded his creation, not as an infant, but as a fully developed miniature adult. Soon, he was carrying her downstairs to dinner, as if expecting her to partake in the dinner table conversation. When, he inquired, would she be able to go out for a drive?

Later, when the baby began to teethe, it was Hollerith who was miserable. The infant appeared to be healthy, but Hollerith was dissatisfied with her progress. He bombarded Dr. Peters with salvos of questions. In defense, the beleaguered doctor ordered milk for the baby to be sterilized. When this did not placate the inventor, the put-upon physician suggested goat's milk. Overruling the complaints of Lu's Aunts Mary and Kate, the inventor marched off and bought a goat, which he staked out in the yard. Hollerith showed the goat to the baby, who gurgled with pleasure at her. Hollerith's regimen, which as usual centered on food, appeared to work. Soon, much to his satisfaction, his little lady was happy and healthy.

In October, members of the International Institute of Statistics took time off from their sessions in Vienna to see Hollerith's machines at work on the Austrian Census. Although most members, out of deference to their hosts, referred to the devices as the "Machine Electrique," Luigi Bodio, the director general of Italy's Imperial Bureau of Statistics, felt no such constraint. Predicting that Hollerith's invention was destined to play as great a part in commercial life as the sewing machine in domestic life, he declared: "The time will come when the railroads, the great factories, the mercantile houses and all the branches of commercial and industrial life will be found using the Hollerith machines as a matter not only of economy but of necessity."

On the spot, Italy's leading statistician made up his mind to visit the inventor in Washington. Contented at home, Hollerith closed out the year by demanding that the baby should have a Christmas tree.

At seven, Herman Hollerith betrays a wistful expression at being dressed up for a formal portrait, perhaps prompting a lifelong aversion to formal occasions. Over the years, he also rebelled strenuously at having his picture taken, despite being an avid camera buff. (Photo: Hollerith papers)

Newly graduated from Columbia College School of Mines and away from home for the first time, Hollerith, at twenty, became something of a man-about-town, entering easily into Washington's relaxed social life. Nevertheless, he rapidly earned a reputation for "superior efficiency" as a special agent in the U.S. Census of 1880. (Photo: Hollerith papers)

By 1888, the freelance inventor had lost out to Westinghouse in the Burlington air-brake trials, despite the superior performance of his brake designs; he had suffered rejection when his brother-in-law withdrew backing for his census machine; and he had experienced the loss of his financée, Flora Fergusson, who died of typhoid. Despite these reverses, his machines were doing actual work for the Census Office in processing mortality statistics at Baltimore and several other cities. The trials were held at the urging of Dr. Billings to ensure that similar statistics gathered during the census year showed no abnormal trends. (Photo: Hollerith papers)

Hollerith's courtship of Lu took a strong technological bent. Armed with a newly purchased camera, he took portraits of the entire family, including this one of Lu, at left, with an unidentified friend. Photography was an important influence on Hollerith. He compared the processing of the Census to the development of a photo, with each step bringing out additional detail. (Photo: Hollerith family)

On his return to Washington from St. Louis, Hollerith met Lucia Talcott, the daughter of a noted civil engineer, while attending the Georgetown Assemblies. He fell in love with "Lu" because she reminded him of Flora Fergusson. This photo was taken several years earlier when Lu was sixteen or seventeen. (Photo: Hollerith family)

Hollerith took eagerly to domesticity, following his marriage to Lu on September 15, 1890. Shortly after, the couple posed in front of their first home on Dumbarton Street in Georgetown. At the time, his machines were being used successfully in the 1890 Census, prompting inquiries from other countries. (Photo: Hollerith family)

Bundled in a fur-lined coat, Hollerith visited St. Petersburg in December 1896 to sign a contract for the use of his machines in the first census of all the Russias. It was a banner year. Besides completing difficult and often frustrating negotiations with the Czar's government, he landed the New York Central as a customer following the earlier rejection of his machines and formed the Tabulating Machine Company to carry out his business. (Photo: Hollerith papers)

Bedecked in favored "Coolie Hat," Hollerith, with son Richard, surveys a strawberry bed near his home at Dutch Tussel, Maryland, a Washington suburb. He grew and ordered such large quantities of food as gifts for friends that on more than one occasion purveyors mistook him for a produce dealer. The year was 1908. (Photo: Hollerith papers)

Hollerith formed a close relationship with his mother-in-law, Theodosia Talcott. Widowed early like his own mother, she also struggled successfully to raise her children. She was one of the first women to work in a government department. Often, she kept the whole family, including Hollerith, afloat financially. (Photo: Hollerith family)

With son Richard at the helm, Hollerith takes an outing in *Reedbird*, one of numerous boats he acquired after buying a farm in southern Virginia in 1909. While doting on his daughters, he raised strong, independent sons. Often, he encouraged them to rummage through the scrapbox at his shop to find materials for building model railway cars and for other projects in a workshop he equipped at home. All three sons became engineers and secured patents of their own. (Photo: Hollerith papers)

In retirement, the city-bred engineer took to raising pedigreed Guernseys as if he had invented the idea. His notion of leisure included putting up more than fifty buildings on his Virginia farm. (Photo: Hollerith papers)

Relaxing his stricture against being photographed, Hollerith posed with his first grandson, Herman Hollerith III, and Herman Hollerith, Jr., at Riverton, New Jersey, in 1924. No longer a consultant to IBM, he had started designing a small, battery-operated tabulating machine for customers unable to afford the company's larger "outfit." However, illness interfered with his plans. He died in 1929. (Photo: Hollerith papers)

8

Setting Up Shop in Georgetown

"A menace to the health of the men . . ."

In 1892, Hollerith moved his business from downtown Washington to an old cooper's shop hugging the Chesapeake & Ohio Canal in Georgetown. The two-story brick building—a third floor was later added and the back of the building extended nearly through the block—would serve as the inventor's assembly and card manufacturing plant for nearly twenty years. When seen in the spring of 1968, shortly before the structure was swallowed up in an "office complex," one side of the building was still graced with two-foot-high black letters, which proclaimed, "The Tabulating Machine Company," the name that Hollerith would adopt for his business in 1897. And below, in smaller letters, appeared the words, "Factories at Endicott, N.Y. and Dayton, O." As the fading words indicated, the shop continued in operation after Hollerith sold his business in 1911, when it was merged with the Dayton Scale Company at Dayton, Ohio, and the International Time Recording Company at Endicott, New York, to become the Computing-Tabulating-Recording Company, the firm that later changed its name to IBM. For a short time, until it was devoted completely to card manufacture, the small building whose windows looked over the towpath toward the water could claim to be IBM's first data processing plant.

The date that Hollerith started up operations in the new building is uncertain. But he made his presence very much known starting on August 25, 1892. For on that date, he wrote to Dr. Hammatt, the Washington Health Officer, and failing to get a reply within a week, forwarded a copy of his missile to the *Washington Post*, which printed it September 7. It reads:

I would respectfully call your attention to the filthy condition of the gutter in front of my shop located at the northwest corner of 31st Street and the Chesapeake & Ohio Canal. . . . The condition of the gutter . . . is such as to be a nuisance and, in my opinion, a menace to the health of the men working for me.

The *Post* goes on to note that, the written remonstrance having had no effect on the authorities, Mr. Hollerith had a photograph taken and forwarded to the Health Office. An engraving made from the photo appears above the article. Conditions at the new shop, as well as its efficient operation were not to be taken lightly.

Inside the structure, the upper floors were supported by heavy wood beams spaced at intervals along the manufacturing floor. At the center, a small steam engine hissed and puffed, powering a driveshaft that ran the length of the building overhead. As was common at the time, numerous belts descended from the driveshaft to power the machinery spaced out along the floor. The shop was devoted to final assembly and repair, as well as serving as Hollerith's development lab. At first, tabulators and sorters came from Western Electric in New York and punches from the Pratt & Whitney Company at Hartford. Around 1905, there were other suppliers. The Hart Manufacturing Company in Poughkeepsie, New York, shipped in key punches; counters came from the W. H. Nichols Company in Waltham, Massachusetts, and tabulators and sorters arrived from the Taft-Peirce Manufacturing Company at Woonsocket, Rhode Island. At first, a large print shop in Georgetown made cards from rolls of paper shipped from Bordentown, New Jersey. Later, the shop was increasingly devoted to card manufacture, a role it continued to perform until IBM built a card manufacturing plant on New York Avenue, in the northeastern suburbs of Washington, just before World War II. After Hollerith had stationed representatives—he would not call them salesmen—in Philadelphia, New York, Chicago, St. Louis, and Detroit, the assembly area also doubled as a school. Men hired in the field learned the business, not by polishing sales pitches, but by taking down and reassembling the product by hand.

Things were tidy enough at the 31st Street plant by early 1893 for Hollerith to want to show it off. When the Columbia College Glee Club gave a concert in Washington, he ordered a fistful of tickets and took a large party. Afterward, the students and guests came back to the brick building for an oyster roast. Mrs. Talcott described the scene:

The men made a big fire and, when it had burnt down to a good bed of coals, they laid an iron grating on it and then shoveled on the oysters and, as fast as they were done, opened them and we all stuffed. We had bread, butter, crackers, slaw, celery, pickles and ale, and had a jolly good time.

After the guests were filled to the brim with both roasted and raw bivalves, Hollerith asked the cabdrivers in from the cold to finish the feast. The inventor was a genial host. "The shop and machinery was very much admired and Hollerith was very happy," his mother-in-law recorded.

During the working day, the atmosphere at 1054 31st Street was distinctly different. From a glassed-in office, to the right of the entryway, Hollerith watched his workmen arrive and leave. Precisely punctual—after the advent of radio, clocks at the inventor's home were synchronized on a daily signal from the Naval Observatory—Hollerith could not countenance the least degree of tardiness in others. A worker reporting as much as a minute late risked a virtual explosion at the door. Discipline was no less required on the job. The inventor installed a system of electric bells, running from his desk to every part of the shop. He expected his men to "step lively" when called. With typical Germanic exactitude, the demanding employer insisted that instructions be carried out to the letter. When a pointed question was answered with an "I think," the inventor thundered back, "Don't tell me you think; tell me you know." He demanded uncompromising quality in any task, no matter how small—which invariably meant doing things according to *his* instructions. As Marion Smith, a long-time gardener on the Hollerith farm, later expressed it, "If you're doin' to suit him, he's all right; if you wasn't doin' to suit him, he'll let you know."

Woe, especially, to the worker who slacked off on the job.

Hearing of an employee who spent an excessive amount of time reading the newspaper in the lavatory, Hollerith devised his own solution to the problem. He drove nails upward through the toilet seat, filing them smooth where they emerged. From their heads protruding underneath he ran wires back to his office nearby, where they were attached to a magneto that sat on his desk. Watching through a peephole from his office for the malingerer to take up his reading habit, the inventor gave the magneto crank a sudden turn, sending a shock along the toilet seat.

Despite his unusual management techniques, Hollerith for the most part commanded the respect of his men. Joseph Langley, employed in the shop around the turn of the century, recalls being fired on the spot after Hollerith mistakenly blamed him for an accident. The youngster was barely out the door when the inventor, realizing his mistake, raced after him to call him back. A week later, Langley, who had been receiving $2.50 a week as a messenger boy, received a two-cent-an-hour raise. Measured against the standards of the day, Hollerith was a fair and even generous employer. When business was good, he regularly granted a 10 percent Christmas bonus. He also advanced considerable sums of money to his men without interest and with little expectation of repayment. Special care was arranged on a farm outside the city, at Hollerith's expense, for the sickly child of an employee—long before the day of company "benefits." The employer's set-to with the health department was far from bombast or bluster. He worried about the health of his men as much as he did over the well-being of his immediate family. After a smallpox scare swept Washington in 1894—a messenger in the Census Office had contracted the disease—the inventor ordered Dr. Peters to vaccinate all the men at the shop. "Mr. Spicer [Hollerith's foreman] fainted and Ned came very near to fainting," Mrs. Talcott reported.

The year 1893 was a busy one. Suddenly, the Census Office wanted more machines for the Agricultural Census. Hollerith and Ned worked until late into the night to get them ready. On May 1, the Columbian Exposition opened in Chicago. Hollerith had planned his own exhibit, but three weeks after the fair opened was still trying to get out of it. "He doesn't want to go one bit," Mrs. Talcott reported, "and will only exhibit his machines in the Census Office exhibit." Despite his reluctant participation, the inventor won a bronze medal. Inquiries for his system arrived from both Italy and Brazil. But Hollerith brushed them aside. Only he and Ned were expert enough to wire up and install the machines, and they could not be everywhere at once. "My, what a fortune Hollerith has in view," his mother-in-law remarked, "if he can only attend to it."

On his way back from the Columbian Exposition in the fall, Professor Bodio, who had admired the machines at Vienna, kept his promise to visit the man responsible for them. "Sunday, Hollerith had three Italians to dine with them," Mrs. Talcott wrote. "One spoke a little English, one spoke a little German, the other spoke only French and Italian." Despite the babble of tongues, the evening proved agreeable and the visit a profitable one. Before leaving Washington, Professor Bodio purchased two machines to demonstrate their usefulness to his government. A newspaper gave a somewhat chauvinistic account.

The effete monarchies of the old world have frequently to beg for advice from this young and progressive republic. Even in minor details of the execution of governmental work we beat the world. The latest instance of it was the visit of Professors Luigi Bodio and Boseo Bonelli to this city for the purpose of finding out how Uncle Sam does his counting.

Clearly, the description was overblown, for, as Carroll Wright had earlier told the American Statistical Association, Professor Bodio had led the way in the constant and rapid publication of statistics covering almost every important feature of social and industrial life. The Europeans were far ahead of the United States in their applications of statistics to everyday life. Be that as it may, the order for the machines meant another trip abroad at a time when Hollerith's family was growing far faster than his income.

When Lu had become pregnant again the previous year, it was Hollerith who became uncomfortable, because Dr. Peters would not let her eat all sorts of things. Frustrated in his gustatory schemes, the inventor occupied himself by filling the windows of her room with pots of azaleas. The birth of Herman, Jr., the previous September had brought comments that the baby's nose was somewhat too full, like his father's. And Hollerith, who doted on his female offspring, promptly labeled the male heir "the ugliest thing I ever saw." However, his admiration was soon aroused when, without prompting, the young man began to eat heartily and well. Now Lu was expecting again. And the baby's birth at the close of the year—a second son, named Charles—seemingly set off another frantic burst of activity. Early in 1894, Hollerith set off for Boston to see the governor of Massachusetts. From there, he took the train to Albany to keep an appointment with New York's governor. His objective: to keep his machines at work, and income coming in, from taking the census of their states. But with no certainty that he could get work in his own country, he once more turned his attention abroad.

Hollerith made two crossings to Europe during 1894. On February 24, he sailed for Italy, taking his foreman Spicer with him, to install the machines that Professor Bodio had purchased for his government. He was a true innocent abroad. If he had found the French "like a big lunatic asylum let loose," he had less patience with what he considered Italian lassitude. No sooner had he landed than he complained:

This is a frightfully slow country. They are all living in what happened thousands of years ago . . . I saw them cutting lumber on the road from Naples to Pompeii, and, when I got to Pompeii, I found paintings on walls showing exactly the same way of cutting lumber. I also saw how they made Italian macaroni, and . . . I don't feel like eating any more.

Not even the horses showed any signs of life. "They are all like cows," Hollerith grumbled, missing his own spirited horse. "How I wish I had Jack here to drive around the country." Hollerith found doing business equally frustrating. "I am struggling along slowly," he wrote. "It is like pulling teeth to accomplish anything."

Professor Bodio wanted him to meet Professor Mengarini, chief engineer of the new electric generating plant at Tivoli, which supplied the power to Rome.

Tomorrow at 2 P.M. [he wrote], Professor Mengarine, or something of that kind, is to call on me. It is not polite enough to say come along and then meet Prof. M. there [at Tivoli]. Oh, no. Prof. M. must first come and pay his respects. Then I suppose he will send me a written invitation and perhaps by next week we will be ready to meet out there. It is all very polite and nice, but it gets very tiresome.

When the meeting did take place, Hollerith found the professor "quite a man in the electrical world." And despite his impatience with social amenities, he found himself enjoying a cultivated and, to him, unconventional circle.

Mrs. Meyer is a German so I got along very well with her. I was invited to smoke a cigarette with her which I did. It was quite a scientific reception, a professor of architecture, another of hygiene, etc., etc., a young lady who is studying mathematics, all people who had some hobby or another. The prettiest lady was the daughter of a marquis, bright and young.

But being feted did not quell Hollerith's impatience "perhaps you think this is all very nice but that I am not trying to finish up and get back," he wrote somewhat guiltily to his wife. Without being rude to his host, it was difficult to break away. Besides, Mengarini might be of some use to him. And he was also to meet the Minister of Water and Commerce and the Under Secretary of State. However, the longer he stayed, the more frustrated and homesick he became. On March 18, he wrote:

I have no longer any interest for Roman antiquities and don't care when this old wall was built or when that old door was made. I would much rather see those three bright little faces with their dear mother.

Without any tangible accomplishment, Hollerith entrained for Vienna. "Just think of it," he reported. "To go to Vienna, I will have to spend two nights, one day in a sleeping car. And what sleeping cars! Still, some people travel in Europe for pleasure." Before sailing home from Le Havre April 14, Hollerith had circled northward to Berlin, Copenhagen, Oslo, and then back to Paris. What he lacked in solid business results, the inventor made up for in buying presents for his family. He bought monogrammed handkerchiefs in Vienna, a hogshead of china from the royal factory in Berlin, a pepper grinder from Paris, a vase from Copenhagen, and carvings and enameled jewelry from Norway. Finally, there was a Norwegian peasant's costume for little Lucia and a full suit of cavalry uniform for Herman, Jr. More crates of presents would follow, arriving for months at the Hollerith household.

While abroad, he had worried incessantly over the health of his family, including his wife's aunts Sophie and Kate. A flurry of cables had sought information on their well-being. The inventor, who would be known for the Hollerith code by which information is recorded into punched cards, had devised still another code for the purpose, in which he had instructed his clerk Otto. "Bumkin," transmitted to Hollerith, meant, "We are all very well, domestic affairs running smoothly." "Bunch," cabled in reply, stood for, "I am very well." In turn, "Sophie Bumptious" conveyed that Aunt Sophie was quite ill. Whereas 'Kate Bouyantly" signaled that Aunt Kate was feeling very well.

Hollerith's fears were not entirely unfounded, for less than twenty-four hours after he arrived home, the doctor decided that Lucia had come down with scarlet fever. The dolls the inventor had looked forward to giving her would have to be withheld, or destroyed after she recovered. To avoid exposure, Herman, Jr., was packed off to Normanstone. "Poor Hollerith came home so happy, so delighted to be with Lu and the children," his mother-in-law recorded, "and this knocked him very flat."

Miraculously, Lucia was soon on the mend, leaving the doctor suspicious of his initial diagnosis. But Hollerith soon had other worries. By early August, the Census Office was finished with his machines. All 105 tabulators, complete with tools, were packed up by Ned and shipped to a warehouse on River Street, below Hollerith's shop near the Potomac. Back from Europe, where his business prospects had come to little, the inventor saw his principal income from the Government come to a complete halt. He left almost immediately for Boston and Albany to try once more for their state census business. And as he would often do when other business failed to come through, he turned his attention to the small adding machine to which he had bought the rights while developing his census machines. While the mechanism had proved too expensive to manufacture at the time, Hollerith kept sorting the problem through his mind. By tinkering with the device and redesigning it, he came up with a machine "embodying the same fundamental principles, but of a different mechanical construction." He tried to hurry it along. "Hollerith now has no income from the government," his mother-in-law reported, "so he is anxious to get his adding machine on the market."

Through it all, the inventor kept up a cheerful front with the children and toward his family. When Lu's elderly Aunt Kate began to lose strength, Hollerith persuaded the spinster to drink ale every day and sent several cases to her. "I think she is better," Mrs. Talcott wrote within a week. "It takes her three days to drink one bottle, and she imagines she is wildly dissipated." And when Lu's older brother Robert Talcott moved out to Garrett Park, Maryland, to begin married life in a house built on a lot that Hollerith had given him, the inventor rolled up a handsome rug from his office floor and loaned it to him. As with other such "loans," this one became permanent.

However, Hollerith's underlying desperation came out early one morning. "Mr. Hollerith has just gone on the 4 o'clock train for Europe," Mrs. Talcott reported.

He went off rather suddenly. He had been talking of it for some time and hated to go, but last week he was cabled to go at once to Berlin to see about using his machines for taking the German Census so went at once. He hopes to get through and be back in six weeks. Then, if they decide to use his machines, he will go later and take his family and be gone several years.

Behind Hollerith's personal crisis was a dire national crisis. The country was caught in deep depression and business had not recovered from the money panics of the previous year. The government, which had been living beyond its means, could repay its obligations only by dipping into a rapidly-dwindling reserve of gold. Businessmen could not raise money; workmen were laid off to roam the streets. Investors everywhere were worsening the situation by cashing in their holdings and demanding payment in gold. Only the previous May, Hollerith and Ned had walked into the city to watch an unusual sight: General Jacob S. Coxey, leading an odd array of men carrying sacks of food and blankets, had marched up Pennsylvania Avenue to make an unheard-of demand. The government, they asserted, should hire the unemployed to build macadam roads all over the country. Failing to get help from Congress, President Cleveland, within two months, would call financier J. P. Morgan to the White House to halt the slide into chaos. Hollerith could have blamed his lack of success on these conditions. He didn't. Instead, he looked abroad once again.

9

Railroad Experiments

"I did not know the first damned
thing about railroad accounts."

Hollerith hated travel. He was unhappy away from his family. He had no real interest in countries or cultures other than his own. His only reason for making a second crossing to Europe in 1894 was that business conditions abroad could not possibly be worse then in his own country. Or so he hoped.

On reaching Europe in early November, he went straight to Berlin. Then it was on to Rome, Paris, and London. Professor Bodio, he learned, had started using the machines for the Italian Government's penal and mortality statistics. Perhaps the Italians did not move so slowly after all! But if Hollerith was encouraged by this development, it did little to alter his mood. He apparently thought too little of his business prospects abroad to mention them in his letters home. Plainly, he was agitated and depressed. And even the change of scene did little to lift his spirits. Ironically, it was at this low point that he received the highest tribute of his career.

He did not record which came first: the invitation to address the Royal Statistical Society in London December 4, or his own application for membership in the prestigious body. His friend John Hyde had submitted nomination paper no. 2,854 on November 22, though without a seconder as required. "Some member of the council," Hyde hoped, "will be so good as to supply the deficiency on the strength of his general knowledge of the candidate." Hyde had also taken another step on Hollerith's behalf. Although honorary members were not allowed to act as seconders, he had gotten Dr. Billings, a distinguished honorary fellow—and the man who had first suggested a census machine to Hollerith—to add his name to the application in a place where it would "at least not vitiate the nomination."

Without knowing whether he had been properly proposed for membership, Hollerith made his way to the society's headquarters at 9 Adelphi Terrace. He may have paused to look over Victoria Embankment Gardens to the Thames, taking in the strings of barges and busy river traffic below. But the chances are his mind was too occupied with the latest crisis that had arisen. Having whetted the society's interest by a promised demonstration of his system, he now faced the experience that any lecturer dreads. His showpiece had failed to arrive.

The next day Alice Porter, wife of the U.S. Census Superintendent, reported to Lu, busy with diapers and baby bottles at home, how well her husband had overcome the unexpected obstacle: "We all wished last night you could have been with us at the meeting of the Royal Statistical Society. You would have been so proud of Mr. H's appearance before that scientific, august and bald-headed body."

No doubt reflecting her British husband's sentiments, Mrs. Porter called the society "the most important of its kind in the world. An appearance before it is the statistical equivalent of a presentation at court for a social aspirant." As for Hollerith's immediate embarrassment, "I can assure you," wrote Mrs. Porter, "he rose to the occasion and in the easiest possible manner and in the most lucid language gave his distinguished audience a clear idea of the machine. It roused success, admiration, and a good deal of wonderment." Mr. Hollerith, as the Society's *Journal* noted, said that "he should be happy to exhibit the machine upon some future occasion."

In his prepared remarks, Hollerith ranged widely over his experience in taking the U.S. Census. And in reply to a question, he revealed something he had never spoken of before: the penalty clause that Porter had inserted in the contracts—that the inventor pay $10 for every day a machine was out of order—had never been invoked. Of most interest to the members was Hollerith's discussion of his latest work with farm statistics drawn from the 1890 Census. The Society's *Journal* noted:

He had been making many experiments upon a considerable scale involving the use of about 5,000,000 cards, on which the amounts, instead of individual items were recorded. One card, representing a farm, for instance, would give the total number of acres, number of horses, value of the farm, and the implements, stock, produce, etc. By attaching to the machine an integrating device, he had been able to make it a species of adding machine.

This led directly into other fields; he was now experimenting on railroad accounts . . .

Hollerith had not been resting on his laurels. The machines designed for the 1890 population Census had merely added up one and one on separate counters, much as primitive man kept track of days by carving notches on a stick. The inventor had first developed a crude device for carrying amounts forward from one digit position to the next in his earlier equipment for the Surgeon General's Office. But the totaling of monthly absences, ranging from one to thirty-one days, was a far cry from the demands of the agricultural statistics. Those were little short of astronomic. They called for the adding up of thousands upon thousands of acres of land, millions of bushels of wheat, and innumerable mules, chickens, ducks, and other livestock—circumstances that, in turn, called for new technology.

While perfecting the Lanston adding machine, the inventor had combined an adding or integrating mechanism with his tabulator. In solving one set of problems, Hollerith made another discovery. He could, for the first time, chart a course toward the unexplored world of commercial statistics. And his first foray into this territory, as he also disclosed to the Royal Statistical Society, would be taking on the railroads. Years later, he recounted the course of development:

While the census [of 1890] was underway, my attention was drawn to the statistics of agriculture. Here was a question of adding, not counting. The only previous work approximating this was . . . some work I did for the Surgeon General's Office . . . The reports were made monthly and any case may have been sick for 1 to 31 days. So I had to develop a machine for this and I followed the same lines in the Agricultural statistics.

Hollerith was proud of the machines he had developed for the agricultural statistics.

They were certainly wonderful machines. They were operated by weights and I had these weights over against the wall and small wires running from the machines over pulleys.

And it was the agricultural machines that suggested the transition to railroad accounting—though the idea was admittedly not his own.

Now while I was struggling along with those agricultural statistics along came J. Shirley Eaton whose brother was a clerk in the Agriculture Census and asked me why I did not use the machines for railroad accounting. I remember distinctly telling him there was one good reason . . . I did not know the first damned thing about railroad accounts.

Following his visit to London, Hollerith set sail for home. He arrived December 13, laden with gifts for his family. He brought dresses for Lu from Paris and Berlin and a pale blue silk dress for his daughter from London. Despite his worries, he had found time to buy Irish point lace cuffs and collars for Nellie, the Irish maid, and arrived holding a bunch of shamrocks to give her.

On the day he came home, the Council of the Royal Society approved Hollerith's application for membership. The supporting letter from Bodio could have done little to hurt his chances. Bodio had written:

I am convinced that the future of statistics lies with the usage of the Hollerith machine, for it permits the utilization of statistical material in a far more comprehensive manner than ordinary methods. . . . The machine supplies numerous combinations between diverse elements in place of simple addition of separate isolated elements.

Citing his recent experience in compiling both mortality and penal statistics, Italy's leading statistician concluded:

The principle of the machine is so flexible that it can be prepared for the most varied applications . . . My experience already confirms the impression that the machine is excellent.

Even if he could have heard the news, Hollerith would not have felt better. He had spent heavily for two trips to Europe during the year. Now, with Christmas less than two weeks away, he and Lu decided they would buy presents only for the children. Even the novel electric lights which Hollerith favored for the Christmas tree would have to be omitted. He didn't have time to wire them and his men were too busy at the shop. Ordinary candles would have to do. His mother-in-law, in whom Hollerith seemed to confide as fully as anyone else, summed up the situation. "So far the foreign countries have not paid him very well. I don't think there is any chance of his going abroad again very shortly." As if there wasn't enough on his mind, the ice-clogged Potomac now threatened to sweep over its banks, destroying his tabulating machines stored in the River Street warehouse.

All else, however, was secondary to Hollerith's interest in the railroads. On February 9, 1885, less than two months after returning from Europe, he picked up the experiments he had described to the Royal Statistical Society. For it was on that day that the officials of the Richmond & Danville were coming to his shop.

Hollerith's remark, made in later years, that he "did not know the first damn thing about railroad accounts," has been interpreted as signifying his lack of interest in their important business. It has even been written that he "brushed aside" the first inquiries from railroads and that, "despite his misgivings, his machines were installed in the offices of the New York Central . . ." His actions speak largely otherwise. While Hollerith candidly admitted his complete ignorance of railroad accounting, he set off in typically energetic fashion to make up for the deficiency. Soon, Mrs. Talcott could report on her son-in-law's first recorded meeting with railroad officials.

Last Saturday, Hollerith had the auditor of the R & D and some other gentlemen to look at a machine constructed for railroad work, also an integrating device. They all expressed themselves as much pleased with it, but Ned says the auditor is evidently timid about making a change in their mode of auditing.

Far from being disinterested, Hollerith had primed himself to satisfy any doubts the railroad men might have, as Mrs. Talcott also reported:

Ned came home quite enthusiastic over Hollerith's quickness and ability. . . . no matter what objections . . . or what questions they had, Hollerith was ready with an answer immediately and could practically prove all he stated.

The inventor clearly recognized that steady employment of his tabulating machines by commercial customers was preferable to their intermittent use in the census. His mother-in-law echoed his thoughts: "Hollerith is very anxious to get his tabulating machines and his integrating devices used by the railway companies. That would give him permanent use of his machines."

Despite Hollerith's readiness to prove out his machines, the R & D officials were reluctant to shed their established ways. A second meeting with them took place on March 13. But the railroad men stood around and fingered their heavy watch chains and did nothing. Soon March turned to April, and, though winter had passed, the railroad officials remained mired in indecision. On April 3, Mrs. Talcott summed up the state of affairs: "Six of their auditors were over at the shop today, but they talk and talk and do nothing, and he has no income."

One blustery March morning, Hollerith set out for the city with $10,000 in securities—virtually everything he had managed to put aside. He drove from bank to bank. As the day wore on, he realized that he could not raise a cent on the certificates. He could not sell the real estate he owned either, and his $100,000 in tabulating machines, instead of supplying income as might be expected, were draining his savings for storage. Although it would have been easy, Hollerith refused to blame his troubles on the depression. During the year, he had gone to Albany and Boston to seek the census business of their states. But he had been unsuccessful. Everything he had tried had failed, he told himself. And it was entirely his own fault. While the adding machine was working smoothly—Professor Brown at the Naval Observatory was trying one—the device still could not be manufactured at moderate cost.

In the meanwhile, Ned had gone to Providence to install a

tabulating machine at the State Health Office. But little Rhode Island could afford to pay only $100 a year. That would help hardly at all. Although the Hydrographic Office and the Weather Bureau were also looking at his adding machine—and talking— they could not make up their minds. And negotiations with the R & D dragged on. By the second week in April, Mrs. Talcott wrote: "So far he has not met with any success either with his railroad work or with his adding machine. I am surprised to see how he keeps up under all this worry and anxiety."

Whatever progress he was making, Hollerith realized, it was too little and too late. There simply wasn't enough money to keep his business going. So he sold his carriage horse. Horseflesh was marketable, even if securities and land were not. Hollerith even thought about selling his buggy horse, Jack. "We all hope he won't feel obliged to do so," Mrs. Talcott wrote. "We are all devoted to Jack. He is a beauty, very fast, smart and knowing." Lu and the two children would not go away for the summer. It was a painful decision for Hollerith, who prided himself on how well he provided for his family. Now, instead of breathing the mountain air at Linville, North Carolina, where they had gone before, Lu and the children would ride out to nearby Normanstone for the day, taking their lunch with them. They would have to get through the steamy Washington summer as best they could. Finally, Hollerith laid off his workmen and closed his shop. He kept on only Ned and Otto, a typist, and a stenographer. The beam-studded room where he had served beer and oysters to the admiring Columbia students was no longer the center of busy activity. The steam engine that had hissed and clattered in the middle of the floor was still.

To lighten the load on Hollerith, Ned applied for another job. Congress had just appropriated money for raising the height of the dam at Great Falls to increase the city's water supply, and Ned thought Colonel Elliott might take him on. As it turned out, the Colonel agreed to hire the grandson of Charles Talcott, the architect whose name was inscribed on the aqueduct's great stone span. Ned would be superintendent of the government quarries at Seneca, from which the stone for construction was hauled. It would be hot and dirty work, and the pay less than Ned had been getting from Hollerith. But the inventor would not have to carry another head on the payroll.

Ned's action was generous and thoughtful by any measure, but Hollerith was furious at not having been consulted. Wasn't he in charge? Boiling mad, the inventor loosed all of his pent-up frustration of weeks and months on his brother-in-law's head. While acknowledging that Ned had paid faithful attention to some of the work, Hollerith upbraided him sharply for neglecting many opportunities. Ned, Hollerith charged, could have made himself a lot more useful, if he had really tried.

Although usually complaisant, Ned stood his ground before the intemperate onslaught. He told Hollerith that he had been difficult and discouraging to work for, always finding fault and never praising him for anything. Hollerith should be thanking him now instead of cursing him out. Surprised at Ned's forcefulness and candor, Hollerith backed down. He admitted that his hot temper made him impatient and exacting. Then he confided his many worries and disappointments. When it was over, the air was cleared, and Hollerith asked his first employee to stay on. He could promise nothing, he said, but some work might turn up if business improved.

In the days to come, Lu eased the strain on her husband by managing the household thriftily and cheerfully. There were also the children. One Saturday, Hollerith offered to pull them out to Normanstone and back in the painted cart he had brought back from Norway. They had promised beforehand to get out and walk up the hills, but on the way home they refused. Coming up Lover's Lane on the last leg into Georgetown, Hollerith was breathing hard. Suddenly the cart got lighter. Looking around, he saw that Herman, Jr., had toppled out. The youngster bounded to his feet and angrily pitched into his father for spilling him out. Seeing a miniature version of himself, the inventor laughed heartily and suddenly the world fell back into place. But such moments when he could forget his troubles were few.

10

Persuading the Russians

*"The principal thing is to get
them to have a census."*

At thirty-five, Hollerith should have relished the honor of being
the only American invited to address the presitigious International
Institute of Statistics at Bern, Switzerland. But having literally
closed down his business along with his Georgetown workshop,
he may have been wondering how he was going to pay for the
trans-Atlantic crossing, the second in less than a year. As he rest-
lessly paced the deck of the liner, on an August day in 1895, his
mind was doubtlessly occupied with the more compelling reasons
for making the trip.

Through an introduction from Porter, he hoped to form an
English stock company while in London to exploit his patents in
the British Isles. He also banked on a second scheme to breathe
new life into his moribund business. Just a few weeks before, Czar
Alexander III had issued the Highly Confirmed Order for the
first general population census of all the Russias. If Hollerith could
convince the Emperor's Imperial Government to employ his machines in counting its untold millions—no one had a notion exactly
how many—the warehouse hugging the Potomac at River Street
might be emptied of its tabulators and sorters put out of work at
the close of the U.S. Census. With business at home still rutted
in deep depression, the inventor was forced to look abroad to
break out of his personal financial doldrums. "So much depends
upon the success of my present trip," he wrote his wife on arriving
in England, "that I hardly dare contemplate the result of a failure."

Porter, who had become editor and manager of the *Cleveland
World* after leaving the Census Office, had tried to pave the way

for his friend in England by appealing to British industrialist Sir John Puleston. The potential backer's reply, forwarded to Hollerith just before sailing, was less than reassuring.

I have great faith in the matter you proposed being successfully done, but in view of all the ups and downs, depression taking place of boom and so forth, affecting every kind of business . . . I did not want to take the absolute responsibility of Mr. Hollerith coming over here without his taking into account that he might be here at an inopportune moment when people are out of town and when for some reason . . . such a transaction might not immediately be carried through.

Hollerith arrived in London on Saturday, August 24, to find that, true to his implied warning, Sir John was out of town. In fact, he was out of the country visiting Hamburg for his health. No one else was in town to conduct business with over a summer weekend, as Hollerith should have known if he had cared about anyone else's way of doing things. So, not due in Bern until Monday, the inventor set off for some sightseeing with his traveling companion Jack Church. If the pair passed by Parliament, the Tower of London, or any of the other familiar tourist attractions, it was entirely accidental. "We went out to Richmond," the inventor wrote, "investigated the Underground Road. Then explored the Underground Electric Road, etc." The inventor was on a busman's holiday. One can easily imagine the two curious Americans—Church had helped Hollerith with his railroad patents—peering at the undersides of British railway carriages to see the braking apparatus they employed.

Hollerith left for Switzerland at 10:00 A.M. Sunday, hoping to catch up with Sir John later in the trip. "I am dead tired and sleepy," he wrote on arriving at Berne twenty-four hours later. "A night's journey is by no means as comfortable as with our American railroads." The inventor yawned his way through the formalities of the Institute's opening session at the Bunderpalais before returning to his room at Bernhoff Hotel across the street for a nap. "As yet," he wrote his wife before retiring, "I have not had a chance to talk business with Troinitsky."

Nicholas A. Troinitsky, the delegate from St. Petersburg, was not only the director of the Central Statistical Committee of his government's Ministry of the Interior, he was also a member of the Czar's Privy Council. But more important to Hollerith, the influential official was an active conduit for new ideas at a time when the capital, known as Russia's window on the West, was looking abroad for new developments in such diverse fields as medicine, music, steam locomotives, and electric power plants. Along with the enthusiastic Professor Bodio, Troinitsky had inspected the "Machine Electrique" at work on the Austrian Census while attending the previous Institute at Vienna in October 1892. Like his Italian colleague, the Russian had also seen through his host's claims to inventing the system. While Bodio had vowed to visit Hollerith in Washington, Troinitsky had even earlier expressed interest in obtaining the system for the Russian Census. As he often did, Hollerith had shared the prospects with his mother-in-law, who passed them along. Complaining of straitened family finances, Mrs. Talcott had written on October 11, 1891, "If Hollerith doesn't get the Russian Census soon, I don't know what I shall do. I spend every cent I can get."

Four years had passed, and Hollerith's principal problem had been getting the Russian monolith to move. In contrast to most other civilized countries, the Empire did not count the noses of its citizens at stated intervals. A census took place only after the Czar issued an imperial edict for the ordering of his subjects— something he had last felt inspired to do in 1851! Hollerith had explained his problem to the *New York Sun* only the previous March.

I have heard nothing definite as yet from Russia, but have hopes of success in that direction. The principal thing is to get them to have a census. There is no special time for taking them there. They take their chances as with other affairs of state and are at the mercy of government officers.

If the Russians were timorous or lackadaisical about launching a census, they had good reason. The geographic area to be covered comprised one-sixth of the earth's surface. Then, too, previous censuses had been based on local counts. Each province kept registers of its citizens by farms, households, or individuals. Not only did the classes of information collected differ, but the local

workers used different manual methods for collecting and recording it. While the census for a particular province might be valid,
when combined with counts from other provinces, the resulting
mass of figures could amount to little more than a statistical mul-
ligatawny stew. While Hollerith fretted at the delay, Troinitsky
had to clear away the amassed custom of centuries in order to
plan the administration, procedures, and format of a modern
census.

After carefully studying various methods used in the West, the
Russians had already reached two conclusions. Their Census, like
that of the United States, would be based on the local gathering—
but central processing—of statistics on individuals. And they
would rely on "the best mechanical devices" for the processing
of the Census. In a report by the Central Statistical Committee,
published at St. Petersburg only the year before, the Russians
disclosed that they had "become acquainted in detail" with the
application of the Hollerith system in the Austrian Census.

No existing devices, the report commented, were sufficiently
developed to give the results the fullness demanded by the administration and by science. Nevertheless, the best hope appeared
to be the Hollerith machine.

Convenience, intelligibility, significant exactness of work, economy of
time, and, most important, large curtailment of expenses . . . are attested
to by the excellent results of the American census in which this system
was first used and by the Austrian census.

Central Committee Senior Editor V. Struve described each unit
of the system in such detail that it was difficult to believe that the
Russians did not intend to use it. But as important as the functioning of the system was the manner in which it changed the way
the job was to be done. While hand methods were slower and less
exact, Struve observed, they were nevertheless more flexible. For
example, questions that had been overlooked might still be included after the job was under way. This became more difficult
when using the machine.

The punching of the cards and the plan of the work of the machine are
tightly connected. As a result, both plans should be composed simul-

taneously before the beginning of the work so as to get maximum use of the machine.

Once properly set up, however, the new apparatus could complete even the most complex combinations with the same ease as simple tabulations, the editor concluded.

Until the present . . . the major . . . time and labor . . . was spent on the composition of tables, i.e., on the apportionment, grouping and tabulation of the cards, and with each increase of number, or with each complication of the tables . . . the work took on increasingly larger dimensions and became more difficult.

Now, said Struve, "even the most complex combinations can be completed with the same ease as simple tabulations."

Hollerith could not help but be pleased with the report. If the Russian bureaucrats were exasperatingly slow, they at least were painstakingly thorough. But the question that had been on his mind for so long remained: was the Russian monolith ready to move?

Rousing himself from his nap at the hotel, Hollerith put on a fresh collar and fixed a broad knot in his tie. After running a brush through his short-cropped brown hair, he set off briskly at 7:00 o'clock to find Troinitsky. His short quick stride and prepossessing manner reflected his high hopes. If he could reach an agreement with the Russian official, his financial worries would be behind him.

Two hours later, Hollerith returned to his hotel room. His conversation with Troinitsky had been highly disquieting. He had learned that the Russians were negotiating behind his back with the Austrians to purchase his own machines from them. He immediately wrote a letter to his wife to explain the situation: "I found that I will have competition from Austria. As you know, I have no patents in Russia and since they [the Austrians] upset my Austrian patents, they can manufacture the machines in Austria and send them to Russia."

The Russians were getting ready to pirate his invention and there was nothing he could do about it.

It has been said that James Watt, the inventor of the steam engine, would rather have faced a loaded cannon than settle an account or make a bargain. Hollerith was similarly disposed: "So much depends upon what Troinitsky will say that I am almost afraid to meet him. Still, on a matter of business, I must impress him with my utter indifference as to whether he accepts or not. It is this above business that I so much dislike. The fact that one can never be frank and sincere." It was a mean piece of business. "I sometimes wish," Hollerith wrote, "I could keep a grocery store and stop quietly at home with my wife and children."

Though close to despair, the inventor was determined that the Austrians were not going to profit from what was rightfully his without a struggle.

I have decided they will not get the job even if I cannot make much out of it myself. They will have to furnish the machines pretty cheap if they want to get the customer. If I can only find out what price the Austrians will build them for, I will certainly cut under these.

The only recompense to this tawdry business, Hollerith told himself, was that he was becoming quite well known. While walking with Church in London, he had stopped by the Royal Statistical Society to look up some books. He had seen constant references to the "Machine Hollerith." Now, at Bern, everyone except the Austrians referred to the "Hollerith Machines". Sitting alone in a strange hotel room far from home, Hollerith wrote to his wife:

This machine or the principles will be potent factors in Statistical Science long after I am gone. Whether I or someone else will do it, this system is bound to be developed in many ways. It will take many years and perhaps it will be something for the two boys (perhaps more than two) to be able to say their daddy originated it. Of course, these are things I don't often speak about. I don't know whether I ever referred to it in speaking to you, but it is constantly in my mind.

The machine, as it exists now may and probably in years to come [will] appear crude and inefficient. Still, it is the genesis. This may appear like conceit and vanity on my part but [you] will understand how I say it, and I have no idea of ever talking like this to anyone else.

Two days went by before Troinitsky paid a return call. Driving a hard bargain, the Russian suggested that he might get some of the machines from Hollerith and some from the Austrians. Perhaps Troinitsky reasoned that, to obtain Hollerith's cooperation—and the latest improvements in his machines—he had to buy at least some of the machines from the inventor. If so, Hollerith was prepared. "My reply," he wrote, "was that in that event, I would prefer him to get them all from Vienna." As distasteful as he found such dealings, the proud inventor had called the Russian's bluff. "He was a little surprised at this," Hollerith observed, rather pleased with himself, "and I believe I gained my point. It is to be either all-American or all-Austrian. The question is which?"

Though he was "sitting on the anxious bench" and would not see Troinitsky again for two more days, Hollerith, having done his best, was now able to enjoy the meeting. Before the closing banquet, he sat for his silhouette, and while it was being cut with a scissors, the director of Swiss statistics, "a nice old man," made up a description to go with the profile. "He called me a 'Statistical Engineer,'" Hollerith recounted, "and, as someone present said, it was a happy designation, I would not be at all surprised if the definition should stick." Hollerith was pleased. In future years, he might, he predicted, be called the first "Statistical Engineer."

At the closing dinner, the end of the room was decorated with the silhouettes, Hollerith's among them. "Mine looked very well," the inventor recalled. One of the statisticians delivered a witty discourse in which he referred to each likeness, winding up with clever references to Hollerith and his machines. Commenting on Hollerith's profile, the speaker quoted a Latin poet: "a fool may have an insignificant nose, but a genius never."

Hollerith's speech left a favorable impression, and Porter quickly recorded the event for an American public that never tired of American technical triumphs abroad. In the *Cleveland World* he wrote:

Dr. Hollerith made a great hit among the European statisticians. Dr. Rauchberg, the statistician who had charge of the Austrian census, spoke . . . on his experience with the machines and their marvelous accuracy. The president of the congress, Sir Rawson Rawson, then called upon Dr. Hollerith . . . who described with considerable detail the operation of these important pieces of mechanism.

The Institute ended without a commitment from Troinitsky. However, Hollerith no longer felt discouraged:

I have . . . made a favorable impression on the Russian representative and I hope I will get the order for the machines . . . Troinitsky has promised to let me know in October.

But it was a bittersweet triumph, as had been his appearance before the Royal Statistical Society the year before. The learned European statisticans might heap honors upon him. But the praise meant little when he had nothing tangible to show for it. Learning that Sir John Puleston had not yet returned to London, Hollerith decided to stay over for a few more days. Along with Bodio, Trointsky, and others who had not hurried away, he stopped off at a beer garden for a friendly farewell. "They have a large table . . . inlaid with the names of various statisticians or their guests," the inventor wrote. Hollerith admired the handiwork of the Swiss woodcarvers and was flattered to have his name inscribed on the table. "It is a rather neat idea," he wrote his wife, "So you see, perhaps your husband's name will be prominent in a beer garden."

Hollerith accorded the Swiss a favorable ranking compared with the "slow" Italians and "crazy" French. Their cleanliness, neatness, and efficiency appealed to his innate Germanic tastes. But even the Swiss could go too far. Moving on to Lucerne, Hollerith described the view from his third floor room at the Hotel L'Europe—and longed for North Carolina, where he had summered with his family:

This is beautiful mountain scenery . . . yet so different from our Linville. It is all artificial. A railroad runs up to almost every peak and everywhere is evidence of civilization. While it is all very beautiful, I don't know but what I prefer N.C.

The man who would systematize much of modern life with his punched card tabulating machines did not himself care for too much order imposed on nature.

Hollerith finally caught up with Sir John in London on September 12, two days before embarking for home. After a preliminary chat, the inventor returned to his hotel to draw up more detailed statements requested by the industrialist for a discussion the following day. But Hollerith set sail without any agreement having been reached. He had been applauded by the Royal Statistical Society the year before, could read enthusiastic reports of the "Machine Hollerith" in technical journals, and had just been honored by Europe's leading statisticians. But the Russians were proving difficult and Britain, the home of the industrial revolution, was apparently not yet ready for punched card tabulation. "As you see," he wrote in a final letter home, "Englishmen can't do anything in a hurry."

11

Taking on the Central

"The more complicated the tabulation,
the more efficient the machine."

Arriving home from Bern, where he had been hailed as the first statistical engineer, Hollerith gave up the house in Georgetown. He simply couldn't pay the rent. When the lease expired at the end of September 1895, he packed Lu and the children off to his mother-in-law's home near the Naval Observatory. "He is at present very hard up for money," she wrote. "As Ned is dependent on him and he is also without means, I am supporting the whole party." It cut into Hollerith's pride that he could not even provide the bare essentials for his family.

Although he had been unsuccessful with the Richmond & Danville railroad the previous winter and spring, Hollerith felt confident enough of his hard-won knowledge of railway accounting by June to approach the two largest lines of the day. He recalled making the proposal many years later.

I made the same proposition to Mr. Riebenack and to Mr. Carstensen [the comptrollers of the Pennsylvania and New York Central, respectively]. . . . at about the same time both decided to give the matter a trial. But Carstensen telegraphed while Riebenack wrote so it came about that I started with the New York Central.

By 1895, Cornelius Vanderbilt's preserves took in New York, Buffalo, Cleveland, Detroit, Chicago, St. Louis, Cincinnati, and Indianapolis. No other rail system in the country, with the single exception of the Pennsylvania, covered so much rich and settled territory. The Central alone processed nearly 4 million freight waybills a year—each one by hand. If a punched card could take the place of the written waybill transcript, as Hollerith proposed, the giant railroad could chart its freight movements—and freight revenues—on a weekly rather than a monthly basis. It could tell on a nearly current basis how many hundreds of tons of freight were moving East—or West; which of hundreds of stations along its lines were profitable; where freight cars should be sent or returned; what freight agents were being paid. It would give the railroad a much firmer command of its far-flung business.

Whether the installation was made before Hollerith left for Europe in August is uncertain. But by the fall, he had set up his machines in Room 612 of the Grand Central Depot, a mansard-roofed structure topped with flags, at the corner of Broadway and 11th Street in New York City. In a patent issued at the time, he described the first application of data processing to the railroad business.

In the tabulation of statistics relating to the transportation of freight the items of each invoice which may be tabulated are . . . first, weight (in pounds); second, proportional charge (in dollars and cents); third, advance charge (in dollars and cents); and fourth, prepaid charge (in dollars and cents). The items are transferred from the way-bills to a record.

Perforations in the record card will . . . correctly represent the items to be tabulated relating to this particular invoice. . . . all the cards belonging to the same series or station are . . . placed together and the items tabulated thereon . . .

Hollerith's almost volcanic bursts of creative activity were ignited by his having to react on short notice to immediate and unmet needs. He developed electrically actuated air brakes when long strings of frieght cars, made possible by increased locomotive power, slammed into each other on quick stops. He developed his census machine in direct response to the impending collapse of the census brought about by a growing population and the desire to know more about it. In his experience, it was a threatened collapse in the current way of doing things that spurred his creation of new technology, not technology itself that prompted change.

In helping the railroads to control the blizzard of paper entailed in freight accounting, Hollerith again sought to bend technology to the job at hand. Most noticeably, he radically altered the layout of the punched card to accommodate information from the way-bill, a change that, in turn, called for the redesign of his machines. For the first time, information would be punched in vertical columns. To enable the operator to read the card, each column was printed with the numerals zero through nine from top to bottom. In addition, groups of vertical columns intended to hold a particular class of information were set off from each other by vertically printed lines, which served as sort of fences. The divisions between them Hollerith appropriately called fields. It was an ingenious arrangement, and one that would endure. Suddenly, the punched card assumed the familiar appearance it has today.

But Hollerith also took care not to design himself into a corner. The fences could be moved to widen or narrow the fields, depending on the number of columns needed for recording figures. In his card for the Central's freight accounting, Hollerith allotted five columns for the weight of shipments, allowing for totals up to 99,999 pounds, while four columns were deemed adequate for advance charges. Other fields varied, according to the space needed. Within a field, the right-hand column was reserved for units, the second for tens, the third for hundreds, and upward. Where dollars and cents were recorded, the two right-hand columns were reserved for cents, and adjacent columns for dollars.

The new card marked an important transition. In the census cards, the punching positions stood for personal characteristics, such as marital status, or numerical quantities, such as age. However, each fact on the new cards had to be expressed in numbers. This meant that in railroad accounting and in other future commercial applications, facts not already stated in numbers would have to be coded or translated into numeric terms. With his newly designed punched card, Hollerith had begun to propel the nation's commercial activity into the world of numbers.

Hollerith had just gotten started at the Central when he received an urgent summons to come to Russia. The contents of the message are unknown, but it must have implied that agreement was close at hand. Should he tear himself away when he had barely gotten a toehold with a rich and important customer? When the machines were scarcely in place and the installation at a critical stage? On the other hand, could he afford *not* to go, considering the probable size of the Russian order—if he could get it? It was an agonizing decision. No matter which course he took, it seemed to be the wrong one.

The inventor left hurriedly for Russia, placing the newly installed machines at the New York Central in charge of J. Shirley Eaton, the man who had sparked his interest in railway work. The dates Hollerith was away are uncertain. But he was determined to make the trip as short as possible. He was home again by October 2, when the enthusiast Porter interviewed his friend "just back from Russia." Porter was quick to tell how Hollerith had brought the Russian Empire to bay.

The Russian Empire next June will take a census and, in all, they expect to enumerate a population of between 120 and 130 million. The man at the head of this work, Mr. Troinitsky . . . after a careful investigation . . . has decided to adopt the same system as that employed for the first time in . . . the 11th Census. Thus, three great European nations, Austria, Italy, and Russia have followed the U.S. in using the Hollerith Electrical Machine.

The quantity of punched cards alone, Porter estimated, would weigh over 300 tons. More important, Porter understood that "the order for these machines will soon be placed with the American inventor and that they will probably be manufactured in this country." The reasons were compelling.

During the past five years . . . great improvements have been made . . . by Mr. Hollerith in methods of electrical tabulation. . . . the machines . . . first used in population work have now been improved and enlarged in scope so that the work relating to mortgage indebtedness was partially tabulated by these machines. Also, the Agricultural returns . . . they [the machines] have been improved . . . so that they can be used to great advantage in the tabulation of railroad accounts. Experiments are now being made by the New York Central Railroad Co. . . . and also by the United States Express Co. and other large concerns that deal with vast masses of data.

To obtain the latest in technology, it was only logical that Russia should turn to the United States. And there was nothing left for

Porter to do except praise the broad-mindedness of the Russian officials "who realize that, in coming to the fountainhead for this intricate mechanism, they take advantage of the wide experience and many improvements since the introduction of electricity into statistical work by the 11th Census."

Hollerith liked the Russians and discovered that they, in turn, had a kindly feeling toward Americans. He was also surprised to find that the Czarist Empire, then building railroads faster than any country except the United States, was more ready to adopt his methods than any other European country. Despite his favorable impression, doing business with the Russians was decidedly strenuous. Serious negotiations, he recounted, didn't start until after midnight, following countless cups of spiced and sugared tea poured from an ever-present samovar and served in glasses set in metal holders. As a consequence, the inventor complained of being dead tired while on his three trips to Russia. He was rescued from sheer exhaustion on more than one trip by the services of a Russian woman secretary—women secretaries were still a rarity in his own country—who worked efficiently over long hours to help him get away. Grateful, he kept track of her whereabouts for many years, and during the Revolution, sent her parcels of food and clothing. Among the souvenirs he brought back from Russia were coffee cups, sleigh bells, and a small enameled drinking cup. Hollerith's Russian friends evidently shared his warm feelings, since they inscribed, at the bottom of the cup: "Out of this small cup to drink, your Russian friends to think."

Porter's enthusiastic accounts might have led some readers to assume that Hollerith had solved all of his problems on his return from Russia in October of 1895. But this was not quite the case. He had come back from St. Petersburg without a signed order for his machines. And, stepping off the boat, he learned another piece of news. In his absence, the New York Central had thrown out his machines. The devices, he was told, were simply not up to the job. The first installation of data processing equipment by the railroad industry had lasted no more than three or four months. It was a devastating blow. Not only had he lost an important customer, but news of his failure at the Central would surely spread.

Under the circumstances, no other line would seriously consider his machines.

Hollerith's reaction to the news is unrecorded. Certainly, he had every reason to be discouraged. Others in his place might simply have given up. However, within four months, he was busying himself at the Western Electric shops in New York. On January 31, 1896, his mother-in-law-reported: "Hollerith is in New York. he is having some new machines built there for the work of the New York Central Railroad. They are to be larger and have quite a few improvements."

The tabulators that were taking shape in the Western Electric shops were notably different from anything that Hollerith had built before. Gone were the familiar clock dial counters of the census machines and of the first railroad machines. In their place, a row of four adding machines peered through a glass-covered case toward the operator. Each electric adding machine was connected through the press of the tabulator to a different field of the punched card. There was one machine for weight; another for freight charges; a third for adding advance charges; and a fourth for the prepaid charges. When the press was pulled down upon a punched card, the amounts in the four classifications were added simultaneously.

Clearly, the capacity of the new machines was greater than that of the integrating tabulator developed for the War Department and improved for the handling of farm statistics. In the first integrator, the closing of the press upon a card caused a cylinder inside the machine to make one complete revolution. Ranged around the cylinder were nine parallel strips of conducting material. A row of brushes was positioned above the cylinder so that an electric impulse was produced each time a brush crossed one of the strips. The brush on the left end of the cylinder came into contact with all nine strips, sending nine impulses to a counter. Brushes further to the right came into contact with progressively fewer strips. Thus, the press had to be held closed while the cylinder made a complete revolution to generate as many as nine impulses. Not only was this operation cumbersome, but the counters of the earlier machines could accept only one impulse at a time, causing further delay.

In contrast to the serial operation of the early machine, each adding device in Hollerith's new system operated independently. Each was backed by a series of nine electromagnets ranged in an arc around the adding wheels. When the press was closed, creating a circuit through a hole in the card, it activated one of the magnets. The pull of a particular magnet, in turn, caused a swinging arm to engage an adding wheel and move it a greater or lesser number of spaces, depending on the position of the magnet in the arc. In one closing of the press, separate groups of figures could be added at once, with the results being shown directly in figures on the wheels of the counting mechanisms.

Armed with his new integrating tabulator, Hollerith stubbornly fought for a second chance at the Central. By May 15, 1896—seven months after his return from Russia—the persistent young man had budged the huge organization, if only slightly, in his direction. It agreed to let him resume his experiments. He would be granted a year's trial and could insist that the tests be continued until the year was up. If the Central was satisfied before that time, it could decide to end the tests in advance and draw up contracts to pay for the machines. In the meanwhile, Hollerith would pay for the tests. It was a one-sided bargain, with the Central risking little, if anything, on the outcome. All it had agreed to was putting up with the nuisance of tests that might be to its benefit. Hollerith, on the other hand, was staking money he didn't have on a newly designed system. He was wagering that his untried machines could do the job.

While he was frantically readying his new machines for the Central, Hollerith heard nothing from Russia, despite Troinitsky's promise of a decision by October. And soon the overly optimistic Porter was playing a far less certain note. Raising the renewed possibility that the machines might be purchased more cheaply from Austria, Porter appealed to the Russians' nobler instincts.

Would such a course be either wise or right? . . . it would be taking unfair advantage which would hardly be a dignified thing for so great and lofty a nation as Russia to do. In the second place, it would be unwise as the Austrian machines are four or five years old and the inventor, Dr. Herman Hollerith, has made some important improvements since then. One automatic improvment alone will save nearly 25 percent in the cost of tabulating over the old machines.

Porter concluded:

It would be a great mistake for the Russian Government . . . to secure anything but the latest inventions and to do this it must come to the United States.

While Hollerith counted heavily on the Russian contract, he concentrated all of his energies at the Central. As if to add to his frustration, auditors from the rival Pennsylvania began calling upon him. And the Express Company was urging him to install a machine. But without capital to pay for workers and to finance additional machines, he could do nothing to take advantage of the opportunities. Businessmen in New York had money put away, he told his family, but were afraid to invest it. With his business at a virtual standstill, he reached a low point in his personal finances.

"Hollerith asked me if I wanted to do something for him and Lu," Mrs. Talcott wrote, "and then told me he had three life insurance policies due the next day and hadn't the money to pay for them." If the policies were not paid, Hollerith explained, he would lose them entirely. The widow paid the $240 that was due. "I thought it over carefully," she said, "and decided that, if allowed to lapse and he should die, then I should have that much more to do for Lu."

What could he do to rise above his seemingly endless troubles? Shortly before the turn of the year, Hollerith had gone to Chicago to visit the "Big Shop," as the headquarters of Western Electric was called. The industrial giant turned out three-fifths of the world's telephonic apparatus. No one else used so much wire, hard rubber, and brass. In a single year, the behemoth business consumed 1,000 pounds of platinum from the distant Ural Mountains; miles of silk thread from Italy and Japan; tons of iron for magnets from Norway; paper tape from Manila; mahogany from

South America; and rubber from Brazil and the Congo. Besides its manufacturing business, the company had also been sought out by scores of inventors such as Hollerith. Some came with little more than pipe dreams; others, with practical models to be turned into products. For thousands more, Western Electric was the largest jobber anywhere. As middleman, it purchased electrical equipment from hundreds of makers and distributed it to buyers of every kind. Page 206 of its *Electrical Supplies Catalogue* for 1896 lists the counters that Hollerith had designed for his census machines. They sold for $5 apiece. And Phenix dry batteries to run them were an extra $1.10 each. To Hollerith, Western Electric had been, at one time or another, manufacturer, supplier, and distributor. Now he asked the company to assume still another role—that of banker.

While in Chicago, the inventor discussed the financing of machines for Russia, as his mother-in-law disclosed: "Hollerith has not yet received a definite reply from Russia, but just as soon as the contract is made, he says that he can get all the money he wants from the Western Electric Company." Another topic had also been broached. The inventor shared it with Ned, who confided in his mother: "Hollerith told him that he wants to sell out to the Western Electric Company and then they are to employ him at a big salary to manage the machines for them. If this arrangement is made, Hollerith would probably go immediately to Russia."

Unable to free himself from continuing financial problems, Hollerith was considering selling out. He was not yet thirty-six—Lu would bake a cake with nine candles to observe his leap-year birthday. But except for three years as a government employee, he had always been his own man. He was the one who barked out instructions, who insisted on exact compliance, who maintained complete control. But lately there had been no resources and no people to command. He had hung onto the little shop on 31st Street in Georgetown, but it was dark most of the time. Busy in New York, he had told Ned to stay at home and to avoid using fuel to heat the building. If there were prospects for new business, he had no way of exploiting them. The giant manufacturing company, he knew, could easily solve all of his problems—and put his tabulating machines on the map once and for all.

It was a tempting proposition.

In March 1896 a ray of sun shone through an otherwise bleak sky. The French government wrote asking Hollerith to make an offer to take their census of occupations. It would, the French figured, cost them a million dollars to do the job without the machines. Hollerith thought he could make money out of the job. But he found himself in his usual predicament. He couldn't even bid for the job unless some money came in from Russia. He had received letters from St. Petersburg strongly hinting that the matter would be decided within the month, but so far the Russians had made no commitment. How could he break out of the tight circle without losing his business?

One day, Hollerith borrowed $20 from his mother-in-law to buy a train ticket to Boston. Once there, he walked from the station to 146 Franklin Street. Feeling his pocket to make sure the letter from the French government was still inside, he entered the offices of the Library Bureau. Founded in 1876, the Bureau was an offshoot of the prestigious American Library Association and had found a good business in supplying library equipment and supplies not available elsewhere. By 1894, the Bureau had made another discovery: "There is hardly a library article on our list," its catalogue confirmed, "that is not also used in offices." To serve "a larger and equally interested clientage in wide-awake, energetic business men and institutions," the Bureau had started a separate department of Improved Business Methods. It now boasted:

Among life and fire insurance companies, banks, railways, large manufacturing establishments, and to representative houses in almost every line, it has not only suggested and installed better methods and improved machinery, but it has also effected great savings in expense.

The firm was one of the growing number of "systemizers." It studied "the unproductive side of the expense account" and considered, "after carefully studying the details of each business, how it is possible to reduce expenses by changes in method or adoption of new devices." The proved value of such services was the basis for its fee.

Of more immediate interest to Hollerith, the firm did business abroad through locations in London and Paris. On March 31, 1896, the inventor signed a ten-year agreement with the Bureau licensing it to use his patents for "Improvements in Tabulating and other Machines and Apparatus" in England, Germany, France, and Italy. He also made an agreement covering his domestic business, though the extent of it is not clear. Several years later, Hollerith would report:

The Library Bureau has made a contract to compile one year's experience of the Travelers' Insurance Company. This, while a small contract, shows the disposition of the Insurance Company to give out such work by contract. Propositions to compile the complete experience of the New York Life, Phoenix Mutual, Mutual Benefit and other Companies are also being considered.

Hollerith's mother-in-law was first to break the news. She wrote on April 14:

Hollerith has made a contract with the Library Bureau of Boston and they are to work up contracts for him and . . . capital to undertake them, and then share the profits. . . . Hollerith will receive $300 per month and . . . the half or more of profits for all contracts.

H. E. Davidson, first vice-president of the Bureau, left immediately for Paris to work out an agreement for the French Census. The Bureau would supply the capital to prepare for the work. However, the Bureau would not share in the big Russian job, if Hollerith got it, except for equipment it might provide. Within a few months, Ned would pack a tabulator and accompany it to Boston to train the Bureau's clerks in the operation of the machine. By bringing his system to the Library Bureau, Hollerith established a prototype for today's data processing service bureaus, firms that do not usually manufacture equipment themselves, but take in the data processing work of other businesses for a fee.

Returning from Boston, Hollerith received a puzzling cable from Russia. It was, he thought, an offer from the Austrian manufacturer Schaefler to withdraw as his rival for the Russian Census for a fee of $4,000. His mother-in-law wrote: "we think that such an offer is a pretty sure indication that they [the Austrians] have lost it and they want to make something out of Hollerith before he is informed that he is to have it." Whatever his other weaknesses, Hollerith seldom lacked decision. But now he hesitated. And for the only recorded time in his business career, he asked his wife what to do. "Turn down the offer," Lu advised, sharing her husband's pride. "Refuse to pay a single cent; never mind what the result will be." Long the bane of his existence, the Austrians, he decided, were not going to profit from his inventions— no matter what the outcome.

The inventor fretted for more than a week after cabling his reply, only to discover that the baffling message had not come from his Austrian rival at all. His mother-in-law was quick to explain:

The Western Electric Company have a branch in Berlin and the manager of it has been to Russia in Hollerith's interest. What he intended by his cable was this: Schaefler, the Austrian, has asked the Western Electric Company if they would manufacture machines for him in case he got the Russian census. So the Western Electric manager cabled Hollerith, meaning that if Hollerith would give them $4,000 they would decline to manufacture the machines for the Austrians and that would cut them off from getting the contract. And when Hollerith refused, they made a contract to manufacture machines for the Austrians.

Once again, Hollerith may have dreamed of running a corner store and staying home with his family. Six years before, the Austrians had broken his patents after he had helpfully sent them a machine to copy. Now they had contracted with the same manufacturer that he himself relied on. Hollerith showed the cable to the Western Electric people in New York, who interpreted it the same way he had. It was small comfort. Schaefler, he learned, had just gone to Russia to work all the harder for the contract.

Surprisingly, the setback had little observable effect. Pleased at the unusual prospect of some income from the Library Bureau, Hollerith was busy moving his family from his mother-in-law's to

General Abbott's house, which he had rented in nearby Garrett Park. If Lu and the children liked living in the Maryland suburb, he would build a home on his own land in the park. He could only be happy in a household that revolved around him.

Like a general supplying an army, Hollerith planned the move meticulously and carried it off in style. He hired a procession of six huge farm wagons to haul his heavy oak furniture. Barrels of other belongings and a hogshead of china were dispatched by train. Each shipment left and arrived at precise intervals, with the inventor barking out instructions. He was firmly in command. "It is a move as is a move," his mother-in-law noted approvingly. "Hollerith bossed the whole shootin' match and was happy."

The ample Victorian house he had chosen was topped by a Norman tower. It had large rooms and a porch that swept around the front. There were banks of roses and other flowers to please his wife as well as asparagus and strawberry beds where Mrs. Abbot had picked 400 quarts of berries the year before. Food in plentiful quantities gave Hollerith a sense of security and well-being, summoning back his childhood, when bins of vegetables in the root cellar had helped tide the family through the severe winters. Now the inventor rented an additional lot at the back of the house and ordered it plowed and planted. He would supply vegetables not only for his own family but also for Lu's brother who lived nearby.

The children were almost as excited as Hollerith with their new home. Lucia helped her mother with the garden. The boys rushed out of the house every time a train roared by at the bottom of the hill, trying to read the number on the locomotive. They hoped to find the engine that pulled the train with their father's air brakes at the Burlington airbrake trials many years before.

May arrived and Ned was in New York instructing the New York Central clerks in the use of the new machines. "There was no trouble with the machines," he reported. "It was the stupid station agents and stupid clerks. The first could not make their vouchers out correctly and the clerks could not learn to use the machines. So, as Hollerith expresses it, 'it shall be a success.'" Hollerith and Ned had been getting in before the clerks arrived in the morning and staying until after midnight. The Central's clerks ran the machines. But Hollerith and his young brother-in-law had to set them up for the next day's work and keep them in repair. When June came, Hollerith sent Ned home for a short rest. Mrs. Talcott summed up the state of affairs:

Hollerith has had a hard time with no end of obstacles and disappointments and at times has been tempted to throw up the whole thing. Ned says that he has been so sorry for him sometimes that he would have sold the coat off his back to help him.

Why Hollerith, with his nervous, excitable temper, has not lost his mind, I do not know. You cannot realize what a strain he has had to bear without one cent for current expenses and yet obliged to spend freely.

Good, plain food in ample quantities was Hollerith's answer to almost any sort of crisis. To weather the ordeal at the Central, he insisted that Ned eat three square meals a day. Ned looked fine, as a result. But the inventor was becoming portly. As the summer wore on, Hollerith still heard nothing from Russia. On his trip to St. Petersburg the previous fall, he had taken along a tabulator to lend to the Committee. Now, almost a year later, Hollerith expressed his fears, which were echoed by his mother-in-law.

I have an idea that as they have one of Hollerith's machines there, they are simply copying it and will make their own machines—a clean steal. But those Russians would not mind a little thing like that! As Hollerith did not take out patents in Russia, I have given up all hope of his getting the Russian census.

In early August, Mr. Davidson cabled Hollerith that he had secured the work for the French Census. Hollerith himself had no idea how much money the job would bring as he had not yet heard the terms of the contract. But the cupboard at home was bare. Lu wrote that she did not have one cent in the house and had not had for a week. By the end of the week, Hollerith managed to send her $20 from New York. How much longer he could subject himself and his family to this self-imposed ordeal, he could not be sure.

On August 20, Hollerith wrote to tell his mother-in-law "of just a few words of conversation between the controller of the New York Central and myself at lunch yesterday."

He said he was willing to contract with me for machines for the entire road for one year provided we could agree on price. He believed in the utility of the system and the possibilities of its development. It has been a desperate struggle for me. I believe that I have nearly won and am determined to win. Knowing what your interest in this matter, direct and indirect, is, I concluded to write you though it is somewhat contrary to my judgement to say much until the matter is decided.

I have no hesitation now in saying that I believe the methods of railway accounting will be revolutionized within the next five years. Here I am doing the very thing I said I never liked to do . . . what I say, however, is simply intended to show you that perhaps your confidence in me has not been misplaced and perhaps, after all, I will come out on top.

I think I have won. I hope soon to be able to say that I have *won* and I want to assure you that I appreciate what you have said and done which often encouraged me when I was nearly desperate.

Victory was at hand. And on September 28, 1896, Hollerith signed the contract with Chauncey M. Depew, the president of the New York Central and Hudson River Railroad Company. A year had passed since his earlier machines had been unceremoniously ejected by the line. It had taken gumption—and an unshakable belief in his new machines—to pick himself up and try again. Six months after his new integrating tabulators had been installed, Hollerith brought the trial to a successful conclusion. Although his new contract did not start until the beginning of the year, the Auditor's Office now wanted his machines applied to all, rather than part, of its work in a "further experiment as to the efficiency of the system." His mother-in-law gave further details:

Now he will have to manufacture some more machines, and be very busy. He will probably now give some attention to the Pennsylvania Railroad. So I hope he is on his feet again though we may all still have to pinch and economize as I doubt he will get much ready money yet awhile.

The contract called for Hollerith to "supply, erect and maintain in good working order" a sufficient number of keyboard punches, gang punches, electric tabulating machines, and electric sorting machines to process up to 4 million waybills during the coming year. He was also to supply trays and racks for handling cards and operator's tables. He would procure these through the Library

Bureau. In return, Hollerith was to receive "the sum of Five Thousand Dollars" in equal monthly installments, starting February 1, 1897. The railroad also agreed to buy all the cards it would require for the machines "at the price of one dollar per thousand." In contrast with his agreement during the trial, the Central bound itself to pay Hollerith a full year's rent for the machines in 1897—no matter how long or short a time it chose to use them.

"It shall be a success," Hollerith had repeated to himself and Ned, and he had finally made it so. However, he did not wait for other machines to be built to expand the work he had begun. Besides the compilation of freight accounts and statistics, his system would be equally available for the processing of passenger and car accounts. To manage the extra load, Hollerith shipped cards punched in New York to Georgetown, where Ned ran them off on machines in the shop and sent back the figures. This early example of remote computing was less expensive than feeding Ned three square meals a day in New York. But Hollerith also had another objective in mind.

The more complicated the tabulation, the more efficient the machine. ... when this system is once introduced into a railway office, and it is learned that statistics beyond the traditional limits ... may be obtained rapidly and at trifling cost, the uses of the machine will rapidly increase.

By supplying his systems more work to do, Hollerith was not only giving the Central its money's worth. He had also found a sound means of expanding his business opportunities.

This time the installation would stick. But it would take somewhat longer than the five years the inventor predicted for his methods of railway accounting to be fully accepted. The breakthrough would be signaled by a rather curious series of events that would come to light on June 9, 1902. And to recount them, we must skip ahead in our story.

It was a time when the Interstate Commerce Commission was tightening its regulation of the roads and had ordered the railroad accountants to furnish it with additional statistics beyond those previously required. On that Monday in June a hearing was being held to give the railroads a chance to reply to the order. "Several of the officers present," it was reported, "were rather violent in their remonstrances, declaring that it would cost the roads millions more than they were paying for such work, as it meant a complete readjustment of their statistical processes." In contrast to the hue and cry from his colleagues, the New York Central Controller took the new demands very much in stride. Mr. Carstensen, it was noted, assured the Commission that "the Central would put in no objection, as he can simply run his figures through his electric tabulator and the additional trouble and cost would be nominal."

The Central Controller's response set off a virtual explosion among his fellow actuaries. Not only were they annoyed at having their position undercut. But they were also mystified at the black statistical arts being practiced in secret by the Central. Controller Carstensen—the man who had wired rather than written to Hollerith at Mobjack Bay—gave his explanation of the event to *Railway World*.

There has been a great deal said to me . . . about the tabulating machines that have been in use of the New York Central. I think there is a misunderstanding on the part of some gentlemen here and perhaps on the part of the Commission as to what we were doing with those machines.

Five or six years ago, they were put into our freight office to see if we could report freight earnings and balance our accounts with them. We tried it for a time and it was a failure. But Mr. Hollerith was very persistent in his efforts to have us use the machines and begged the opportunity to put them back in without any expense to the railroad company and experiment a little more with them. We consented and he did so.

About a year ago he asked whether I would send back the five machines as he wanted to clean them. I sent word to the auditor of the freight office to have the machines returned. He came to me with a very long face and said that if he did that, he would have to hire twenty men. They [the machines] had become useful."

Always the conservative engineer, Hollerith did not care to boast about the prospects of machines still under development. Experimenting with automatic feeders in 1902 to take the place of the hand feeding of cards into his systems, the inventor still felt there were difficulties to be overcome. "The news which has just come out," it was reported, "had been held back by the desire of Mr. Hollerith to wait until some experiments . . . in . . . feeding machines as well as running them by electricity should reach greater perfection."

Despite Hollerith's reluctance to promote his machines, the nation's leading lines would be placing orders faster than he could fill them a little more than a decade after his early experiments at the Central. Replying to a friend's offer to propose him for membership in the Railroad Club in July 1905, Hollerith would write:

I do not think it is worthwhile wasting any energy in this direction We have the machines fully established at the New York Central Railroad, and there is hardly a railroad auditor of any consequence in the country who has not seen them in use.

The man who had started off by admitting he "did not know the first damned thing about railroad accounts" would succeed by meeting their requirements to a remarkable degree.

12

The Russian Census

"Russia . . . has a foundation for so much larger a country than ours . . ."

On November 12, 1896, a black cat strayed into the Hollerith home at Garrett Park. Black cats meant good luck, Nellie the Irish maid told Lu. The following day, Friday the thirteenth, a second black cat arrived just as mysteriously. It was decided that both Herman, Jr., and Charles could have one. As if to prove Nellie's premonition, Mrs. Talcott received a letter from Hollerith in the noon mail that day and immediately sat down to share the news with her brother. "At last, we have met the Russians and they are ours," she reported.

It was true. Hollerith had finally won the Russian census order, and Lu invited her mother, brother, and cousins to Sunday dinner at Garrett Park to drink to the Czar's health.

Hollerith, who had dreamed of the moment for years, was in something of a quandary when his moment of victory arrived. His dilemma revolved around a cup. It was one of the handleless white enamel cups, stamped with the Imperial Eagle, that had been passed out by the cartload as royal souvenirs at the coronation of Nicholas II the previous May. On receiving it as a present from Lu's Aunt Nannie, the inventor, shedding his usual caution, had vowed to drain the five-inch-high vessel on winning the Russian Census contract. Now he carefully filled it to measure its volume and, determining that it held more than a pint, backed off from his rash pronouncement. Nevertheless, spirits were high. Both grownups and children pitched into the feast—Lu had reluctantly killed her ducks for the occasion. A good time was had by all.

"I am very delighted," Hollerith's mother-in-law recorded, "and hope that it is the beginning of better times for us all."

Earlier in the day, the inventor had walked over to look at some wooded property on the other side of the railroad track. The five acres, set on a hill, had more room than his land in the residential park, and he talked of trading his lots for it. Then he could build a shop in the country and do his experimental work there. The load that had sat on his shoulders for so long was beginning to lift. Once more, he could look confidently ahead. He was in an expansive mood. "What is the use of living in the country," he remarked, "unless you can have some ground?"

The gay family celebration at Garrett Park was tempered only when Hollerith announced that he had to leave for Russia in two weeks to sign the formal contract with Czar's government. The November 25 sailing date meant that he would be away from his family for both Thanksgiving and Christmas.

Meanwhile there was much to be done. Though Hollerith had signed the New York Central contract on September 28, he still had no money. To make matters worse, a windstorm had rampaged through Washington on October 1, blocking the streets with broken trees. At the Hollerith home, the attic window was blown in and Lu had watched the windmill come crashing down. Damage was even more severe in Georgetown. "Hollerith's shop is entirely unroofed—open to the sky," his mother-in-law had reported. "The warehouse on Water Street had the south end blown in and the roof taken off . . ." Hurrying back from New York, Hollerith had the roofs made watertight. Though he had tamed the New York Central, the inventor was still helpless before the forces of nature.

Even with the Central contract in his pocket, Hollerith found it impossible to raise money to break through the depression that had weighed down business for so long. He believed that the presidential election might change conditions for the better, and on November 3, he and Ned walked into the city from Georgetown after dinner to hear the latest returns. Although the count was not yet complete, they returned at 11:00 P.M. and the inventor went to bed happy. McKinley's election over Bryan seemed assured. For years a staunch Democrat and Cleveland man, Hollerith had given up on his party's ability to cure the nation's and his own hard times.

His hunch may have been right, for a leavening of optimism swept through the land. And before sailing, he managed to get his hands on some money. "He spent all of Saturday and Monday going around paying bills," his mother-in-law reported, "and was delighted to do so." Still, the advance was a few drops falling on parched ground. And that Hollerith saw his way clear of his financial doldrums for the first time was all the more frustrating. He would not receive his first payment from the Russians until late January, and the rental from his Central machines would not start until the beginning of February. In the meanwhile, for a second year he could not afford to celebrate Christmas. "As the whole family is in the same fix," Mrs. Talcott wrote, "we will just have to make up our minds to do without and not give any presents."

Once out on the ocean, Hollerith seemed to throw off his worries, and, as it often did, his mood changed from one extreme to another. By the time he reached Russia, he appeared to be in cheerful, even playful spirits. By his own calculations, he had arrived at St. Petersburg *before* sailing from New York. Pleased with himself, he wrote to his wife from the capital city on the Neva:

The time in St. Petersburg is about seven hours ahead of your time so when I arrived here at 4:30 P.M. it was only 9:30 in the morning with you. It is today the 25th of November (Russian Calendar) and as I sailed on the 25th at 10 A.M. you will, I think, admit that I arrived here before I left New York.

Evidently enjoying himself, Hollerith was even amused at the circumstances of his arrival.

You will no doubt be surprised to know that I am wearing another man's undershirt and that of an entire stranger. Troinitsky met me at the depot in Berlin and told me of having helped an American, a stranger, get his tickets, and told the man that I was on board. So he looked me up and at night, when he learned how thinly I was clothed, he got one of his Jaeger shirts and insisted on my putting it on over my cotton shirt. I have every reason to be thankful for I believe that, were it not for that, I would have a much worse cold that I have got.

The temperature had dropped from 60 degrees F. in Paris, where Hollerith had entrained, to zero at St. Petersburg. Concerned about his head cold, Hollerith invested in "some Jaeger flannel, a fur cap, and a fur coat."

What I will ever do with the coat I cannot imagine when I leave here, and it is rather expensive for so short a time. Still, I thought it better to take no chances with my health. Could the children see me in this getup, I think they would be amused. If I get a chance, I will send you a picture.

As a rule, Hollerith stubbornly refused to have his photograph taken. To an unsuspecting editor who asked for one, he once retorted: "Should I ever decide to have a picture taken, which I very much doubt, I will try to remember to send you one. . . . I regret to disappoint you in this matter, but I do not see how I can help it." However, he apparently approved of the snapshot taken in St. Petersburg. It shows him almost totally enveloped in the double-breasted, fur-lined coat. The high fur collar cuts cross his cheeks and is turned up well over his ears. The round fur cap is pushed down low on his forehead. Perhaps Hollerith favored the photo because so little of himself is revealed. Only a pair of bright, sparkling eyes, his roundish full nose, and a portion of bushy mustache emerge from the fur collar and cap. But the expression in the eyes hints at a smile on the hidden mouth. In contrast to most earlier portraits, which convey a solemn if not doleful look, this one is confident and happy. It catches Hollerith at a triumphant moment of his career.

For once, the inventor even enjoyed traveling, a frequent source of complaint. On his way to St. Petersburg, he had a close-up look at Russian royalty in the person of one of the towering uncles of the twenty-six-year-old Czar.

On the train coming up from Paris was the Duke Alexis. It afforded some little interest, and I must say I admired the man for his magnificent physique and plain simple manners. I had seen and admired the man but would never have suspected he was anybody had not the conductor told me who he was. I had a good opportunity to observe him, for at the table in the dining car, the conductor gave me a seat diagonally opposite to him. He was dressed in plain clothes, but as soon as we struck the Russian frontier, he appeared in full uniform of a Russian Admiral. While he got on and off as any individual might while in France and Germany, in Russia a step was brought to the car, carpet laid, etc.

The inventor might have been less impressed had he been aware that the admiral was known for his "fast women and slow ships." But Hollerith was equally taken by the reception accorded an ordinary American citizen.

Just before coming into St. Petersburg, another American and myself were standing talking along side of an old officer, evidently an Engineer officer. He had occasion to say something to me in very broken English. The result was an attempt at conversation. He asked were we English and evidently took us for English. When I replied no, not English, American, he immediately unbuttoned his glove, took it off and gave us each a hearty handshake. The whole thing was so simple and sincere we could not help be impressed. While he thought we were English, he was polite, but as soon as he knew we were Americans, he was cordiality itself.

On December 15, 1896, Hollerith signed the contract with Troinitsky "to furnish you for the Russian Government electrical tabulating machines of my invention." In contrast with his usual rental policy, he agreed to sell the Russians thirty-five "new" machines. It did not matter that title to them would pass with the sale. Hollerith had no patents in Russia at the time, and he could not have brought suit if the Russians had pirated his machines. However, the "new" machines did not include the integrating device the inventor had perfected for commercial work. The feature may not have been needed for census work where counting units rather than adding larger sums was involved. But after his difficult dealings, the inventor may have been taking no chances. Although far larger than any census machines he had built before, the "new" tabulating systems were far less sophisticated than the equipment that Hollerith had recently installed at the New York Central.

Priced at $1,700 each, the tabulators designed for the immense Russian count came equipped with eighty counters, thirty relays, and two sorting boxes apiece. They were exactly twice as large as Hollerith's system for the 1890 U.S. Census, which came with forty counters and one sorting box. The "new" machines even topped the tabulators modified for the Austrian Census, which had housed seventy counters. To further enlarge their capacity, Hollerith agreed to furnish sixty-three additional relays with each machine. When properly set up, the "new" systems were capable of processing more combinations of data in a single run of cards through the tabulator than any system he had designed before.

Hollerith had won his gamble that the systems were to be "all-American." Although the "new" machines would be assembled at St. Petersburg, all the parts would be made in the United States.

The warehouse on River Street would also be relieved, as Hollerith had hoped, of some of the "old" machines returned from the 1890 Census. His contract called for him to furnish thirty-five "old but thoroughly serviceable" tabulators, each with forty counters, thirty relays, and one sorting box. As part of the deal, the Russians would have free use of the old tabulators until April 3, 1900. But the Committee agreed to pay the shipping charges, marine insurance, and duties on all the machines to St. Petersburg—and return passage for the old machines. Despite the onrush of technology, Hollerith intended his machines to last. He was also a keen businessman. He insisted that the Russians have the old machines returned to his own country on time to take part in the next U.S. Census.

Besides furnishing a total of seventy tabulating machines with sorting boxes, Hollerith sold the Russians five hundred keyboard punches at $12.35 each. Admittedly, the price was low. But to save on shipping costs, the wooden bases for the punches would be made at St. Petersburg at the Committee's expense, with Hollerith supplying the pattern, jig, and fixtures for their manufacture. The contract also called for the inventor to furnish spare parts and maintenance tools for his machines. The latter included complete sets of wrenches and an india rubber bellows for each five machines. The bellows was to clean out the press of the tabulators. Dirt, or small flecks of paper from the cards, could cause the press to make faulty electrical contact and register incorrect totals on the counters. The Russians could order additional dial counters at $5 each, the same price charged in the Western Electric catalog. Extra sorting boxes were available at $200 each.

All told, Hollerith was to receive $67,571.30 under the contract. Of the total, $59,500 was for the "new" machines. He would get the first payment of $22,000 in New York "upon presentation to the Russian Consul or designated official" of the bill of lading for the thirty-five "old" machines. The "old" machines and keyboard punches were to be shipped by January 19. The second payment of $23,000 would be made in New York, in the same manner, after shipment of the parts for the "new" machines not later than March 29—and arrival of the "old" machines in St. Petersburg. The final payment of $22,571.30 would be given to Hollerith's representative at St. Petersburg after acceptance of all machines and parts.

It was a colossal order for a colossal job.

Hollerith would return to Russia for a third time the following August to see his machines start to consume the mass of statistics collected by 900,000 enumerators more than a year before. Besides the army of enumerators, a staff of 2,200 persons would help the inventor's machines digest fourteen separate categories of information on 129 million persons from schedules printed in forty-four languages. The data would include: name; sex; marital status; age; position within the household; group or class of population (gentry, clergy, merchants, peasantry) or status; place of birth; religion; native language; literacy and extent of education; chief and secondary occupation or trade; position in given occupation or trade; and physical defects.

It was the first uniform description of all the Russian people. Maligned when his own census count fell below popular estimates, Porter would look on, not without a twinge of envy when the Russians reported a grand total of 129,211,113 people. On June 19, 1897, he wrote:

The distinguished statistician at the head of the census department of Russia, if the spirit of progress is abroad in the Russias, should be a happy man just now, for he has found no less than 9 million more population in that vast empire than he expected when conversing with a friend on the subject last winter. Perhaps a million one way or another does not affect a nation after it exceeds the 100 million mark, for which, by the way, we may have to struggle on for many years ourselves.

Perhaps unknown to Hollerith and Porter, the Census had not been taken without some opposition from the suspicious Russian peasants. Some non-Christians, it was reported, feared it was a Czarist plot to baptize them, while certain Christian sects viewed it as "the net of anti-Christ."

Like the Americans, the Russians would issue preliminary bulletins of population totals before the job was completed. These were impressive compared to the U.S. Census of 1890. St. Petersburg, with 1.3 million inhabitants, closely rivaled New York with 1.5 million and surpassed Chicago with 1.1 million. Moscow, at 990,000, nearly matched Philadelphia's 1 million, while Warsaw, with 610,000, was rapidly catching up with the mighty city of Brooklyn, still a separate metropolis, which counted 810,000 souls. Since its last census in 1851, Porter noted, Russia had added nearly 62 million—a gain almost equal to the total population of the United States in 1890. With an increase of 92 percent, Russia had come within 5 million of doubling its population. Observing its incomparable natural resources and "the vast areas of Russia less occupied than our Western states forty years ago," Porter predicted:

As her development of Siberia and Central Asia proceeds, Russia will have such vast hordes of Asiatic labor and skill to draw on, and she has a foundation for so much larger a country than ours, that even our growth does not offer a parallel to the opening up of the new country.

In contrast, Hollerith would look at the speed and efficiency of the Russians and be considerably less impressed. Buttressing his annoyance was a belief that the Committee had ordered far too few of his machines for the job at hand. "The work of tabulating the census returns of the Russian Empire has been started," he would tell a gathering at the Shoreham Hotel in Washington the following October, "but they are in a habit of taking things in a lesiurely way over there." By the summer of 1897, when Hollerith would return to St. Petersburg to watch his machines start the work, more than a year had elapsed since the enumeration. The Russians would not issue their first published report, for the Province of Archgelsk, until January 28, 1899—nearly four years after the beginning of the census. Nine years after its start, the Committee would still be busy at work. It had taken only three years to complete the U.S. Census of 1890.

Hollerith was right that the Russians had underestimated the job. And he would take satisfaction that they would come to him for more machines—this time his Automatic Tabulating Machine developed for the U.S. Census of 1900. By 1903, he had been issued a patent in Russia. And, perhaps for this reason, he would lease rather than sell the extra machines. The proposed rental was "22 cents per thousand cards counted, furnishing labor ourselves; or for 17 cents per thousand, the labor to be furnished by the Russian Government."

The arrival of the new devices would prompt a visit to the Census Bureau by His Imperial Highness and heir apparent, the Grand Duke Michael Alexandrovitch. On February 6, 1904, *Novoe Nremya* would report the event.

His Highness . . . examined the sorting of cards and the tabulating of them on Hollerith electrical machines. He displayed special interest in an automatic tabulating machine which [counted] over 10,000 cards per hour. When the inspection was ended, all the young ladies in the office to the number of over 700 poured out into the street in a dense crowd and saw the heir-apparent off with a display of enthusiasm expressed in hurrahs and the singing of the National Hymn.

The flourishings and trappings of royalty meant little to the plain-spoken inventor. Perhaps ungraciously, he criticized the manner in which the Czarist government paid its census workers.

The compensation of $6 allowed the Russian enumerator for two weeks' work seems very meager. But the government tickled the vanity of the people who did this work by giving each employee a bronze medal, and so the honor was enough to balance a good deal of cash.

Disgruntled or not, Hollerith had enabled Russia to take the first census of its fifty governments spread from Poland to the Bering Sea. Within a score of years, the young Czar, whom Hollerith had toasted, and his family would be slaughtered and the entire Imperial Empire swept away. And Russia would have to wait another thirty years for the next "ordering of its citizens" in the first Soviet Census of 1926.

However, despite the flood tide of revolution, the American

tabulating machines would leave a deep impression, and the name of Herman Hollerith—or more precisely "German Gollerith," since there is no "H" in the Russian alphabet—would survive the Revolution. Eugene F. Saber, who headed IBM's marketing efforts in Russia in the early 1930s following U.S. recognition of the Soviets, recollects:

The name of Hollerith was still well known. . . . At the place in Moscow where I arranged to show our machines, they still kept, as a museum piece, one of the very early Hollerith tabulators with the clock dials. It is probably still around.

Hollerith did not remain long in Russia in December 1896. After cabling Ned that he had signed the contract, he set off for Paris, resting for a few days with Lu's aunt in Vienna. The French officials had started their Census of Occupations the previous fall with only $40,000 allotted for the work that it projected would cost more than $1 million by hand. Arriving at the French capital, Hollerith was greeted with good news. The Chamber of Deputies had reported favorably on the census in progress and passed a further appropriation for the work. Eager to see his wife, Hollerith wrote from Paris urging her to meet him in Baltimore on his way home. "It is . . . quite likely I will call you up and talk to you from New York on telephone. . . . So watch out and don't get frightened if you are sent for to come to the telephone."

Hollerith was back in the United States before January 13, when his mother-in-law could report: "Ned is more than busy getting machines on order and packing them to send to Russia. Thirty-five are to go now and thirty-five later."

Through sheer determination and force of character, Hollerith had accomplished what he had set out to do. As he had approached his thirty-sixth birthday only a year before, he had considered selling out. Less than twelve months later, he had reversed his defeat at the New York Central, contracted to take the French Census, and won the long-sought-after Russian job. In a period when large business organizations were becoming commonplace and the formation of trusts the order of the day, it was most amazing of all that he had done these things virtually by himself with little in the way of resources and no organization behind him.

13

The Tabulating Machine Company

*"He has formed a stock company in
New York to manage his inventions."*

One day shortly before leaving for St. Petersburg to sign the Russian Census contract, Hollerith sat down at his desk, a ruled yellow pad before him. Near the top, in firm pointed handwriting, he wrote "Library Bureau," the name of the Boston firm he had recently contracted with to help carry out his business. Directly under, he jotted down "Russian Contract." Then, after thinking it over for a few minutes, he ran a line through the last two words. Still further down the page, he wrote "French Contracts" and, in a following parenthesis, "Library Bureau." As a final item, he penciled in "New York Central Contract." On four lines of the sheet—most of which remained blank—Hollerith had totaled up his entire business as it stood in late November 1896.

He was pondering what parts of it to include in the company he was about to form.

Almost certainly, he had considered a matter of such consequence before, although there is no record that he had. Be that as it may, Hollerith had reached his final decision in the twelve short days since hearing of the Russian order. For it was not until November 24—the day before setting sail for St. Petersburg—that he signed the legal documents empowering his attorney and friend Samuel G. Metcalf "to act for me in . . . the formation and organization of a corporation to take over and carry out my present business." For once, the speed of events caught the seemingly omniscient Mrs. Talcott flat-footed in calling a turning point in her son-in-law's career. In fact, it was not until Hollerith's return from Russia—a month and a half later—that she could report: "He has formed a stock company in New York to manage his inventions."

The decision marked a fundamental change. Since he had started paying rent on Room 48 of the Atlantic Building on the eve of the 1890 Census, Hollerith had done business for himself under his own name. It was always "The Hollerith Electric Tabulating System," and all the patents were held directly by him. Now he was changing this state of affairs. While he was out of the country, his attorney had been instructed to set up a New York State corporation. The name Hollerith had chosen for it was the Tabulating Machine Company. He would assign to it all of his past and future inventions "relating to counting, adding, sorting, recording, calculating, classifying or tabulating machines." The company about to be born would one day be the keystone in the formation of IBM.

What lay behind the decision? Since Hollerith seldom shared his inner thoughts, one can only speculate from broader outlines. Some men have interests that run beyond their business or profession—they are avid golfers or collectors of postage stamps, or, perhaps, leaders in their church or their community. Even when he had the leisure, Hollerith was never among them. Outside of making gifts—he planted several acres of asparagus for distribution to friends—Hollerith had no hobbies. As one contemporary put it, he was "a peculiar sort of man, reserved, not easily approachable, and living for his family and his work alone." These two interests underlay his decision. His mother-in-law came closest to explaining: 'He said it would be the best thing to do as it would give him money to work with, and, if anything should happen to him, they would manage things for Lu."

Chartered December 3, 1896, the Tabulating Machine Company started life with a capitalization of $100,000 made up of 1,000 shares of common stock with a par value of $100 each. Hollerith would be general manager, holding a controlling 502 shares. But more than by assets, a company is characterized by the men behind it. What kind of associates did this loner choose? What caliber of men were willing to stake their savings on Hollerith's future? While stopping over at the Transportation Club in New York, Hollerith had written his attorney a letter of introduction to George Mead Bond. Bond's tie with Hollerith's business, and later with IBM, would span half a century.

By 1879, the year Hollerith graduated from Columbia, Bond, the expert of the Pratt & Whitney Company, had drawn the attention of the engineering world as coinventor, with astronomy professor William A. Rogers of Harvard, of the Rogers-Bond Comparator. The device could make measurements, with certainty, down to a fifty-thousandth of an inch.

While American craftsmen had long been concerned with exact measurement—both Eli Whitney and Simeon North had fashioned revolvers with interchangeable parts—the twin notions of standardization and interchangeability of parts became even more critical as the nation moved toward mass production. The Comparator, a slide-shaft mounted with two microscopes trained upon scratches in the master yard, could translate the standard into usable form. While Hollerith was developing the interchangeability of standardized units of information through his punched card, Bond's Pratt & Whitney Standard Measuring Machine, based on the Comparator, was rapidly becoming a master standard for exact measurement in toolrooms throughout the world. Interchangeability in production and the handling of information were linked through the friendship of the two men. Perhaps significantly, both the U.S. mode of production and Hollerith's machines were often called "the American system."

It was to the Stevens Institute-trained engineer that Hollerith had turned in the early 1880s to see whether the Lanston adding machine, which he had purchased, could be cheaply manufactured. And Bond had closely supervised the construction of Hollerith's keyboard punch for the 1890 Census. Now, the Pratt & Whitney engineer subscribed to seventy-one shares in the new venture at $70 a share. His $4,970 commitment, except for a $500 down payment, would be paid in installments, and $60 in bills that Bond had paid for Hollerith at Pratt & Whitney credited toward the purchase. The difference, possibly advanced by Hollerith, could come later. Bond was a friend worth carrying, worth having in his company. Charles C. Tyler of Hartford, an acquaintance of Bond's, subscribed to another fourteen shares for $980.

While Bond lent professional luster to the new enterprise, financial respectability was assured by a second backer. Ferdinand W. Roebling was the youngest brother of Washington Roebling, the man who built the Brooklyn Bridge. "F.W.," as he was called, had been delegated by his family to stay home and tend the business that turned out three-quarters of the wire rope in the country. The name "Roebling" was one of substance—and of magic—in the worlds of industry and engineering, dating to John A. Roebling, the German-born engineer who designed the bridge his oldest son completed. A stark Old Testament figure with piercing eyes, John Roebling had been inventor, spiritualist, philosopher, and founder of the dynasty carried on by his sons. "Their grounds cover fourteen acres," a visitor wrote after touring John A. Roebling's Sons at Trenton, "and within the walls are five wire rolling mills, and all the buildings needed for their three hundred and fifty workmen and office purposes . . ."

Hollerith's association with the youngest Roebling might have come about in a number of ways: through Professor Trowbridge, at one time a bridge designer and vice-president of the Novelty Iron Works; or because the younger Roebling, a businessman of some acumen, was steering the family firm into the new field of electrical wiring and Hollerith might have purchased supplies from the Trenton company. Regardless, the secretary and treasurer of the family firm was already a firm believer in Hollerith's future, before the birth of the Tabulating Machine Company. The seventy-one shares of stock and $31 in cash that he received was in full repayment of a $5,000 loan that Roebling had previously advanced to Hollerith.

Other associates, from early days, would soon take up shares in the venture. Henry C. Adams, chief of the Transportation Division in the 1890 Census and now chief statistician for the Interstate Commerce Commission, would buy twenty-five shares. A handsome man with a trailing mustache, Adams had lectured on political economy at the University of Michigan, Cornell, and Johns Hopkins. He had recently been elected president of the newly formed American Economic Association. J. Shirley Eaton, the man who had whetted Hollerith's appetite for railroad work— he was now auditor of the Southern—would subscribe to ten shares. And finally, M.I.T. Professor George F. Swain, Hollerith's oldest and closest friend from Census days, would back him as a stockholder with fifty shares. A total of 743 of the 996 available shares—the 4 remaining shares went to incorporators—had been subscribed to. The rest would be held in the treasury for futher distribution.

Although he held only a single share as an incorporator, no one was more important to the company and to Hollerith personally than Harry Bates Thayer, the manager of Western Electric's New York City plant. It was Thayer who at twenty-six had personally supervised the inventor's order for "twenty-five or thirty thousand dollars worth of apparatus" for the 1890 Census. More recently, Western Electric's New York shop had turned out the improved machines that enabled Hollerith to fight his way back at the Central. Although the friends contrasted physically—Thayer was a lean New Englander and Hollerith a rotund, food-loving German-American—they had more than a little in common. Both came from good families of relatively modest means—Thayer's father was a small-town banker. Both inherited little except high standards and had to succeed on their own. Both graduated from college the same year—Thayer was Dartmouth '79—at a time when college men were considered ducks out of water in the business world—law, medicine, and the ministry were suitable callings for the educated man. Perhaps for this reason, too, they sought each other's company. Both were hard-driving and ambitious, though not overtly so. But if there were similarities, there were also differences. It was the qualities and expertise that Hollerith lacked that made Thayer's presence all the more valuable. A rising star in a large organization, Thayer was sophisticated in the ways of big business; Hollerith was not. While the inventor could be blunt and tactless with subordinates, Thayer was adept in dealing with people at all levels. Indeed, over the years, he would offer Hollerith diplomatic advice on many matters: from how and when to give out raises, to the handling of delicate negotiations with the Census Office. Thayer was knowledgeable in all aspects of manufacturing. And what he didn't know he could soon find out. Drawing on his company's vast resources, he advised his friend on everything, from the annealing of Norway iron cores used in the electromagnets of Hollerith's machines to suggesting new sources of supply when Western Electric could not take on a job. Above all, while Hollerith was temperamental and quick to anger, Thayer proved an emotional counterbalance, remaining calm in any situation. Thayer's unusual composure on a trip to Russia with Hollerith was described by Thayer's stenographer, E. W. Rockafellow:

Czar Nicholas' brother the Grand Duke had been assassinated, and there had been two or three funerals for the public and other nations to attend, when one night Mr. Thayer was left alone in his hotel attired in formal dress prepared to meet Mr. Hollerith.

As he left the hotel . . . two men . . . took his arm and, without uttering a word, accompanied him into a chapel. . . . The occasion was so solemn that it would have been risky to explain who he was, so he just sat down two or three seats behind the Czar and Czarina, and sat during the ceremonies as though he was one of the family. After the services . . . the two men who escorted Mr. Thayer . . . took him back to the hotel . . . and left him exactly where they found him.

Mr. Thayer never inquired how it all happened. He only conjectured he had been taken as one of the family on account of his dress, and . . . it was better not to explain, than to have a scene with a consequence that no one could foretell.

Under similar circumstances, Hollerith might well have exploded.

From Western Electric, Hollerith drew the mainstays and most active members of his company. Thayer brought with him his protégé and assistant manager, Albert Lincoln Salt. A cheerful, outgoing young man, Salt, the son of a Brooklyn lumber merchant, had given up a projected career in the ministry at age fifteen— Brooklyn was the city of churches—to enter the still unfathomed field of electricity. He had already risen from office boy to manager of the promising business of telephone purchases and sales. Soon he would become general purchasing agent for Western Electric, a post in which he would often perform double duty for Hollerith as well. Besides furnishing such staples as electric wire and magnets for tabulating machines, Salt was called upon for such diverse items as a complete set of records for *La Traviata* and Edison Electric Lights for the Hollerith Christmas tree. Despite Hollerith's taking advantage of Salt's position, the purchasing agent would never lose his cheerful disposition.

On December 16, 1896, the incorporators of the Tabulating Machine Company met for the first time "to organize, elect officers and adopt by-laws"—despite the fact that the two most important members of the new concern, Thayer and Hollerith, were out of the country. By prearrangement, Roebling was elected president. Though he was too occupied with his family's business to play an active role, his name would lend respectability to the fledgling enterprise. Salt was named vice-president; Thayer, treasurer; and Metcalf, secretary. Thayer and Salt would serve on the executive committee along with Metcalf.

Instead of joining forces with Western Electric the year before, Hollerith had borrowed two stout ribs from its side. Thayer would later rise to become a noted president and chairman of the entire Bell System, Salt, to president and chairman of Graybar, the supply subsidiary of Western Electric formed in 1926. By forming his own company instead of joining with Western Electric, Hollerith had maneuvered one of the great "what ifs" of industrial history. If Hollerith had gone over to Western Electric, taking his patents with him, the Bell System might well have emerged as the leading supplier of punched card data processing equipment, as well as furnishing the country's telephone service. There would certainly have been no IBM as it is known today. By sticking to his guns and remaining independent, the inventor bent, if not permanently altered, the course of American enterprise. Be that as it may, Hollerith's mother-in-law looked approvingly at the new developments. She wrote: "There are no salaried officers except Thayer and Hollerith. The latter is to receive a salary of $500 per month and hold a controlling amount of stock. He hopes to begin New York Central work February 1, and from that he will receive $500 per month."

When Hollerith sketched out his company on the yellow pad before leaving for St. Petersburg, he had crossed out the Russian contract. He had been trying for the Russian business since 1891. The trips abroad had been expensive and the endless negotiations a source of strain and worry. Why should he toss it in the pot with his other business? Back from Russia, he apparently changed his mind and brought a duplicate of the Russian contract to his company's second board meeting on January 12, 1897. He would, he told Bond, Salt, and Metcalf, assign all rights under the contract to the company—if he was paid his actual expenses in securing it. This included "compensation at the rate of $500 per month for his services from November 23 to January 1," the period preceding the start of his term as general manager. The proposition was reasonable, the directors agreed. The Tabulating Machine Company would take over both the obligations and the profits of the Russian contract. But to avoid confusion at St. Petersburg, "Mr. Hollerith as General Manager was authorized to carry out the contract in his own name without notice to the Russian Government of any change of interest . . ." As a final item of business, the board approved the resolution made at the previous meeting, under which the company purchased Hollerith's assets, at a fair valuation of more than $100,000, in consideration of issuance of the authorized stock.

Hollerith had done well for himself and his family. Just turned thirty-seven, he was the principal stockholder and operating head of his company. He had surrounded himself with associates of scope and accomplishment—men who were also his friends, who could share his worries and give him sound advice. He now had the resources he needed to develop his machines and the means of raising more capital to expand his business. Last but not least, he should, for the first time in years, be able to count on a steady income. Lu, who had not bought a hat, coat, or dress for a year, could shop for new clothes. "He is on his feet again," his mother-in-law declared, "and in a fair way to make a great deal of money."

By any objective standard, Hollerith should have been pleased at the launching of his company. Instead, he seemed to forget immediately that its formation was *his* idea. With every apparent reason to be confident and hopeful for the future, he suddenly became fretful, worried, and depressed, lashing out at those around him. Highly logical as an engineer, he was something less than that in governing his emotions in business activity. Until now, no one else had worked closely with him and shared in his decisions. With the exception of his mother-in-law, he had depended almost completely on himself. While in the eyes of family and friends he was firmly in command of a promising new business, inwardly he was apprehensive and torn by doubts. In sharing his business, had he given up too much control? Had he ceded too much of himself?

After Sunday dinner at Garrett Park in February, he rushed off through the snow to put his mother-in-law on the train. It was slippery and slow walking down the hill. The engine pulled in before they got to the station, and Hollerith ran ahead to hold the train. Afterward, when he discovered the train had arrived one minute ahead of schedule, the inventor shot off a complaint to the office of the line. "I don't think it is worthwhile to be always complaining and finding fault," his mother-in-law advised, "particularly when you may at some time want favors from that road."

Irritable with his immediate family, the disgruntled inventor saved most of his anger for Ned Talcott. His brother-in-law had packed off the machines to Russia and was just starting on the New York Central work when Hollerith asked how much he owed him. The young man, who had turned down another job at Hollerith's request, had not been paid for more than two years. Part of that time, Ned had worked long hours at the Central. He had also gone to Boston to install the machine at the Library Bureau and instruct the clerks in its operation. But when Hollerith had told him there was no work to do, he had stayed home tending the chickens and the bees. In April, Ned presented Hollerith a bill for the entire period, including the time he had not worked. It came to over $2,000, a considerable sum.

Infuriated, the inventor told his employee that he did not have the money, but would pay Ned every cent as soon as he did. Instead of discussing the situation calmly and arriving at a settlement, Hollerith laced into the young man for his lack of ambition and his inattention to detail. Before he had left for Russia, Hollerith charged, he had given Ned instructions for laying out two new wiring diagrams to be ready on his return. The work, he said, had not been touched. Finally, Hollerith announced that after Ned was paid, they had better part company. Ned told him he would save him the trouble and leave right away. To show that he did not have to depend on anyone, Hollerith had summarily fired his first employee, who was also his wife's younger brother.

No sooner had he taken the hasty action than Hollerith regretted it. He offered Ned some work in Boston. After the young man turned it down, the inventor urged Porter, who had headed the 1890 Census, to call on President McKinley. Perhaps with Porter's help, he could get his brother-in-law a lifetime post as a naval engineer. The matter drifted along until July 2, when Mrs. Talcott wrote: "Porter went to the Navy Department in Ned's behalf. He saw [Theodore] Roosevelt, assistant secretary who was in charge of this matter, and he told Porter that he would be glad to do anything he could for Ned." But as it turned out, Porter's influence was of no avail. Ned did not score high enough on the competitive examination to get the job.

In the meanwhile, work had not been going well at the Central. The railroad had already postponed the start of its contract from the beginning of the year to February 1. Even before Ned was fired, Thayer had suggested that "it would be for the best interest of the Company to employ a reliable and capable man to take charge of the machines in the office of the New York Central . . ." On March 12, Hollerith was authorized to employ one H. C. Jordan at $15 a week. Hearing of the inventor's troubles, Ned offered to go to New York at his own expense to lend a hand. It was a generous gesture, but Hollerith was unable to swallow his pride. Mrs. Talcott summed up the situation on April 29:

The work is not going well at the Central and Hollerith really needs Ned. But you know he would never say so. He is very much afraid anyone will say Edmund is necessary to him.

. . . Hollerith has worried himself sick over small details . . . that Ned has always relieved him of and now he has no one to depend on. . . . Altogether he has too much to do and is not well.

Hollerith's strength was his weakness. He knew far more about his machines than anyone else, and the only way to get things done right, he believed, was to do them yourself. If you depended on others, they only let you down. But if he wanted the Tabulating Machine Company to amount to anything more than the corner store he sometimes thought of, Hollerith had to learn to delegate, to share responsibility, to train others and trust them to do the job. It was a lesson he could never completely absorb.

Hollerith's mood resumed an upward curve by August 1897, when he left on his third trip to Russia to attend the International Institute of Statistics at St. Petersburg. He would have a chance to see his machines start the processing of the Russian Census— "Elles sont toutes prêtes," Troinitsky would tell the delegates who were invited to inspect the mechanisms. In contrast to the last Institute at Bern, when he was striving desperately for the Russian business, Hollerith would now be a celebrated guest at the Russian capital. For once he was eager to shed his business worries. With the trip approved and paid for by his company, he was happy to get away. On August 23, he wrote his wife:

I have arrived at St. Petersburg and so has the President of France. Now I have nothing against the President of the French Republic, but I wish he had come some other time. In the first place, today is made a holiday so I can do nothing. The streets are all full of people shouting and yelling. All, of course, unintelligible to me.

Hollerith's first order of business was to see Heisler, his agent. For his contract with the Russians had stipulated:

The testing of the machines and of their parts will be made by persons appointed by the Committee in the presence and with the assistance of Mr. Hollerith's representative and all detected defects that can be remedied will be made so by Mr. Hollerith . . . at his expense.

Had his machines passed muster? And, more important, had he been paid the final installment under his contract? Hollerith didn't say. But as no complaint was forthcoming, the inventor presumably found everything in order. If so, he could thank Harry Thayer, who had almost certainly paved the way.

By 1897, Western Electric had purchased a one-third interest in N.C. Heisler & Co. and by the following year would buy the firm outright for 100,000 rubles. The company had a booming business in Russia and soon the outlet would be known as "N.C. Heisler Electro-Mechanical & Telephone Works Co." Almost certainly Hollerith's new machines had been assembled in the firm's imposing five-story brick factory. Some years later, Francis R. Welles, general director of Western Electric's foreign business, told the history of his company's plant in Russia, and the ultimate fate of Hollerith's agent:

In 1891 I fixed up an arrangement with Mr. Heisler after which I took a third interest in his business. One night during the Revolution, two Bolshevik soldiers came to the door and shot him. . . . After Mr. Heisler died, Mr. Joseph, capable factory manager, married Mrs. Heisler. We built a good factory in Petersburg in the early '90's. We made our capital as the business developed. From 250,000 francs, our business grew to 30 millions.

Western Electric's St. Petersburg plant evidently had everything in order. Having no further business, Hollerith reluctantly entered the round of ceremonial functions planned for the delegates. On August 30, he wrote:

I have just received an invitation which reads: "Leurs Altesse Impériales Monseigneur le Grand Duc Constantin Constantinovich et Madame la Grande Duchesse Elizabeth Mavoikrivna vous invitent de vieur au Palais de Marbre le 18 Août à 8½ heures du soir."
As I will not often be invited to visit Grand Dukes, I suppose I ought as a matter of curiosity to go and I will do so.

The next day Hollerith told his wife about the reception at which the Grand Duke and Duchess received the delegates:

I was standing pretty well to the rear as I had no gloves. . . . Troinitsky, however, made me come forward and so I shook hands with the Grand Duke and said a few words . . . Troinitsky wanted also (for me) to be presented to the Grand Duchess but I avoided this as I was afraid my not having gloves would be too conspicuous.

Once again, Hollerith was the shy, uncomfortable five-year-old who rebelled at dressing up for a formal portrait. Though he had now gained international recognition, he found it painful to assume the public role.

A few days later, the delegates cruised down the Neva to Cronstadt to visit the cruiser *Russia*. From there, they visited Peterhof, the summer palace modeled after Versailles that Peter the Great had erected on the Gulf of Finland. Ignoring this royal and splendid setting, Hollerith nevertheless shed his reserve long enough to enjoy "little pig boiled whole and covered with a sort of aspic or jelly." He noted the recipe and sent a flower from the table home to Lu. But away from his family and his business, the inventor only longed to return. When Troinitsky gave him a railroad pass, he wrote: "I suppose I ought to take advantage of my railroad pass and visit Moscow, but I am afraid that this desire to get back is stronger than my curiosity for sight-seeing."

In the city where Pavlova and Nijinsky were appearing with the Imperial Ballet and Rimsky-Korsakov was conducting the symphony orchestra, Hollerith's only thoughts, as he strolled down the Nevski Prospect, were to be back with his family. He wrote: "You may rest assured that I am on my way home if it is by any means possible. Under the circumstances, I might even be willing to travel on a French steamer."

In all likelihood, Hollerith was paid by the Russians while abroad. For only five days after returning home, he took his wife, her Aunt Mary, and her mother on a shopping expedition to Philadelphia. He had the sales clerks at John Wanamaker's Department Store scurrying about as he ordered table linen, blankets, comforters, towels, rugs—and dresses for all the women, including Aunt Mary. He was in a jovial and expansive mood. "I just looked on," his mother-in-law reported, "while they spent the money."

Hollerith's small family of shareholders had also been rewarded. At the Tabulating Machine Company's first meeting, it was decided that no dividends would be declared while "any money loaned to the company remained unpaid." Six months later, the new company was apparently in the clear. It dispensed a semiannual dividend of 4 percent, a sign of heartening progress. But while the company's directors may have taken some satisfaction at its income from abroad, they may also have wondered whether their company was, in fact, doing any business at home. Since he had dismissed his workmen and closed his shop some two years before, Hollerith's domestic business, except for the Central, had been in virtual eclipse.

Whenever Hollerith's other business ebbed, he returned to his adding machine. "It is strong and serviceable," he now declared, "and can be built in quantities at a cost not exceeding $8.00." He had pressed forward steadily to get the machine on the market. In March, his directors had agreed to "have a perfected sample machine constructed at the earliest possible moment. . ." By early April, he had reopened his shop on 31st Street and had a man and a boy at work on it. Back from St. Petersburg in September, he carried the completed machine to New York for inspection by his Board. They approved the sample and authorized him to obtain estimates for 100 complete machines. Now, suddenly, he was stopped short by a patent interference. The marketing of the machine would have to wait until the matter was resolved.

Was there any other business? Before closing down his shop in 1895, Hollerith had sent Ned to Providence to install a machine for morbidity statistics at the State Board of Health. But as Rhode Island recorded no more than 8,000 deaths a year, Hollerith figured he could charge the small customer only $100 a year rental. More than two years had passed and the inventor had heard nothing—either from the Board or the Library Bureau, which had assumed the contract. Now he suddenly recalled the small installation and wrote directly to the State Board of Health. On January 19, 1898, its secretary replied:

In regard to the tabulating machine placed in office a few years ago, I will state that it is still here and in use. Present bill and same will be audited by this department.

Assumed that you had become so absorbed in foreign contracts that you had forgotten our little machine in Rhode Island.

When there hadn't even been enough money for groceries, the inventor had forgotten about one of his only customers. Matters would have to be straightened out, but it wasn't that simple. Puzzled, Hollerith wrote to Metcalf for advice:

The question now is where does this $200 go, and what would be a proper way under the terms of our contract with the Library Bureau for collecting same? Then, where does the Tabulating Machine Co. come in and where do I stop?

Hoping you can answer this conundrum . . .

The attorney's reply discloses the Tabulating Machine Company's relation with the Library Bureau: "It seems clear that . . . we are entitled to 90 percent of the rental after the rental amounts to the price of the machine and, on the termination of the contract with the Providence people, 90 percent of the machine is our property."

Although Hollerith would not have been entitled to any income, clearly, the company would have to have a closer command of its domestic business—if it was to have any at all. Not only had the Rhode Island installation been overlooked, but there were other customers to be attended to. Hollerith had shipped a complete tabulating machine to London for the Library Bureau in 1896. A record of key punches shipped, presumably to be employed with tabulators, showed that thirty-two had gone to Paris, nine to Boston, one to the Hartford Board of Health, and ten to the New York Central. While Hollerith had separate contracts for the French Census and the New York Central, he should have been receiving some rental from the other installations. He was also to be paid 50 percent of the profits from cards furnished to customers by the Library Bureau. Yet his income from the Bureau had never matched the $300 a month agreed to under his contract. And for the first quarter of 1898, the Bureau had failed to send him any statement at all.

On May 3, the Tabulating Machine Company served notice on the Library Bureau that it would terminate the ten-year agreement that Hollerith had signed some two years before. For a company with so little business, it was a spirited, though perhaps relatively meaningless, action. However, the declaration of independence meant that the little stock company intended to grow its own business. It would control its own destiny, whatever it might be.

It would take another five years for Hollerith's company to begin to make good on the premise. "The Electrical Tabulating System," it would claim by 1903, "is now in successful operation for: Auditing freight accounts; Computing shop costs; Sales accounting and analysis; Distribution of expenditures and Special requirements demanding analysis of a considerable volume of detail . . ." But the growth of new uses for its machines would have to wait the trial of new technology in the Census of 1900, which was now at hand.

14

1900: Putting Information on the Assembly Line

". . . operations . . .
are all entirely automatic.

As the U.S. Census of 1900 drew near, Hollerith—and the country—were motivated by a specific and urgent need. Half the country's labor force still worked the land, compared to less than a twentieth today. The widespread crop failures of 1894 had bred severe discontent. For the first time, Populist "agitators" from the farms were banding together with angry factory workers to form a political force that had to be reckoned with. If the census planners did little else, they had to save their political skins by shedding light on the nation's largest—and sickest—industry.

Surprisingly, most of the data needed to understand the nation's farm crisis had been gathered in previous censuses; it had simply lain fallow. "No census office in the past," Harry T. Newcomb, the expert chief of the Agriculture Division, pointed out, "was equipped [for] the tabulation of these data in the elaborate manner necessary to realize the possibilities. . . ." As a consequence, the one thin volume of farm statistics from the previous census told nothing about the relative productivity of large and small farms; whether tenant farmers worked as effectively as those who owned their land; or whether blacks grew more cotton on land that they owned or leased than on a plantation owned and managed by a white man. There was, he concluded, "an imperative demand for a new scheme of tabulation . . . far more extensive than any previously adopted."

The decade before, Hollerith's machines had kept the Eleventh Census from being curtailed and saved the government more than $5 million. Now, William R. Merriam, the former governor of Minnesota and newly appointed Census director, forecast that mechanical tabulation "is apparently capable of responding to all the demands for many years to come." There could be no serious question of returning to hand methods, although Congress was less than enthusiastic about the new system. In its wisdom, it had cautiously provided that "in case the Director deems it expedient, he may contract for the use of tabulating machines for tabulating purposes." As before, a competitive test would be required before any system of tabulation was adopted. Accordingly, Merriam appointed a commission on May 18, 1899, "to make a practical test of all electric accounting machines or tabulating machines or other devices which might be presented." No mention was made, or consideration given, to the special requirements or devices that would be needed for farm statistics.

To Hollerith, the processing of population and vital statistics was bread and butter work that he had easily mastered before. Moreover, reemployment of his old tabulators—thirty-five would soon return from Russia—would be highly profitable. Those that had served in two censuses had already paid for themselves several times over. The inventor looked forward to the tests with a confidence that was reflected by his mother-in-law, who wrote: "There is to be a test of all the different machines and methods of tabulating, but there is little doubt that Hollerith will get the contract."

His only competition, Hollerith soon discovered, was from the same Charles F. Pidgin whose manual "chip" system he had beaten ten years before. Hollerith had nothing but scorn for his rival. And when the chief clerk of the Massachusetts Bureau of Labor Statistics presumed to enter three new tabulating systems into the fray, Hollerith promptly dubbed his rival's devices "Pidgin Coops."

In retrospect, Pidgin, whose diverse talents included the production of a comic opera, *The Electric Spark*, performed more than 3,000 times in England and the United States, deserves better than the "also-ran" reputation he received at Hollerith's hands.

For tabulating population statistics in the Massachusetts Census of 1885, the Boston inventor had devised a "punch card and pin board . . . so called because it was fitted with steel pins which passed through the punched holes in the cards and indicated their classification." For no apparent reason, he had given up this line of development—which closely resembled the circuit-closing press of Hollerith's tabulator—to return to the manual "chip" system for the U.S. Census of 1890.

The devices Pidgin now put into competition were his Automatic Mechanical Tabulation System, the Pin Board Electrical Tabulation System, and the Electrical Typewriter Tabulator. Descriptions of the systems are incomplete, and since none survives today, it is impossible to assess their worth. But in the tests, which began June 12, Hollerith's system completed the sample material in 185 hours, 53 minutes, while Pidgin's Automatic Mechanical Tabulation System required 452 hours—or well over twice as long. Tests on Pidgin's Pin Board System were stopped by mutual agreement when it was found that its rapidity was practically the same as that of his Electrical Typewriter Tabulator. The test of the third system was discontinued at 163 hours with two tables and part of a third, out of twelve, incomplete and none of the results yet transcribed to tables. It was clear that the device could not match the Hollerith system. On July 27, 1889, the Commission reported: "The superiority of the Hollerith Tabulating System for the compiling of individual data in the forthcoming census has been clearly and fully demonstrated."

With the test out of the way, Director Merriam contracted with the Tabulating Machine Company for fifty machines, similar to those used in 1890, at an annual rental of $1,000 per machine, the same terms Hollerith had gotten ten years before. The director also reserved the option of renting an additional 100 tabulators of the 1890 type to complete the tabulation. The extra "old-style" tabulators, as it would turn out, would never be employed because of the "new and extraordinary instrumentalities" that Hollerith was developing for the special requirements of the farm statistics.

In the tabulation of population statistics, the old-style machines were only required to count—that is, add up one and one over and over again, rather than total larger sums. Individuals, described by various facts—such as age, sex, place of birth—were tallied in this manner. In contrast, the agriculture statistics demanded that Hollerith's machines be able to handle both qualitative descriptions—such as the type of tenure under which each farm was held—and quantitative items, such as the acreage of each farm and the hundreds or thousands of bushels of corn or wheat that each farm produced. The totals for such items were staggering. For each farm, quantitative amounts included total area, improved area, total value of the buildings, value of improvements, value of implements, value of products, value of livestock, and amounts expended for fertilizers and labor. "The far greater portion of the labor required," it was pointed out, "is expended in the aggregation of the facts which are to be stated quantitatively so as to secure from the multitude of descriptions of single farms descriptions of the agricultural activities of separate communities, such as counties, and states and of the nation." It was inconceivable that the same machines could handle both population and farm statistics.

Significantly, the competition that Hollerith had won had been confined to systems for tabulating such "individual" data as population statistics. No test had been demanded for compiling the much larger figures contained in the agricultural and manufacturing data—since the machines would differ—requiring a separate test. Why a second test was omitted is not entirely clear. But the census officials evidently decided there was no legal requirement to match tabulating machines against adding machines, which could also do the job. They were also persuaded by Hollerith's recent railroad work to turn to devices "somewhat similar to those that had been in successful use, experimentally and in a not wholly developed form" at the New York Central. Recommending the adoption of Hollerith's new integrating tabulator being used at the Central, Assistant Director Wines wrote to Merriam on June 11:

You should understand that the Hollerith machine is an adding machine . . . the only tabulation required is the taking off of the totals upon result slips and inserting figures in their proper places on the tables . . . mental computation is almost totally eliminated.

For the Central, Hollerith had replaced the drum integrator of his early War Department machine with a row of four electric adding machines that could total as many classes of information simultaneously. Now he drew from this line of development, as he recalled many years later: "Now the railroad work reacted on the census work in that when the Census of 1900 came along we used machines such as were used in the R.R. for compiling the Agricultural Census."

What kinds of machines were needed? To Hollerith, the punched card was never a separate entity, but an integral part of his system. His machines, in turn, were designed to accommodate the amount of information required on the card for any particular job. The design of each was flexible, but the two were inseparable. When one was altered, the other had to change with it. For the farm cards—divided into ten fields to record as many classes of information about each farm—he would build twelve tabulators, each incorporating ten electric adding machines. For the smaller crop cards, which contained three fields, he would construct eighty-six smaller tabulators, each with three adding machines. He decided this at the outset. But the existence of machines that could add such vast quantities of information posed other questions.

Wines estimated a need for one "farm" card per farm, or six million cards, to record the general facts for each farm. On top of this, he figured an average 15 "crop" cards per farm, or a total of 90 million cards, to record the totals for crops and livestock. The work of punching, it became clear, would place a staggering and unforeseen burden on the census clerks. How in the world, census officials asked, could nearly 100 million cards be punched and run through the machines in the two years allotted by Congress? Here, too, the officials looked to Hollerith's experience at the Central where he was trying a new form of punching device.

Mr. Hollerith [holds] the opinion that one clerk can punch on the average 1,200 crop cards per day . . . the number of cards punched on an average by each clerk in the office of the New York Central Railroad where the same machines are used.

Where would Hollerith turn for the final development and manufacture of his latest designs? In 1890, he had relied on Western

Electric for his tabulators and sorters and on Pratt & Whitney for his keyboard punches. Now he thought the matter over and came to a critical decision.

Just five years before, Edwin J. Peirce, Jr., a skilled mechanic and the son of a maker of wooden patterns, and Daniel W. Taft, a wealthy Uxbridge, Massachusetts, wool merchant, had formed the Taft-Peirce Manufacturing Company, "for the sole purpose of performing contract manufacturing, engineering and toolwork of high precision." The capital for the Woonsocket, Rhode Island, firm had been supplied by Taft, who bought the business to provide a career for his son, D. Wendell Taft. However, the operating head and guiding spirit of the new firm was Peirce. As manager of the predecessor Wardwell Sewing Machine Company, he had added to the manufacture of sewing machines "models, tools and parts of small patents in which skilled labor is demanded." The advertisement the partners ran in the 1900 Woonsocket city directory described their business:

THE TAFT-PEIRCE MFG. CO., CONTRACTORS FOR THE MANUFACTURE OF MACHINES AND MECHANICAL SPECIALTIES WITH PARTS INTERCHANGEABLE. ESTIMATES FURNISHED FOR SPECIAL TOOLS AND MANUFACURE . . .

In all likelihood, Hollerith was steered to Taft-Peirce by his friend George Bond, who had advised him on the manufacture of the Lanston adding machine. It was Woonsocket firm that more recently had developed the keyboard and controls for Lanston's highly successful Monotype Machine. Philip P. Merrill, who later worked for Hollerith, explained:

It was during the '90's that Hollerith expanded his basic principles in the direction of mechanization and automaticity. Possibly through his friend George M. Bond, designer of the original Pratt & Whitney measuring machine, or perhaps simply because Taft-Peirce by that time was well known as a source of accurate machine work, Hollerith brought his design to Taft-Peirce to have the first automatic tabulating machines perfected and manufactured.

Interchangeability of precision parts, the specialty of the New England firm, was once again linked to the development of machines that could handle interchangeable units of information. And as before, Hollerith's friend George Bond, inventor of a measuring device, proved the link between the two. In coming to Taft-Peirce, Hollerith was looking not only for manufacturing capability but for engineering skills as well.

The unlikely answer the firm supplied was a slight, dark-haired young man without a day of technical schooling. Even the accent of Mississippi-born Eugene Amzi Ford seemed out of place among the harsh nasal twangs of the New England mechanics. Yet the meeting was fortuitous. Though Hollerith was notably reluctant to rely on or admit the help of others, it would later be said that many improvements in his machines originated in the brain of Eugene Ford. The young man had an irrepressible inventive bent. While working as a "chain man" on a Texas surveying crew, Ford had devised a measured cartwheel attached to a tabulating mechanism. When rolled along the ground, it proved as accurate in gauging distances as the conventional chain measure—and far less taxing in covering the vast western landscape. As a stenographer in a Louisville, Kentucky, law firm in 1887, Ford came up with another invention—one of the first visible printing typewriters, so called because the operator could see what she typed as she went along.

While Ford's typewriter would fail to find a secure niche in a crowded market—Taft-Peirce dropped it as a standard product within a few years—Ford put his facility with keyboard devices to good use in the final development of Hollerith's key punch, a machine that would remain basically unchanged for more than forty years.

The machine, which operated like a one-handed typewriter, was a radical departure from Hollerith's keyboard or pantograph punch designed for the 1890 Census. In the earlier punch, the operator swung the arm from the upper left corner of the punched card across the top, and then from right to left across the bottom. The census card was laid out so that the operator would get to those hole positions first where data was most frequently recorded. But for railroad accounting, the inventor had ruled off the punched card into the now familiar vertical columns. The new format required that numbers might be punched anywhere in a column—from a zero at the top to a nine at the bottom. And the operator had to be able to move across the card from left to right to record information in successive columns or fields. In designing his new card, Hollerith made the earlier punch obsolete.

Hollerith had tried the earliest models of his key punch at the Central. But it was not until May 17, 1901, the start of the Agricultural Census, that he applied for a patent on his improvements in "Apparatus for Perforating Record-Cards." He wrote:

My invention . . . comprises a traveling carrier for the card, a series of key-operated punches arranged at right angles to the path in which the carrier moves, so that in any position of the card either the cypher or any of the nine digits may be punched by the operation of the proper key.

The device had eleven keys, ten for punching the numerals zero to nine and an additional key marked "X" for skipping over positions to be left unpunched.

In designing his key punch, Hollerith borrowed heavily from the typewriter. A carriage, holding the card, moved from right to left past the punches. The key punch similarly contained a mechanism for automatically moving the carrier to the next punching position after a key was pressed. A release freed the carrier entirely, so that it could be moved without punching. However, unlike a typewriter, in which the keys, driven by lever action, were not strong enough to punch through paper, Hollerith's punches descended directly downward upon the card, enabling them to cut through it. Hollerith and Ford built well. The key punch would later be improved and electrified—well before the advent of the electric typewriter. And legs would be added to the tabletop device, perhaps to enhance its appearance and justify a higher rental. In 1968, a desk-top unit, identical in appearance to the model built by Hollerith and Ford nearly three-quarters of a century before, was still in daily use at a Harrison, New York, IBM office.

With his key punch, Hollerith speeded the preparation of punched cards for processing by his machines. But, considering this, would each of the 100 million agricultural cards still have to be inserted and removed by hand from the tabulator press, as in the 1890 Census? By improving one unit of his system, had the inventor, in effect, piled too much work on another, throwing the whole system out of balance?

The inventor had, indeed, anticipated the heavier demands by designing an automatic feed for the tabulator to be employed toward the end of the 1900 Census. But, in the meanwhile, the Automatic Tabulating Machine he was designing was preceded by a little-known Semi-Automatic. Few of the transitional devices were built and none survives today.

In the Semi-Automatic, the pin box mechanism was set on edge and cards fed one by one into the sensing mechanism by the operator. Opposite the pin box was a reciprocating plate "which operates in much the same manner as a printing press." An electric motor under the desk-top work surface of the tabulator closed the plate upon the pin box and then moved it away to allow for the insertion and sensing of the next card. Hollerith described the machine's operation:

As the plate recedes, a card is dropped upon fingers which hold it in position before the pin box, against which it is pressed by . . . the plate, so that when the pins encounter cards, they are pushed back into the pin box, but where there are holes in the card, the pins pass through and establish electrical connection which operates the adding machines.

The fingers fall as the plate recedes, allowing the card to drop into the receiving box below, but if the card is defective or has been carelessly inserted, no tabulation occurs, and the fingers retain the card.

Hollerith had begun to speed the flow of information through his machines with the Semi-Automatic, but it was not until early 1902, well after the start of the Census, that he "perfected" his tabulating machine "by the addition of automatic feeders." On April 19 of that year, the *Scientific American* reported:

The latest development of the Hollerith System is the automatic machine in which the work of separately placing each card beneath the pin box, depressing the pin box, and removing the card is performed automatically . . . instead of by hand.

Set upon an upright stand by the side of the tabulating machine, the automatic feed was a cube-shaped unit about eighteen inches on a side. The operator placed 400 to 500 cards on a feeding platform at the top. Held firmly by a pressure plate, the cards were pushed downward one at a time by knife edge into the vertical pin box, where they were sensed by "spring-pressed conductive pins arranged to cooperate with a corresponding number of electrically connected spring-jacks." After electrical contact was made through the holes, the cards were fed downward into a receptacle. If a card was improperly punched or sensed, it was directed automatically into a reject box for further examination.

While developing his automatic feed, Hollerith envisioned still more automatic operation. In a patent, filed on March 13, 1901, he wrote:

After the cards are placed in position and the apparatus started, the subsequent operations, including the feeding of cards, the compilation or the tabulating of the data thereon, and the removal and the sorting of the cards are all entirely automatic and are all controlled by the records themselves.

In August 1900, a year after contracting for fifty of the old census machines, the inventor signed a second contract for fifty of his "improved automatic" machines for compiling the agricultural statistics. Henceforth the old census machines would be called "hand" machines. Hollerith charged $1,500 a year for the "automatics," half again as much as for the "hand" machines—but it was estimated that they would do six times the amount of work. Although not fully perfected until the Philippine Census in 1904, the automatics, employed toward the close of the Twelfth Census, were soon tabulating up to 415 cards a minute. They averaged 80,000 to 90,000 cards a day, including stoppages for the reading of counters and the transcription of information.

To handle the new demands of the Census, Hollerith had developed the key punch to speed the preparation of cards and an automatic feed to hasten their flow through his tabulating machines. But curiously, he had overlooked devising a comparable sorting device to arrange the staggering quantity of agricultural cards for subsequent processing. It was done by poking through holes in the cards with an ordinary knitting needle.

His failure to anticipate the greatly increased requirement for sorting is especially curious since he had developed a "sorting box" for his hand machines as part of his system for the 1890 Census. Soon automatic sorters would be an essential unit of his punched card systems, so much so that no future census would be attempted without them. Yet Hollerith was strangely reluctant to mechanize this major part of the data processing job. In April 1903, a year and a half after the successful introduction of his first automatic sorter at the Census, the inventor still appeared to cling to older methods.

Sorting . . . of cards is one of the most important features of the system. The card is designed to contain certain basic facts, qualified by modifying facts, thus by grouping and regrouping the former by the latter, and tabulating, the results desired are secured.

Sorting by any given field is accomplished very rapidly by drawing off the cards with a knitting needle, and the accuracy of the grouping is indicated at once by the fact that it is possible to see through the hole or holes by which the sorting has been made. . . . If the sorting requirement is large or expensive, automatic sorting machines will be supplied.

At the start of the 1900 Census, Hollerith was either too busy developing the other units of his system to bother with the automatic sorter, or perhaps did not believe such a unit would be profitable. But other evidence suggests that the inventor clearly saw the requirement for rapid sorting several years before the census, when he first applied, his integrating tabulators at the New York Central. Charles W. Spicer, who worked for Hollerith as a foreman, would later recall:

When we were working on these freight integrating machines . . . we had in mind the necessity of a sorting machine for . . . rearranging the cards. In fact, the idea of the sorting machines had been . . . in our minds continuously.

Whatever his reasons for neglecting an automatic sorter earlier, Hollerith would make his subsequent rapid development of the unit appear to be a casual afterthought. In 1919, he told how it came about:

At luncheon with Governor Merriam [the director of the 1900 Census] he called my attention to the enormous work . . . in sorting the agricultural cards. I said he ought to use a machine and, in reply to his question, I said I did not have one but could build one . . . to save time I was to build him some machines and he was to pay me cost plus a profit of ten to twenty per cent.

Through oversight or deliberate delay, Hollerith had backed himself ino a corner. He must now bring out his sorters on a crash basis or jeopardize the other work his machines had performed. Robert N. Holley, a clerk at the Census Office, summed up the somewhat chaotic situation at the Census Office:

The tabulating machines were made idle a good portion of the time waiting for the hand sorting. . . . Immense possibilities were being dissipated in the delays and, if maximum advantage of electric accounting were to be achieved, the elimination of this bottleneck was a prerequisite.

Although Hollerith had shown that the successful winding up of the Agricultural Census depended solely on him, the future business cost would outweigh any satisfaction he may have derived. Instead of renting the machines as he usually did, he sold the twenty sorters at cost plus a small profit. The outright sale permitted title to the new inventions to pass to the government. In his haste, he also failed to patent the new machines until two years after they were installed. His carelessness would come back to haunt him later when the government was trying to develop its own line of machines. Looking back, he would say, "I think this was the worst mistake I made in a business way."

The first of Hollerith's automatic sorters arrived at the Census Office in October 1901, and the remaining machines the following month. Each of the horizontal units was equipped with a feed device similar to that of the automatic tabulator. The sensing of a hole position in a card activated a magnet, so that the card, which traveled through the machine on a belt, was steered by a guide channel into a particular pocket. The machine could sort cards into twelve pockets, which ranged along its length. Though crude by comparison, the sorters nevertheless bear a distinct resemblance to those employed to sort bank checks today.

The usefulness of the sorters is a matter of dispute. Appearing in court ten years later, Hart Momsen, expert chief of the Division of Agriculture during the Twelfth Census, would testify:

[The] machines were installed in the latter part of . . . 1901 and were continuously used . . . until the completion of the census; [the] machines were operated under two shifts . . . and [they] sorted many millions of record cards; . . . [and] saved the Government both time and money; and [Momsen] doubts that the census work could have been finished on time without these machines . . . unless the sorting force had been greatly increased [which] was impossible on account of lack of room.

Contrary accounts, however, would be given by other witnesses. No longer with Hollerith, Spicer would swear the machines were "mechanically faulty due to hasty construction . . . made a great racket and destroyed a great many cards." Katherine T. West, in charge of nine of the machines as an assistant in "Dr. Hollerith's Work-Shop" at the Census, would add that "none of the sorting machines in my charge was capable of doing complete and satisfactory work."

No doubt, the truth lies somewhere in between these and other statements given in the heat of litigation. Certainly, the machines were untried and complex and required careful adjustment and care. But there was no real question—before Hollerith's suit against the Census Office a decade later—that the sorters performed their basic job. Hollerith would be paid $9,200 for the twenty sorting machines on March 6, 1902—without any objection being raised. And in 1903, the Department of Commerce, which had charge of the Census Bureau, would report that "automatic electric sorters were also used to great advantage" in the preparation of the agricultural statistics.

Looking over the inventor's shoulder, Auditor William T. McCullough of the New York Central ordered several of the horizontal sorters in 1902, a few months after the first machines were installed at the Census Office. "They proved indispensable to our work," he later recalled, "and greatly aided us in the prompt, accurate compilation of our accounts."

Before the Census ended, Hollerith developed and built still more sophisticated sorters for population work. The rapid advance from his first automatic sorter further suggests that the inventor's concepts ran far ahead of his implementation. Referring to his early sorters used in agriculture and railroad work, Hollerith later recounted:

I then developed and built some vertical machines for sorting population cards. The problem here was very different than . . . Agriculture and

R.R. In the latter case we only had to sort to locations of a hole in a column. In the case of population cards, we had to sort according to combinations of two or more holes. One . . . might be at the top of a card and the other at the bottom. Besides . . . they might be in different columns.

As I recall it, I built only two of these machines and instead of selling them or even renting them to the Government, I ran them on a basis of so much per thousand cards sorted. It was a good paying business. . .

There is no doubt that these machines are the very best type I ever developed and the only reason I did not continue to use them was that they were rather complicated and . . . would have tied up a lot of capital in building them . . .

Little is known about the population sorters. But machines that could sort more than one hole at a time were not introduced for commercial use for more than twenty years. Writing in 1919, Hollerith wondered why his main competitor had failed to follow his lead.

The wonder to me is, as these patents have or are about to expire, that Powers or someone like that don't take them up. . . . I don't think [Powers sorters] would be worth considering along side of a machine built on those old lines.

All told, 311 tabulating machines, 20 automatic sorters, and 1,021 punches of various kinds had been supplied by Hollerith for the 1900 Census. With the help of the census clerks and his repairmen, tall, skinny "Doc" Hyde and Clarke Hayes, who reconnected the machines and kept them in good order, Hollerith completed the major reports of the Census in two and a half years. More than 120 million cards were run through the machines. Without them, the population statistics alone, it was estimated, would have occupied the time of a hundred clerks for seven years, eleven months, and five days.

As for the all-important agriculture statistics demanded by Congress before the Census began, the figures pointed to a revolution perhaps more astounding than that taking place in the country's machine shops and factories. The value of farm implements and machinery had risen 54 percent over the previous decade. Not only had the number of farms grown, but for the first time since

1850, their average size had increased as well. In forty years, "the crop producing area has increased so much faster than the natural population," it was reported, "that the country now supplies its people with more and better food and with more material for clothing than ever before, and at the same time exports agricultural products to an extent that was impossible in recent years."

A near-fanatic in guarding against error, Hollerith was especially proud of the accuracy of the tabulations. Toward the close of the Census, he ingeniously wired eight of his automatic tabulators with a large number of relays so that they would reject cards that might contain any of hundreds of possible inconsistencies, such as children inadvertently listed as married, or naturalized citizens also classified as being native born. The chore of wiring the machines turned out to be far more complicated and time-consuming than he anticipated, and Hollerith's sensitivity to criticism may have led to more checking back of cards against schedules than necessary. But his new scheme of verification assured that the 1900 Census was more accurate than any before. In contracting for the special machines, the inventor departed from his usual practice. Instead of charging an annual rental, he charged for amount of work done—at 65 cents per thousand cards counted. If it was a profitable arrangement, Hollerith was willing to back his scheme to the hilt. He guaranteed that the eight machines would make at least 6 million tabulations a year.

Reviewing the Twelfth Census in his annual report, the Secretary of Commerce and Labor would conclude:

The application of mechanical appliances in large statistical undertakings enables work to be completed in at least one-tenth of the time required to do it by hand, at about one-third the cost and with marked increase in efficiency.

On this basis—Hollerith received $428,239 for his machines and services—it could be conservatively estimated that he had saved the government well over a million dollars. Many years later Henry Ford's production expert Charles Sorenson would write: "Whereas the car evolved from an idea, mass production evolved from a necessity; and it was long after it appeared that the idea and its principles were reduced to words."

A similar observation may be made of Hollerith's approach to the handling of information. The census system he had devised the decade before had closely resembled a manufacturing job shop that turned out a product through a series of well-planned manual and mechanical steps. Now, through a series of gradual alterations, he was putting his system through a "sea change." Responding to the new demands of the 1900 Census for handling high volumes of information, Hollerith made the sensing of the punched card itself control its passage through the machine—without human intervention. Partly mechanized before, the handling of information was set on its way toward becoming a continuous process, a trend that Hollerith would hasten further during his lifetime and that would be continued by others in the future. Although he had no way of knowing it at the time, Hollerith may have taken the first steps toward the still distant age of data processing.

H. HOLLERITH.
APPARATUS FOR COMPILING STATISTICS.

No. 395,783. Patented Jan. 8, 1889.

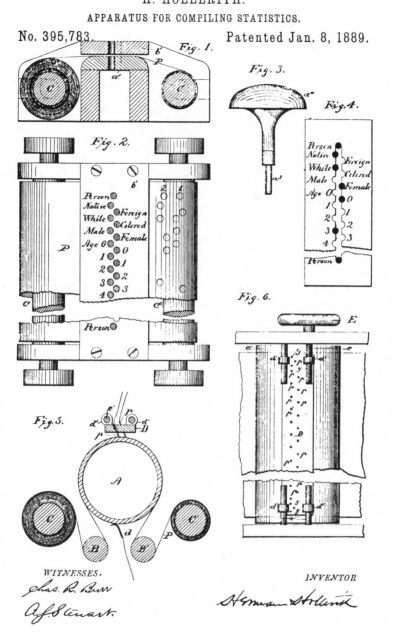

Fig. 1.

Fig. 2.

Fig. 3.

Fig. 4.

Fig. 6.

Fig. 5.

WITNESSES,
Chas. R. Burr
A. J. Stuart.

INVENTOR
Herman Hollerith

Hollerith found a mechanical solution to processing the census while an instructor at M.I.T. during the academic year 1882–83. His device employed a continuous paper tape. He recorded statistical items for a person by punching holes through a template in a line across the tape, the hole positions standing for various personal characteristics. Then he ran the paper tape over a metal drum, making electrical contact through the holes to activate counters for corresponding hole positions. (U.S. patent drawing)

Before the Census of 1890, Hollerith substituted a punched card for the continuous tape, "because you would have to run miles of tape to count a few chinamen." His first punched cards, for mortality statistics at Baltimore, had hole positions only around the edge because the conductor's punch he used could not reach the center of the card. However his pantograph punch, developed for the 1890 Census, could punch holes anywhere in the card. Here, an operator employs a pantograph punch in the Census of 1920, more than 30 years after the punch was introduced. (Photo: IBM Archives)

Hollerith developed a complete system of interrelated units to process the 1890 Census. The pantograph punch, resting on the counter of the tabulator, at left, was used to punch data into a card. Then the card was placed in the circuit-closing press, on the right side of the counter. The upper half of the press, equipped with yielding pins, was pulled down on the card. Where the pins met with the card surface, they telescoped upward into the lid of the press. However, where the pins were aligned with holes, they passed through them into cups filled with mercury, which acted as a conductor. Below each cup, a wire led from a binding post to a counter. As a pin entered the mercury, electricity passed through it, completing a circuit and actuating a counter in the upper portion of the tabulator. The wooden unit, at right, is a sorting box, divided inside into numerous compartments. When the tabulator press recorded a card with particular characteristics, the lid of a corresponding box popped open. By placing the just-registered card in it, the operator was able to presort cards for subsequent processing with her right hand while operating the press with her left. (Photo: IBM Archives)

Hollerith relied on Harry Bates Thayer, at desk of his New York City Western Electric Company office, to build $25,000 or $30,000 worth of tabulators and sorters for the 1890 Census. Later, Thayer, who rose to become president of AT&T, and Albert E. Salt, at left, became officers of Hollerith's Tabulating Machine Company when it was formed in 1896. With Western Electric becoming increasingly devoted to telephonic equipment, Hollerith turned to the Taft-Peirce Manufacturing Company of Woonsocket, Rhode Island, to supply his equipment for the 1900 Census. Others in photo, taken in 1893, are C. E. Scribner, center, and W. M. Sage. (Photo: Western Electric Archives)

By 1892, Hollerith had moved his business to an old cooper's shop hugging the Chesapeake & Ohio Canal on 31st Street in Georgetown. It served as his assembly and card manufacturing plant, as well as a development lab, for nearly twenty years. A demanding employer, Hollerith was concerned about the health of his men, seeing that they were innoculated when a smallpox scare swept Washington. (Photo: IBM Archives)

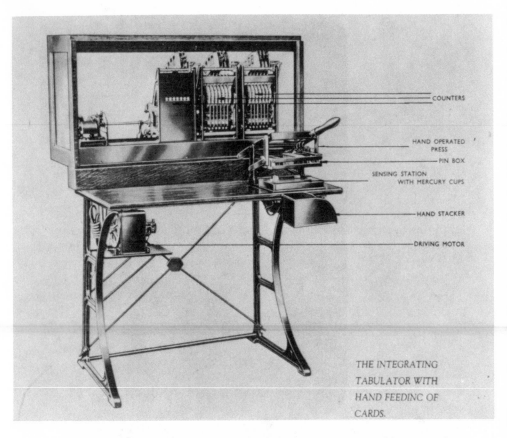

COUNTERS

HAND OPERATED PRESS

PIN BOX

SENSING STATION WITH MERCURY CUPS

HAND STACKER

DRIVING MOTOR

THE INTEGRATING TABULATOR WITH HAND FEEDING OF CARDS.

Hollerith's almost volcanic bursts of activity were spurred by immediate needs. To handle the large aggregate totals demanded by farm statistics and railroad accounting, he developed an "integrating tabulator" housing separate adding machines—the upright units—that could simultaneously add totals recorded in separate areas, or fields, of a punched card. In contrast, his census machine could only tally, or add up, one and one over and over again. (Photo: IBM Archives)

No. 682,197.

H. HOLLERITH.

APPARATUS FOR PERFORATING RECORD CARDS.

(Application filed May 17, 1901.)

Patented Sept. 10, 1901.

(No Model.)

2 Sheets—Sheet I.

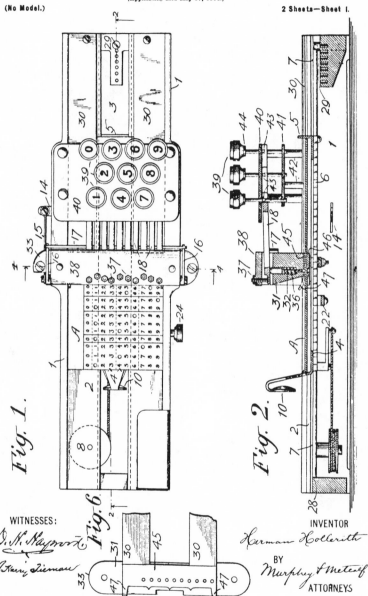

Fig. 1.

Fig. 2.

Fig. 6.

WITNESSES:

INVENTOR

Herman Hollerith

BY

Murphey & Metcalf

ATTORNEYS

The new tabulators called for a different type of punch which could punch or skip over any hole position in a card from left to right. The result was the first key punch. It was employed experimentally at the New York Central and shortly after in the 1900 Agriculture Census. (IBM Archives)

Toward the close of the 1900 Census, Hollerith speeded the processing of information by adding an automatic feed to his tabulator. It fed cards downward into the unit through a circuit-closing press, Later, the pins of the sensing unit were replaced by brushes to further speed the flow of information and information punched in the cards began to control the operation of the units. Hollerith had begun to put information on the assembly line. (Photo: *Scientific American*, 1902)

To break Hollerith's "stranglehold" on the Bureau, Census Director North began development of an "independent" system of tabulation in 1905 based on Hollerith's expired patents. Among those hired by the Census machine shop was the little-known Russian-born inventor James Powers, shown with a punch he developed for the 1910 Census. A talented inventor, Powers later sold out to Remington Rand, providing Hollerith's company and later IBM with its first serious competition in the United States and overseas. (Photo: IBM Archives)

HOWE & ARTHUR
PHOTO 8488

Because the other railroads viewed Hollerith's successful installation at the New York Central as a "white elephant," he turned to other fields, developing applications in shop cost accounting, sales analysis, and inventory control. Later, Hollerith got revenge by letting the railroads "cool their heels" by giving priority in deliveries to other customers. Despite it all, railroad installations became a major portion of his business before he sold it in 1911. This installation at the Chicago, Milwaukee & St. Paul is pictured around 1918. To suit conditions in crowded railway offices, Hollerith stood his sorter on end. The vertical sorter was knicknamed the "backbreaker" because of the need to bend over to retrieve cards from the lower pockets. (Photo: IBM Archives)

Who is the fastest key puncher? That's what these young women are determining in a competition in Berlin in 1928. Although this IBM key punch resembles earlier Hollerith models, electricity had been added to lighten the job of punching. Like Sholes' typewriter, Hollerith's systems opened up an important new field of employment to women, starting with the 1890 Census. (Photo: IBM Archives)

Standing in front of IBM's newly opened New York show-
room at 310 Fifth Avenue in the 1930s are Thomas J. Watson,
president of IBM, and financier Charles R. Flint, who formed
the firm (known as C-T-R until 1924) from four companies,
including Hollerith's, in 1911. Although he would be best
known for his marketing and management skills, Watson had
an instinctive understanding of inventors and what made them
tick. Among his first moves with the new company was the
establishment and staffing of a well-equipped development
laboratory. (Photo: IBM Archives)

15

Probing the Commercial Market

*"There seems no reason why the cost of the machine should
be so great as to prevent the use of
several in a large works. It is no
more complicated than a Jacquard loom."*

In August 1901, Hollerith bought a controlling interest in the
Taft-Peirce Company that was turning out his machines for the
U.S. Census of 1900. No doubt he liked being the proud proprietor of the Woonsocket firm with its neatly burnished oak
woodwork, glistening lathes, and highly trained mechanics. By
acquiring the manufacturer, he may have been grasping an opportunity to branch out in his business. But there was a more compelling reason for the decision. Hollerith and his fellow officers
of the Tabulating Machine Company had been asked to supply
increasingly large sums of money to ensure the solvency of the
firm that was making their urgently needed key punches, automatic tabulators, and sorters for the Census that was already under
way. They may have been forced to act to protect their investment.

Behind it all was the fact that Edwin J. Peirce, Jr., the superintendent of Taft-Peirce, was a man of outstanding mechanical
ability and fine human qualities. He walked through the shop each
morning to greet each of his men by name. But he was nevertheless
a poor businessman. "Never mind what the first lot costs," he was
fond of saying. "If we do a fine job, the customer will come back."
It was a worthy idea—in theory—but not always highly practical
in fact. By mid-1901, his copartner, Daniel Taft, had had enough.
Through an option to Peirce, he sold his right, title, and interest

in the firm to Hollerith, who acting as trustee also assumed a portion of the company's debts. On August 31, the *Providence Journal* took note of the event, though it misspelled the inventor's name.

The big machine shops of the Taft-Peirce Company . . . were yesterday sold . . . to Herman Hollerich of Washington, D.C. The Company will be incorporated and it will continue, under Mr. Peirce's efficient management, to be one of the prized industries of Woonsocket. The concern employs . . . 300 hands, nearly all . . . skilled, well-paid mechanics. Under the new regime, it is intended to further push the business.

The deal was promising, an independent expert assured Tabulating Machine Company stockholders. "Machinery and tools," he reported, "are in first class order and have been well kept up. Their average age is less than two and a half years, the greater portion having been purchased for use in the new building completed January 1, 1900." Although the net value of the property came to more than $300,000, the Tabulating Machine Company would acquire a $200,000 interest for only $100,000. Peirce would stay on as general manager of the reincorporated company for five years at a salary of $5,000 per year.

Although Taft-Peirce dwarfed Hollerith's own shop on 31st Street, the question would later be asked how he could persuade his directors to become interested in acquiring the nearly insolvent firm. The answer supplied was that Hollerith, a gourmet and tastevin of great distinction, paid his directors fees in the form of sumptuous dinners at Solari's Restaurant in New York. In its golden days, Solari's—near the theater district at 80 University Place—had been the stamping ground for such notables as Leonard Jerome, William R. Travers, Boss Tweed, and Jim Fisk. The starchy inventor's penchant for the worldly establishment—with its marble statuary, red velvet upholstery, and discreetly curtained side entrance—appears incongruous with his outwardly punctilious manner. But Emanual Solari's famous bisques of lobster and other shellfish and his unusual selection of wines drew as surely as the electromagnets of Hollerith's machines. However, the attraction between the inventor and the Swiss restaurateur was mutual. On the menu, along with planked shad, English mutton chop, and other specialties appeared an ingenious side dish called "Hollerith potatoes." Passed through a grid, with holes punched in them, the potatoes were a bow to the celebrated patron's punched card.

With his purchase of Taft-Peirce, Hollerith assured himself a major manufacturing outlet for the next decade. But he had yet to carve out a commercial market for his newly developed tabulators and sorters. As in the past, he hung his hopes on the solidly successful railroads. In forming his company in 1896, the inventor had kept apart a special interest in the New York Central contract. Now his fellow officers of the Tabulating Machine Company recognized this claim when, in May 1889, they formed a separate subsidiary to conduct their railroad business. Called the Auditing Machine Company, it was licensed to employ Hollerith's machines to compile statistics "relating to transportation by rail, water or otherwise of persons, goods, merchandise and other property." In recognition of his special interest in the Central's business, Hollerith received 500 shares of stock in the new company, valued at $100 a share.

At the Central, Hollerith was demonstrating how a railroad could keep close control of its freight movements and its revenues. Timely information, he sensed, could be as important to increasing a railroad's profits as the coal, timber, wheat, and other commodities its engines hauled. But the same railroads, which were creating a vast demand for technological improvements of every kind along their thousands of miles of track, were not yet ready to apply the latest technology to their own front offices. Hollerith's expectations for their business proved overly optimistic, as his directors soon agreed. In 1902, three years after the birth of the Auditing Machine Company, they devalued its stock to one-tenth its original value. While the Central had been quick to adopt the new automatic systems—its contract for 1902 would bring in $3,000 to $4,000 from fifteen machines and another $3,000 from cards—the more conservatively minded competition was reluctant to follow suit. In signing the new agreement with the Central, President Roebling undoubtedly reflected Hollerith's scaled-down hopes. "I hope this will lead to a contract with the Pennsylvania Railroad and other companies," he wrote, "so that the

Auditing Machine Company will begin to have an income." The railroads, the bluest of the blue chips that made up Mr. Dow's industrial average, could not be hurried. Looking back a few years later, Hollerith realized his mistake. "We started to use the machines in commercial work some time ago," he wrote. "At first, I met with a good deal of opposition. Unfortunately, I selected the railroad field first, and some of the men around the country referred to the tabulating machine . . . at the New York Central as a 'white elephant.'"

Frustrated, Hollerith had to start all over again. And the easiest place appeared to be at home. So, shortly after purchasing Taft-Peirce, he put Philip Merrill, whom he had just hired, to work. The job: designing a punched card machine installation for cost accounting. If new methods were not yet accepted in railway offices, they might be more welcome on the factory floor.

At the time, 80 percent of Taft-Peirce's work was special order. No two jobs were likely to be the same. Each order varied in volume, size of individual pieces, character of work, complexity of parts and other particulars—in all, a difficult operation to "systematize." To add to the complexity, the labor for each job had to be recorded. Also to be figured in was the cost of jigs, fixtures, and special tools used in the work, which in Taft-Peirce's business were charged to the customer. However, one fact was of considerable help to Merrill in devising the first cost accounting application for data processing machines: most of the information required was already written on time tickets filled in by the men.

From the tickets, the key punch operator recorded the date, man number, contract number, job number, lot, class of work, and time consumed. A separate card was punched for each job. If a worker divided his time between three separate jobs, that number of cards was punched. The next step was sorting the cards to man number. An initial tabulating run then verified the payroll and the correctness of the time and money expended. After tabulation, the cards were again sorted, first by job number and then by lot and class to show the money spent for each.

The result was a running account of the company's business. At any point during a job, costs could easily be run off, letting the customer know where he stood. The system would be further refined at Taft-Peirce over the next decade until the *American Machinist* could report:

In the contract manufacture of light machinery and metal specialties having interchangeable parts, it is necessary to keep most complete card records of costs—records up to the minute in every respect . . . The use of the tabulating machine system (at Taft-Peirce) . . . has made it possible to provide not only the regular daily, weekly and monthly reports, but also special reports as may be required to form the basis of proper charges to a customer for work done on any particular job or series of jobs.

While applying his machines to cost accounting, Hollerith met a Canadian-born accountant with the odd name of Gershom Smith. No one, with the possible exception of Italy's leading statistician, Dr. Bodio, had so immediately and profoundly grasped the potential of the punched card machines. What was more, the recently appointed auditor of the Pennsylvania Steel Company of Philadelphia was eager to apply the systems to his new employer's operations. While the word "salesman" would remain an anathema to Hollerith, he would depend heavily on the forward-looking young man to develop machine applications that would serve as invaluable benchmarks for other customers.

Like Merrill, Smith was intent on applying the new systems to better control of manufacturing. "Accounting departments," he would say, ". . . must present the records to management sufficiently promptly to enable those in charge to check excess costs, stimulate production and use the facts before they have become ancient history." However, Smith's special interest lay in overturning a commonly accepted fallacy. Although machines were increasingly taking on the labor of workers in the factory, wage costs were still used as the principal measure in determining indirect manufacturing costs. The producing unit, Smith contended, should not be the worker alone. It should be the worker *plus* the machine. Starting in 1904, Smith began putting his new theories, and Hollerith's machines, to work at Pennsylvania Steel. And the inventor could soon report on the application that combined the measurement of human and machine efficiency. In 1907 Hollerith wrote:

They punch cards in which they have, first, the number of hours and quarters and, second . . . burden or charge [for] machine tools . . . used in the work and, third, . . . the amount they paid [for] labor.

These cards give a record of the number of machines on which any given piece of work is done—the first figure in the number indicating the kind of machine, as milling machine, planers, etc. Then there is a field . . . in which the amount of burden is punched, . . . depending on the value of the machine used. . . .

These cards always furnish a ready analysis as to the number of hours machines were used . . . and, I believe, have sometimes been used when claims were made by foremen that more machinery was necessary. I also believe that at the Pennsylvania Steel Works these cards are analyzed with reference to operations and the number of machines and, in this way, the office often detects that high-priced machines are being used for operations which could be done on cheaper machines.

The railroads that had snubbed him could be damned! Hollerith was finding a receptive market for his new machines by carving out the first applications in industrial accounting. In faraway London, the journal *Engineering* looked at how Hollerith's "mechanical accountant" could marshal facts like a highly drilled army and extract their meaning with great rapidity.

Suppose that in a works a 100-horsepower engine has been turned out and that . . . it has cost less than a similar engine constructed three years ago. The manager wants to discover the cause of the economy.

It may be due to new tools . . . to . . . lower . . . wages paid, to a speeding up of the tools, or to better methods and discipline by which output of the men is increased, or to a combination . . . of these causes. To get this information from the books would be an onerous business. . . . But when the data are punched on cards, the job can be put in the hands of a girl.

Comparative figures could be obtained by simply passing the cards one or more times through the machines. "There seems no reason," the writer concluded, "why the cost of the machine should be so great as to prevent the use of several in a large works. It is no more complicated than a Jacquard loom."

That Hollerith was succeeding in the factory may have been due to ideas planted a few years earlier by a man he never met. The man was Frederick Winslow Taylor, another mechanical engineer, whose business card read, "Systematizing Shop Management and Manufacturing Costs a Specialty." Before Gershom Smith installed Hollerith's system at Pennsylvania Steel Company in Philadelphia, Taylor, working in the steel industry in the same city, had expressed the same idea that Smith espoused: that higher productivity could come about through the most efficient use of both labor *and* equipment.

Armed with a stopwatch, Taylor had analyzed such simple operations as picking up and putting down a bolt. He made a study to determine the exact amount of time a worker should take for doing the job the right way. While Taylor's famous time and motion studies started with the individual worker, and Hollerith's attention focused on efficient use of the machine, their interests came firmly together on the common ground of statistics. Taylor's methods could not be proved without accurate and timely cost accounting; conversely, the application of Hollerith's machines depended on the prior rationalization of work. In Taylor's view, accounting was not something to be grafted onto manufacturing. Lucid, clear, and readily available information should, he believed, make the plant operate as an organic whole. To this, Hollerith, and the pioneering Gershom Smith, could only have said amen.

Hollerith's second major commercial application was in quite a different field. Before he was born, nearly everything that the customer bought was either one of a kind or, like the bolts of cloth and many other items in dry goods stores, was purchased in raw form. It took the Civil War to bring about standardized sizes of clothing for military uniforms. Now cheap standardized goods of nearly every kind were available in large quantities. As a result, distribution, retailing and sales methods were undergoing rapid change. Already, the new demands placed on merchants and bankers had spurred the development of cash registers and key-driven calculating and adding machines of many kinds.

Few grasped the new trends more surely than the Chicago merchant Marshall Field, who was turning a small dry goods firm into the largest department store of the world. An innovator, he had begun to advertise directly to women, installed a bargain basement to sell "less expensive but reliable" goods, and even opened a restaurant in his store, serving up chicken salad and other delicacies with a complimentary rose. "Give the lady what she wants," he said. But with a growing assortment of goods, what exactly did the sometimes fickle shopper want?

Earlier, Hollerith had tried his machines for sales analysis in the New York and Chicago shops of Western Electric, which sold an impressive array of items to manufacturers and inventors. But the first really thorough job of sales analysis, in his view, was that initiated by Marshall Field. And he was especially proud that the order from this important customer came to him unsolicited. Many years later, he recalled how it happened:

This came about in a peculiar way. Mr. C. E. Martin of Marshall Field was in the East and called on a friend at Wanamaker in New York (Mr. Comstock). Martin asked what was new and Comstock reached down in his desk and showed Martin a reprint of an article that had appeared in the *Railroad Gazette* describing the accounting of the New York Central. Martin went back to Chicago and wrote me from there.

The *Gazette* article came out in the summer of 1902. By the following spring, the Tabulating Machine Company was ready to tell its other prospects about "one large industrial enterprise which uses the electrical tabulating machine for sales analysis."

For each invoice a carbon is made and on this is added the class and item numbers of the goods sold. This information and all related information . . . desired is transferred to punched cards. When the cards first reach the tabulating machine they are arranged by days. The results of the first tabulation by days are checked up with those of the bookkeepers. The cards have now been verified as to accuracy of amounts punched. Red cards are used for credit cards and these are accumulated until the end of the month.

There are now on hand cards for every item sold during the month. In addition to articles by class and item numbers and value, the card also carries such other facts as . . . date, customer, state, route, branch, etc.

With a month's sales thus carded, it is clear that to make the business actually done tell its story, it is only necessary to group by any one fact or combination of facts.

While obtaining the order from Marshall Field, Hollerith was building a large house at Dutch Tussell, named after a tavern that once stood on the site in the Maryland suburbs. Soon, wagonloads of newly ordered quilts, blankets, towels, beds, and other furniture arrived by express from Marshall Field. The relationship to a valued customer was not to be taken lightly. One should be as loyal to the customer as to members of one's own family. Hollerith took pains to impress this policy upon his directors. When, in 1902, he wanted an automobile, his officers agreed that he should make use of this latest invention and allotted up to $5,000 for him to buy one. However, in obtaining the vehicle, preference, if practicable, was to be given to one of the company's customers.

Whatever its merits, the policy seemed to work; it certainly did no harm. By 1906, Hollerith received an encouraging letter from the same C. E. Martin of Marshall Field who had read of his system in the *Railway Gazette* in 1902:

Our experimental work with your system of auditing seem[s] to warrant extension of same . . . forward at once by express, 20,000 manila cards, 480,000 same by fast freight, two key punches and one tabulating machine . . .

Our present plan is to take on two ledgers at a time and do one side of the work, that is, tabulate the sales by terms and departments and check with the old system department by salesmen. We have been doing two ledgers and today are trying four. As soon as the operators are qualified, we shall take on two more and extend the system gradually in that way.

We see no reason . . . why the system should not be a perfect success . . .

Employing his automatic machines developed for the Census of 1900, Hollerith was finding that he could take on more than the straightforward statistics of government work. Having swallowed his initial disappointment with the railroads, he was probing the large and profitable worlds of commercial bookkeeping and industrial accounting. His company had taken its first small steps in this direction by April 1903, when it bravely announced: "The Tabulating Machine Company does not claim to possess a panacea for all accounting ills. It unquestionably does offer, for many classes of large concerns, better, quicker and more accurate results at reduced expenditure."

By the spring of 1903, the small company had worked out some tentative uses for its new machines. But it still had little idea how to go about contracting for commercial business. How much, Hollerith wondered, should he charge for his new machines? And what services should he offer to business customers? Should rentals be governed by the size of the machine, as in the Russian Census? Or should rates be determined by the amount of work done? Did he have to go to the bother of having standard contracts printed for customers he did not yet have? On April 27, the puzzled inventor wrote to Metcalf:

In what shape do we want to make such a contract . . . as, for example, with the General Electric Company? Do we simply want to embody these terms in a letter and have the customer acknowledge receipt of the letter and accept the terms, or in what way should we make the terms a matter of record?

Past practices were little help. Hollerith had simply charged a flat annual rental of $1,000 for his hand machines in the 1890 and 1900 censuses. The fee had also included services. But he had also worried about being square with a small customer. And the Rhode Island Board of Health had been charged only one-tenth the rental for the same system.

The pricing of the new automatics for the 1900 Census did not offer much to go on, either. For the first fifty machines, he had charged $1,500 annual rental. But for other machines, he had charged according to the number of cards tabulated. And he had sold the twenty automatic sorters outright. Only one thing was certain. Because the automatic machines were more than twice as fast as the hand machines, they consumed more than double the number of cards. As the speed of the machines increased, the selling of cards, in itself, became a proportionately larger and more profitable part of his business.

In a small, neat hand, Hollerith drafted a proposed contract, setting a policy that would last for many years. He would furnish tabulating machines "on condition that all cards . . . are purchased from this company." He also inserted a second condition: the customer must employ the machines for a specific, well-proved-out application, such as orders or payroll. With limited resources at his disposal, Hollerith insisted on carefully picking and choosing customers. If an installation failed, he was keenly aware that the resulting criticism would hurt his reputation, impeding the acceptance of his machines. A few days later, he had further developed his thoughts. On April 30, he wrote to Metcalf:

We put the machine in at Woonsocket, and today they may use a large number of cards because they are busy, and tomorrow less because they are slack. We really are indifferent as to the number of cards they use, provided all they do use are purchased from us and provided they continue to use the machine for their shop costs. The moment they stop compiling their shop costs on the machine, the license should cease. 10,000 cards a month might perhaps be as much for the Taft-Peirce as 100,000 for the Pennsylvania Steel Co., and I think it would be hard to establish a minimum number of cards. But I would like, if possible, to have some clause framed to show that the license for the machine ceases the moment they stop using the machine for the particular accounting. After all, though, is a concern such as we are dealing with likely to keep the machine standing around if it is not being used?

Hollerith decided not to charge for the machine at all, but only for the cards, the rate per thousand determined by the length of the cards used. His new contract stated:

The price paid for the cards includes a free license to use said machines for the work aforesaid, which shall terminate if the use of the machines . . . for which they are installed is discontinued, or upon any failure to purchase cards . . . therewith from this Company. By charging only for the cards, the amount paid for the use of the system is proportionate with the amount of work done.

If the contract expressed the peculiar prejudices of the inventor, it also reflected a rudimentary fairness. No large and wealthy customer, Hollerith decreed, could command a better price than a smaller concern. Hollerith showed the same inclination to reject price breaks for larger customers—even when the customer turned out to be himself. In placing orders with the Jones Dairy Farm in Wisconsin, he discovered that a case of sausage weighing twenty-five pounds cost less than twenty-four pounds purchased separately. Outraged, he ordered the twenty-five pounds, then stubbornly insisted that the firm throw away the extra pound.

Hollerith also held singular notions about raising prices—where loyalty to an old customer was involved. Once you gave your word, that was that—even though changing economic conditions might have boosted costs. "I do not see how you can increase the prices of the machines or cards to any of our old customers," he would write Thomas Watson in 1917, after Watson had assumed control of the business. "I think there is a moral obligation, even if not a legal one. Of course, as far as new customers are concerned, you can make any price you please." The only excuse for raising prices was better value, as he also wrote to Watson:

My idea of meeting this increased cost of paper would be to bring out as soon as possible an automatically controlled tabulating machine using a smaller card. The fact that the machine would be automatically-controlled would enable you to make new contracts at any price you saw fit.

Besides determining how he would charge for his commercial machines in 1903, Hollerith detailed the services his customers could expect. Characteristically, he backed his relatively untried devices to the hilt. His identification with his creations was so complete that to do otherwise would have been to admit a similar flaw in himself. Thus, repairs were made free of charge for the first six months following free installation and connection of the devices. After six months, any repairs were made at cost. Perhaps it was an old-fashioned notion. But Hollerith could not conceive of the idea of profiting from his own failure to design and build quality into his machines. One can only wonder at the epithets the perfectionist engineer might have reserved for the meretricious manufacturers of a later day, those who profit as much or more from repairing and replacing the faulty wares they produce as from selling the products in the first place.

At last, having worked out the conditions for doing business with commercial customers, Hollerith came to a somewhat anticlimactic conclusion. In June of 1903, some three months after raising the question, he recognized that there weren't enough business prospects around to bother with printing a standard contract. He wrote to Metcalf: "Regarding the general form of contract, my idea is to write a letter in each case where we make a definite proposition. For the present, there is not enough of this to make it worth while to print the proposition."

While preparing for the business that had not yet arrived, Hollerith had to attend to still another important chore. He was constantly speeding the flow of cards through his machines. "The record on the automatic sorter today is 140,448 cards in 6½ hours," he wrote to Metcalf on April 21. Although he had decided to charge customers by the number of cards they would use, Hollerith had not yet assured himself of a reliable means for producing the millions of cards they would need. Joseph Langley, who came to work at Hollerith's Georgetown shop on May 2, 1902, recalls: "The paper came in a big ream and we cut the cards with a big cutter. Later, when the paper came on wide rolls, we used a slitter to make narrow rolls the width of the cards, then cut them to length. Next, we cut the half-inch corners." It was a primitive hand operation. Some cards were printed; others, such as those used in the Agricultural Census, were not. While some concerns, such as the Library Bureau, employed automatic machines for making cards, Hollerith still relied on hand methods. Now he set about to make up for the deficiency.

In August 1902, The Tabulating Machine Company had paid its president $2,000 for a card printing press. Roebling had agreed to sell his company a second press for $1,750 when business required. In April 1903, Hollerith took further steps to assure an ample supply of cards. "Mr. George W. Swift was here this morning," he wrote Metcalf. "I had a long talk with him and I think the matter is fully covered." Swift would build a slitting machine at his Bordentown, New Jersey, shop. It would cut the wide rolls of card stock into strips 3¼ inches wide, the width of the cards, for rewinding on cores. The narrow rolls of stock could then be used on card cutting and printing machines Swift had designed.

The Tabulating Machine Company would supply the paper f.o.b. Bordentown. Swift would guarantee to furnish a minimum of 750,000 cards daily on each machine.

Despite Swift's assurances, Hollerith worried about his customers' being able to depend on an uninterrupted supply of cards. What if Swift's machines should fail? How long would it take him to get them back into operation and make up for the lost supply? Swift proposed that he have at least ten days to repair a machine. Dissatisfied, the inventor launched a sarcastic letter at his Bordentown supplier.

I cannot help being a little amused that "the party of the second part shall have at least ten days to recover from [an] accident." I suppose you may have meant "shall not have exceeding ten days." You will readily understand that ten years would be at least ten days but it would not answer our particular purpose.

Hollerith was obdurate. If the supply of cards should halt, the machines would quickly shut down and their income disappear. Within a short time, Hollerith would supply all of his own cards. In the meanwhile, he wrote teasingly to Metcalf:

Your unfortunate paragraph is apparently causing Swift to lie awake at nights. . . . Won't you please . . . amend it so that he will have a maximum of ten days to recover from any accident, on condition that in the next ten days he furnishes at least double the quantity.

The inventor would prove equally demanding and cantankerous with his paper suppliers, for poor quality paper could make the machines register incorrectly. Years later, he would advise, "I always like to keep two paper mills 'on the string.' Once in a while we would get some bad paper from one mill, then we would call on the other mill. The first mill would then take the paper back."

In whipping his suppliers into shape, Hollerith was completing a period of careful preparation. At the start of the 1900 Census, he had purchased Taft-Peirce, assuring himself a major manufacturing outlet. Then he had test-marketed his automatics for specific uses with a handful of carefully chosen commercial customers. With their help, he had carved out new applications for his systems that could easily be adapted by other firms. Finally, he had determined how he would charge for and service his equipment and provide the vast quantities of cards that they would consume. By 1904, Hollerith was ready to burst out of the narrower confines of government statistics to take on the larger and more profitable world of commercial accounting.

It was a happy and satisfying time during which Hollerith's personal life blended easily and often indistinguishably into the busy activities at his Georgetown shop. His family had grown to include Nan and Virginia, who joined their older sister Lucia. And Richard, the next to youngest child, now formed ranks with Herman, Jr., and Charles. Often, Hollerith would load the two older boys into his car and proudly drive them down to the three-story brick building on 31st Street to see for themselves what their daddy was doing. One day, while rummaging through the attic at Normanstone, the inventor came across some brass wheels for a model train. Soon, he put his mechanics to work making lead patterns for a locomotive and passenger cars. And shortly after, a half mile of track was laid at his Maryland home. The boys gleefully rode in the cars, which were boxes set on wheels. Soon, they had their own well-equipped shop, where they turned out models that won prizes at local fairs.

While Hollerith lavished attention on his sons, his daughters also benefitted from the by-products of his shop. In economic fashion, he saved the triangular corners cut from the punched cards and ordered bags of the scraps bundled off to the girls' school, where they came in handy for paper chases.

At Hollerith's command, the shop also fashioned patterns for the shirts that he wore. "Bill Barnes made boards for them," Joe Langley recalls, "and his shirt had to fit right over the board." Forms were also carved by the men for the special order shoes that Hollerith decreed for himself and his sons. His kids wore the same kind of shoes that he had," Langley comments. "They were slip-ons with square toes. He always said that he wanted his sons and himself to have a pair of shoes that would fit." Neat and precise in everything he did, Hollerith was carefully building for the future.

16

Getting Started in Britain

"The staff whistled the 'Dead March.'"

Robert Percival Porter, the man who had staked his reputation on Hollerith's machines in the 1890 Census, possessed an extraordinary range of talents. Added to these was an equally rare capacity for friendship. Applying both, the English-born journalist, since resigning as head of the Census, had become the close friend, adviser, and one of a score of biographers of the popular President McKinley.

In 1898, the versatile Porter had served as the President's special fiscal and tariff commissioner to Cuba and Puerto Rico. The following year, he had successfully taken on the delicate task of inducing General Maximo Gomez to disband the Cuban army. By 1901, Porter's political star was at its zenith, when McKinley was assassinated and "that damned cowboy"—as Mark Hanna labeled the forty-three-year-old Theodore Roosevelt—entered the White House.

The death of the President also signaled the end of Porter's political fortunes in the United States. Shortly after, he left for England to join the London *Times* as the first editor of the newspaper's engineering supplement. Before he sailed, Hollerith asked him to see if something could be started with the company's patent rights in Great Britain and the Colonies.

Seven years before, Porter had tried to line up backing for Hollerith in England. But the inventor's negotiations with Sir John Puleston in 1894 had been frustrating and short-lived. Hollerith had attempted to cultivate business in Great Britain once again when the Library Bureau installed a system in London in 1896, but without apparent success. While the Czarist Empire eagerly adopted American technology for its Census, Great Britain, basking in Victorian prosperity, remained oblivious to, if not downright disdainful of, the advent of punched card tabulation.

This time, fate, which had intervened with the killing of the President, appeared to be on Hollerith's side. Porter had a wide circle of friends. In search of an office in London, he walked from the *Times* on Fleet Street to the Westinghouse Building, at Norfolk and Strand, where he met one of them, Ralegh B. Phillpotts, secretary of the British Westinghouse Company. They discussed what Porter had been doing in the United States and Porter happened to mention Hollerith's machine. Phillpotts took more than a passing interest. The man who agreed to be a backer would later become the first chairman of the British Tabulating Machine Company.

Back home, Hollerith broached the renewed possibility of forming a company in Great Britain at a special meeting of his board on January 30, 1902, when the matter was "carefully discussed." Matters moved quickly, and in less than three weeks, the officers instructed Metcalf "to prepare a suitable contract with Robert P. Porter, giving him the exclusive option, for the period of six months, of forming a company in Great Britain." The agreement, dated February 24, called for Porter to proceed at once to organize and capitalize a company in Great Britain with exclusive rights to the system in that country. He would raise £20,000, half of which would be issued as stock to the British backers, the other half to be paid to the U.S. company in return for the assignment of patents. Of the latter amount, £5,000 would be set aside by the U.S. company for the purchase of tabulating machines over the next five years. The systems would be sold to the British company at cost plus a 10 percent profit.

Getting started is never as simple as it looks on paper. Not only would capital have to be raised, the principles of the machines and the business would have to be transported across the Atlantic in someone's head. Whose would it be? On January 22, 1903, Phillpotts wrote to enlist the services of a young man.

My idea was that your knowledge of handling small electrically operated machines would suit you to understand the working of this machine. If this attracts you, I must ask you to understand that the above business is here in an underdeveloped state as yet . . . and possibly nothing may come of it.

However, I saw my friend Mr. Porter . . . and he is inclined to agree that it might be well to suggest to Dr. Hollerith . . . that you should go to America to see if you could learn the operation of the machine in order to demonstrate it on this side and be fitted to take up employment with the Machine Company when formed.

If this plan developed and seemed agreeable to you, some arrangement would be proposed with regard to your expenses in going to America.

The young man who received the letter was C. A. Everard Greene, known as "Ever-Green" to his friends. In search of adventure—he was also considering enlisting in the Boer War—he quickly accepted the offer. Soon the future general manager and director of the British Tabulating Machine Company set sail for America on the steamship *Minnehaha*. On reaching Hollerith's plant on 31st Street, he was immediately put to work. As he later recalled:

The first job was taking to pieces and reassembly of one of the most important units on the Tabulating Machine. After a few weeks I became reasonably sure of this, and the next move was the . . . assembly of the various components comprising a machine. These, when assembled on a base and table, required a motor, and had to be wired in accordance with a wiring diagram. When complete, the machine was tested with punched cards, and after adjustments to remove any faults . . . it was . . . ready for final inspecting and testing.

The regimen that Hollerith prescribed for Greene was probably similar to that given to other "representatives," such as Merrill, Hyde, and Hayes, on the equipment "loaned to the company for educational purposes." The training centered on tearing down and rebuilding the machines to learn every part and how it fit with every other. It may have led to this advice, accorded the company's repairmen in 1913:

All parts should go together without forcing them. If, for any reason, you are unable to assemble any of the parts, you should examine them thoroughly and locate the trouble. You must remember that the parts you are assembling were disassembled by you. Therefore, if you cannot get them together again there must be a reason. By all means, do not use a hammer.

Greene learned quickly. But soon he found that he required more than a mechanical familiarity with the system. "In addition, there was the need for studying the planning of system and cards [and] the operating of the machines to produce required results." He recalled in later years:

The [British] Tabulating Machine Company's staff had to be such a versatile body of lads. They needed not only a good knowledge of the Hollerith Punched Card System and the construction of the machines, but also to understand commercial and other organisation in order to be able to apply the system to any kind of work. In fact, the individual had to be versed to some extent in Accountancy, Engineering (electrical and mechanical), Organisation, etc., procedures, so as not to offend principles.

The second part of the young man's training was to inspect the Tabulating Machine Company's installations in customers' offices. He was somewhat surprised to discover that the company that he was meant to duplicate abroad "was of no great size and was, in fact, busy securing customers for their own development." He made a brief stop at the Census Office, where Hollerith was processing the Philippine population statistics. But of greater interest was the New York Central installation, where he was in care of John Hyde, who represented the company in New York.

It was arranged that I should go to the New York Central and Hudson River Railroad where Integrating (or Adding) machines for adding varying amounts and weights were installed for auditing Freight Accounts and Statistics. This was a great deal more interesting to me than Census Work, for it appeared to be of more commercial interest and likely to have greater application in England.

Before experimenting in his own country, Greene was determined to test the capabilities of the commercial machine, since he also found it was far from being in general use: "nothing was excluded from my attempts to prove that the scheme would work under all conditions—and that is what satisfied me in the end. I was unable to expose a flaw anywhere in the system." From the Central, Greene traveled to New Haven to visit new installations at Yale & Towne Manufacturing Company and Niles Bement, Pond. Returning to New York, he took in another new installation at the Long Island Railroad. Then he was off to inspect the Pennsylvania Steel works at Steelton, near Harrisburg, Pennsylvania.

Gershom Smith, the controller of the company, had the courage to try out Hollerith equipment in their Frog Switch and Signal Department and Rolling Mills and also at their Bridge Construction Department. In the latter department, they were used for Costing, Labour and Materials analysis of manufacture and gave very good results.

Greene arrived home a few months after setting out, and in 1904, the Tabulator Limited was formed. The private syndicate, assembled by Phillpotts, Porter, and a few friends, was a far cry from the company that Hollerith and his directors had envisioned only two years before. Instead of the £20,000 in capital called for in Metcalf's 1902 contract, the British backers had raised a scant £2,000, or one-tenth the amount. Customers also were not exactly queuing up for the new machines. However, Greene did manage to find a prospect willing to accept a trial, and was now eager to prove out the experimental installation at the Woolwich Arsenal Ordnance Factory.

He made careful preparation. The machine was tested, cards drawn up, and punch operators obtained to tabulate wages and production costs at the arms factory. But no sooner was the system in place than the young man ran into difficulties for which he had received no prior instruction from Dr. Hollerith.

It was not unusual for Machine Operators to find that the machine would not run due to failure of the electricity supply to the Machine Room. It was not long before it was realised that the supply cable passed through the room where the staff was working, with the result that wires were cut and the Hollerith machine disconnected from time to time and this, of course, considerably upset results and hampered efforts.

This went on . . . over a period of several months and eventually it became difficult to make any progress at all. So much so, that the Authorities came to the conclusion that the machine "did not offer sufficient advantages over hand methods to make it worthwhile to introduce them."

Greene stood by helplessly as the units of the system were dismantled, packed, and removed one by one. "During their conveyance through the offices," he later recalled, "the staff whistled the 'Dead March.'" The young man, whose future was apparently being carted away with the machines, may have thought of the experience of Richard Arkwright 150 years before. Hearing ominous rumblings while exhibiting his new loom at the town of Preston, and remembering the fate of Hargreave's spinning jenny pulled to pieces by a Blackburn mob a short time before, Arkwright had wisely decided to remove himself and his machine to a safer locality. A century and a half later, Hollerith's fledgling enterprise in Britain may have been fortunate to retrieve its first tabulating machine unscathed.

Was Greene's experience unusual? Hollerith himself had never encountered outright sabotage of his machines. In contrast, he was the one who seemed, at times, to resist the penchant of his own countrymen to gobble up every bit of new technology before its usefulness was fully proved. Only once, had his efforts to install his system been blocked by a fear of its job-displacing effects. Hollerith had visited Berlin on the heels of the U.S. Census of 1890. He had brought a punch, some tabulator counters, punched cards, and photographs of his system with him. But despite designing a comprehensive application for the processing of criminal statistics, the young engineer had been unable to budge the Prussian Statistical Bureau. By 1895, Hollerith had successfully installed a system in the Berlin Customs House for the processing of import/export statistics, yet the Prussian Bureau refused to employ a system he had loaned it free of charge for its large special censuses. Six years after Hollerith's initial visit, Privy Overstate Councilor Blenk explained why:

The most important reason . . . I have not introduced the machine in Prussia is socio-political. In both of the last large special censuses . . . in the Empire and in Prussia . . . I have employed 1,000 persons . . . from one to three years. The help is comprised mainly of people, who through special circumstances or bad luck, are unable to support themselves. If our Imperial Regime . . . thinks about and works with all its strength to help the victims of unemployment, we have work security. . . . it appears to me it is our duty to oppose the replacement of man by machine.

Despite the rejection of its bellwether installation at Woolwich, the Tabulator Limited soon convinced the Messrs. Vickers of Sheffield to try out their system at the firm's Don River Works. Here the persistent Greene encountered still another obstacle:

"it was a big surprise to find that no means at all existed for handling English currency except by use of fractions. Counters had been designed for most fractions but not $\frac{1}{12}$ths, so that pence presented the main difficulty to begin with."

Greene returned to the United States to consult with the inventor, who had failed to anticipate the seemingly obvious problem.

Eventually, it was agreed with Dr. Hollerith that the recording of pence should take place on two separate wheels representing $\frac{1}{2}$ a shilling and $\frac{1}{6}$ths (6 pennies to 6d or $\frac{1}{2}$ shilling). . . . At first sight it appeared a sorry makeshift, but, after a little practice, to copy what was shown on the counter wheels as "1&5" as "11d," "1&1" as "7d," etc., became a matter of habit.

The Vickers application—tabulating the money and time to be charged against each job—was similar to that at Taft-Peirce. However, "the reception at Sheffield was somewhat frigid," Greene reported. "But after nine months a contract was signed, machines supplied and from then on a very successful organised system of punched cards was run for some years." Other customers followed: the Lancashire and Yorkshire Railway, where the machines calculated locomotive mileage and coal and oil consumption; the Great Western Railway; the Calico Printers Association; and the British Westinghouse Company. In December 1907, the small syndicate became the British Tabulating Machine Company, a publicly owned firm with a capital of £50,000. BTM, as it was known, would, after Hollerith sold his company, remain tied to IBM until 1949. The following year IBM formed a separate subsidiary, IBM United Kingdom, which operated in competition with both BTM and Powers-Samas (which marketed Remington Rand's punched card machines). Later, BTM and Powers-Samas merged to form International Computers, Ltd. (ICL). Ironically, ICL, started on Hollerith's patents, as was IBM, has been IBM's principal rival in the United Kingdom for many years.

Meanwhile, despite its progress, the British Tabulating Machine Company would not become firmly established until after it took the British Census of 1911—twenty-one years after Hollerith's machines had made their bow in the U.S. Census! In contrast to their American cousins, the British traditionally viewed the census as a threat to the last vestiges of English liberty, a sentiment expressed by William Thornton in the House of Commons on March 30, 1753.

To what end . . . should our number be known, except . . . to be pressed into the fleet and the army, or transplanted like felons to the plantations abroad? And what purpose . . . to know where the kingdom is crowded, where it is thin, except we are to be driven from place to place as graziers do their cattle?

In any event, Hollerith had tried his impatient best in 1904 to win the census business for his British company. After reading what he considered to be an unjust criticism of his system in the *Journal of the Royal Statistical Society,* he sought to rebut it by supplying comparative figures from the U.S. Census, where his machines were used, and from the British Census Office, which still employed hand methods. But he was rebuffed. Fuming, Hollerith wrote, "Regretting that the Honorable Registrar General would not furnish me data as to the accuracy of hand tabulations," and added:

In the Journal . . . the Hon. J. A. Baines states: ". . . there seem to me . . . two chances of error. . . . In the first place, the whole operation is dependent upon the punching of the cards used and, unless this be subjected to continuous test either by re-doing or by some other method, an initial error is established which vitiates the subsequent record throughout.

"Again, . . . in feeding the machines very quickly there is a chance of missing connection in the current. Altogether the machine . . . is by no means infallible, and where clerical labor is cheap, I confess my personal preference for the soaring human boy provided . . . that the amount of human supervision is such that will prevent his thoughts from straying into the fields of original research."

Annoyed at the criticism, Hollerith replied:

I have obtained . . . complete data as to the percentage of errors made in punching cards from records in the 12th census. I have also complete data relating to the errors made by clerks punching the cards for the census of Cuba and Puerto Rico. . . . Therefore, if I could have obtained from your office data as to the percentage of errors made by your clerks,

I would have had a unique comparison of the relative accuracy of tabulating by punched cards and tabulating by hand. This would, I think, have been the most effective reply to Mr. Baines' criticisms.

Referring to the remark that Mr. Baines makes about missing connection due to feeding machines very quickly, I can easily demonstrate the absolute absurdity of his criticism because I have in operation machines which feed cards automatically at a speed of from 200 to 300 per minute, whereas the fastest clerk feeding cards by hand would probably not exceed 60 cards per minute.

The inventor's salvo had no recorded effect on the complacent British officials. But despite the English reluctance to give up "the soaring human boy," Hollerith and his handful of British friends had succeeded. With the help of McKinley's assassin who drove Porter abroad to seek a new career, the former Census head, Phillpotts, and Greene had overcome complacency, doubts and outright hostility to plant the seeds of the computer industry in Great Britain.

17

"My Row with North"

"He simply wants to humiliate me."

Hollerith looked to few people as heroes in his passage through life. But he more than made up for the deficit on one side of his personal ledger by compiling a growing list of villains on the other. First came Westinghouse. That "scoundrel" had somehow cheated him out of the rightful benefits from his air brake patents. Later, Edison entered the lists. Hollerith may not have known him, but that seemed to matter little. Any inventor who hired hordes of others to do his inventing for him was automatically beneath contempt. As the year 1903 opened, a new name topped Hollerith's tally of those variously dismissed as "rascal" or "scoundrel." The new target of the inventor's wrath was one Simon Newton Dexter North. Hollerith's world, to paraphrase Emerson, could not move ahead without rogues.

To most eyes the latest miscreant was the model of respectability. A descendant of Simeon North, the first official pistol maker of the United States, North had been educated at Hamilton College in upstate New York. While there, he displayed ability in journalism and on graduation became managing editor of the *Utica Morning Herald.* He was one of the first in his profession to make regular use of a typewriter.

It was a time when journalism, as Porter had demonstrated, often served as a graduate education for other fields. Accordingly, North employed his newspaper days to fit himself out with a more than passing knowledge of statistics. For the Census of 1880, he had prepared an extensive report, the first ever, on the history and current condition of the newspaper and periodical press.

Moving to Boston in 1889, he became secretary to the National Association of Wool Manufacturers. Quickly mastering wool prices and other industry statistics, North in short order turned out a report on wool manufacture for the 1890 Census. Soon he was also testifying to Congress on tariff matters. His progress was such that, within a decade, he had climbed the census hierarchy to the post of chief statistician for manufacturers for the Twelfth Census. Well connected as well as talented—he had served on President McKinley's Industrial Commission between censuses—North took the final step on June 8, 1903, when he succeeded William R. Merriam as director of the U.S. Census. The appointment set the stage for a cataclysmic battle with Hollerith that would redound through Congress and the courts and even lead to the White House. Before long, "North must go!" became a war cry in the Hollerith household.

The temperaments of the two men made conflict between them almost inevitable. Both were highly susceptible to that rarefied Victorian state known as moral indignation. Once a matter of principle was seized upon, each became unalterably attached to his own point of view. If either had been more flexible, more tolerant, the self-defeating encounter might have been avoided or muted, despite the real differences between them.

The spark for "my row with North," as Hollerith called it, had been struck several years before and had lain smoldering. In winning the competitive test for the 1900 Census, Hollerith had applied his machines only to the simple tallying of individual data required for population and mortality tables. The Commission had required no separate test for the handling of aggregate totals, such as adding the acreage of farm after farm. Though the question of a second test had been left open, Hollerith had been awarded the contract for the Agricultural Census on the basis of a detailed report comparing the performance of his integrating tabulator at the New York Central with two types of adding machines. "The Hollerith system," Census Director Merriam had concluded, "is far better adapted to work at hand as well as much more economical."

As chief statistician of a Census division that did not use tabulating machines, North had no real interest in the decision. Yet he immediately championed a complaint by Hollerith's rival Pidgin. Shortly after the tests, the Boston inventor had written:

Mr. Hollerith . . . never has had any machine constructed and in operation for the tabulation of statistical data contained upon agricultural schedules. If he had had such a machine, the Commission would certainly have examined it instead of confining their inspection to a machine employed in the office of a railroad company in doing an entirely different kind of work.

Pidgin claimed that he had brought his tabulating and adding machine to Washington at great expense. For five weeks, it had sat in the Columbian Building, where the tests were being held, but the Commission had never examined it. Though Walter Willcox, a member of the Commission, denied that Pidgin had even entered his device into the competition—the Commission later examined the system at Boston to atone for a possible oversight—North was undeterred. He went over the Commission's head, appealing to Assistant Director Frederick Wines and to Census Director Merriam himself.

Hollerith explained:

Mr. North wrote a letter to the Assistant Director . . . and following from this, there were certain happenings which resulted in Wines and North becoming estranged. . . .

It was difficult for me to keep my balance . . . my sympathies, my sense of justice . . . were for Wines. North's letter, if it should have gotten into the hands of Pidgin, might have embarrassed us. Wines stood up for me like a man; North did the other thing.

. . .from that time on, although I kept up the appearance of friendly relations, my friendship for North had ceased.

The private feud had been kindled. Never one to withhold his prejudices lightly, Hollerith soon heaped fuel on the fire. When Merriam resigned from the Census Office, Hollerith came out strongly for Willcox over North to succeed him. As an outsider, he had no more business meddling in Census Office politics than North had in contesting the decision over the machines. But Hollerith was incapable of letting a quarrel subside; he had to have the last word.

Regardless of what had gone before, North faced a major challenge in taking over the Census. On July 1, 1902, the Office had become a permanent bureau of the government. It had been moved from the Interior Department to the newly formed Department of Commerce and Labor. To avoid duplication between the two agencies, George Bruce Cortelyou, Secretary of Commerce and Labor, had already shifted to the Census Bureau the annual processing of statistics of cities and the compilation of immigration figures. "It is my intention," the former private secretary to McKinley stated, "to transfer other important branches of statistical work to the Bureau of the Census."

The transformation of the Census Bureau into the great statistical laboratory of the nation was an idea that appealed strongly to the new President. Despite an outwardly bombastic manner, Theodore Roosevelt had a keen appreciation of solid fact as the bedrock for social legislation. And soon he was commanding the Bureau to supply him with statistics on a wide range of subjects: from the condition of natural resources to the number of lynchings in the South. When North proved understandably reluctant to risk the safety of his workers in gathering the latter, the President reinforced the director's waivering resolve:

Before we can deal successfully with crime and criminals, we must know the underlying facts; and if some special phenomenon in crime, such as lynching, presents problems of peculiar difficulty and seriousness, it is all the more important that the facts be fully known.

The change of the Office into a statistical clearing house should have been a windfall for Hollerith, who could look forward to the steady and growing employment of his machines. Both he and North had everything to gain. Instead, the new permanent status of the Bureau brought them into head-on confrontation.

On taking office on June 8, 1903, the director found contracts for eight automatic tabulating and verification machines already in effect for the fiscal year 1903–4. The rental for the automatics was 65 cents for each thousand cards tabulated. On November 27, North signed the first contract in his own right with Hollerith's company. It was for seven automatic tabulating machines at the same rental and also for two automatic sorting machines at 18 cents per thousand cards sorted. The agreement ran through June 30, 1904, the end of the government fiscal year. A second contract was signed by the director on April 19, 1904, for not more than twenty hand machines at $3.60 per day for such time as the machines might be used.

Although he had continued the old terms, North became increasingly dissatisfied. "At the time I executed the contract of November 27," he later explained, "the returns of the Philippine Census were in the office waiting tabulation, and there was not time for sufficient investigation." The changed status of the Bureau, he believed, should result in an altered relationship to its supplier. But he waited for more than a year before bringing the matter to a head. After granting a two-month extension to the contract for the eight automatics, which ended June 30, 1904, North wrote:

The permanent Census Office introduces entirely new factors. . . . As it is probable that the Census Office hereafter can make more or less use of the tabulating system . . . between census periods, and thus would become to a certain extent a steady . . . customer, we more nearly approximate the commercial conditions . . . therefore the rates or royalties . . . ought to be substantially the same as those given to other parties.

The director now demanded a great deal of information. What were the reasons for the different rates Hollerith had charged the Office in the past? What was the relationship between the rentals of the automatics and the hand machines, and their relative capacities? How much was Hollerith charging his commercial customers? And, finally, on what terms had Hollerith recently offered his automatics to the Russian Government? The director concluded: "All that I desire to be satisfied of is that the government is given as fair and as liberal terms as those embodied in the company's contracts for commercial work or for work that it does for other governments."

Since President George Washington had signed the first census law in 1790, those who had run the Census had come under fire for excessive spending and for conducting the Census as a political boondoggle. Most of the arrows had been aimed at the dispensing of jobs to politically chosen enumerators. Only recently had they been brought under the new Civil Service laws. But North could be equally open to criticism for allowing Hollerith's company to prosper unduly at the taxpayers' expense. The director intended to avoid not only actual wrongdoing but the appearance of wrongdoing.

Even before the close of the last Census, the *Brooklyn Eagle* had noted that "a surprisingly large portion of the total cost . . . was due to the use of various punching, adding and tabulating machines for which excessive royalties were demanded by the inventor." It noted:

An investigation of this matter . . . showed that the government paid a pretty penny for the privilege of using the automatic devices for census work, but nothing like as much as has been represented. . . . For the past two years [Hollerith] has had several hundred machines in constant use and . . . received $1,000 to $1,500 a year for each. At the present time he has in operation only 182 machines, for, as the work decreases, he is required to take off the machines.

At that, Mr. Hollerith has probably received well on to $700,000 for the use of his machines. When the census work is concluded the contractor will, of course, have a lot of practically useless machines on his hands. But he has a scheme on foot by which he hopes to close a contract with the Russian Government for use of some of them.

The $700,000 was one-third again as much as Hollerith had been paid for the 1900 Census. However, North was in a poor position to rebut such attacks, if he wanted to. No one else besides Hollerith could supply the equipment the government needed. On the other hand, it was inconceivable for the Census Bureau to consider going back to hand methods. North was in an untenable position.

It mattered little how much Hollerith's machines had saved, or the more accurate and current information they supplied. The highly visible fact to the public was the large amount of money the inventor was receiving. Rightly or wrongly, North felt compelled to take action against what he sensed was a grasping monopoly that was getting rich from patents the government itself had granted.

Adding to the director's zeal was a self-righteous distaste for profit in any form. In 1905, North would complain that

unlike the majority of inventors, Mr. Hollerith had been richly compensated. . . . his company had been paid nearly three quarters of a million dollars (from the Eleventh Census through 1904–05). The capital stock of the Company is $100,000, and . . . it has sometimes paid dividends of 100 percent. The United States Government has paid the Company more than seven times the amount of its capital stock.

That Hollerith was at last earning money from his inventions might have been a cause for commendation, rather than castigation, in another time. But in 1903, Roosevelt was making ungentlemanly attacks against the malefactors of great wealth, against the Sugar Trust and the Tobacco Trust, the railroads, and, eventually, the giant Standard Oil. While Hollerith's small company could hardly be classed with the great industrial combinations, such moral crusades left little room for subtle distinction. There was something increasingly suspect about profit in any form. North concluded:

Large sums of money have also been paid the company by railroads and other corporations which have used the machinery during this interval of 17 years and are still using it. It is plain that the Government has done its full duty in the protection of Mr. Hollerith's rights under his original patents.

To make matters worse, another situation had arisen that was a personal embarrassment to North. Although a year had passed, Governor Merriam, his own predecessor as director of the Census, had in July 1904 become the president of Hollerith's company. This meant that in granting an extension to the current contracts, North was, in effect, being forced to accept terms worked out between Hollerith and the man who was now the head of Hollerith's company. North wrote: "I was much embarrassed in making this second contract by the fact that my predecessor as Director of the Census had in the meanwhile accepted the presidency of the Hollerith Tabulating Machine Company and had entered upon the duties of that position." To avoid outright condemnation, North would have to subject any future agreements with Hollerith to the closest scrutiny. The director felt trapped. Though he realized the value of Hollerith's machines, he was determined to break the inventor's stranglehold on the Bureau.

By mid-1904, North had two factors going in his favor. First, the work of the 1900 Census and the Philippine Census was virtually complete. He was also aware that on January 8, 1906—well before the next Census—the basic patents on Hollerith's hand machines would expire. After that, anyone could manufacture or use such equipment without making any royalty payments at all. Stating that he was unwilling to approve a renewal of the old contract until satisfied that the proposed rentals are equitable and reasonable, he wrote: "While there is considerable work pending on which your machines can undoubtedly be used to advantage, none of it is of great magnitude, and all that the law requires this office to do could be done by hand."

The battle lines were formed. There could be no turning back. Surprisingly, Hollerith, who usually relished a fight, was depressed and out of sorts. Not only had North turned against him, but everything else was also at sixes and sevens. Taft-Peirce, which had promised to bulwark his business, had proved a leaky sieve. More than $56,000 had been sunk into the manufacturing arm of the Tabulating Machine Company, with Roebling and Bond advancing large sums on their personal account. But Hollerith had been unable to turn it around. At the beginning of the year, the directors had put it into receivership. To lighten the burden on Hollerith, Merriam had been hired for a five-year term "to assume general charge of the business and commercial affairs of the company." Roebling, busy with the affairs of his family business, had obligingly stepped aside. As director of the Census, Merriam, the former governor of Minnesota, had been known for his organizing ability and willingness to delegate. For his services, he was promised the right to subscribe to 250 shares of Tabulating Machine Company Stock at $100 a share. The firm's capitalization would be increased from $100,000 to $200,000, with another 250 shares available to the stockholders.

No sooner had the agreement been signed than Hollerith regretted it and feared losing control of the company. On August 3, he wrote to Metcalf:

If I could have seen the condition of affairs . . . today, I would never . . . have negotiated with Governor Merriam. . . . all of my negotiations were based on the supposition that the Pennsylvania Railroad business was a success. I find now that we are going to lose the Pennsylvania Railroad. . . .

Then with regard to the Census Office, I find North in a vindictive mood . . . and he is going to cause me all the trouble he can.

Everything was going wrong. Even Hollerith's machines appeared to have turned against him.

I have had a good deal of trouble with machines . . . and my brilliant assistants seem unable to connect up these machines in such a way that they will work for any length of time. Perhaps it is my fault in not designing the machines satisfactorily. . . .

Instead of increasing our business, we will probably have to struggle along in a small way. . . . but I still believe in the end the machine can be worked out satisfactorily. I, however, may land in a lunatic asylum before that time.

At Metcalf's urging, Hollerith made what, for him, was a generous concession. Burying his pride, he admitted that he might have been mistaken in his feelings about North. And on August 10, he called at the Census Bureau to have a frank talk with the director. "I went in absolutely sincere and frank," Hollerith reported. "My reception was anything but cordial."

I was indifferently asked to take a seat and, after I stated the object of my call, I was informed by North that he would prefer to have me make my statements in writing. . . . I told him the matters I had come to explain could probably be made clear in his mind in conversation but not in writing. . . . Mr. North insisted, however, that he could see no reason why it could not be written. . . .

. . . in short, he simply wants to force me to write a letter which I do not propose to do. I am more convinced than ever that my surmise of North's position is correct, that he simply wants to humiliate me.

North would recall the meeting somewhat differently.

Mr. Hollerith expressed his willingness to explain verbally certain of the discrepancies referred to; and I replied that, since the matter must finally be determined by the Secretary of Commerce and Labor, it was necessary that his reply should be in writing. The answer was that I would take it verbally or I would not get it at all.

The two men had come together like flint and steel. Instead of healing the breach, the meeting only served to widen it. The diplomatic Thayer, or almost anyone else, would have been a better choice to send to the meeting. Perhaps it had been suggested. But Hollerith was "Mister Census." He had been given a free hand to negotiate the contracts for the 1900 Census. And, with his many friends in the Bureau and his extensive knowledge of census affairs, it would have been out of the question for anyone else to represent him. In all likelihood, he would not have permitted it.

North left on vacation following the meeting, hoping to find a revised proposal from the Tabulating Machine Company on his desk at his return. He had taken a tough line, and he half expected his opponents to back down. Realizing the value of the Hollerith system, he had no desire to press the battle to its conclusion. However, finding no letter on his return, he was forced to make the next move. On September 17, he wrote:

It is important to know at once whether or not this office is to carry on its work during the remainder of the year by the agency of your mechanical apparatus, or by other mechanical devices now under consideration. Estimates for the appropriations for the next fiscal year must be submitted . . . not later than October 1, and these . . . cannot be made until this question is determined.

North gave the Tabulating Machine Company ten days to reply. In the meanwhile, he would submit his own proposed agreement.

I have reached the conclusion that, pending the receipt of the information . . . and for the remainder of this fiscal year, I will be justified in agreeing to a contract . . . on the basis of a reduction of approximately 25 percent from the royalties fixed in the last two contracts . . .

Instead of 65 cents per thousand cards tabulated, the director would pay 50 cents per thousand for the automatic tabulating machines. Rental for the automatic sorters would be reduced proportionately, from 18 to 13 cents per thousand cards sorted.

Significantly, it was the first time that North had threatened directly to employ other mechanical means to process the Census, though no comparable system to Hollerith's existed. He ended his letter:

I will submit such a contract for . . . approval . . . provided I receive the decision of your company thereon . . . on or before September 27.

In the absence of a definite reply . . . I shall assume that the Tabulating Machine Company prefers to terminate its business arrangements with this office, and proceed to make other arrangements.

North's letter had an unexpected effect. It drove a wedge between Hollerith and his fellow officers of the Tabulating Machine Company. During the past weeks, Hollerith, deeply depressed and worried, had become almost irrationally suspicious of Merriam. The new president had been hired, with Hollerith's blessing, to put the company on a firmer financial footing. But when Merriam had routinely deposited $30,000 in company funds in the American Security and Trust Company—where Hollerith usually made such deposits—the inventor had complained. As the majority stockholder, he should have been consulted. Now all his friends and business associates appeared to be arrayed against him. They had decided to go along with North. Hollerith wrote:

Governor Merriam informs me that the . . . directors instructed him to make the best contract he could with the Census Office. He will, I understand, submit for your approval a contract for the use of automatic tabulating and sorting machines at 50 cents and 13 cents as against the former price of 65 cents and 18 cents. . . . it is stupid for us to accept these terms.

When Hollerith was hopeful, he pushed for new methods and new technology and had faith they could be relied on. When his fears overtook him, as they did now, he distrusted even his own machines. Comparing the automatic tabulating machines, employed successfully in the Philippine and Agriculture censuses, with the earlier hand machines, he wrote:

We have automatic machines in stock which are constantly requiring attention, subject to wear, delicate in adjustment, and requiring continual and constant nursing. We also have . . . an ample supply of the old hand machines. . . . requiring very little attention . . . if we compared the gross income to us from the work to be done during the balance of the year, we will receive less money for the work done on the automatics under the proposed contract than if the work was done with the old hand machine under the old contracts as made years ago.

Hollerith had little hope that the board would listen. In fact, he now realized that basic decisions about his own business were being removed from his hands. Was he only a hired hand engaged to carry out orders? Or was he going to have a say in this and other matters? The same day, Hollerith wrote a second letter. He proposed to buy out Merriam's contract, saving up the money by waiving the dividends on his own stock. He would reassert control. Two days later, he made still another proposal that showed that he could steer his own course.

Would it not be the best thing . . . to give me the same privileges in Germany that you have given Mr. Porter in England? If this is done, I will undertake to make a living in Germany and relieve the Tabulating Machine Company of the burden of carrying me.

My ideas regarding the conduct of negotiations with the Census Office are so entirely at variance with those expressed by Mr. Thayer, as actually carried out by Governor Merriam, that it seems unreasonable to expect me to execute . . . a contract . . . I consider a personal humiliation.

Hollerith felt that his own board, like North, was trying to humiliate him. In actuality, he was acting like a spoiled and petulant child. If he could not have things his own way, he wasn't going to play.

Thayer carefully penned a letter that only a good friend could write. He began it by assuring Hollerith that "Bond, Metcalf, Salt and I are your friends. There isn't one of us who would not go the limit to meet your wishes in the affairs of the company if we could possibly believe that what you wished was for your real interest." Thayer continued:

Sometimes a man gets so fagged out with work that everything looks black. For months we have not been able to discuss with you with any frankness the affairs of the company because you have been in a state of mind in which our best intentions would seem to you wrong. I have written and rewritten letters to you in the effort to avoid giving any offense. . . . If I was the only one who had had that difficulty I should think that it might be me and not you, but as you know, I am not the only one.

Thayer quickly got to the heart of the matter.

Five years ago, you would have been the last man to let a personal quarrel influence a business matter. Now your quarrel has produced a condition in which you and North cannot do business and instead of the Census Office being as friendly as in the past—it is rather on the defensive.

Now which is the truer friendship: To back you up in your quarrel at an expense to you of the Census Office business or to back the Governor up in trying to save something out of it for you?

Next, Thayer took Hollerith gently to task for his attitude toward Merriam. The governor had been hired after careful consideration, he reminded the inventor, to attend to the financial side of the business, "and leave you to the technical and scientific end."

We had no more than made the agreement than you . . . commenced to look for trouble and you have resented everything the Governor has done without consultation. It was to relieve you that he was hired. If he had run to you with every question, where would the relief have been?

Finally, Thayer brought up Hollerith's future with the company.

We all of us fully recognize . . . that your connection with the company, if you work with it cordially and hopefully, is the company's best asset, and we believe that there is a bright future. If you should quit or . . . if you should stay . . . in your present frame of mind, I don't know what is going to become of the company.

If Hollerith wanted to go to Germany, become rested, and, incidentally, work up some business, Thayer would urge the others to go along. They would pay his salary and expenses and even hold his stock indefinitely so that he could regain control of the company.

Thayer had been warm, honest, compelling, and tactful. Hollerith read the letter carefully through his steel-rimmed glasses, then slowly put it down on the oak surface of his cluttered desk. He would stay with the company. But the decision did not mean the directors were going to back down. Against Hollerith's wishes, Merriam signed a contract for the remainder of the fiscal year ending June 31, 1905, at the reduced rates proposed by North.

Was peace at hand? Unfortunately, the Census director proved more inflexible than his adversary. Although North had proposed the new rates himself, he now found them "excessive and exorbitant." What was more, the Tabulating Machine Company, North believed, would still be able to fix any rates it chose for the Thirteenth Census in 1910, as it had in the past. "Mr. Hollerith," North declared, "was apparently seeking to place himself in a position where his company could control, nor merely the Thirteenth, but all subsequent censuses for all time to come."

For the first half of 1905, North's actions appeared baffling and at times contradictory. Eager to break Hollerith's hold over the Bureau, he applied to Congress and on February 3 received approval for a $40,000 appropriation, effective in July, "for the cost of experimental work in developing tabulating machinery." At the same time, he was apparently trying to contract with Hollerith for the further use of his tabulating machines in the coming fiscal year. On June 17, he wrote, "I now feel at liberty to . . . submit a draft of a contract for the use of your machinery which will be satisfactory to me."

If North was trying to have his cake and eat it too, he was blocked at the last minute by his own superior. On June 28, 1905—just three days before the start of the new government fiscal year—the director was forced to withdraw his letter of June 17. The reason the Secretary of Commerce and Labor gave was that Hollerith was ineligible to contract with the Census Bureau because the inventor had refused to enter his system in competitive tests the year before. Hollerith had snubbed the requirement to compete because the only other system entered in the tests was the same Pidgin machine that he had trounced five years earlier.

In the meantime, Hollerith had also been trying to break the logjam. In March, he had submitted a contract draft for the continued use of his machines at the reduced rates. However, it had stipulated that, if the government carried on any experimental work on tabulating machines or any apparatus covered by his patents, Hollerith would have the right to withdraw his machines from the Census Bureau. It was an impossible condition, and Hollerith may have known it at the time. Having just won approval of his appropriation for experimental work, North could not very well thwart the will of Congress by deciding not to use it.

What stung Hollerith most were his enemy's charges that he was profiting at the public's expense, that his company was a grasping monopoly. Hollerith had always prided himself on being scrupulous in his business dealings. If the government wanted its own tabulating system, he would sell it not just his patents on the hand machines, which were about to expire anyway, but exclusive rights to all his inventions for use in any government department. The amount to be decided by arbitration.

The offer, made in March, was repeated in April. If accepted, the government could have his proved system instead of spending money on experimentation. The offer, and similar offers in the future, were also turned down. As the deadline approached, both Hollerith and North worked for the same objective—the continued use of Hollerith's machines. Neither could fully believe that the other would refuse to back down. But both had been too stubborn, too inflexible to agree. So on July 1, 1905, the inconceivable but inevitable result of "my row with North" finally came about. All of Hollerith's rented machines were withdrawn from the Census Office.

North said it was "because of failure to reach agreement as to the rental." "The real reason," Hollerith contended, "was the reluctance of the Tabulating Machine Company to leave its patented devices where they could serve as models for experimental work and as the convenient means for testing the potential or problematical operations of possible competitive machinery." Whatever the reasons, it was a defeat for both men, perhaps ordained from the start.

Without waiting for the dust to settle, North immediately contracted for fifty to one-hundred of the detested "Pidgin Coops" for three months at a rental of $20 a month for each machine. Earlier, he had championed Pidgin's cause. But, soon, the director was bitterly complaining to Cortelyou, who had barred him at the last minute from contracting for Hollerith's machines. ". . . the withdrawal of the Hollerith machines from the Census Bureau," he wrote, "compelled the substitution of an untried system of mechanical tabulation known as the Pidgin system in an important branch of Census work—the compilation of immigration statistics—at much inconvenience."

Hollerith was incredulous. On July 18, he wrote to Swain: "You may be interested to know that Mr. North has made a contract with Pidgin and . . . has either bought or rented a number of his 'Pidgin coops' which were tested in competition with our old hand machines in 1900." Still unbelieving, the inventor wrote a second letter to his friend a few days later:

The Machines North has fired out of the Census Office are the automatic machines, which are far and above the old hand machines which were tested in competition with Pidgin in 1899.

   . . . North has not the slightest conception of . . . population, vital or social statistics . . . If he knew anything of the details of this work, he certainly could not take up with Pidgin's devices . . .

Damn the whole business! While losing his Census contract, Hollerith had gone out and bought a four-cylinder, air-cooled Waltham-Orient automobile. And for some time, he devoted more attention to his car than to running his business. But instead of proving the diversion he had hoped, the purchase only added to his deeper frustration. Soon he was firing off complaints to its maker.

Many thanks for your favor. . . . Regarding the luck on my car, I should say it is very rotten. I nearly wore my arm off trying to start the engine; finally succeeded in starting it, and ran the car altogether on Saturday and Sunday about 20 or 30 miles. Now I am absolutely unable to start the engine, and have been unable to use the car since Sunday.

   I was disgusted to find that when I was running the car the fender was loose. I found a bolt had jarred out and dropped along the road somewhere. Inspection afterwards showed me that there were eight bolts to this machine with a single nut and without cotter pin. Right in the front of the machine, the bolt which holds the spring on one side had a cotter pin, while on the other side the bolt had no cotter pin. I found that the four nuts that hold the clamps of the rear axle on one side had all jarred loose, and apparently the axle had shifted.

   After you left, I found that the governor did not control the engine when I threw the clutch out. In other words, the engine would race. The spring around the governor rod was compressed, and it had taken such a set that it would not work the valve for throttling the engine by the governor.

   I found that there was about one-eighth of a revolution play in the steering wheel. Such inspection as I could make did not show me how I could take up this slack or lost motion.

I am afraid that life is too short to trouble much with an Orient machine.

At times, God and machine, as well as Simon Newton Dexter North, seemed to be conspiring against him. He would just have to wait for the fitful mood to pass.

18

Commercial Success

"I am simply taken off my feet."

With his thinning hair turned steely gray, Hollerith looked fully his forty-five years as he peered out at the world through steel-rimmed glasses. His battles and worries had taken their toll, which was reflected in his rapidly changing moods. "You never know what he will do," one of his workers was heard to remark. It was rumored that the doors on his home were built extra strong so that they wouldn't fly off their hinges.

Since he had written "my invention is no longer a crude idea" as a young man twenty-one years before, Hollerith had counted on the Census Office as the main proving ground for his ideas. He had relied on its hundreds of clerks and ample resources to provide a record of practical work performed. And "Dr. Hollerith's Work-Shop" at the Census Office had been a staging point for both the hand machines and the newer automatics. The unique demands of the census more than anything else fueled the creative drive that pulled his business ahead. Suddenly, in mid-1905— when the Census Office, now a permanent Bureau, was becoming the statistical clearing house for the government—Hollerith found himself looking in from the outside. Suddenly, he had to rechart his life at mid-career. "After my row with North," Hollerith would later recall, "I devoted myself entirely to commerical work."

Where many men would have caved in at defeat and spent time counting their losses, Hollerith released a store of restless and explosive energy. "I have been working for some time with the Pennsylvania Railroad, trying to get them into shape," he wrote

Swain, eighteen days after his machines were expelled from the Census Bureau.

We have started using the machines at the shops of the Atchison, Topeka, & Santa Fe. . . . [and] at the Denver Gas & Electric and I am also in correspondence with Brown & Sharpe. . . . The Regal Shoe Company is also coming along.

The seeds that Hollerith had planted in defining his first commercial applications a few years before were beginning to grow. Even the railroads, which had derided his "white elephant" machine at the Central, were starting to show some life. In 1904, Hollerith had feared losing the Pennsylvania, but inch by inch he was winning over its affiliated lines. In August 1903, the Long Island Railroad started experimenting with his system. In 1904, the West Jersey & Seashore Division had come aboard in March; the Northern Central in June; the Philadelphia, Baltimore & Washington in August; and the Philadelphia & Erie in September. The total had grown in 1905: the Buffalo & Allegheny in January, and the United Railroads of New Jersey in May. Now Hollerith was closing in on the parent Pennsylvania itself: "They are using the machines, but . . . not . . . for the entire system and, therefore, in a certain sense, must be looked upon as still experimenting. Ultimately, I want to get the shops at Altoona to use the system for cost accounting."

At his urging, the Pennsylvania's comptroller, Max Riebenack, wrote to Gershom Smith on July 11.

We are experimenting in the office of our Auditor of Merchandise Freight Receipts . . . and I am advised by Mr. Hollerith that you are using these machines at your plant at Steelton with great success. . . . Will you . . . advise me the definite kind of work that you have adapted this machine to and the results.

Inviting the railroad official "to visit our works . . . to show you what we have accomplished," the Pennsylvania Steel Company's comptroller replied: "We are making a daily distribution of all our labor (9,000 men) at Steelton, also of our stores and supplies, and, partially as a result of our using this machine since January, 1904, we have gained 14 days' time on our monthly costs. All of the work, Hollerith's friend reported, was now proved out daily and at less cost than under the old system. Three departments were also tabulating detailed costs of shop orders. Smith concluded: "To enable us to do this, we have one pretty good man at the head of the Tabulating Department who is selected for his executive ability and not loaded down with details. Most of the punching of the cards and the reading of tabulations is done by boys to whom we pay salaries of from $25 to $30 per month."

In later years, Hollerith was fond of saying that after he lost the Census contract, "one customer brought another." While the inventor's personal distaste for salesmanship barred him from soliciting business himself, he nevertheless found it permissible, and dignified, to have others speak for him. And who could do so better than an enthusiastic and knowledgeable customer? In mid-1905, the proselytizing Smith was also penning letters to Browne & Sharpe and to his former employer Pope Manufacturing Company, the bicyclemaker at Hartford. A year later, another convert, Pierre Bontecou, who had been employed as a tabulating clerk at the New York Central in 1900, wrote Hollerith from Yale & Towne, eager to know "all the different ways the machine is being used . . . If I can interest the firm to handle the tabulating work on a large scale, it will make a good thing in the way of promotion for me and would also make a market for the machines."

Recalling the young man favorably, Hollerith replied, describing the Pennsylvania Steel installation and enclosing "a number of different cards used by some of our customers." Among them was the card the Studebaker Brothers at South Bend, Indiana, were trying for keeping an inventory of their lumber supply: "In their case, they make quite a use of the cards for keeping a running inventory of their stock on hand. In the case of lumber, of course, the question is not only quantity, but how long in stock. In other words, the question of seasoning is important." Soon, Yale & Towne was expanding its installation and Bontecou was winning a reputation for which his future fellow IBM sales representatives would hail him:

Oh, he's strong for the system;
He makes it pay,
He carries great schemes in his hat,
He got seven raises last year,

So they say,
Now what do you know about that?

Although he was disdainful of hiring salesmen—"If the machines are any good they will sell themselves"—Hollerith was not beyond reacting when an important prospect failed to show interest. Annoyed that he had never heard from any of the New England railroads, he wrote to Swain: "If you would get Mr. Tuttle (President of the Boston & Maine) to write to the Fourth Vice-President of the New York Central Railroad, or if you could get him to write to the Pennsylvania Steel Company regarding their use of the machines at Steelton, I think it would be a great point for us. Can you not arrange to do that?"

At the same time that he was encouraging friends and admirers to seek new business, Hollerith was also keeping a weather eye on possible competition, though he had little to worry about in 1905. He reported to Swain: "I had understood . . . that Pidgin was trying to get into railroad work. Of course I am sorry, for his efforts in this direction will probably simply result in bringing the tabulating machines into ill favor, due to his ridiculous ideas." Ridiculous or not, Hollerith was taking no chances. He had copies of the Census Commission's Competitive Report for 1900—in which he had defeated Pidgin—printed up and distributed to his friends. He also asked Swain: "If you can in any way get some idea of what Pidgin is driving at, it will be of great service to me."

The stirrings among his new commercial customers buoyed Hollerith's spirits. But by far the most important activity that engaged his renewed flood of energy was the impending birth of a new line of machines. He wrote to Swain: "we are developing an entirely new line of tabulating machines for commercial work which I think promises much better results than the old forms. While we have lost the Census Office contract, as you know, there is plenty of work in other directions."

Taft-Peirce, which had floundered two years before, had been wrested from bankruptcy almost single-handedly by its acting receiver, Frederick S. Blackall. A bear of a man, who stood six feet three in his stocking feet, the shrewd and energetic Blackall had not only paid off all the firm's debts in two years' time—the receivership was terminated August 22, 1905—but had repurchased the Tabulating Machine Company's 1,970 preferred shares. The transaction, in which Hollerith's company received almost what it had paid for the stock, was the best of two worlds. Under Blackall, vice president and general manager of the reorganized company, Taft-Peirce would continue to manufacture Hollerith's automatic sorters, tabulators, and key punches. Though it had parted with its interest in Taft-Peirce, Hollerith's company held onto its most valuable asset. On May 1, 1905, it employed Eugene Ford "as a mechanical engineer for . . . developing, improving, and perfecting" the machines and devices employed in its business.

While Hollerith respected the talents of few people, he had a high regard for those of the Mississippi-born engineer. When Ford, who was married to a local girl, insisted on working "within 40 miles of Uxbridge, Massachusetts," Hollerith agreed, paying $25 a month for work space that Ford selected. He nevertheless cleared out a large light front office next to his own in the Georgetown plant, which he reserved exclusively for Ford's infrequent visits. On his part, Ford considered himself more than another "hired hand." Though paid the handsome salary of $150 a month for the first year—he would receive $200 the second—Ford was also eager to have a stake in Hollerith's company. Earlier, Swain had told Hollerith that he wanted to dispose of a few shares of his Tabulating Machine Company stock. Hollerith replied:

Regarding your stock . . . Mr. E. A. Ford . . . who is now engaged in making designs for the newer forms of machines on which I am now working, is the one who wants to purchase this stock. Ford knows the condition of the Census Office contract, and as he is anxious to buy some of the stock . . . his opinion of the newer development of the machines must be quite favorable.

The "new forms" of machines, although basically refinements of the automatics developed for the 1900 Census, differed markedly in appearance. The automatic feed unit that had perched on a separate stand by the side of the tabulating machine had lost its makeshift appearance. It was now joined solidly to the left side of the machine. The counters, or adding machines, which had peered at the operator through a glass case at the rear of the console, were now sunk downward into the base of the machine. Only the counter wheels, raised slightly above the work surface, remained visible. A crank, not unlike that for starting a car, appeared on the right side of the tabulator. By turning the handle, the operator cleared the adding wheels and reset them to zero. Brushes, similar to those already in use in the sorter, took the place of the reciprocating pin box; as in the sorter, they could sense cards in motion. Gone completely in the new models were the oak and ash covers of the earlier machines— and the homey feeling the wood imparted. Instead, impersonal metal panels, mounted on steel frames, lent a functional and strictly businesslike appearance to the new commercial line.

For the most part, Hollerith had neatened up his older designs. But there was a new and useful element, borrowed from the telephone switchboard. It was the plugboard used by operators to route calls before automatic dial systems came into use. In Hollerith's earlier machines, connection between the counters and the mechanism that sensed hole positions in the card had been hard wired. And the resoldering of wires, a delicate and time-consuming chore, had been necessary to set up the machine for different jobs. Now Hollerith could "reprogram" his machine for different jobs by simply unplugging and replugging wires in a panel. The rewiring of back panels was a task that would become familiar to generations of people who worked with tabulating machines over the years.

While he was drastically changing the appearance of the tabulator, Hollerith was also altering the sorter—almost beyond recognition. The railroads had complained that the horizontal sorter, designed for census work, had taken up too much room in crowded stationmasters' offices. So the highly practical Hollerith literally stood the assembly on end. In his new "vertical" sorter, cards were fed downward from the top of the five-foot-high unit into a series of twelve chutes corresponding to the twelve positions in the column of a card. In addition, the machine was speeded by giving its feed mechanism a continuous rather than an intermittent action. Because it was difficult for women operators in tight-laced corsets to unload the bottom or "nine" pocket, the machine soon became known as the "backbreaker." But despite complaints, the new vertical sorter was what the paying customer wanted. Amusingly, Eugene Ford, who had worked on Hollerith's earlier horizontal sorter as well as the new vertical machine, would make news as an IBM inventor some twenty years later when he developed what was widely and mistakenly hailed as the first horizontal sorter. Women operatives, perhaps abetted by some portly males, would prevail in the design battle after all.

Hollerith's actions in bringing out his new commercial line show a curious mixture of the cautious engineer and the bold entrepreneur. At times, one appeared to be at war with the other. On occasion, he was, once again, the inventor who in 1902 adamantly refused to disclose his work at the New York Central "until some experiments . . . in the way of feeding the machines, as well as running them by electricity, should reach greater perfection." At other times, stung by the loss of his Census business, he seemed almost over eager in his pursuit of commercial success.

A model of the new tabulator had been completed by June of 1905, when the inventor sent a photograph of his latest progeny to Swain. "I was glad to receive the cut showing your new machine," his friend replied, somewhat uncertainly. "It looks quite complicated." Hollerith labored over the prototype for another year and a quarter, at which point he received a letter from the general auditor of the Union Pacific Railroad. On September 8, 1906, auditor Erastus Young had finally gotten around to reading the *Railroad Gazette* of July 4, 1902, describing Hollerith's application at the Central. It was the same article that had led Mr. Martin of Marshall Field to install a system three years earlier. Young wrote: "I would like to have you advise me if the machines can be adapted to our requirements and, if so, what the cost would be to install them and supply the cards. If adopted for the Union Pacific, and their use proved satisfactory, I would have them used by the other lines also." The Harriman lines, as they were known, included not only Union Pacific but also the Central and Southern Pacific routes. It was a tempting prize for the small Tabulating Machine Company. With uncharacteristic confidence, Hollerith almost arrogantly prescribed his untried system for the important customer.

Kindly allow me to postpone replying to your letter in detail until we have completed the experiment . . . in regard to the new style tabulating machine.

I believe you have seen the machines at the New York Central Railroad and will probably remember that these machines operate at a speed of from fifty to sixty cards per minute, and each machine requires an operator. The machine we are now building . . . is arranged with automatic feed, and tabulates cards at the rate of from 180 to 200 per minute.

In view of the vast improvement, and the probable early completion of this machine, it would . . . hardly pay to equip such a large railroad as yours with the old style machines.

Only three months later, the cocky businessman was replaced by the cautious engineer. Reluctant to let his new tabulator go into production while any improvements could still be made, Hollerith asked Thayer's advice on bringing out the new product. On December 12, the Western Electric executive replied:

It is better to go ahead and get some new machines out than to wait for the last touch. We will probably never be able to get out a machine in which we will not see chances for improvement in a later lot. But . . . the difficult and important thing is to decide whether it is worthwhile to interrupt business in order to try to get perfection.

On the kind of stuff that we make, we try to get it in as good shape as possible and get it into process of manufacture. Then, we periodically round up the thing in view of our experience and the experience of the people using the apparatus and make changes at the convenience of the shop. Of course [in] the case where we find that something is radically wrong . . . we have to make changes at once.

It was good to be able to rely on the level-headed and sensible Thayer, who had only recently been made vice-president of the largest manufacturing company in the world. Thayer, Salt, and Metcalf, sitting as the Tabulating Machine Company's executive committee, approved and ratified the action of their general manager in ordering twenty-five automatic machines from Taft-Peirce.

The Woonsocket mechanics worked with care on the delicate new mechanisms. It was not a job that could be rushed. Jigs and patterns had to be made; new tools ordered; armatures for the magnets and other parts procured from Western Electric and a host of other suppliers. But nine months later, the demanding inventor wrote Thayer, apparently pleased with the progress. On May 24, Thayer replied: "I am glad to hear that the tabulating machine is coming out so satisfactorily." Then, a few days later: "I would like to go to Washington to see that new machine, but have found it a little difficult planning ahead."

Meanwhile, nearly a year after its inquiry, the Union Pacific was beginning to wonder about the new-style machines whose early completion Hollerith had predicted. And its freight auditor inquired of his superior: "Do you know in what shape that Washington Machine (Statistical) matter is at the present time?" Hearing from the line, Hollerith confidently announced on August 7 that the first shipments had been made. " Our preliminary tests satisfy us that we have finally perfected this machine and that the same will work satisfactorily. Unless we meet with some difficulties in the use of the machine . . . we will be prepared to furnish machines of this type about December 1st or January 1st."

The corner had been turned. And Hollerith could hardly wait to report the news to Swain. "I intend to put the new machines in use at from 150 to 180 cards per minute," he declared, "and in a big works one clerk can take care of more than one machine." Though the speed was slower than the 180 to 200 cards per minute that the inventor had confidently ventured to the Union Pacific the year before, Hollerith was evidently satisfied. He recounted:

Some two or three years ago I started work on an improved machine, and I am just finishing up ten of these new automatic tabulating machines. These ten machines I will put around the country in different places. The first one has already gone to the Eastman Kodak Company. Another will go to Maryland Steel Company. The third will go to Marshall Field & Company; another will go to the Pennsylvania Steel Company, and another to the Topeka shops of the Atchison, Topeka, and Santa Fe.

In other words, I am going to put out about 15 or 16 of these new type machines in different parts of the country and, in that way, will make sure of what I believe is correct: namely, that these machines will work excellently in actual use. I have thoroughly tested them here in my own shop . . .

Once more the exacting engineer had taken over from the bustling businessman. At least ten of the machines, thoroughly tested, were ready. The Express wagon would call for them at the Georgetown shop in the next two to three weeks.

While Hollerith the engineer was bending all his efforts toward the mechanical perfection of his new tabulators, Hollerith the businessman had almost neglected to work out a suitable means of charging for them. It was a scant three weeks before the first customer shipment that the directors of the company got around to adopting a rental plan.

In offering his first automatics to commercial customers four years earlier, Hollerith had charged only for the number of cards ordered. The price had included a free license to use the machine for the application specified. In this way, customers paid for the amount of work actually done. The fairness of the old plan depended on the ability of each machine to handle the same amount of work. However, the new machines varied greatly in size and capacity, since each was practically custom built. Depending on the customer's requirements, a tabulator could now be ordered with anywhere from two to five counters, or separate adding mechanisms, for totaling as many different classes of information. Within each field of information, the customer would, in turn, require a varying number of columns, depending on the number of digits in the figures to be added. Therefore, Hollerith offered the counters with from two to seven counterwheels—one for each column to be added. Because one of the new tabulators might do twice as much work as another, while using the same number of cards, the new rates were pegged to the size and capacity of the machine.

Each customer, Hollerith decided, would be asked to pay a standard fee of $35 a month for the base, or main frame of the tabulator. Each counter, or adding mechanism, was $3 a month additional. And each magnet, which controlled a column or digit of an adding field, was 50 cents a month more. A typical tabulator, Hollerith figured, would rent for $40 a month. In contrast, the sorters, which were all alike, rented for a flat $10 a month.

How did the rentals for his machines relate to their costs? Hollerith explained:

If we can build these machines in reasonable quantities, the outfit of a sorting machine and tabulating machine would cost $700 to $900 at the very highest. Out of this, the sorting machine would cost about $300. We charge only $10 per month rental for the sorting machine, but for the tabulating machine the average rental will be about $40 per month, this being dependent upon the size of the machine.

While today's computers pay for themselves in approximately seven years, Hollerith's tabulators would earn their keep in twenty months, while his sorter would pay its way in thirty months. It looked like a good paying proposition, though Thayer worried about the relatively lower charge for the sorter. He wrote: "In regard to . . . sorting machines, . . . it is all right to get all you can for them until we can find out what they really ought to cost. It is evident that the present price is not enough in proportion to the present cost. Is Ford doing anything to get new estimates on the machinery?"

How would Hollerith charge for servicing the new machines? For his earlier automatics in 1903, the inventor offered free installation and service and repairs "at cost" after six months. Still more confident of his new machines—Hollerith built with the soundness of his German locksmith ancestors—the inventor promised "to make all necessary repairs and replacements" at his expense except where negligence was involved. But if the Union Pacific at Omaha and the Southern Pacific at San Francisco became his customers, Hollerith would have new costs to worry about as his business spread westward across the country. "The customer pays all the charges for transportation," he now decreed, "and all traveling expenses in connection with our representatives." His new policy would prove a sound one from a business standpoint, as Hollerith would later recall. "Always make a customer know that he is to pay the freight and all other details in connection with the order, and you will avoid a lot of trouble." However, in 1907, some customers worried about getting any service at all. Before placing his order a few months later, the Union Pacific's auditor would write to his superior:

If it can be arranged to have repairs made at the Union Pacific Shops here in Omaha, I think it should be done. Mr. Hollerith may, however, object to this. If so, and it is necessary to return the machines to the factory for repairs, I think we should ascertain if they can be made promptly, as it would place us in a rather serious predicament to be without either an Assorting or a Tabulating Machine.

There was some doubt whether Clarke Hayes, Hollerith's man in Chicago, could make it as far west as Omaha. Fortunately, repairs to Hollerith's machines, other than routine maintenance, would become virtually unknown. Asked in 1916 to tell a company sales convention how to handle repair calls at distant points, Clark Stoddard, Hollerith's first representative in San Francisco, felt compelled to decline. He had made only two repair calls the previous year and these were for minor adjustments. The company's newspaper would comment:

Many . . . installations . . . which Mr. Stoddard has supervised are located in such remote places as the copper mines of Arizona, in Mexico, lumber concerns in the Northwest, etc. Yet these users are able to trust the figure-handling of their business to Hollerith Tabulating Machines with practically the same degree of security as the Wall Street corporations within speaking distance of our New York Office.

In 1907, as before, the supplying of cards remained an important and profitable part of the business. "Under the contract," Hollerith explained, "the customer buys all of his cards from us." Sulphite paper cards, printed in black ink and properly cut, came in two lengths, $5\frac{5}{8}$ and $7\frac{3}{8}$ inches.

These cards we sell at 85 cents and $1.00 per thousand, according to size. The cards which we sell at $1.00 per thousand cost us about 30 cents per thousand to make, and you will therefore see that, besides the rental of the machines, we get a good profit on the cards.

. . . When you see that customers like Marshall Field & Co., Simmons Hardware Co. and others would use at least 10,000 cards per day, you can see that profit on the cards will amount to quite a considerable item.

The more work put on his new machines, the greater card production would be, as Hollerith explained:

I have an actual order from the Southern Railway, the information for which work will be temporarily put on about 200,000 cards per month, simply because I cannot furnish the machines. But the plans are that as soon as I can furnish the necessary machines, they will use about 550,000 cards per month. After we get started, we will put on another piece of work, which will mean an additional 500,000 cards per month. Besides this, they have other work in mind, so that right in sight and ready at any time we can furnish the machines, the Southern Railway has plans involving the use of close to a million and a half cards per month.

Other business in sight could give the cards with holes still wider currency.

I am also going to make a test for the Commission on Post Office business methods. . . . This is for auditing Post Office money orders, and should this go through . . . it would mean 65 million cards per annum.

Several years before, Hollerith had moved the first automatic card machines into his shop. The meeting was not altogether friendly, as Joseph Langley, who worked in the card printing operation, recalls: "I remember the old man getting a new machine in there. He was a great one for tinkering. He started it up and it knicked the end of his finger. Back it went to the factory." Later machines would prove more amenable, as Langley recounts: "Around 1909, he bought two big Kidder presses made by George W. Swift. We used to take and put a roll of paper on them and then it was slit and it would come right out and cut off the cards. The cards were printed at the same time."

Though Hollerith would later land the Post Office business— Langley recalls printing the short money order cards—he would have been too busy in 1907 to attend to it.

Since he had lost his Census contract two years before, Hollerith had been actively pushing his commercial business. Suddenly, in mid-1907, it was beginning to push him. While the railroads had been unimpressed with his earlier systems, the new automatics had apparently tipped the scale, as he reported to Swain:

I have urgent requests for machines from the Southern Railway, the

Chicago Great Western, the Chicago & North Western, the Great Northern and the Northern Pacific.

The Union Pacific have asked me to send a representative to Omaha and the Southern Pacific have sent their chief statistician from San Francisco to see me and he is now in Washington.

Having fought for the railroad business so hard, Hollerith was immensely pleased by the lines' sudden interest. Having been kept waiting for so long, he was also content to let them cool their heels while he took care of his other customers. Perhaps untactfully, he informed the Southern Pacific's auditor that since the railroads were so slow in taking up his system, he had commenced to develop the mercantile and manufacturing lines. Among his present customers, he informed the auditor, were Marshall Field, Eastman Kodak, National Tube, American Sheet & Tin Plate Company, Pennsylvania Steel, Western Electric, and Yale & Towne. Negotiations were also in progress with Simmons Hardware, Heinz Pickle, Regal Shoe, and Carnegie Steel. With no more machines in sight until after the first of the year, Hollerith might have done better to hide his evident satisfaction. Southern Pacific Auditor Hathaway reported on his vist with Hollerith to Erastus Young, general auditor for the affiliated lines at Omaha:

I found him quick, alert and apparently very eager to push his business. As evidence, he apparently took a great deal of pleasure in showing his letters and the increasing demands for his machines. But . . . in many cases, there was an urgent request for more machines or more supplies which he was obliged to put off.

While in the East, Hathaway had dropped by at the Southern and at the New York Central. ". . . everyone using the machine," he found, "is more than satisfied with the results." But there were some doubts about the inventor's ability to stay on top of his business. Mr. Peabody, the Santa Fe's statistician, who had put his order in before his cohorts, was "making all of his statistics by four distributing and three computing machines." But "he was better pleased with the machines than with Hollerith." Mr. Peabody said that "a good-size stock company ought to take it and manage it and let Hollerith go on with his experiments." But, in

Peabody's view, "Hollerith will not listen to any proposition that takes the management out of his hands."

In point of fact, Hollerith's success was reaching crisis proportions. Not only was he unable to deliver the new commercial line to his railroad customers in the summer of 1907, he was even "hung up" in finding enough of the old hand machines. The auditor of the National Tube Company complained:

We are up against a very nasty proposition at two of our mills . . . due to the non-receipt . . . of two of the four tabulating machines I ordered last December. At National Works . . . we are going to get into serious trouble in case we are unable to secure an additional machine of either the old style or one of the new design. The same conditions prevail at Lorain, although to a lesser extent.

While we know you are being hounded all the time for machines, this is a special case and I would like to know when we may count on receiving one or the other of these machines.

While some customers were grumbling angrily, others adopted a plaintive tone. Auditor Frank Hewitt of the Heinz Pickle Company would start factory cost accounting and stock keeping "as soon as I can secure an outfit." He would not, he explained patiently, press Hollerith for that. In the meanwhile, he implored the inventor for a hand machine to analyze "all orders received, all shipments and sales made and every conceivable kind of entry touching customers' accounts. . . . for one Hand Tabulator, one Assorter and probably three key punches, also one gang punch, we are in the position of simply 'throwing ourselves on the mercy of the court' and begging for early delivery."

Swamped by orders, Hollerith told the Union Pacific in December 1907 to expect a two- or three-month delay. On February 15 of the new year, he again postponed delivery to July 1908. On July 21, he was obliged to write again after numerous tracers from the company. "We have met with unforeseen and unexpected delays in getting the new lot of machines completed. The Taft-Peirce Company, who are manufacturing parts for us under contract, are behind in their deliveries, so that it is not entirely our fault . . ." But the fault went beyond Taft-Peirce. The Woonsocket company was in turn relying on Western Electric and other suppliers for parts that Hollerith was trying to chase down himself.

Although he had become the head of a booming enterprise, the inventor was still acting as his own expeditor and getting Thayer—now president of Western Electric—to do the same! In a typical communication, Thayer wrote: "After hearing from you by telephone last Friday, I got promptly after the armatures and had 428 of them expressed that day by Adams Express to Woonsocket. I neglected to tell you but hope that the armatures were received in good shape."

Besides rushing delivery of parts, the two men were busily looking for new sources of production. Louis de Gaul, the president of the Rowland Telegraph Company, called Thayer. The Baltimore concern, he reported, did not have enough work for its seventy-five to one hundred people. Thayer relayed the message to Hollerith. "From what he told me about his equipment, it occurred to me that it was the kind of shop which might be able to do some work for you to good advantage." Western Electric's Chicago plant might be able to take on some of the new sorters that Hollerith was developing for his larger capacity forty-five-column punched card. Union Pacific Auditor H. J. Stirling summed up the situation after visiting Hollerith's shop on 31st Street:

There are a large number of orders awaiting to be filled and Mr. Hollerith has had a great deal of trouble with parties to whom he has let out contracts for making of the different parts. . . .

At his own works in Washington, he practically does nothing but print and cut the tags [cards]. . . . The setting up is also done at his shops in Washington, but the manufacturing of the parts is let out on contract elsewhere.

Though he was opening a major market for his machines, Hollerith was still running his business like the proprietor of a neighborhood store. The spectacle of the world-renowned inventor and the Western Electric president scrambling after parts might have been amusing, if it hadn't begun to hurt. On May 8, 1908, the Bullard Machine & Tool Company's treasurer wrote: "It is true we are anxious to install a Hollerith machine but unfortunately are unable to get any satisfaction whatever that the makers can supply us."

While the Tabulating Machine Company would rescue the Bullard order, they were in deep trouble with another customer. Hollerith explained to Bontecou:

Referring to the General Electric Company, when they first took up the question at Schenectady, we did not want to put out any more hand machines; in fact, our stock was all in use and the automatics were not yet ready. We tried to postpone this work on account of the automatics and, finally, we had correspondence. . . . You will see that the matter was not dropped by us but by the General Electric Company which stated that they had a satisfactory system.

Two GE representatives were now inspecting the installation at Yale & Towne and were then coming on to Washington. Perhaps the order could still be saved.

The production bottleneck was not the only problem. With the rush of orders, Hollerith's company did not have the capital to pay for building more machines. He was already aware of the problem, and trying to solve it, when he wrote to Swain in August 1907:

In view of this extraordinary demand for machines, I would like to go ahead and build quite a number of them. This would take additional capital, and I do not want to lose control of the company, and I, myself, have not enough money to furnish my share of the additional capital.

Therefore, it may be that we shall issue some preferred non-voting stock, 7% or even more, if necessary. . . .

One stockholder of the Tabulating Machine Company (not Roebling or anyone of exceptional means) virtually agrees to take $10,000 worth of such preferred stock. If we can get the money, it will undoubtedly pay us to build these machines and put them out just as quickly as possible.

With the market sinking on Wall Street—1907 was the first bad year in a long time—Thayer was not nearly as sanguine as Hollerith about floating the preferred stock issue. Few of the directors, he believed, could take up the issue. And, under present conditions, it could not be made attractive enough to attract outside capital.

So many good stocks and bonds . . . can be bought at prices now which seem reasonably sure of large returns . . . so that any one buying pretty near anything on the stock market would be comparatively sure of getting a good return and a chance to sell later at a profit.

Besides, Thayer pointed out, there was no need for getting in even as much as $100,000 in advance of requirements.

We do not want any money immediately. All that we want is to . . . have it available when there is machinery to be paid for. . . . by the time we will want money for a lot of 50 or 100 machines, we could probably borrow what we need to pay for them. And, having got them into service, we could make some earnings that would, perhaps, take care of further extensions of the business.

Perhaps Thayer was right. Who would want to invest in a small company, with no solid earnings record and not even a public market for its stock? There were, as Thayer suggested, other ways of raising money.

If you or Eaton or any other stockholders have money that you would put into preferred stock, would you not be equally willing to lend it to the company at a higher rate of interest? Considering the prospects of large profits . . . I would not hesitate to vote in favor of paying stock-holders 10% on money that they would lend to the company.

Between August and December, the market panicked; banks went under; and brokerage firms closed their doors. Only J. P. Morgan seemed able to stem the rout. President Roosevelt, who did not know what to do, stopped railing at businessmen long enough to invite Morgan to the White House to dine. But despite the dire economic crisis, the Tabulating Machine Company's orders held firm, and on January 16 the directors declared a 400 percent stock dividend. The capital stock of the company was increased from $100,000 to $500,000 to correspond more nearly with the value of its assets. Two days later, the directors authorized the issuance of 2,500 shares of nonvoting preferred stock at $100 par, increasing the company's total capitalization to $750,000. However, on February 7, the board decided that $100,000 of preferred would be ample for the company's needs. The company had acted to raise the funds to "purchase the new machinery now so imperatively needed."

No sooner was the financing complete than the general manager was instructed forthwith to place an order not exceeding $40,000 with the Taft-Peirce Manufacturing Company for automatic sorting and tabulating machines. On April 3, 1908, Hollerith wrote to Bontecou:

I closed a contract for the construction of 90 tabulating machines and 80 sorting machines last Saturday. These ought to come along in from two and a half to three months. That is to say, the first one will be delivered within that time and the last ones within four to five months. Of course all of this is subject to the vicissitudes of an ordinary manufacturing plant. At the same time, manufacturers at present are not hampered with too much work.

While in June of 1908 Hollerith was "not placing any machines as the new lot are not yet finished," by the start of 1909 his business was back in balance. There was, Hayes informed the long-suffering Union Pacific, only a two-month order backlog. Having waited two years for its order, the railroad discovered that its requirements had grown. It now requested three, rather than two, tabulating machines and three improved sorters at $30 a month each in place of two older machines at $10 each. With time to attend to his customers, Hollerith would soon inquire "if the Southern Pacific at San Francisco is any longer interested in tabulating machines?" He wrote:

My object in asking for this information is that I have a request for a machine from an insurance company in San Francisco. . . . The point is, we would have to send some one to San Francisco, and, while the insurance company is willing to pay a considerable portion of this expense, we hardly feel warranted in undertaking this one proposition alone . . . if the Southern Pacific was still interested, this might be an opportune time to consider the matter.
Hoping that I am not troubling you too much . . .

Less than four years after losing his Census contract, Hollerith had bounded back to create a solid commercial base for his business. He had turned the once-reluctant railroads into enthusiastic users of his equipment. In enlisting the leading companies of the day as pioneers in applying his new methods and relatively untried line of commercial machines, he had released new forces that would propel his business forward at an increasing velocity.

Emerging from the cyclone he had kicked up, the inventor who disdained to hire salesmen recalled the words he had written to Swain on an August day two years before: "I started in to create this demand for machines. At first, it apparently would not go at all. Now, it comes with a rush and I am simply taken off my feet."

19

An Unusual Competitor: the Government

"The benefits which inventive genius has conferred upon this country cannot be . . . tabulated in mere figures. It is the basis of our commercial greatness."

Hollerith's growing success with commercial customers, following the loss of his government business in mid-1905, might have tempered the hurt to his pride if Hollerith had been more like other men. But he wasn't reasonable, in any ordinary sense. Years went by, yet his inventions remained highly personal creations bound up with and inseparable from his innermost feelings. More engineer than entrepreneur, he still found financial reward important, but only to the extent that it proved the unfolding of his original vision, as it gave evidence of the imprint he wished to leave on the world. Thus, as acceptance of his systems and methods grew, the pain Hollerith felt at the rejection of his machines by his own government only became that much more acute.

Hollerith's reaction to what he considered unjust treatment by the government bears a striking resemblance to that of another erratic genius, the Englishman Charles Babbage, whose calculating machine had been rejected by the British government some fifty years before. Circumstances differed. Babbage's machines, never completed, had been a constant drain on the exchequer. Hollerith's, in contrast, had functioned smoothly from the start and saved his government substantial sums. Yet, the behavior of the two men is closely parallel. Both were proud and sensitive to an almost abnormal degree. Both could imagine slights where none may have been intended. And both provoked monumental rows, largely ignoring the advice of their friends. Instead of letting things settle down after the loss of his government business, and perhaps working out a deal, Hollerith loosed an acrimonious campaign to oust Census Director North and get his machines returned to the Bureau. Over a half dozen years, the prickly inventor would literally wage war against the entire United States Government, each of its several branches, with the newspaper press a Greek chorus accompaniment in the background.

The first thrust, a subtle maneuver, was launched in early 1905, even before Hollerith's machines were finally dismissed from the Bureau. The years following the turn of the century were a less complicated time when the President of the United States, if so inclined, could still mingle with the residents of the city of Washington. He was, in fact, a familiar presence to the men in Hollerith's shop, which hugged the C & O Canal. "Every morning we looked out the window," Joe Langley recalls, "and there come Teddy Roosevelt. He would go along the towpath on his horse with his Rough Rider's suit on. He used to stop to talk to us." Whether Hollerith struck up an acquaintance with the President through such meetings is unknown. Langley believes he did not. But Hollerith could not help but be aware of Roosevelt's special interest in statistics as part of the arsenal for reform.

In his recent annual message, Roosevelt had urged the compilation of statistics on marriage and divorce from 1887 to the present. The information had been collected but not processed in previous censuses. The President's proposal, Hollerith was quick to realize, presented a further opportunity. Why not combine the statistics on marriage and divorce with those on the number of children born and living, information also collected in the 1900 Census but never used? Combined, the two sets of statistics could provide a revealing portrait of the American family. On February 4, Hollerith wrote to the President:

Your repeated expressions concerning . . . social questions centering in the family, the marital relation, the birth rate, etc., show such a profound interest that I . . . [call] your attention to the opportunity greatly to contribute to the sum of knowledge on these matters.

What was the relative birth rate among different elements of the population? How did the real birth rate among native women of native parents compare with that of native women of foreign parents? Were more or fewer children being born to the wives of professional men than to those of mechanics? What was the average number of dependents in each class of population? A vast store of information collected at great cost to the taxpayer was lying untouched. Having appealed to the President's interest, the inventor then launched a projectile at his arch enemy, Census Director North. "No effort is being made by the present head of the Census Office to utilize this information . . . and unless those outside the office who perceive its value persuade him of the advisability of a different course, he will continue to ignore its existence." It was an ingenious sally. Only five days later Presidential Secretary William Loeb, Jr., responded that the Chief Executive was "greatly interested" and "would take the matter up and see if he can have the figures worked out as you suggest." Even before his reply, Secretary Loeb had prodded North, who agreed that the two sets of figures must go together "to make them both complete."

Hollerith had struck with a two-edged blade. At the same time that he had exposed North's shortcomings to the President, he had also made the Census director more dependent on tabulating equipment. And he had done so at a time when North was trying to break Hollerith's "stranglehold" on the Bureau.

Within a year, Hollerith opened a second front in his battle against North. This time the attack was launched in the Congressional arena, where the inventor tried to strike down a further appropriation "for experimental work in developing tabulating equipment." Although North had spent $3,354 to rent the detested "Pidgin Coops" as replacements for Hollerith's machines, the rival devices had been discarded within six months, presumably because they were next to useless. And North set about developing an "independent" system of tabulation based on Hollerith patents about to expire.

If North was determined to copy Hollerith's system, he was also circumspect in avoiding the appearance of any wrongdoing. Shortly after the money for experimental work had become available in July of 1905, the director transferred to his staff from the Patent Office one Harry H. Allen, an expert skilled in patent law and especially conversant with electrical patents. He wrote to Allen:

I ask you to advise me as to the nature and scope of any patents for tabulating apparatus . . . issued to Herman Hollerith, or to any other person or corporation, and whether . . . there are any such tabulating machines or systems which may have become public property by reason of the expiration . . . of patents covering same.

Allen gave North the reassurance he was seeking. On or after January 8, the public would have the right to build what was known as "the hand machine." What was more, since the means of feeding cards automatically was old and common knowledge and had acquired a distinct status in the arts, it would also be lawful to employ an automatic feeding device with a hand machine. "The way is already clear," North reported to the Secretary of Commerce and Labor in the fall of 1905, "along which new and improved mechanisms can be devised which will not intrude upon the rights of patentees in this line." Moreover, North also confided privately that "he intended to advance the art a long way beyond Mr. Hollerith's mechanisms."

On whom would North rely for this important work? The director's second step in developing an "independent" system was to staff the new Census Machine Shop located in the Bureau of Standards. The names of the new employees had a familiar ring, as Robert Holley, working in the shop as a skilled laborer, confirmed.

One of [the Census Bureau's] first acts . . . was to secure the services of Charles W. Spicer, a former employee of Mr. Hollerith for 12 years during part of which he was foreman of the Hollerith concern. Mr. Spicer thereupon secured the services of Mr. Eugene M. LaBoiteaux and O. Lewis Cleven, both former employees of Mr. Hollerith's to assist him in establishing the mechanical laboratory and in carrying out its purpose.

If, in the past, Hollerith had appeared to suffer from a near obsession with threats that seemed more real to him than to his associates, his fears in this instance turned out to be solidly rooted in fact. His former employees not only knew every detail of the old "hand" machines, they were also closely informed of the improvements that their former employer was developing for his new line of commercial machines. LaBoiteaux had left Hollerith less than a month before. Hurt and angered, Hollerith wrote to his old friend George Swain of "North's retaliation on me." In his letter he cited the Census official's boast that, with the new system, the next Census could be compiled with great rapidity and a more economical basis of cost. Then Hollerith brought up the hiring of his former employees. "I think it is a perfect outrage," he concluded, "to use the Bureau of Standards for this purpose."

Besides having to worry about his former employees helping the government, Hollerith soon learned about a still more ominous threat. The Census mechanics would be required, as is traditional, to make their inventions available for government use. However, in a change of policy, they would be granted exclusive patents to exploit the same inventions against private citizens—an unusual arrangement then and now. While North was taking the surest and quickest route toward developing an "independent" system by hiring Hollerith's former employees, it also appeared that he was underwriting his rival's future commercial competition—at government expense!

Something had to be done. For the issues, by early 1906, could no longer be viewed in purely personal terms. Should the government be able to enter the field of invention against an individual? If so, why should it single out tabulating machines? Why not steam locomotives? Steelmaking? Or generating electric power? Should the government have the right to threaten patents awarded by itself under the Constitution? Hollerith huddled with his lawyer. And in phrases that bear a juridical imprint, he wrote:

Protection of inventors is the settled policy of all civilized countries. . . . It is part of the delegated power conferred by the Constitution upon the Federal Government. The grant thereof exercised under wise patent laws is not a bounty.

The benefits which inventive genius has conferred upon this country cannot be . . . tabulated in mere figures. It is the basis of our commercial greatness.

The first notes for an impending legal battle were being struck. But Hollerith had not yet exhausted his other remedies. On February 27, 1906, he wrote to Lucius N. Littauer, the wealthy Gloversville, New York, glove manufacturer, who headed the powerful House Appropriations Committee, in an effort to choke off funds for the government's experiments. In the letter, he renewed his company's offer to sell all of its patents to the government for all government uses for $200,000—forestalling the need for further experiments to develop an "independent" system. The Tabulating Machine Company, he suggested, could be paid at $40,000 a year, the same amount requested by North. There would be no need, he pointed out, to increase the appropriation.

Friends and associates were also asked to write to members of the House Committee. Roebling dwelt on the propriety of the government's hiring Hollerith's former employees. Resulting improvements would injure Hollerith, he pointed out, not only in government work, but also

in respect of the large commercial field to which his existing invention and patented approvements clearly apply. . . . if the government undertakes to furnish its own machines with the aid of assistants formerly in Mr. Hollerith's employ, it would thus seem that it was not only entering unjustly into the field of invention, but doing so under circumstances which do not savor of high propriety.

The words, from a member of a family preeminent in the worlds of engineering and manufacturing, should have carried considerable weight. In addition, Hollerith's friend George Fillmore Swain—chairman of M.I.T.'s Department of Civil Engineering, consulting engineer to the Massachusetts Railroad Commissioners, and member of the Boston Transit Commission—appealed to his fellow Bay Stater John Sullivan, another member of the Committee:

I have known Mr. Hollerith for nearly 30 years. He was an instructor at this Institute for a short time and lived in the same house with me at the time he invented this machine, and we worked together on the Tenth Census. His invention has saved the Government hundreds of thousands of dollars besides enabling it to do much more that could not have been done without it on account of expense.

Swain called his friend an honest and reasonable man who had not become rich through his invention. He was ready, Swain added, to make a reasonable arrangement with the government, and the government "should not interfere with the business developed by an honest man as his life's work." Similar letters followed, and Hollerith's attorney appeared before the House Committee—as did North. Hollerith waited. On March 17, Swain heard from Sullivan. "I voted for the item," the Congressman wrote, "because the hearings indicated that there was sufficient ground for its inclusion." The Committee had included the appropriation in the Legislative, Executive, and Judicial Bill, ensuring continuance of the experiments.

North had won. He had gotten the money to continue his experiments. Hollerith, he had told the committee, "has received from the government the fullest protection under patents already expired . . . [and] broad claims, introduced into later patents in the hope of extending the original monopoly, cannot be permitted to defeat a fundamental purpose of the patent law, to limit . . . monopoly to 17 years."

Perhaps more persuasive than legal or technical arguments was the changing public mood, which North had read correctly. Rich and powerful business interests had had their way for too long. Railroad men, steel barons, bankers, sugar kings literally ran the country. And they did so with little regard for the ordinary citizen. If Hollerith was not among them—his Tabulating Machine Company was in fact dwarfed by other enterprises of the day—he was, nevertheless, profiting from their support. Profiting handsomely, according to North. The government had paid the company nearly three-quarters of a million dollars over two censuses, North had pointed out, a sum seven times greater than its capital stock: "Meanwhile, the company has received and is receiving great sums from commercial corporations for the use of its mechanisms. It is rare that any inventor is so richly rewarded for his labor and ingenuity."

In early 1906, Hollerith had barely gotten a toehold with commercial customers. But North's argument fit the temper of the times. The Census Office, the *Washington Times* informed its readers,

proposes . . . simpler, cheaper and more expeditious machines than any yet devised, which the Government can build and operate for about 10 percent of the sum it must otherwise pay in royalties. . . . The appropriations committees of Congress are greatly pleased with what they see in the new scheme. It accords also with President Roosevelt's idea of how public business should be transacted.

To Hollerith, the world was turned upside down. Row your own boat, he had been told by his father many years before. He had taken the advice to heart—he had worked incredibly hard in pushing his ideas, taken little from others, and been scrupulously honest and aboveboard in his dealings in a period when business morality was next to nonexistent. Now he felt unable to fight back against malicious and unfair statements. "Assume for the present," he wrote to Swain "that I am a fool and that North is the most virtuous and honorable gentleman that ever was, and let it go at that. I am evidently beaten."

He gave up on pursuing the matter in the Senate, even though Senator Orville Platt of Connecticut, had promised to present his case. Swain believed he might also win over Senators Crane and Lodge. But in Hollerith's view it was little use.

The best thing to do is . . . to forget that the Census Office ever existed, and wait until . . . the next census comes around. I believe I have a number of valid patents of later forms of tabulating machines, especially of the automatic machines for compiling population statistics . . .

When the next Census came around, Hollerith believed, North would pay for the trouble he had caused—with interest. There was no way that the director could get along without his machines.

Throughout it all, the level-headed Thayer remained unruffled. Reading in the *Washington Times* how the government would revolutionize census taking by supplying its 10,000 enumerators with a punch, instead of a pen, to prepunch cards, the affable vice president of Western Electric assured his friend: "If this represents all that has been accomplished by North, I do not believe it is worthwhile for us to lose any sleep. Anyway, this seems to be more in opposition to the fountain pen than it is to the tabulating machine."

But Hollerith was incapable of laughing away his troubles. It has been written that Charles Babbage spoke "as if he hated mankind in general, Englishmen in particular and the English Government most of all." Hollerith would be similarly embittered. Many years later, the inventor complained to Swain about his experience with the government, to which the latter replied: "I . . . fully appreciate what you say about government work. It is, I am sure, most unsatisfactory. . . . Your own experience, however, I think has been somewhat exceptional in that it had a personal character not often present."

20

Enter Mr. Powers

*"The aid of a man of Mr. Powers' remarkable
inventive gifts . . . will be invaluable."*

In the spring of 1906, Hollerith's friend and business associate
Harry Bates Thayer had reassuringly poked fun at the government's efforts to develop its own tabulating system. "I do not
believe it is worthwhile for us to lose any sleep," he had told the
inventor. But within a year, Hollerith had new cause for worry.
In March 1907, Census Director North had moved the bureau's
Machine Shop, set up two years before at the Bureau of Standards,
to more spacious quarters in the Census Bureau itself. The shop
had been enlarged, North proudly reported. Construction and
equipment had cost $17,483, a considerable sum: "it is one of the
most complete shops of its kind in the country and admirably
adapted not only for experimental work, but for the construction,
testing and repairing of the tabulating machines."

As if to underscore the importance of the move, the Census
head placed a new man in charge of the operation. His choice was
both curious and unsettling—the same Harry H. Allen who, two
years before, had been transferred from the Patent Office to give
advice on Hollerith's patents. Rather than scour the country for
an outstanding engineer to fashion the government's new "independent system" of tabulation, North had selected the man most
knowledgeable in Hollerith's advances—and how to get around
them.

The work force itself was also enlarged. The newest recruit,
one Askel Hensen, had gone to work for Hollerith only three
years before. A mechanic and electrician, he had resigned from

the Tabulating Machine Company on March 29, 1907, a few weeks after the new laboratory had been established, to join the Westinghouse Electrical & Manufacturing Company of Pittsburgh, Pennsylvania. But finding "the climate of Pittsburgh was injurious to my health," he had returned to Washington within five months. Robert Holley, who worked in the laboratory, comments:

This indirect method of securing . . . another employee of Mr. Hollerith was all pre-arranged. Its purpose was to preclude Mr. Hollerith from accusing the Office of enticing another one of his employees. . . . In later years, several other employees of Mr. Hollerith were employed in the laboratory.

What had made Hollerith's employees defect with such seeming readiness? Evidence is scanty and one can only guess. Working for the temperamental inventor, a demanding perfectionist, could certainly have been no sleighride. Then, too, there was no place else, in the year 1907, where one could apply a special knowledge of tabulating machines. Comments made several years later during Hollerith's suit against the government shed only partial light. "I did not think there was much chance for advancement," said Hensen when asked why he had resigned. And to the same question, Eugene LaBoiteaux would reply, "I could no longer stand the methods and manner of Mr. Hollerith."

Be that as it may, by the spring of 1907 developments at the new shop in the main Census Building at B Street between 1st and 2d were emerging from the purely experimental stage. Part of the thrust came from North's determination to rid the Bureau of dependence on Hollerith. But technology also received a boost from the country's new vision of itself as a force in the world. A few statesmen—William Jennings Bryan for one—questioned the rectitude of meddling in the affairs of peoples living thousands of miles from U.S. shores. No one, however, doubted the wisdom of counting the natives of other lands once they came under the civilizing sway of the United States. Just as Hollerith had seized on the Philippine Census a few years before to further prove out his automatic machines—he had taken it under a special arrangement with the War Department—so North took advantage of the Cuban Census. Roosevelt's dispatch of Secretary of War William

Howard Taft to set up a provisional government on that island gave North an opportunity to take stock of the government's new system of tabulation. He reported:

The Cuban Census has . . . permitted a thorough testing of several of the new designs of tabulating apparatus invented in the Office for the Thirteenth Census. The results have exceeded my most sanguine expectations. Notwithstanding the fact that the machines had to be hurriedly constructed to meet a contingency unforeseen, and that at the start many mechanical difficulties, impossible to foresee, had to be overcome, the machines did their work perfectly, and indicated beyond question that that they are adapted to handle the great work of a decennial enumeration more quickly, more economically, and more satisfactorily than any mechanisms heretofore employed for this purpose.

Imperialism could aid in the launching of tabulating machines as well as dreadnoughts.

The first new machine to emerge was called the semiautomatic tabulator. While the machine, which was fed by hand, could not compete with Hollerith's hopper-fed automatic—in which a stack of 500 to 600 hundred cards were sent flying past sensing brushes at 150 cards per minute—even slight improvements, when aimed at ease of use, might result in large gains in productivity. In fact, the government's first such innovation, a button, gave its semiautomatic not only its name but also a distinct edge over Hollerith's old "hand" machine invented some twenty years before. Rather than pull down the circuit-closing press of the semiautomatic by hand, the operator simply touched a button that connected the movable portion of the press to a drive mechanism. The force of a small motor brought the press down automatically upon the card, saving elbow-bending effort by the operator, often a female employee.

More important was a second feature added to later models. It was a printing device that Hollerith did not offer on any of his machines. In place of the familiar clock dial counters of his "hand" machines, the government mechanics installed printing counters similar to those on a stock ticker. Instead of being read from the dials and manually recorded, the results of a tabulation were printed on rolls of two-inch-wide paper pressed against the type by hammers. The main advantage: the printers made it unnecessary to stop the tabulator while the operator laboriously copied forty to sixty numbers from the dial counters. Also, the printing counters could be set back to zero by a single lever in place of resetting each of numerous dials.

Why hadn't Hollerith installed a printer on any of his tabulators when electric printers, such as the telegraph printer, had been well known since he was a student in engineering school? Was the omission a simple oversight? Perhaps. Yet, it is difficult to believe that the otherwise farsighted inventor had not previously considered the utility of a printer, especially for the heavy volumes of figures turned out in commercial accounting. Could it be that this compulsive Germanic figure, so demanding on others, harbored an illogical lazy streak within himself?

Hollerith had indeed seen the need for a printer many years before and, in fact, had conceived a practical design for one. But as with the development of his automatic sorter—also an essential element of punched card data processing systems—he simply had not bothered to follow through until after he had allowed a crisis to arise. It was almost as if he was waiting for the world to tell him how much it needed his talents, so that he could impress it by pulling the invention out of a hat. On January 4, 1899, he had written to his patent attorney:

I have for many years considered the future tabulating machine to be one in which the counters were arranged with numbered wheels, very small and close together, the wheels being provided with raised numbers or type. These counters to be placed in rows, side by side, so that when the cards for a given district are passed through the machine, an impression is taken from all those counters. In other words, the result is printed direct on a sheet, without the intermediate reading and setting down of numbers by a clerk.

Some years ago, I built a small counter, bringing the face of it within about one inch by three quarters. It would show that a small counter could be built for this purpose. We simply had plain wheels on this counter, and no type, but the intention was to represent a counter with type wheels.

This counter, unfortunately, got lost in the Western Electric Company's moving, and I cannot lay hands on it, although many people saw it. I could, if necessary, prove its existence in that way. It occurs to me, however, that if the combination of a tabulating machine with counters provided with a type wheel and a printing attachment for printing such a record is proper subject matter for a patent, perhaps we ought to proceed with an application covering this broadly. Please give me your advice in this matter.

Hollerith enclosed in the letter a detailed sketch showing print wheels in combination with an ink ribbon, paper, and an impression roller—all linked to a tabulating machine. But he apparently never received a patent. His oversight, or that of his attorney, helped the government beat him to an important innovation. Years later, after he had sold his company, the oversight would cause severe competitive problems for IBM when it was competing with another firm that offered printing tabulators.

During its first two years, developments that came out of the Census Machine Shop may have largely reflected Hollerith's own plans, since the shop was staffed by his former employees. However, July 19, 1907, marked a clean break with the past. On that day, the shop's mechanics shook hands with a new expert, who had no previous association with Hollerith. Little is known about him. No photographs have been found to show what he looked like. Yet in a few short years James Powers would leave a deep imprint and then just as suddenly disappear, proving even more of an enigma to future students of the industry than Hollerith himself. Adding to the mystery is that his name would often be confused with that of Le Grand Powers, chief of the Agriculture Division of the Censuses of 1900 and 1910 although James Powers, the inventor, had had no previous connection with census work.

The barebones facts show that James Powers was born in Odessa, Russia, on February 12, 1871, making him eleven years younger than Hollerith. He displayed mechanical talents early, graduating from the Technical School of Odessa, before emigrating to the United States at the age of 18. For a time, he worker in a mechanical shop connected with the University of Odessa, where he helped fashion scientific instruments for the university's physical laboratory. It was exacting work, the kind not often entrusted to a young man still in his teens.

On coming to America, Powers settled in Brooklyn and worked in the New York area for such well-known firms as the Carrin Machine Company, Western Electric, and Bergman's Electrical Works. At the last-named firm, he had charge of some eight-five different automatic machines. He displayed a growing talent for innovation, as his letter of application to the Census Bureau reveals. He had helped perfect a letter-registering machine, cash registers, typewriters, and adding machines, taking out a number of patents for diverse and somewhat fanciful inventions—among them, an automatic toothpick-cutting machine, a glass breadbox, and a coin-operated photographic machine. It is uncertain how much Powers benefited from his efforts, since the rights to his inventions were often assigned to others.

His approach to machine design contrasts with that of Hollerith. It would later be said that where Hollerith employed more sophisticated electric technology, Powers would come up with a simple mechanical solution for the same problem. Whatever the range of his talents, the Census Bureau eagerly sought them out.

When Powers balked at an initial salary offer of $1,200 a year, the Bureau upped the ante to $1,400, which he accepted. Although officially hired on May 25, he was allotted a generous two-month hiatus to dispose of a partnership in a small experimental shop in Los Angeles where he was working at the time.

Like Hollerith, Powers shunned the role of "hired hand," remaining on the government payroll for only a brief period. During this time, he made sure that articles appearing on his new devices for the Census also mentioned their commercial utility. He appeared to be sure of his talents and of his ability to convince others of them. Citing some difficult unsolved problems in connection with the invention of the sorting machine, North informed his superiors that he had found the man who could solve them: "The aid of a man of Mr. Powers' remarkable inventive gifts, especially in lines of closely-related machinery, will be invaluable, and his employment will be in the interests of economy by expediting the work."

Although Powers was hired primarily to work on the sorter, the Russian-born inventor's more immediate claim to fame was a mammoth and radically different punch for preparing data. It resembled a huge typewriter—so large that when seated behind it, the operator was almost obliterated from view. The *Scientific American* wasted no time in sizing up the monstrous machine.

The new machine is built on the plan of a typewriter with 240 keys. The operator, instead of punching one hole at a time, presses as many keys as may be necessary. After all the facts have been thus recorded . . . a bar resembling . . . a space bar on a typewriter is pressed, which brings an electric motor into play, whereupon all the holes are punched at once without any effort . . .

In concept, Powers's punch was superior to both Hollerith's early pantograph punch, which continued to be used for census work, and to his later commercial key punch, developed for railroad work and employed in the previous Agriculture Census. Its greatest benefit was protection against punching errors by the operator, as the magazine also noted.

In the old punching machine, a hole was punched in a card every time a key was depressed. If an error was made, the card had to be thrown away. . . . In the new machine, each key is depressed independently . . . and can be released at will without punching a hole . . . until the operator is ready to press the motor bar which punches all the holes at once.

As he had with the earlier Pidgin machines, Hollerith took the birth of a rival's device as a personal affront. Especially galling to him was the electrified key mechanism. The addition of any such frills, he contended, could only cause needless problems. In 1914, when Hollerith finally got around to electrifying the operation of his earlier key punch, he launched a humorous defense of his earlier manual device in a mock patent application.

The punch shown in my patent No. 682,197 is capable of being operated by persons in commercial establishments with little or no difficulty, the keys requiring about one-tenth the pressure employed for operating type-writing machines and one-fifth that demanded in playing pianos. Nevertheless, not being wholly self-operating, they have not been favorably regarded by those occupying sinecures under the United States Government, and in consequence complaint has been made that the manipulation of the punches, coupled with late hours, has produced a large crop of nerves. Of course, I could provide for operating the punches pneumatically, that is, with hot air, but this would seriously interfere with conversations while working. Then again, I might resort to mental suggestion, but, in this, conflict might arise because of the absence of mentality. Therefore I have fallen back upon electricity which is not automatic, in that it will not work by itself of its own free will, but with the expenditure of one-one hundreth the pressure heretofore required, it is hoped to spare the nerves epidermis of the fair manipulators, if any.

Scornful or not, Hollerith would continue to respond to the creative proddings of his first serious rival. The little-known Powers, had supplied the missing stimulus of competition. And each man would try to outdo the other over ensuing years, bringing dynamism to a young industry. In the meanwhile, Powers's efforts were such that they apparently soon exceeded the resources of the new Census Machine Shop. Within six months of joining the Bureau, he moved his experiments to 15 Murray Street, New York City, to the laboratory of Francis H. Richards which "specialized in making models, patterns and machines." Powers's large expenditures for labor—$15,319 for the punch alone—suggest that additional skilled assistants were hired to help perfect his designs. Richards may also have supplied capital to develop the commercial potential of the devices. It is significant that his name appears with that of Powers on a number of patents granted Powers after he left the Bureau.

In New York, work progressed at a rapid pace; within eleven months, a working model of the Powers punch had been installed in the Bureau. By February 25, 1909, R. L. Laffin, chief of division, could report the results of a trial covering eighty-three working days. "There can be no doubt," he assured the director, "as to the possibility of punching twice as many cards on the Powers electric punching machines as on the old Hollerith." As if to add insult to injury, chief expert Allen would add:

We have found that the Powers punch is capable of doing substantially three times the daily work that could be done on the old style Hollerith pantograph punch. Not only this, but the Powers punch does infinitely better work . . . than could be done on either the Hollerith pantograph punch or what is known as the Hollerith commercial punch.

North was elated—so much so that he had already reported by the close of 1908, two months before the conclusion of the test, that plans were practically complete for the machinery to tabulate the next population Census. "The new mechanisms invented," he proclaimed, "are novel in plan and design, are of greater speed and efficiency than those they supercede, and can be built and operated at a large saving of money."

What was more, the director asserted that savings in the hiring of clerks, due to the greater efficiencies of the new machines, meant that the Thirteenth Census could be done for less money than the previous two censuses.

For the past two and a half years, Hollerith and his business associates had found themselves very much in the dark. Despite the government's glowing progress reports on the development of its own system, they found it almost impossible to assess the real nature and extent of the threat to their business. Was the Census director actually infringing Hollerith's patents? In reporting to Congress on the successful use of the semiautomatic, North also told of some progress "on various other machines automatic in their character." On the other hand, he had spoken of making some inventions and throwing them away, because there was some question as to whether they invaded Hollerith's broader patents for automatic machines.

The question of commencing suit against the director of the Census Office for infringing the company's patents had been discussed at length at an executive committee meeting of the Tabulating Machines Company's board a year earlier. But first, the officers had to have a clearer notion of what was actually taking place. On December 2, 1907, they had, in fact, authorized the general manager, at his discretion, "to employ detectives to ascertain the facts in regard to the infringing." Nine days later, the question was raised again and a decision reached: "in view of the uncertainty as to exactly what the director is doing, the expense of a suit, the condition of the company's funds, and the fact that any remedy open to us is totally inadequate, it was decided to take no present action."

Hollerith faced an extraordinary dilemma. Even if he had been able to walk into the Census Machine shop in broad daylight and inspect the vaunted new mechanisms at first hand, he probably could not have done anything about it. In 1907, the laws of the land contained no provision under which an inventor could sue the government for patent infringement—unless he had a prior written contract with the government. In other words, even if Hollerith could prove that North was stealing him blind, he could not legally prevent him from doing so. Not only was Hollerith forced to stand helplessly by while his former employees were trying to put him out of business. On top of that, the government was sponsoring the entrepreneurial efforts of an ambitious new competitor, perhaps equal in ability to Hollerith himself, in the person of James Powers.

The law had to be changed. But could it be?

21

The Growing Impasse

If North had lost, had Hollerith won?

Surprisingly, Hollerith found strong and immediate Congressional support for strengthening the laws protecting inventors. John Dalzell, a ranking member of the House Rules Committee, sponsored a bill providing that whenever a U.S. patent had been used by the United States without a license, its owner could recover reasonable compensation in the U.S. Court of Claims, the traditional forum for claims against the government.

In the Senate, a companion measure rode on the shoulders of Philander Chase Knox, who had already gained national prominence by turning down the post of Attorney General, offered by McKinley in 1900, because he was too busy assembling the giant Carnegie Steel Company. However, he promptly accepted the post when it was reoffered the following year. And in a reversal of roles, the attorney had gone to the Supreme Court to halt James J. Hill, J. P. Morgan, and their associates from gaining control of railroads covering the entire Northwest through a holding company. "The success of the Northern Securities case," President Theodore Roosevelt would later recall, "definitely established the power of the government to deal with all great corporations." It would also give Roosevelt a reputation for "trust busting."

In championing the individual inventor, Knox was once again striking out at the large and impersonal forces that now seemingly threatened the well-being of the citizen. Only instead of the faceless corporation, the target this time was government itself. But it was left to Congressman Dalzell to sum up best the intent of the new legislation.

The United States Government issues patents, and it insures to every patentee the exclusive right to use his invention. The Supreme Court . . . says, also, that it is within the constitutional provision that protects property from appropriation without compensation, and yet, in the very same sentence, it says that the patentee can not protect his property, because there exists no court into which he can go.

After pointing out that the Court of Claims should have such jurisdiction, Congressman Dalzell concluded:

Every civilized government . . . with the exception of Russia and the United States, has provided a tribunal where a patentee and his government may settle . . . their respective rights . . . the right of the patentee against the government for the appropriation of his patent.

The bill passed the House on May 12 and sailed through the Senate three days later. Soon after, Patent Commissioner Edward Moore gave it his unqualified backing. The imminent passage of the law was heartening news to Hollerith. Although he and his fellow officers of the Tabulating Machine Company had no immediate plans to bring suit, since it was unclear whether Hollerith's patents had been infringed, the new law would greatly strengthen their bargaining position. But if the inventor and his associates celebrated the action of Congress, their self-congratulations were premature.

Roosevelt failed to sign the measure, which had been passed in the closing days of the session, possibly because the Justice Department questioned whether the Court of Claims would be the proper tribunal for the settlement of such disputes. In so doing, he killed the legislation. Now Hollerith resumed his letter writing campaign to the President. "The Census Office has completed the investigation of marriage and divorce," he wrote on December 11, 1908. "This is the investigation which Mr. North assured you in 1905 was to be 'illuminated' by the results of inquiry concerning children born and living. It now transpires, however, that that illumination is not to be granted."

North had broken his promise. There would be no illuminating portrait of the American family, as Roosevelt had agreed there should be. But the President, now a lame duck, turned a deaf ear to the querulous complaint. Hollerith had failed in his indirect strategy of getting his machines back in the Bureau by creating conditions that demanded their use. Instead, he met with his attorney and, in a document that amounts virtually to a legal brief, summed up all of his complaints against the government. This time, he was appealing to the President's sense of justice and fair play and, incidentally, laying the groundwork for possible legal action. In the letter, dated January 9, 1909, Hollerith:

—pointed to inaccuracies in North's report on operations for 1907–8 implying that his machines were relatively inefficient and extravagantly costly in use;

—complained of the new policy permitting Census employees to acquire patents in their own names to make use of as they pleased after their use by the government. "Applications for such patents," Hollerith wrote, "are believed to be pending and it is, therefore, reasonable to presume that these mechanisms will ultimately enter into rivalry for private business";

—cited the hiring away of employees who "held confidential relations with me" and "were largely informed concerning my plans and ideas concerning further experiments and development . . ."

Finally, noting that North had made inaccurate statements to the press, Hollerith reproached the Census head.

It is highly improper . . . that the authority of high position . . . shall be utilized to support and disseminate . . . statements . . . intended to injure the business of the company in the field of private industry and to support the pretensions of owners of rival patents whose experimental work has been conducted at the expense of the United States Government.

Having appealed to the President's "sense of justice," the inventor asked for "prompt and adequate redress." The letter was turned over to Secretary of Commerce and Labor Oscar S. Straus for reply. Straus, a lawyer, former minister to Turkey, and a member of the noted New York merchant family, who was also North's superior, essentially denied every charge that Hollerith had made. The Census director, he responded, had scrupulously respected Hollerith's personal and patent rights; his main purpose was "to serve the interests of the government and to reduce the cost of Census tabulation." Whatever the merits of the appeal, Straus slammed the door firmly shut on Hollerith's hopes.

Roosevelt's role, if any, in the dispute is unknown. In all likelihood, absorbed in other matters, he paid little notice to the letter, if he was aware of it at all. But Hollerith's reaction to what he considered a rebuff by the President was highly personal. He was raised on the notion that success was the reward for energy, frugality, and perseverence. He especially believed in fair play. If you went by the rules, justice would be done. The manipulations of the railway barons, meat packers, and Wall Street financiers that were rapidly bringing all business into disrepute were completely foreign to this somewhat eccentric loner, who insisted that small as well as large customers benefit equally from his machines. Now, the man who espoused a "Square Deal" for every citizen had suddenly and unfairly thrown up an insuperable barrier in his path. And something inside Hollerith gave way.

It was said of Teddy Roosevelt that one of the things that most rankled those who did not like him was that they could not get rid of him, even in the inmost recesses of their minds. So it was with Hollerith. The inventor's hatred of the President became almost pathological. One day, he read a newspaper account about the President's riding in Rock Creek Park on Thanksgiving Day. A group of young women from the National Cathedral School, which Hollerith's daughters attended, galloped past the President in an apparent breach of etiquette. Spurring his horse, the President overtook the young ladies and, in so doing, reportedly struck the flank of one of their horses with his riding whip. The horse reared, nearly throwing its rider. Hollerith clipped dozens of copies of the article and passed them out to his friends. But there was no way he could really get back at the man who had thwarted him or shake Roosevelt's grinning, toothy visage from his thoughts. Especially galling was that Hollerith, with his bristling gray hair, steel-rimmed glasses, and outwardly bellicose manner, was sometimes mistaken for his latest nemesis.

Years after Roosevelt was out of office, Hollerith was still eager to settle the score. In reply to a letter to his lawyer, which has been lost, the inventor received the following letter dated November 23, 1921.

The letter which I wrote to President Roosevelt is so long that I feel pretty sure the *Sun* would not print it. There is no reason, however, why I should not send them a copy. I shall be glad to have my file of correspondence with President Roosevelt . . . when I see you. We will discuss . . . what, if anything, it is desirable to do.

But in the spring of 1909, with the portly and affable William Howard Taft moving into the White House, Hollerith was far from ready to concede. He renewed his efforts to get the legislation that Roosevelt had killed through Congress. This time, he wrote to Wisconsin's Senator Robert LaFollette, chairman of the Senate Committee on the Census, asking that the Census Act be amended to give a patent owner the right to sue in the Court of Claims. He also urged that no patents be issued for work conducted at government expense. The Department of Agriculture, he pointed out, was among the executive departments that forbade their employees to take out patents—unless any citizen could use the patented article or process without royalties. Private enrichment was wrong for those under the comfortable shelter of the government's payroll.

If private inventors . . . are to be subjected to competition supported by . . . a great and rich government, mere patent rights will, in most cases, have little value and the encouragement . . . which the patent laws are intended to supply will be counteracted . . . by the threat of such competition.

Hollerith made a similar appeal a few days later to Congressman James A. Tawney, chairman of the House Appropriations Committee, and renewed his company's offer to make its proved machines available at bargain rates. In the meanwhile, Census Director North was having problems of his own.

With the Census less than a year away—its start had been moved up to April 15—the Census head had little time to contract for the machines required to process it. Yet the House appropriations bill that would release the funds to pay for them was tied up in committee; some thought the measure might not pass at all. In the meanwhile, North was spending heavily on parts and supplies for further experimental work when it was uncertain what machines would be built, how the machines to process the Census would be paid for, and whether they could be completed in time. Everything was at sixes and sevens.

To make matters worse for Hollerith's enemy, the change in administration brought a shift in command. On March 5, 1909, Charles Nagel, a dark and dapper lawyer, replaced Oscar Straus as Secretary of Commerce and Labor. Whereas Straus had supervised the Census Bureau with a loose rein, Nagel took a different view of his duties. The new Secretary felt responsible not only for the general operations of the Bureau but also for close control of its spending. Shortly after Nagel took office, his deputy dropped by at the Census, as the *Washington Post* related:

During a brief absence of Mr. Nagel . . . the assistant secretary . . . heard that Mr. North had made contracts for the manufacture of Government tabulating machines, and, as no authority had been given by the Secretary of Commerce and Labor, the assistant secretary asked Director North for an explanation . . .

Director North explained that he had made contracts with several firms for manufacturing parts of the proposed tabulating machines with the idea of having those parts assembled in Washington. The assistant secretary . . . maintained that Mr. North had no right to make any contracts except with the approval of the Secretary of Commerce and Labor. When Secretary Nagel returned . . ., he took the [same] view his assistant did . . . and ultimately brought the contention to the attention of President Taft.

A showdown was near. Never one to avoid a good fight, Hollerith leaped in. On April 30, he wrote to Nagel in an attempt to deepen the split.

There has been a great deal in the newspapers . . . to the effect that delays in the publication . . . of the past censuses were attributable to the fact that the Director was not endowed with sufficient . . . authority.

The truth known to everyone acquainted with census work . . . is that the vast saving in time that has been effected is attributable to the machinery invented by Mr. Hollerith, and it is also to this machine that those who make use of the census results are indebted for more detailed classification and the greater accuracy of the data supplied.

Hollerith was trying to catch the besieged census official off balance. In the meanwhile, a flanking move was under way to bring North's procurement methods to President Taft's attention. Here, the moving force was Frederick S. Blackall, president of Taft-Peirce, which made Hollerith's tabulators and sorters. Through a mutual friend, Dr. Henry C. Coe of New York City, Blackall obtained an introduction to the President. Mentioning that the head of Taft-Peirce was already known to Secretary of Commerce and Labor Nagel, Dr. Coe wrote, "I have no knowledge or interest in the matter about which Mr. Blackall desires to see you. But he is a strong, true man after your own heart on whose integrity and business ability you can thoroughly rely."

If the physician was unacquainted with the subject of Blackall's visit, Hollerith's attorney was more fully informed. On May 3, Samuel Metcalf wrote to the industrialist: "If the President has as high an opinion of Dr. Coe's friends as I have of his surgical skill, he might feel like turning over to you the order for all the census machinery without even competition."

The situation is far from clear. Since Hollerith's company no longer owned Taft-Peirce, it appears unlikely that the inventor would have benefited directly from Blackall's procuring the Census business; it is also not known whether Blackall planned to furnish machines based on Hollerith's designs. However, what appears likely is that Hollerith, unable to land the business for himself, was helping a friend in an effort to forestall the government's development of its own machines. In the process, he saw another means of discrediting his arch enemy North. A letter from Blackall to Nagel, dated April 6, appears to support this view.

Learning that the Census Bureau had been conducting . . . experiments looking to the development of mechanisms designed to take the place of the Hollerith machines in the Census of 1910, I have several times during the past two years called at the office of Mr. North, . . . for the purpose of bidding upon the manufacture of such machines.

While most of his visits had been with the chief clerk of the Bureau, Blackall also saw Mr. North, who showed him an automatic punching machine belonging to the department. Blackall continues:

At that time, Mr. North assured me that when . . . the Bureau was ready for bids, my company would be afforded an opportunity to submit proposals on the same basis as other manufacturers . . .

A few weeks ago, I was informed that . . . "The Funding & Development Company," with an office at 40 Wall Street, New York City, had been awarded . . . a contract for 200 punching machines.

I went to New York and met a Mr. Elmer Sperry—said to be connected with the Funding & Development Co.—who delivered me a set of blue prints made from working drawings of the Punching Machine that Mr. North had shown me.

Mr. Sperry requested me to look the drawings over and to submit prices to his Company for lots of 200 and 500 machines, respectively. Mr. Sperry first stated that the contract had been awarded to "his people" but subsequently admitted that, while he and his associates were not actually in possession of the contract, they could get it, or, if they so preferred, could, as they had control of the patents, covering the machine, determine to whom the contract should be awarded.

It was a strange way of doing business, Blackall pointed out to Secretary Nagel. It seemed to him that the government would be better served without middlemen. What was more, he had been told that the Census Bureau had awarded, or was about to award, a contract for the punches on the basis of a fixed price per hour with no maximum price limit stipulated for completed machines. Such a procedure was highly unbusinesslike, he also pointed out.

Under such a contract, it is the experience of all manufacturers that, as the method of charging and payment presents no incentive to keep the cost of machines within reasonable or fixed limits, there is actually an inducement and opportunity for the contractor to make the cost of the machines as high as possible.

Blackall's letter evinced that North's methods, if not illegal, were at least highly wasteful of the taxpayers' money. The head of Taft-Peirce concluded: "there would seem to me no reason why proposals could not be solicited and an award made to the lowest responsible bidder best qualified to do the job." If Blackall had been pleading Hollerith's cause instead of his own, he couldn't have been doing a better job. In the meanwhile, he had also written to Assistant Secretary of Commerce Ormsby McHarg of the dangers of using untried equipment in the Thirteenth Census. Knowing nothing about the government's machines, he was "unable to venture an opinion as to whether the machines will function properly." But as someone who had manufactured almost every type of light machinery, he advised the official to proceed very carefully: "I would have to be shown before I could bring myself to approve the use of machines whose efficiency, capacity and durability superiority over other and well-known types have not as yet been fully demonstrated."

While these efforts were under way, Hollerith was somewhere behind the scenes fanning the flames, a matter that did not remain entirely unobserved. Picking up a dispatch from the *Boston Transcript*, the Waterbury, Connecticut, *American* observed, "There is a 'nigger in the woodpile' in the matter of the elimination of S. N. D. North as head of the Census." The former paper had commented that Hollerith's company was trying to push its machines upon the government while North was carrying out experiments to develop a comparatively inexpensive tabulating system. "On this account," said the *Transcript*, "it is charged that the Hollerith people have long been after North's scalp. If this is true, it should . . . be a strong reason with President Taft for going slow in the matter of North's removal." Hollerith's lawyer wrote to the *Transcript*, correcting facts in the article. He added, "Mr. Hollerith is a very clean, upright gentleman whose extraordinary genius has been very profitable to the Government and of much less benefit to himself than would probably have been the case had his efforts been expended in some other direction." The *Transcript* editor, R. L. O'Brien, replied somewhat contritely: "On the face of it, the purpose of the director to get along without paying royalty to a private concern would seem commendable, but nobody connected with the *Transcript* had any thought of doing any injustice to the gentleman you represent, whom I remember most pleasantly."

While the dispute swirled in the headlines, North battled for his survival. "Strong efforts to keep him in office have been made for several weeks, ever since it became known that he was under fire," reported the *Washington Star*. "North has a powerful backing in the Senate," the *Washington Times* added, "and the members of Congress went to the White House in droves to ask that he be retained." The Census head, it was reliably reported, even had the support of Vice President James Sherman, who, like himself, hailed from Utica, New York.

As the days went by, it was rumored that the fight between North and Nagel had been amicably settled. By May 26, the level of Washington gossip had more or less settled down to its normal level. So the announcement that day took the capital city by surprise. Unknown to the public, Secretary Nagel, a few days earlier, had put the matter squarely up to the President: either he or the Census head would have to leave.

"Director North Out," headlined the evening *Star* of May 26. "North Gives Up Place As Director of Census Today," affirmed the evening *Times* of the same day. After hearing both sides, the President had left the matter for Nagel to investigate and had followed the recommendation of his cabinet officer.

The following day, statements from the White House and the Census head appeared side by side in the morning papers. "Mr. North's resignation," said the President, "was based on the ground that, on account of conditions existing and likely to continue, his administration of the Census Office would not probably be successful." Commented North; "I am convinced that circumstances which now exist and which are apparently likely to continue render it difficult, if not impossible, for me to conduct the 13th Census of the United States."

By all accounts, North's departure was a dignified affair. Standing behind a desk covered with roses, the deposed official shook hands with each of the clerks as they filed through his office. Falling back on statistics, he said, "I really feel that ninety percent of the clerks were sorry to see me go . . ." Then, in a farewell address, he added: "Men may come and men may go, but great scientific movements like this one for the standardization of official statistics depend upon no one man. They are bound to advance for they are at the root of an advancing civilization." Far from skulking from public view, he would the following year assume the presidency of the prestigious American Statistical Association and later serve as assistant secretary of the Carnegie

Endowment for International Peace until 1921, when failing health would force his retirement.

However, in Hollerith's view, the sacked official had, at long last, received what any scoundrel deserves. As the head of the Census Bureau, North had been the personal cause of Hollerith's troubles for seven years. And the feud went back farther than that: to the Census of 1900 when North, as chief statistician for manufactures, had gratuitously championed the infamous "Pidgin Coops."

No sooner had North's removal been announced than Hollerith rounded up his friends for a victory celebration. The menu for the formal dinner, dated May 26, 1909, is embellished with head-lines cut out and carefully pasted on the cover: "Taft Forces Di-rector North Out," "North Resigns," "North Out," "North Quits as Census Chief," "North Loses." Ironically, Roosevelt, who might earlier have settled Hollerith's problems, was reported by the same issue of the *Star* as "resting from the hunt" in faraway Africa, where his slaughter of wild animals had prompted the Michigan Society of Humane Societies to withdraw a resolution thanking the former President for his protection of Michigan birds.

But if North had lost, had Hollerith won? "Mr. North's contention about the tabulating machines has, in a measure, been accepted by Secretary Nagel," the *Washington Post* of May 27 reported. Even if he had exceeded his authority, North had prevailed, for the plans for the government machines had immediately been submitted to Director Samuel Stratton of the Bureau of Standards, who approved the designs as feasible. Bids for the construction of the machines would be advertised at once. The only string attached, according to the *Star*, was that the bids "shall be rea-sonable, assuring the government the saving of money from the renting of the tabulating machines that have been in use for so many years." There seemed to be only a slight glimmer of hope for Hollerith and his company. "If the bids do not come up to expectation, the Secretary reserves the right to reject them and take other steps," the *Star* concluded.

If Hollerith had any chance to recoup, it would be through the ascension of North's successor, Edward Dana Durand, who appeared to be a reasonable man. The former deputy director of the Bureau of Corporations was, from all appearances, an executive of quiet competence and modesty. He was also equipped with a dry sense of humor. "I was," he said referring to his work at the Bureau of Corporations, "supposed to be an economic and statistical expert." Perhaps with a new and independent official in charge, it was not too late to change the government's position.

A chance meeting between a member of Hollerith's board and William Rossiter, chief clerk of the Bureau under North, seemed to offer some encouragement. Albert Salt reported to H. T. Newcomb, an attorney for Hollerith:

> He referred more than once to our friend Hollerith's inventions and told me that he did not see how the compilation of the next census could be accomplished economically and expeditiously without Hollerith's equipment, especially the sorting machine; and that the tabulating machine which had been devised by the Census Bureau was merely a modification of Hollerith's hand machine, which could not, of course, compete from any standpoint with the new automatics.

Rossiter disclosed that he had, in fact, prepared a draft of a contract that he believed would have met both North's and Hollerith's approval for substantial use of the inventor's machines. The letter from Salt to Newcomb was dated October 16. But unknown to the two men and to Hollerith, a contract had already been awarded on August 19 to the Sloan & Chace Manufacturing Company of Newark, New Jersey, for 300 Powers punches. Shortly after, the Bureau had contracted with the same company for 100 of the semiautomatic tabulators. It looked as if Hollerith was already out in the cold.

However, opinion within the Census Bureau was not quite unanimous. A surprising dissent from the effort to freeze out Hollerith came from Census Machine Shop chief expert Allen, the patent attorney hired by North to steer safely around the Hollerith patents. Although he had played a personal part in devising the semiautomatic tabulator, he was the first to admit that the unit was essentially the old Hollerith hand tabulator with a power-operated pin box added. Now he saw a still more serious flaw in the government's plans. There was little point in running cards rapidly through a tabulator, he informed his superiors, without a similar ability to sort them automatically. And in Allen's view, the new Powers sorter was too slow for the job.

The Powers sorter is a mechanical sorter strictly and cannot be compared in speed or compactness with an electric sorting machine. Its speed is entirely governed by the number of compartments used; . . . the further the compartment . . . from the feeding device, the slower the machine, for . . . a card must be fed out of the pile, submitted to the action of the controlling fingers, directed to its proper compartment and placed in that compartment, and the control fingers set back to their original position before another card may be fed forward for sorting.

It would, he concluded, take thirty Powers sorters to do the same work as ten of the latest Hollerith machines. Not only did the rival mechanical device operate at one-third the speed, there was another important consideration: "so far as I can discover . . . Mr. Hollerith was the first to automatically sort cards, one by one, to two or more compartments, with means controlled by the card for determining into which compartment said card should be deposited."

In the patent attorney's view, to build the Powers sorter at all, the Census Bureau would first have to obtain a license from Hollerith. There appeared to be only three courses open:

—repair the twenty old agricultural sorters purchased from Hollerith at the last Census to do population work—that is, to accept the larger cards used for population statistics;

—obtain a license from Hollerith to proceed in building the new Powers sorters; or,

—simply buy the latest sorters from the Tabulating Machine Company.

A practical man, who apparently was not caught up in the personal feud between Hollerith and the former Census head, Allen came out for the third course. If negotiations were opened with the Hollerith Company, he now proposed,

It might be well to endeavor to purchase outright their best type of sorting machine. . . . not over ten would be needed . . . and we could offer to pay as high as $4,000 for each . . . and . . . save money; by so doing, we would be relieved of . . . either repairing the agricultural type of machine, building the Powers type, or building a new type of sorting machine.

Allen's letter was written to Assistant Census Director William Willoughby on September 25. What happened over the following months was far from clear to Hollerith and his business associates. They could not be certain which machines the Census Bureau was actually building or planning to use or whether the Bureau had already infringed the Hollerith patents. The picture was clouded further by various newspaper accounts. While reporting that contracts had been let for 300 Powers punches and 100 semiautomatic tabulators, The *New York American* of November 21 observed. "the census experts are now at work on a tabulator designed to be wholly automatic in its action, which will feed cards from a magazine and receive them into another magazine."

The article seemed to imply that the government was pirating Hollerith's latest designs. The inventor was angered by another article, which appeared under the by-line of W. Osgood, an expert special agent of the Bureau. It boasted about the latest improvements in the government's machines; nowhere did it mention that Hollerith was the originator of tabulating machines. The inventor clipped it out and sent it to Durand demanding an explanation. Similarly, the *American Machinist* in its issue of May 5, 1910, described the goverment's new machines. "The tabulating machine," commented the publication, "is the result of the combined efforts of several experts employed by the Census Bureau." Not once in three lengthy pages was Hollerith's name mentioned. In describing the punching machine, it said, "Mr. Powers has been allowed United States letters patent, and is preparing to place the machine on the commercial market." As if to bait Hollerith further, the author added: "Mr. Powers is also the inventor of a tabulating and sorting machine which is wholly automatic and purely mechanical in operation. It differs from the Census machine in that it has a computing mechanism for commercial work." Not only might Hollerith never have lived, as far as the newspaper accounts were concerned; Census Bureau employees were exploiting their position with the government to promote the commercial possibilities of the rival devices. North might have been thrown out of office, but he was still accomplishing what he set out to do.

Trying to set matters straight, Hollerith's friend Gershom Smith took the *American Machinist* to task:

One could infer that before the machines which were manufactured for the government were installed, the compiling of census statistics had to be done in the old way, by hand. As a matter of fact, the credit for the invention of tabulating machines for this purpose is wholly due to Dr. Herman Hollerith. . . . practically the only thing new on the equipment referred to is the punch.

In the meanwhile, H. T. Newcomb, a former Census official and a friend of Hollerith's was trying to bridge the widening gap. He appealed directly to the Census director, who reported:

Mr. Newcomb suggests that . . . when the Census Bureau completes its automatic and sorting machines, the Secretary write to the Hollerith Company furnishing an accurate description of such machines, stating that the Government proposed to use them, and stating that if such machines were subject to the Hollerith patents, the Government would pay a reasonable compensation.

By late November, Hollerith had learned that the Census Bureau was altering his old agricultural sorters in order to fit them for population work. Although the government owned the machines, the changes it was making might or might not have infringed his patents. Less certain was whether the Bureau was invading Hollerith's patents by developing a true automatic tabulator. Only one thing was clear. No matter what types of tabulating machines were used in the forthcoming census, they would require sorters. "Each of these types of machines," chief expert Allen had pointed out, "needs a sorting apparatus of some type for them to properly perform their function." While the government could freely build the basic hand tabulator on which the patents had expired, there seemed to be no way it could use Hollerith's sorters without invading his rights.

What could Hollerith do? What legal remedies did he have if, indeed, he had any at all? Congress had still failed to amend the Census Act to give him the right to sue the government for damages. In fact, there was still doubt several months before the Census whether the act would pass at all. But Hollerith had learned of two court decisions that might support his cause. The Harris Automatic Press Company had barred the government from infringing the patents on an automatic press by means of an injunction. However, in that case, the company had obtained the ban against a rival supplier, the Potter Printing Press Company—not against the government itself.

More pertinent was a case brought by the giant Krupp armaments company of the German Empire against William Crozier, chief of ordnance of the United States Army. Here, the Army had admitted that it was making guns and gun carriages in violation of Krupp patents. But it also said that the Krupp company had no right to stop it, a claim that was supported by the lower court. Nevertheless, on October 7, 1908, the Court of Appeals of the District of Columbia reversed the lower court, deciding that the Krupp firm was entitled to an injunction. As Mr. Justice Robb ruled: "We cannot believe that in the eyes of the law it is any less obnoxious for an officer of the Government to appropriate property for the benefit of the Government . . . than it would be to appropriate it for his own personal use."

"Any less obnoxious." The words had a satisfying ring to Hollerith when he thought about the government stealing what was rightfully his. But practically speaking, although Hollerith had friends inside the Bureau, he had still had no exact idea what was taking place inside its machine shop. Was the Bureau merely "repairing" the old machines, which it had every right to do? Or was it making fundamental changes that would constitute a patent infringement?

On this question, Edward Durand appears to have been an eminently reasonable and fair-minded man. While he had every intention of readying the Bureau and its equipment for the processing of the forthcoming census, as his duties required, he had no intention of denying Hollerith's legal rights. The new Census director met with Hollerith's attorney, Samuel Metcalf, in late

November. Following Newcomb's suggestion, he agreed to permit inspection of the sorters to clarify the question of infringement.

On December 8, Metcalf returned to the Office with Frank N. Waterman, a Cornell-trained mechanical and electrical engineer often called upon to testify in court cases. The expert now compared one Hollerith sorter, which had been altered, with nineteen other machines apparently left in their original condition.

While the sorters that Hollerith had sold to the Bureau were capable of handling only the 5 5/8-inch-long cards that had been used in the Agriculture Census, Waterman found that the one machine had been "wholly rebuilt or reconstructed" to accommodate the population cards, which were an inch longer. Widening the machine to accept the larger cards, he concluded, required new shafts, new crosspieces, and wider separation between the card guides. To make such changes, Waterman determined that "it was necessary to dismantle and then reconstruct or rebuild the machine." The changes were not those that might be called for by ordinary wear. In fact, Waterman found that the machines showed little wear at all.

Without delay, Metcalf hurried the report to Frederick P. Fish of the Boston firm of Fish, Richardson, Herrick & Neave. The State Street lawyer, he wrote Durand, was without question "the recognized leader of the patent bar in this country." Were the reported changes in the sorter the kind that any owner of a machine could make, the Boston lawyer was asked, or were they so vital that they transformed the old machine into a new one?

Both sides were testing the legal waters. After years of acrimonious debate, Hollerith hoped that an opinion from an authoritative and respected source might result in a just resolution of the dispute before the Census swept down on the land. Frederick P. Fish met the issue head on. "The altered apparatus," he wrote, "clearly infringes many claims of the Hollerith reissued patent and, assuming that this patent is valid . . . as seems to be conceded by everyone, there arises no question of the validity or construction of the patent or of the infringement."

There it was. On the last day of the year, Metcalf wrote Durand of the receipt of the opinion, "which entirely confirms the opinion I expressed to you orally . . ." He enclosed a blueprint showing changes in the sorter, a statement of facts submitted to the Boston attorney, and the opinion itself. A number of legal opinions, including that in the Harris case, were forwarded as well. It was all very correct and cordial. Metcalf closed his letter by wishing the director the compliments of the season.

Durand was not impressed. By January 10, Hollerith received word that the Census Bureau would go ahead with the widening of the sorters and that Durand would confer with the Attorney General on the advisability of making further changes to speed up the operation of the machines. "The question now for the Tabulating Machine Company," Hollerith wrote to Metcalf, "is at once to decide whether or not we should go to the Court and ask for an injunction restraining the Director from making these changes in the sorting machines we sold them ten years ago." "If my opinion is desired in this matter," Hollerith added, "I would say that we should undoubtedly take steps at once to enjoin the Director from making these alterations." He went on to cite the Krupp and Harris cases as his reason for believing that an injunction might be secured.

The following day, Metcalf wrote to board member George M. Bond in Hartford, urging him to attend the Friday night meeting of the directors. "Thayer will be unable to attend because he is ill," Metcalf explained, "and I do not know whether Roebling will attend or not. Without them and without you," he continued, "there will be no quorum . . ." What was actually said at the meeting is unknown. But on January 14, 1910, the directors voted unanimously to authorize the general manager to commence suit, should Durand reconstruct the sorters. The decision appeared to be the most important that Hollerith's small group of associates had ever made. But, in fact, it had already been taken out of their hands. For the day before Durand had written, "I beg to inform you that I have given instructions to resume experiments with respect to the repair of the 20 automatic sorting machines which are owned by this Bureau and that I expect to direct the repair of all the machines as soon as these experiments are completed."

Thus began the incredible case of the *Tabulating Machine Company, plaintiff,* v. *Edward Dana Durand, defendant.* Incredible because the larger issue of the dispute—whether an inventor had recourse against the government—had dragged on since North became head of the Census some seven years before. Incredible because Hollerith had already fought the battle through Congress and to the White House. Incredible, especially, because one stubborn man and a handful of associates now fought to bring an arm of the United States Government to a halt less than three months before it was to fill its Constitutional duty of counting the citizens of the land. As Durand would later report to the Attorney General, the Bureau could not tabulate the population without electric tabulating machines and these, in turn, depended upon sorters to separate the cards into groups. The cost of doing the sorting by hand, the Census head later reported, might have reached half a million dollars, if it could have been done at all. Reliance on tabulating machines, only twenty years after they were introduced in the Census of 1890, made it impossible even to consider returning to the age-old way of doing things.

22

Tabulating Machine Company v. Durand

*"Unless this defendant be restrained, others will . . .
similarly disregard the rights of the complainant."*

Anyone rightly in command of his senses could not realistically
believe that one man, no matter how just his cause, could actually
prevent the U.S. Government from following the Constitutional
mandate of counting its citizens in the 1910 Census. But Washington residents picking up their newspapers on the evening of
January 24 of that year might at least have been given pause.
"Court Restrains Census Director," headlined the *Washington
Times*; "Temporary Injunction Prevents Durand Rebuilding Sorting Machines." Without the machines, census operations would
be crippled. It was far from certain that the job could be done at
all.

A quixotic cause? Perhaps. Yet that morning Hollerith's lawyers
had gotten Justice Job Barnard of the Supreme Court of the
District of Columbia to issue a temporary restraining order. The
judge had given Census Director Edward Durand four days to
show why a further injunction should not be granted until a trial
could be held. The case of *Tabulating Machine Company* v. *Durand*
was under way.

It was a peculiar sort of struggle—one certainly out of keeping
with the times. The least government, the fathers of the Republic
had long ago agreed, was the best safeguard of individual liberty.
But 134 years later, business combinations, unforeseen by the
early statesmen, had grown so large that many citizens believed

them to be more wealthy and powerful than government itself. Clearly, a strong and determined administration was essential to stem the flagrant abuses of business power that seemingly rose on every side. "President Taft Opens Trust-Busting Campaign," screamed the headlines the day after Hollerith filed his suit. With the Beef Trust already under fire and the Standard Oil and American Tobacco cases before the U.S. Supreme Court, the government was mounting a campaign unequaled since the Sherman Act was passed twenty years before. With public attention focused on bringing free-wheeling businessmen and their corporate combinations into line, the climate was hardly conducive to protecting the rights of an obscure businessman.

In its bill, Hollerith's company repeated the already familiar technical arguments. Changes to the altered sorter went well beyond repairs. Moreover, such alterations duplicated features that Hollerith had recently introduced in his commercial machines, violating his patents. One such pirated improvement consisted of redesigning the sorter's card-carrying mechanism to give it a continuous instead of an intermittent movement, thereby greatly increasing its speed. In a sworn statement, Hollerith would say: "The Company has made and leased a large number of sorting machines . . . in use by many of the largest industrial and railroad corporations of the country . . . and found to be almost indispensable in tabulating work of any magnitude." No one besides his company, the inventor added, had attempted to place such machines on the market. He demanded that the government be halted from altering the remaining nineteen sorters. ". . . unless this defendant be restrained," he concluded, "others will be led to similarly disregard the rights of the complainant."

For years, the Bureau had been scrutinizing Hollerith's patents in an effort to steer safely around them and presumably to be ready to defend itself against possible legal action. It therefore came as a surprise when the government on January 28 asked the court and was granted more than a month's delay. It would present its arguments on March 14—exactly a month and a day before the Census began.

The reasons for the legal maneuver soon became clear. Previously the government had freely admitted altering the single sorter to suit it for population work. With admirable open-mindedness, Durand had permitted inspection of the modified machine. Now the Bureau shifted its ground. The original sorters that Hollerith had delivered to the Bureau in the fall of 1902, it now contended, had been so crude and imperfect that repairs had been necessary to make them work at all. Hollerith, the government charged, had schemed to dump useless machines on the Census Bureau!

As might be expected, the new line of argument generated bitter and often conflicting testimony. LeGrand Powers, the man in charge of the Agriculture Census in 1900, had once called the machines "one of the finest pieces of mechanism I have had the pleasure of examining . . ." He had also said that they had more than paid for themselves. Now he asserted that the sorters had not been necessary at all. His earlier statement, he explained, had referred to tabulators, not sorting machines. Next on the stand was one-time Hollerith foreman Charles Spicer, who had accompanied the inventor to Italy. He now called the machines "mechanically faulty" and added that they made "a great racket." Edgar Nelson, an electrician who had been responsible for running wires for supplying electric current to the machines, recalled that cards were often crushed and mashed. "Many times," he said, "I saw baskets of cards which had been ruined in the sorting machines as we had used them in the 12th Census." However, another government witness, who had actually operated the sorters in the previous Census, unexpectedly came to their defense. Commented Vergne Potter: "They worked about as nearly perfect as was possible with any machinery requiring careful attention." The gist of the government's testimony was that it had already been necessary to make improvements in the machines to make them useful in the first place.

Replying to the charges, Hollerith pointed out that the government had never before complained about the sorters. ". . . no question as to the efficiency of the machines," he testified, "was at any time raised either before they were furnished to the Census Office or thereafter, up to the time of this litigation." Quite the opposite, in fact, was true, he contended. In its booklet *American Census Taking*, prepared for the Columbian Exposition, the Census Office had stated that tabulating machines, with adding attachments, were employed for the statistics of agriculture "in connection with which automatic electric sorters were also used to great advantage."

Despite differences with Hollerith, William R. Merriam, the head of the Bureau during the Twelfth Census and later president of the Tabulating Machine Company, said that the sorters were continuously used until completion of the census. ". . . at no time," he commented, "was any report made to him . . . that such machines were not rendering satisfactory service." Had such a report been made, he added, he "never would have authorized payment for such machines." Another Hollerith witness was William T. McCullough, auditor of freight accounts for the New York Central. He had leased several of the early sorters in 1902, several months after similar machines were installed at the Census Bureau. "These machines not only operated to our entire satisfaction," he said, "but they proved indispensable to our work and greatly aided us in the prompt and accurate compilation of our accounts." They were used continuously for several years, he commented, until Hollerith had developed the improved vertical sorting machine. "We installed the new machines in place of the old only because of their greater speed and not because of any dissatisfaction with the horizontal machine."

During the hearings, machines were brought into the courtroom, standing mute while opinions of mechanical experts, testimony of other witnesses, and arguments of counsel were offered over them. Less than a decade after their development, they were already becoming relics of the past. The continued progress of technology was oblivious to the legal goings-on.

When all was said and done, Justice Barnard summed up the arguments and rendered his opinion. Clearly, the government had the right to use the machines; there had never been any question about that. Moreover, the machines had not been patented at the time that Hollerith sold them to the government. But even if they were covered by the inventor's later patents, there had been no infringement. The judge then bore in on the finer points of patent law.

Widening of the feed mechanism, he ruled, did not destroy the identity of the devices, for the size of a machine is not covered by the patent. In addition, the substitution of mechanical devices to make the sorters work with greater facility also did not destroy their identity, since the new mechanisms did not contain anything new that was patentable. "The changes that have been made, or that are contemplated," Justice Barnard concluded, "do not in my judgment destroy the identity of the machines." The judge refused to impose a further injunction pending appeal.

That evening, the *Washington Star* announced the decision: "Court Rules Durand May Alter Machines." But the court's pronouncement mattered little in practical terms. It was March 15—seven weeks since the hearings had begun. The Census Machine Shop had already altered a second machine.

Hollerith had previously been authorized to appeal an adverse ruling. He had also been given free rein by his directors to bring suit for infringement against any supplier that the Census Bureau engaged to make machines that violated his patents. Despite the expected course of the litigation, he may have been totally unprepared for the decision that the Court of Appeals rendered on April 15. Exactly a month to the day after the lower court had acted, the higher court overturned its ruling. Its decision was based on the *Krupp* case, in which the German armsmaker had successfully barred the Army from making gun carriages based on its patents. Legally speaking, things were back where they began. But other events were already overtaking the decision the day it was handed down.

"A bright young census enumerator called at the White House, the *Washington Times* reported, "and asked to see 'the head of the household.'" Starting with the nation's first citizen, swarms of census takers were spreading throughout the land. The Thirteenth Decennial Census of the United States had begun, and soon the systems that Hollerith had pioneered would be required to compile the results. Although the Tabulating Machine Company's case was set down for trial, nothing, it appeared, could prevent the use of the modified sorters in the Census.

No records relating to the case of *Tabulating Machine Company v. Durand* are found covering events of the next two years. One source says that further hearings were held. If so, the Federal Records Depository at Suitland, Maryland, where otherwise complete records of the proceedings are stored, does not have them on file. Apparently, matters drifted along unresolved until May 23, 1912, when the case that Hollerith had brought against the government twenty-eight months before ended quietly by agreement of counsel on both sides.

The precipitating event took place on April 8. On that date, the U.S. Supreme Court reversed the decision of the Court of Appeals in the *Krupp* case and reinstated the decision of the Supreme Court of the District of Columbia. The government, the high tribunal ruled, had a license to take the Krupp patents under the right of eminent domain. Therefore the German company had no right to prevent their use through an injunction. The plaintiff's remedy, the court decreed, was to sue the government for damages in the Court of Claims.

As was so often the case throughout his life, Hollerith had proved to be his own worst enemy. The legislation that he had so assiduously fought to push through Congress—and that Roosevelt had killed by a pocket veto in 1908—had, on June 25, 1910, become the law of the land. And it was this legislation, providing an avenue of relief for inventors against the wrongful use of their patents by the government, that now proved pivotal in the Krupp case and his own. Because the Krupp case was in all respects similar, and thought to be controlling, Hollerith's remedy, he was told, was to sue "without prejudice" in the Court of Claims. From a strictly legal standpoint, the outcome had been a draw. It did not matter that Hollerith had filed his case *before* the legislation was passed. An injunction against the future wrongful use of patents by the government, the Supreme Court ruled, could not be allowed.

The decision, when it finally came, drew little notice. In a one-inch squib at the bottom of page 5, the *Washington Herald* noted, not entirely correctly, "Court Upholds Durand." The *Post* of the same day buried the item midway down page 12. Few people read the news—or cared, for public attention was directed elsewhere. Changing his mind, Teddy Roosevelt was battling in the primaries to oust Taft, the man he had handpicked to run for the presidency four years before. The friendship of years, the *Post* commented, was shattered by the bitterness of the political struggle. From faraway London, the *Daily Telegraph* called the campaign one of "personal vituperation which shocks the unaccustomed ears of Europe and is deprecated by all sober minds in America."

Although Hollerith had failed to prevent the government from wrongfully modifying his machines, the question has often been asked why he did not sue for damages in the Court of Claims. Over the years, researchers have tried to resolve the apparent mystery. Typical of later accounts is that made by Census Director Durand in his memoirs: "The case never came to trial. No damages were ever paid by myself or the bureau. I suppose the plaintiffs simply dropped the matter."

Actually, Hollerith never had any intention of going to the Court of Claims. On January 10, 1910—two weeks before filing suit against the government—he had written his attorney.

I sincerely hope that we will never be put to the necessity of going into the Court of Claims. . . . first, it will be . . . very difficult . . . for us to prove the extent of our damages. It will require a good deal of our attention and will probably demoralize us in the conduct of our regular business. This is due to the fact that the Census machines were special; they were built 10 years ago, and no one around here now knows anything about these machines.

Hollerith also pointed out that in view of the offers he had made at different times to sell and license the machines, damages would probably have been very restricted. "In order that my opinion in this matter might be of record," he continued,

if we cannot get an injunction restraining the Census Office from . . . rebuilding the sorting machines, and building automatic tabulating machines, then we had better stop the whole Census question, for . . . I do not believe we will ever get enough money from them to pay our legal expenses.

Perhaps Hollerith was not as quixotic as he seemed. His real objective in bringing the suit, he disclosed, was to put the Census director "in a position where he would be obliged to negotiate with us." In retrospect, this seemed a real possibility. His final reason for believing he might succeed appears to reflect his personal predilection more than anything else. "To take the census with the old hand machines," he concluded, "would disgrace the Office."

What had the bitter and protracted struggle accomplished? Was Hollerith, in part, compensated by the perverse satisfaction that the Census could not be effectively processed without his machines? Although four years before, North had boasted that plans were practically complete for the mechanisms to tabulate the next population census, and the job could be done for less than at the two previous censuses, the new devices, for the most part, fell down badly on the job.

Sloan & Chace had built 300 of the new Powers punches at a cost of $250 each. Late in arriving, the power-driven mechanisms, despite successful earlier tests, displayed a disconcerting tendency to jam in actual use. The advice given by William Blackall to President Taft to go slow in applying untried equipment had proved all too wise in practice. As a consequence, one-third of the punching during the Census was done on the old Hollerith keyboard punches first employed in the Census of 1890. Ten years later, the Powers punch, although superior to Hollerith's in concept, would be rejected entirely in favor of a modified version of Hollerith's commercial key punch. And the vintage keyboard punches, proving that more modern technology does not always prevail over simpler, more trustworthy designs, would continue to see active service through the Census of 1920.

The decision to hire Powers had been based on his promise to perfect a sorting machine. He did deliver one to Washington in the summer of 1909, some nine months before the Census began. However, it was never used. According to Director Allen of the Census Machine Shop, the Powers mechanical sorter was only two-thirds as fast as the modified Hollerith agriculture sorters that were actually employed and only one-third the speed of the Hollerith commercial sorters. Of more concern, Allen was convinced "without a doubt" that the Powers machine infringed a Hollerith patent taken out in 1901.

The Bureau had considerably more success with its 100 semi-automatic tabulators, also furnished by Sloan & Chace. They operated without apparent difficulty. The power-operated press and the printing counters of the semiautomatics may have offered substantial savings in labor over the Hollerith tabulators, which lacked these features. However, as Allen also pointed out, the devices were basically hand machines based on Hollerith's expired patents. As such, they lacked the highly productive automatic feed. "The Census Bureau," former Census official H. T. Newcomb pointed out, "was the only large establishment, public or private, in which the Hollerith method was in use, that did not have the benefit in time and money that have accompanied the substitution of the automatic for the manual feed."

During the Thirteenth Census, the use of tabulating equipment was confined to population and vital statistics work, where it had been employed extensively before. Of course not all of the difficulties with the Census could be attributed to the quirks of new machinery. But it seems clear that the Bureau might have saved itself considerable pains, as well as time and money, by striking a last-minute deal with Hollerith. Three years after the start of the Census, only two out of eleven final reports had been published. The *Journal of Political Economy* of July 1913 commented:

The complete data are not available, despite the circulation of many bulletins and outlines. . . . Moreover, it is unlikely that these data will ever be available. Many of them are already old and out of date. Appropriations . . . are wanting. It is doubtful whether they will ever find their way into the hands of the public.

From a local newspaper published three years after the Census began, Hollerith culled a letter for his files. "We are now so far on the road to the Fourteenth Census," it said, "that the details of the Thirteenth, still unfinished in tabulation, might as well be abandoned." The inventor's main recorded reaction, forty years later, was one of regret that he could not stay in Census work.

It had been a titanic battle. In its course, Hollerith had gotten rid of North. He had fought the government to a legal draw. Along the way, he had helped give individual inventors recourse against a government that invades the patents it awards. Finally, he had proved that the successful processing of census data depended, to some extent, on his machines. But he had made another contribution of which he was still unaware. His bullheaded persistence had furnished a fledgling industry its first real competition.

While Hollerith was still embroiled in his lawsuit, the mysterious and little-known inventor James Powers resigned from the Census Bureau, after four years of government service. He was to be engaged by a newly organized company, he explained, where he would devote himself to further development of his inventions, not only in the line of punching, but particularly in tabulating and sorting machinery for application to statistical and commercial work. Powers had entered the employ of Sloan & Chace. However, such a move was only an intermediate step for the restless and ambitious "expert." Two years later, Hollerith would learn that his onetime foreman James Spicer had also left the government to become associated with the Powers Company. No less than Hollerith, Powers was his own man. Although his inventions had proved only a partial success in the Census, he was soon to prove a formidable rival, first under his own name and later under that of Remington Rand. As Hollerith had feared, the government had afforded his potential competition a singular opportunity to develop and exploit a rival technology at government expense.

While contemplating all these events, Hollerith, now fifty-one and well established in the commercial world, arrived at a far-reaching decision of his own. Before the final disposition of his suit against the government, he sold his business.

Hollerith Sells Out

"Mr. Flint is a gentleman I have known for a good many years, and his business is putting together industrial consolidations."

About the time that Hollerith decided to sell his business he had been advised by his doctor to give up working and lead a more leisurely life. He almost certainly was prone to high blood pressure, a condition that could not have been aided by a penchant for rich food, expensive cigars, and an explosive temper, not to mention the worries of managing a growing business. He may also have begun to suffer from an accompanying heart disorder; his son Charles, at least, reports that he went to a heart specialist in Washington for a good many years. The physician's somewhat unusual advice was to "saw wood," and Hollerith promptly went out and bought a saw for the purpose. However, as with the bicycle he purchased years before as a weight-reducing implement, there is no record that Hollerith ever put the saw to use—perhaps fortunately for his health. He almost certainly would have benefited from a strict regimen of mild exercise, a salt-free diet, and the taking of various drugs not even contemplated in 1911. But it is far less certain to what extent he would have followed any doctor's advice, now or then.

Besides Hollerith's own health, there was a second reason favoring a sale. In recent years, the company's other officers found that they had less time to devote to the affairs of the Tabulating Machine Company. Hollerith himself, never capable of delegating, found it increasingly difficult to stay on top of a growing business. By 1909, Harry Thayer, Hollerith's closest advisor, had advanced

from Western Electric to become a vice president of the parent
AT&T, and it was an ill-concealed secret that AT&T President
Theodore N. Vail was grooming him as his successor. As early as
April 7, 1907, Thayer had urged Hollerith seriously to consider
selling out. Discussing an offer from a man named Mitchell,
Thayer had written:

I've wondered whether you've ever reflected on the peace of mind which
goes with, say, $150,000 invested in good securities bringing in, say,
$10,000 per annum. If there was also some shares in a new Tabulating
Machine Company, so much the better.

Other alternatives should be considered. Perhaps they should sell
the American patents, Thayer suggested, and continue to run the
foreign business. In the background was a larger reason: "I can't
forget that we are getting toward 50," Thayer mused, almost as
an afterthought.

Later the same year, the company's executive committee had
considered a proposition, perhaps the same one, from "parties in
Wilmington": an offer to purchase the company's business, for
$100,000 in 6 percent bonds and 40 percent of the profits from
the sale of cards up to 200 million. On December 2, 1908, the
board turned down the offer. Only four years later, they would
accept an offer of cash on the barrelhead for twenty times the
amount.

Despite Hollerith's questionable health and his directors' proclivity to sell, it remains unlikely that he would have reached a
decision in 1911 without the intervention of a third force. For
like many others who have built up enterprises in their image,
Hollerith found it practically impossible to let go. As the Santa
Fe's James Peabody had said "Hollerith will not listen to any
proposition that takes the management out of his hands."

The magnetic third force appeared in the person of Charles
Ranlett Flint, a remarkably adroit and energetic man, who held
the view that competition among many small firms in the same
industry was essentially wasteful. Great benefits, in contrast, were
to be gained from consolidation, among them the centralizing of
manufacture and distribution. At a time when mass markets were
rapidly developing, the industrialist foresaw that it took large,

efficient enterprises to serve them. Almost single-handedly, Flint had assembled scores of combinations from lesser firms. Most notable were the giant United States Rubber Company and the American Woolen Company, for many years a blue chip repository for the savings of upper-crust Bostonians. To Flint, the forging of consolidations was not only an occupation, it was well nigh a religion. When, years before, Republican politician Mark Hanna had asked Flint to defend industrial combinations before the Illinois Manufacturers Association, the industrialist had proclaimed: "A combination of labor is a trades union; a combination of intelligence, a university; a combination of money, a bank—a combination of labor, intelligence and money is an industrial consolidation—Work, Brains and Money."

The next morning, a Chicago newspaper had printed Flint's picture and, above it, a new title, "The Father of Trusts." And in the heat of his campaign with Bryan, McKinley had ordered half a million copies of the speech printed and distributed across the land. The title "Father of Trusts" had stuck.

One can only guess at the strange chemistry that brought together Hollerith, who detested business dealings, and the free-wheeling entrepreneur, who was said to be able to consummate six business deals before breakfast and then steam up the Hudson on his forty-five-knot steam yacht *Arrow*, the fastest in the world, to complete another deal before lunch. Although there was no evidence that Flint was anything less than scrupulous in his dealings, on occasion he attained a degree of notoriety that might have shocked even his peers in the business world. As an arms dealer, the industrialist found himself, at one time, representing two South American republics that happened to be at war with each other, a situation that others might have found discomforting. When the Brazilian Navy revolted in 1889, threatening to reestablish the Empire, Flint rounded up a fleet of vessels, fitted them out with the latest dynamite guns, secured crews, and dispatched the private armada posthaste. The first vessel sailed within three weeks; the rest within six, soon enough to tip the scales in favor of the beleaguered Republic. Flint was fast, no doubt about it. Too fast, in fact, for some of the Tabulating Company's stockholders. And his reputation would raise distrust and even alarm.

"Flint and Company," one would write, "sounds to me like Wall Street, which means to me that if there is more money to be made by manipulation than by carrying out this business the slow straight way, they will do the manipulating."

However, Flint displayed a genuine enthusiasm for technology that was bound to appeal to Hollerith. In 1906, he had worked out a deal to represent the Wright Brothers outside the United States. His enthusiasm was such, in fact, that he would have flown with them except for his wife's pleadings. Plainly, Flint was a man of action and adventure, as well as intelligence. The financier, who was on speaking terms with many of the world's leaders—from Teddy Roosevelt to the Czar of Russia—was quite possibly the mover and shaker and the man of affairs that the more conservative Hollerith might have liked to be.

Be that as it may, Flint first swept into the affairs of the Tabulating Machine Company on January 7, 1911, when word of a proposition for the company's stock was received. Six days later, Roebling wrote to Hollerith, "Mr. Flint is a gentleman I have known for a good many years, and his business is putting together industrial consolidations." At first, Salt had suggested asking $400 a share. But he was overruled by the more astute Roebling, who proposed $750 a share, "not with the idea of getting it, but with the idea of having a price which might be reduced."

On his part, Flint wanted to know what annual sales amounted to. The reply was approximately $350,000. "He knew the amount of our outstanding capital, both common and preferred," Salt wrote to Hollerith, "and didn't seem a bit inquisitive." Not outwardly inquisitive, perhaps. The financier had done his homework, finding out in advance all that could be learned about the small company. But the following day, two of Flint's experts, Rice and Hastings, turned up at Grand Central Station in New York to look at the machines. "Mr. McCullough saw them personally," reported Salt, "and says they were greatly impressed by the work that was being done."

Following the visit, Flint called Salt with a message for Hollerith: "He would like to talk with you in the hope of getting an option on your stock . . . He said that he had been in the habit of getting options." The strategy was clear. If Flint could purchase Hollerith's shares and those of a few other major stockholders, he would gain a controlling interest and the other stockholders would have to follow along, accepting what they could get for their shares. The tactic had worked successfully before. But if Flint had counted on it now, he seriously misread the man he was dealing with. For Hollerith stubbornly refused. In letters of authorization drafted for the sale of his company's stock, he would carefully stipulate that "I receive for my stock the same amount per share that is paid to every other stockholder." At the turn of the century, the word "square" was still applied to someone who was honest and aboveboard in his dealings. (not as it does today, to someone who does not fit in, who is not "with it"). Just as Teddy Roosevelt's Square Deal was a program intended to benefit all the citizens in society, rather than just a privileged few, Hollerith had chosen to remain loyal to his small family of stockholders rather than turn a fast dollar. Eugene A. Ford would write: "Please accept my thanks for procuring me the same price for my stock as for your own. I have been wondering how much more you could have gotten for yours if you had let the minority make its own deal, and also how many men there are who would have acted as you did." And from Cambridge, Mass., the inventor's old friend George F. Swain would join in: "Few men would have been so honorable and unselfish and fair." Stockholders had yet to become a vaguely defined constituency. At least in Hollerith's small company, they could be family and friends, and were treated as such in principle and fact.

But if in early 1911 the inventor had already decided to sell his company, his behavior in the months that followed showed a strange ambivalence. While negotiations involving millions of dollars were in progress, Hollerith hid himself away at his farm in Southern Virginia where he was busy "building things." His attorney, Samuel Metcalf, who represented the Tabulating Machine Company in the sale, was equally inaccessible, summering hundreds of miles north in Kennebunkport, Maine. If the pair had been trying to scuttle the deal, they could not have succeeded in creating a more awkward situation for those trying to assemble the new company.

Under the subscription agreement, dated June 7, Flint had to raise a minimum of $4 million before options on the stock of the participating companies expired in July. Yet Hollerith took no action, and his shareholders were waiting for him to move. On June 19, W. P. Rice, a representative of Flint & Company, wrote to the inventor: "We have been somewhat embarrassed because none of the parties interested in the Tabulating Company have subscribed while parties interested in the Scale and Time Recording companies have subscribed very liberally." After characterizing the investment as a very fine one in which large profits would be made, the businessman added: "A subscription from you at once will surely enable us to hasten the matter . . . Quick action is exceedingly important."

Reluctant or not, the Tabulating Machine Company's stockholders had agreed by July 6, 1911, to accept $450 a share, or a total of $2,312,100, for the company's 5,138 shares of stock. It was $50 a share higher than Salt had proposed initially, but not nearly the $750 that Roebling had put forward as a bargaining position at the start of negotiations. Hollerith received $1,210,500 for his 2,690 shares.

His attitude toward the merger may be reflected by the fact that only three of the Tabulating Machine Company's approximately twenty-five stockholders cared to take up shares in the newly formed company. They were Mary Swain (George Swain had kept the shares in his wife's name), who subscribed in the amount of $10,000; Clarke L. Hayes, one of Hollerith's oldest employees, who would work for the new company and who invested $4,000; and Hollerith himself, who subscribed to $100,000 in new shares—less than one-tenth the total he received for his old shares.

While he was not going to commit himself substantially to the new company, Hollerith was reluctant to let go of the old. He truculently held onto his interest in the Auditing Machine Company, the subsidiary he had organized years before to carry out the Tabulating Machine Company's railroad business. It did not go into the merger. Because of Hollerith's stubbornness—the Auditing Machine Company was also bringing in good income—

this corporate appendage would continue to exist as an accountant's nightmare, and a thorn in the side of the new management, for many years. To complicate matters further, Hollerith later assigned his interest in the subsidiary to his sons and daughters and, in typically obdurate fashion, refused to tell them what to do with it. They would eventually sell their interest in the railroad subsidiary to IBM for a million dollars—almost as much as Hollerith had received for his Tabulating Machine Company stock several decades before.

The new company, chartered under the laws of New York State, began to do business as a consolidated unit on July 5, 1911. Its name, drawn from its separate components, was the Computing-Tabulating-Recording Company, more familiarly known by the initials C-T-R. Although today, IBM accounts say that three companies went into the merger, the actual number was four. The name "Computing" came from the Computing Scale Company of Dayton, Ohio; "Tabulating" from the Tabulating Machine Company; and "Recording" from the International Time Recording Company of Binghamton, New York. The fourth, and often forgotten, component was the Bundy Manufacturing Company of Endicott, New York. In what was to become a long-standing company joke, it would be said that, while the other companies gave their names to the newly formed company, the Bundy Company contributed the word "company" to the merger and little else. However, Harlow Bundy is recognized as one of the pioneers of the business, and the tiny Bundy Building, enveloped by but still identifiable in the huge IBM computer plant at Endicott, is still pointed out proudly by employees working there today.

Of the many consolidations he accomplished, Charles Flint would be proudest of C-T-R. Most of his mergers, he pointed out, had brought together companies within the same industry. But this one was different. "It was neither horizontal nor vertical nor circular. In fact, it was so uncommon as to almost justify the description *sui generis*—in a class by itself." In good times, he pointed out, any of the three lines of business—scales, tabulating machines, or time recorders—might contribute to the profits.

However, in bad times, the company, because of its diversity, would have three chances, instead of merely one, of meeting its obligations and paying dividends. Wielding this premise, Flint had successfully appealed to the Guaranty Trust Company of New York for a $4 million loan to float the new enterprise.

The new company was off to a start, but it was hardly an auspicious one. Although the International Time Recording Company and the Computing Scale Company were larger than the Tabulating Machine Company, both brought with them a substantial burden of debt. In fact, in merging the companies, Flint had saddled the newly hatched C-T-R with a debt that totaled three times its current assets—a heavy burden for a fledgling enterprise to carry.

Looking back on the merger, one writer has said that the Computing Scale and International Time Recording companies were the most healthy, and that "only a seer or a madman" could have predicted the future of tabulating machines. The facts at the time of the merger speak largely otherwise. Not only had the Tabulating Machine Company largely financed its growth internally over the years—as IBM was to do later—it also brought with it a steadily rising tempo of revenues. For each six-month period, from December 1909 to May 1911, rentals and sales, the *Commercial and Financial Chronicle* reported, had averaged an increase of approximately 20 percent over the previous period. Perhaps more important, although the Tabulating Machine Company had greatly increased its manufacturing capacity and had made no effort to solicit business, it was "largely behind on the execution of its orders."

The Tabulating Machine Company was far from being a weak reed at the time of the merger, and it is difficult, with the benefit of hindsight, to understand why its stockholders should have chosen to throw in their lot with purveyors of butcher scales, coffee grinders, and time clocks—products long since discarded by IBM. Hollerith himself may have harbored second thoughts after receiving a letter on July 7—the day after Flint had exercised his option to purchase the company's stock. The typewritten note was from James Peabody, the statistician of the Santa Fe, who years before had urged Hollerith to sell his company and go on with his inventions. After commenting that he had had the Tabulating Machine Company in mind for the last five years, Peabody wrote:

> If I were a stockholder in your company, which unfortunately I am not, I could object to disposing of my stock for the price or in exchange for stock of the suggested new corporation on any basis. It is evident that the Tabulating Machine Company is to be made to carry those other companies and, if I were a stockholder, I would prefer to keep the Tabulating Machine Company as a separate proposition and extend its business rather than unite it with anything else.

Peabody, undoubtedly speaking for others, then asked at what price Hollerith would consider selling his stock. Hollerith's reaction, if any, is unrecorded. And with the decision made, it is pointless to speculate on what it might have been.

From Gershom Smith, who had pioneered the machines at Pennsylvania Steel a decade before, Hollerith received a letter thanking him for the check for his five shares and adding, "My only regret is that I did not make a strenuous effort to make the investment a great deal larger when I had the opportunity."

Swain had also written from Cambridge. "I never had such luck before," the inventor's old companion commented. "Now can't you invent something else and let me go in with you again?"

24

A Life of Leisure

Bulls, boats, and buildings

At fifty-one, Hollerith became a millionaire. Through hard work, he had amply illustrated the Horatio Alger legend. Following the sale of the Tabulating Machine Company in 1911, he could live in any style he chose. Yet despite a fortune that might have turned the heads of some men, the inventor's tastes underwent little change. He had always enjoyed good food and solid comfort for himself and his family, and sharing whatever material benefits he might derive liberally with friends. Yet he had little taste for luxury as such and none for its outward display.

He did buy a place in Georgetown, most probably to please his wife and to give his daughters a "social life" that was lacking in the country. Soon, the inventor, who had purchased one of the first Edison phonographs and convinced Western Electric's purchasing agent to buy a complete set of *La Traviata*, began attending concerts and theater in the city—despite an abhorrence of dress-up affairs.

The parklike three acres of land that Hollerith purchased off 29th Street contained a brick and white trim house dating to 1740. However, any plans to live in the graceful structure were scrapped after Hollerith discovered that its foundations were not strong enough to support the additions he planned. In a new house he now planned for the property each of his daughters would have a room of her own and there would be an attached greenhouse for Lu, as well. His new home, Hollerith decreed, should have big rooms, lots of windows, and proper electrical outlets. The building he now planned to put up, he instructed a somewhat startled architect, should be somewhat "like a factory"—una-dorned. Other motives were also at work. A house that was too fancy, the thrifty Hollerith decided, would surely attract the at-tention of the tax collector and, therefore, be assessed at a higher rate. A quiet struggle ensued between the inventor and his ar-chitect. The latter, a man of reportedly aesthetic sensibilities, did get in his licks when a few artistic touches were applied to the front of the building. But as the stolid brick structure testifies, Hollerith largely got his way. But would he outfox the tax col-lector? "It was not so much the architect's gee-gaws, or the house itself that foiled the plan," the *Washington Post* would report in a later day. "It is rather the three acres of land around and under the house that interest the tax assessor." For many years, the property has been listed among the ten most valuable in Washington.

If Hollerith's building plans were somewhat constrained in the city, he soon found more ample scope for his expansive visions in the country. For years, the family had summered at Mathews, a small community near the edge of the Chesapeake in Tidewater, Virginia. The sleepy county seat, 165 miles from Washington by road, has a courthouse, a post office, and little else. It was the kind of a place where, at least in summer months, life barely moved. Once in a while, a dog wandered across a dusty road seeking shelter from the sun.

The inventor and his family, on first coming to Mathews in 1895 had stayed at Poplar Grove, a rambling boardinghouse owned by a Judge Garnett. The place overlooks a tidal mill, dating to Revolutionary times. A huge wooden wheel is turned one way by the rising tide pouring into a cove, and the other way by the water running out. It was pleasant enough. But as his business blossomed, Hollerith wanted to leave his own imprint on the landscape. The *Gloucester-Mathews Gazette-Journal* of August 13, 1909, recorded an event of some interest to the neighborhood. Mr. Jim Campbell's fine farm "Brighton" on the East River had been purchased by Mr. Herman Hollerith of Washington, D.C., for $15,000. Hollerith soon bought an adjoining tract of land because he did not like having to enter his own property through so many gates.

The following year, the family spent its first summer at Brighton in a farmhouse already standing on the property. It was situated on a point of land bordered by the East River on one side and Tabb's Creek on the other. Like many of the local farmhouses, this one was surrounded by poplar trees and topped by a tin roof. From all appearances, it was a setting that invited repose. But Hollerith soon discovered that the leaves of the poplar trees rustled noisily with the slightest breeze; drops of rain falling on the tin roof caused an unrelenting din; and a perennial plague of cicadas, a type of locust, set off a grating crescendo of shrill notes. If he was looking for peace and quiet, Hollerith, whose taut nerves were unstrung by the slightest noise, had come to the wrong place.

At first, the inventor threatened drastic retaliation by chopping down the trees. But his wife, to whom all growing things were sacred, would not hear of it. Seemingly dissuaded from violent retribution, the inventor instead carefully calculated that the house itself faced the wrong way. It fronted west, looking across the East River—rather than Southwest, looking down the river with a grander view of Mobjack Bay, an arm of the Chesapeake, beyond. So Hollerith had the house demolished. Down with it came the noisy tin roof, and in clearing ground for a larger structure, the trees, which closely surrounded the smaller farmhouse, had to give way. This time, the offending poplars were cut off without a protest. In their place, the inventor planted willow oaks, a more obliging local species with small, rustle-free leaves—but the noisy cicadas remain to this day. The new house was large enough for the eight members of the family to have their own bedrooms, without doubling up.

With preliminary sorties out of the way, the inventor's onslaught on the landscape began in earnest. Decked out in his invariable uniform of khaki trousers, white shirt, and white duck hat with a brim all the way around, Hollerith dispatched a platoon of carpenters commandeered from Washington. The din of hammers rent the air. Nothing resembling the clatter had so shaken the sleepy countryside since musket-bearing infantry had battled their way up and down the peninsula during the Civil War. Barking out commands and cursing out the men when they weren't working fast enough, Hollerith was in his element. As if his goading were not enough, heat and mosquitoes were fierce. The first structure, a screened bungalow the inventor was building as a present for a banker friend, was only halfway up when the workers stalked out, taking the first boat back to Washington, with the banker due to arrive in a week. The inventor, also having to leave for the city, conscripted his sons to finish the job. When they found the beams of the building too far apart to accommodate precut panels, the boys—all to become engineers—took a sledgehammer and knocked the supports closer together. Despite the questionable construction methods, never revealed to their father, the building would be standing strong more than half a century later.

Soon other workers were found, and under Hollerith's prodding, the once empty countryside became a small city under construction. A dairy house, a shed for the propane gas lighting system, a machine shop, cattle barns, windmills for pumping water, boathouses, piers all appeared. Whenever Hollerith decided that another shed or shelter was needed, it was fashioned and erected in record time. To this day, the inventor's family has had only limited success in dismantling the myriad structures that fill the landscape.

Hollerith was happy building things. And if it was a strange notion of retirement for most men, he was making the most of it. Buying a book on surveying, a transom, and other tools, he laid out roads and fields. Wire for the fences came special order from Roebling & Sons in Trenton. On the hottest days, Hollerith labored under a "coolie" hat, an ingenious type of headgear he admired because the straw crown was held aloft from the head by a harness allowing free circulation of air underneath. He kept a stack of the hats, as well as a pile of the more familiar duck sun hats, on ready reserve in the attic.

The first new home to go up was a two-story, four-bedroom structure. Hollerith had given his youngest daughter Virginia a general notion of what he wanted and left her to sketch it for the architect. Satisfied with a smaller house he had built, the inventor told the architect merely to double it when he was building a larger residence to replace the demolished farmhouse. Taking Hollerith at his word, the architect followed instructions to the

letter, turning out a house with eight upstairs bedrooms as prescribed—although to get from the bedrooms on one end of the
house to the other, it was necessary to go downstairs and climb
back up again. In doubling the smaller house, the architect had
never thought of providing a connecting upstairs hallway—and
nobody had suggested one.

Hollerith filled the new home with cheap but sturdy oak furniture straight out of the Wanamaker catalog. Hickory porch
chairs, resembling bentwood furniture, came from a place in Pennsylvania. For the mantlepieces, the engineer ordered liberal quantities of electric clocks, some from General Electric, which had
supplied the motors for his tabulators. Like the early tabulators,
they were powered by batteries. Later, when power lines reached
Mathews, he bought plug-in Telechron clocks, which are still running fifty years later.

While Hollerith's building program would have strained the energies of most men, he had not come to the country merely to put
up a place for show. If you bought a farm, you had to farm it, he
reasoned in logical fashion, And that meant livestock and crops.
Back in 1896, when hard times had forced him to close down his
shop, his brother-in-law Ned Talcott had helped to support the
family by selling eggs at 20 cents a dozen. Hollerith, raised in the
city, had scorned the effort. But his mother-in-law had reported,
"He is very much interested though he pretends not to be. He
cannot be persuaded that the fine breeds are any better than the
common stock."

Now Hollerith took up the breeding of pedigreed stock as if
he had invented the idea. Deciding to raise swine, he joined the
American Duroc-Jersey Swine Breeders Association and, with
perfectionist fervor, filled his bookshelves with their journal.
However, the newly arrived sows, not having read the books,
rolled over on their piglets and, to Hollerith's horror, ate some
of them. Disgusted, he ordered the pigs returned.

Next, he imported a special breed of sheep from upper New
York State. As well as providing lamb chops, the sheep could
keep the lawns surrounding the house closely cropped, as they

do on estates in England. Once again, the animals failed to oblige. They climbed up and down the wooden porch steps at night, keeping the inventor awake; they contracted lungworms and were chased over the landscape by the dogs. Soon, the sheep went the way of the swine.

Undeterred, the inventor bought three Guernsey cows from a Judge R. H. L. Chichester of Fredericksburg, Maryland, only to have one killed by lightning. Despite the ominous sign, he soon purchased three more and went so far as to import another three directly from the Channel Isle of Guernsey. This time he struck gold—or, rather, butter, which he treasured more. To a friend he wrote:

The butter on the market was so poor that I recently started Mrs. Fletcher down on the farm making butter for me. . . . The only trouble is I like it so well and eat so much of it I am getting fat. I now weigh stripped 197½. It is altogether too much and yet I don't want to tell Mrs. Fletcher not to make the butter so good.

Hollerith ordered records kept of the butterfat content of the most promising animals' milk. Soon, he could report of Daisy of Mobjack: "I think she produced 36 pounds of butterfat in excess of any cow of her class." After Daisy was written up in the *Guernsey Breeder's Journal*, he proudly sent copies to his friends.

In 1914, a prize bull was also acquired. And by the end of Hollerith's life, in 1929, a total of sixty-seven cows and forty-eight bulls had been born and registered. Not only did the purebred cattle furnish butter and cream for the inventor's favorite recipes; bull calves were also given to friends, and the inventor sold some cows to improve the local herds. Hollerith's efforts at livestock improvement were such that the county later deemed the herds of sufficient quality to warrant the building of a creamery. The inventor's daughters sold cream to it for many years following their father's death.

Besides enjoying his cattle and his friends, Hollerith took a philanthropic interest in the local farmers and fishermen. "He done a lot to help the local fishermen," recalls Captain Henry Owens. "I know of one particular man. Mr. Hollerith had a nice boat built [for him] and put a nice engine in it. The man done quite well and made a lot of money."

Hollerith befriended another man, named Omega Powell, who worked at Diggs Wharf, where the Norfolk steamer came in, by setting him up in the feed and grain business. His interest went beyond his business loans, on which he seldom expected repayment. "He was always giving us things," says Powell's daughter, Mrs. Vivian Hugins. "Who would think of stocking anyone's pantry with canned goods and all sorts of things? Dad told me that he was the best friend that anyone ever had."

To Marion Smith, a gardener at Brighton, Hollerith gave a Model T Ford. He would buy the Fords, use them for two years, then give them away. His benefactions became such, in fact, that Hollerith came to be known as something of a soft touch in the neighborhood, a reputation that the usually thrifty inventor did nothing to dispel. Once when a local character known for his footloose ways told the inventor that he was going to start a jitney service, Hollerith asked him who was going to pay for it.

"Why, you are," came the reply.

Hollerith laughed heartily and obliged, although he had little hope of seeing the money again.

In the country, Hollerith also took to boats. At first, it was a matter of necessity, since roads in the Tidewater country were few. In contrast, numerous inlets and bays made travel by water the natural way to get around. He bought the first craft, a New England dory, to teach the boys about boating when the family stayed at Poplar Grove. It was called the *Luvina*, from the beginnings of his daughters' names, Lucia, Virginia, and Nan. Next came the *Brighton*, a locally built, flat-bottomed workboat; it was his first motor-powered craft. As Hollerith's fortunes grew, so did the length of his boats. The year he sold the Tabulating Machine Company, he bought the *Regina*, a forty-five-foot, gasoline-powered craft, which he renamed the *Luvina*, after his first craft. After buying a still larger yacht, also the *Luvina*, he turned over the forty-five-footer to the boys, rechristening it the *Matoaka*, after Lu, sometimes called that because of her distant descent from Pocahontas.

In buying the new boat, which at eighty-five feet was nearly twice the length of the old, Hollerith came closest to acting like a millionaire. However, there was also a practical need since steamboat service to Washington was poor and roads barely passable. Because of its draught, the yacht was too large for the boathouse on Tabb's Creek. So Hollerith built a wharf, wide enough to drive a wagon down and with a waiting house at the tip, several hundred feet out into the deeper East River. Hollerith used the big boat to take friends up and down the bay. Because it was the correct thing to do, he had a private signal designed with the initials "H. H." and china specially made in the same design. To run the craft, he engaged a Norwegian crew of five with a Swedish engineer. Uniforms—white duck for summer and navy for winter with matching yachting caps—were ordered from Appel & Co., yachting outfitters at 18 Fulton Street in New York. A small boy was kept busy running the signal flags up and down.

By all appearances, the craft made a splendid impression. "I don't see how a boat could be fixed up any nicer," says Alonzo Hugins, who worked on Hollerith's boats. "It had the finest trimming you ever saw. I think it was every bit mahogany." The reality was something else. As often as not, the large craft was laid up with mechanical difficulties. After a time, when things were getting shaken down, Hollerith discovered that some of the crew were getting kickbacks on provisions. When World War I came along, the inventor in a patriotic gesture offered to donate the boat to the Navy. He was bitterly disappointed when the offer was turned down.

Despite the fact that he had more than earned it over the years, Hollerith was not cut out to lead a leisurely life.

25

The Rise of IBM

"The king is dead . . . the king is dead!"

One day following the sale of the Tabulating Machine Company, Hollerith walked down to his shop on 31st Street. "Well, I sold the business," he told the men. Walking among the machines, with their pulley belts stretching toward the ceiling, he first stopped to talk to his foreman, John Sullivan. Next came Bill Barnes, the man who, some time before, had lost an arm putting a belt on one of the machines. The inventor, who brooded over the accident, had always been solicitous. "Then he came over to me," recalls Joe Langley. "He said, 'I sold the company,' and went into his pocket and pulled out a piece of money. I looked at it and it was a $50 bill," said Langley, then still a youngster. "I thought I was a millionaire."

At first, Langley and the others at the Georgetown shop worried about changes being made, about strangers coming in, and about the possibility of losing their jobs. But Hollerith assured each of the men that he would continue with the new company. "We went on and on," says Langley, "just like we did before." There was, in fact, little noticeable change following the sale of the Tabulating Machine Company. Hollerith came to work. The business prospered. And, as if to underscore Flint's assertion that the company would be "a mighty strong factor in any combination," the directors declared a special dividend of 10 percent on the stock at the request of parent C-T-R.

Still, a bar had been crossed. And as vibrations from a ship's motor strike the shallow bottom and bounce upward against the hull, shudders of change were bound to be felt. On October 24,

1911, Hollerith stepped down as general manager of the Tabulating Machine Company. He was replaced by Gershom Smith, who had applied the machines so imaginatively as controller of Pennsylvania Steel. Although Hollerith had almost certainly handpicked his successor and was to stay on as consulting engineer, the letter he sent out announcing his retirement on November 7 stirred a ripple of concern among a few of the company's approximately 100 customers. D. G. Scott, Secretary of the American Iron and Steel Company, wrote from Lebanon, Pennsylvania, to express regret that "we will probably not come in personal contact with you to the extent that we did," adding: "We have always felt that what problems we have in connection with the Tabulating Machines would receive your very careful consideration and assistance would be given if assistance were possible." Who would look after Scott and his machines after Hollerith was gone? The customer was, at least, mildly anxious. Nevertheless, he was also relieved that Hollerith would stay on as consulting engineer. "We will know," he continued, "that the mastermind of the Doctor is still directing the development of the tabulating machines consistently in the direction of greater usefulness."

An officer of the Phoenix Mutual Life Insurance Company employed his letter of farewell to get in a last-minute business request:

I would like to ask you if it is not possible for you to use your influence toward having a mechanical man locate with headquarters at Hartford. I believe there are seven or eight machines at Hartford and several more are ordered and there seems to be a growing demand for the same. As there are so many insurance companies here, it would seem worthwhile to keep a man here.

No doubt, Hollerith would be missed, for he had always taken any failure in his machines as a personal shortcoming. There was little that a customer could want, or need, that was not immediately forthcoming. But in stepping down, Hollerith was in little danger of setting himself completely adrift in an unfamiliar life of leisure. Although he had his boats, bulls, and buildings in the country, he had carefully arranged to have as much or as little of the business as he might want. His contract called for him to stay on as con-

sulting engineer for a decade at the salary of $20,000 a year. Soon,
he asked for and got his board's agreement that all proposed
changes in the design of the machines were to be submitted to
him for approval—before being offered to the company's customers. He also intended to keep tight-fisted control over some
other matters. When the board approved the purchase of land
near the Georgetown plant for a new building, it was on condition
that both its purchase and construction "be first approved in all
respects by Dr. Hollerith."

He had relinquished his title and presumably his duties on
stepping down as general manager. But emotionally, Hollerith was
entirely incapable of loosening his hold. The wording of his contract as consulting engineer shows his ambivalence: "The Individual shall not be subject to the orders of any officer or other person
connected with the Company, and shall be allowed to perform his
services in such a manner and at such a place as the Individual
may decide." In his singular way, he had almost certainly com-
pounded a prescription for future chaos. For it was inconceivable
that the Tabulating Machine Company could continue to revolve
solely around him.

In the meanwhile, he began attending board meetings in his
new post as a director of C-T-R. At them, he sat next to men like
Edward Canby, an Ohio businessman who operated the computer
scale company and was its president, and Harlow Bundy, the lawyer from Endicott, New York, who had helped start the Bundy
Manufacturing Company to turn out his brother Willard's time
recording machine. It was said that Bundy was so thrifty that for
many years he deducted from his wife's allowance the price of the
vegetables she took from her garden for the dinner table. The
directors were businessmen, financiers, lawyers, inventors. And,
for the most part, they were strictly small-town, self-made, and
of no exceptional prominence. A notable exception was the Honorable George W. Fairchild of Oneonta, New York. A Republican
Congressman from the state's Thirty-Fourth District and publisher
of the *Oneonta Herald*, Fairchild, an imposing man with a generous
moustache, was president of the International Time Recording
Company, which he had melded together in 1900 from a number
of smaller firms. He was also the largest backer of the new com-

pany, with a stake of half a million dollars. While it was Flint who had negotiated the merger that resulted in C-T-R, Fairchild gave the new firm character and respectability. It was only fitting that he should be its first chairman and acting president.

Meeting together, the directors of the new company took up the kind of problem that other firms would like to have. Even without the help of enthusiastic and well-trained salesmen, demand for the Tabulating Machine Company's equipment had risen so rapidly that it had not been able to keep up with the rush of orders. The directors would have to put its manufacturing on a firmer footing.

Since the U.S. Census of 1900, Hollerith had relied on the Taft-Peirce Manufacturing Company as his main supplier. Now, to ensure a steady supply of machines and take advantage of the economies that Flint had envisioned, the C-T-R board took an important step. On November 9, 1911, it authorized Harlow Bundy, general manager of International Time Recording Company, one of the firms that made up C-T-R, "to duplicate tools, dies, etc. now in use by Taft-Peirce at Woonsocket, Rhode Island, in constructing the sorting machine." Soon after, a duplicate card manufacturing facility was approved for the scale company's Dayton, Ohio, plant.

Such far-reaching changes are always easier to order than to bring about. Not only must dies, blueprints, and other equipment be copied and moved to a new location, but hard-gained knowledge and skills must be taught to the workers now called upon to build the unfamiliar machines. Here, the directors apparently left little to chance. "James O'Brien, a friend of ours, came over from Woonsocket," recalls Joe Langley, who later moved from Georgetown to the Endicott plant. O'Brien, as it turns out, was a foreman at Taft-Peirce. He was also the man most intimately acquainted with the manufacture of Hollerith's machines. At Endicott, he became superintendent of machine production for both the Hollerith sorters and the tabulators. Finally, there were subtler obstacles to be overcome. "The International Time Recording Division of C-T-R was the clock business," Langley recounts. "They didn't know about the tabulating machines. And they didn't want them in the Endicott plant." It would be some time before the hostility against the strange new product would disappear. When, over the years, men were moved up from Hollerith's plant to help out at Endicott, they often were treated and felt like outcasts.

"In 1912, we were building 235 sorters for Hollerith," says F. Steele Blackall III, the grandson of the man who ran Taft-Peirce in Hollerith's time. "By the end of August, 135 had been delivered and, by the end of September, 55 more—with another 45 to go. It all ended in the middle of 1912," he affirms, with no further deliveries. Why? Besides the projected economies, a second reason appears. The year that Taft-Peirce ceased to be Hollerith's main supplier, it was building $46,522 in sorters, punches, and tabulating machines for Hollerith's arch rival, James Powers.

Some other matters also needed tidying up. Just as domestic affairs appeared to be in disarray when Hollerith had formed his company in 1896, the foreign business was now at sixes and sevens. To set things right, the C-T-R board appointed a special committee. Its first discovery was that the British Tabulating Machine Company was $25,000 in arrears on royalties. Prompt payment was demanded. But despite insistent urgings, the British company would soon slide into default.

Then arrangements in Germany required attention. In 1910, a German businessman named Willy Heidinger, an agent for adding machines, had become enthusiastic about the Hollerith machines after seeing a demonstration by R. Neil Williams, an engineer sent from the United States by Hollerith. Heidinger successfully financed a local company. And almost from the start, the Berlin-headquartered Deutsche Hollerith Maschinen Gesellschaft, more familiarly known as Dehomag, had been a remarkable success. Not only did the Germans take avidly to the precise methods inherent in the equipment, they also tacked on their own improvements, seemingly oblivious to Hollerith's patent rights. In addition to Germany, Dehomag agents roamed Switzerland, Denmark, Norway, and Sweden, paying the Tabulating Machine Company $6,000 a year for the territory. The contract also called for a charge of 10 percent over the cost of the machines and 25 percent of gross rentals. With the agreements up for renewal, would the German company agree to take on Holland, Austria, and the Balkan states?

Much to the C-T-R directors' dismay and alarm, the German company now hesitated. With an unmistakable air of independence, it questioned whether it should be required to sell the Hollerith machines on an exclusive basis. The reason? The threat of competition from the Powers Company! Only after protracted negotiations and visits abroad by C-T-R officials did the German company relent and renew its contract. However, as a consequence of internal differences, R. N. Williams, who had been comanager of Dehomag with Heidinger, resigned to represent Hollerith's rival James Powers in Europe.

As for the rest of Europe—France, Spain, Portugal, Belgium, Italy, Russia, Greece, and Turkey—its business could be handled by a separate agency. In what today might appear to be an unusual arrangement, the directors awarded this potpourri of countries to one of their own members, Charles Flint, who would handle it with an associate, Hart O. Berg. Almost as an afterthought, the C-T-R Board discussed the matter of exploiting the Tabulating Machine Company business in South America. The president and Mr. Flint, it was recommended, "should take the matter up with a Mr. Nolte, who is at present in the Argentine Republic, and see what could be done." The Mr. Nolte who would look into things in the faraway lands was one George H. Nolte, another employee of the Flint firm. Clearly, Flint & Company not only benefited from its initial role in assembling the new company, it was also hoping to profit a second time around by acting as an overseas agent for the fledgling concern.

Such were C-T-R's beginnings. In its first three years, the company acted to expand production of tabulating machines and to gather up the threads of its overseas business. It also saw to it that inventor Eugene A. Ford, who had gone into business for himself, was rehired at the not inconsiderable salary of $6,000 a year. In the meanwhile, Hollerith, apparently freed of his business worries, was able to concentrate his energies on development. By December 9, 1913, Chairman Fairchild could report, "Mr. Hollerith had about completed certain improvements which would be very advantageous to and largely increase the earnings of the Tabulating Machine Company."

So it was until May 1, 1914—the day the company officially hired a new man. His name was Thomas John Watson. And despite an enviable record, he had lately been fired as sales manager of the National Cash Register Company (NCR). Not only that. Along with twenty-nine other officials of the Dayton, Ohio, firm, including its stormy and eccentric head, John H. Patterson, he had been indicated for criminal violation of the Sherman Antitrust Act. Although the case would shortly be dismissed and a new trial ordered (it was never held), the cloud over Watson's reputation was such that he was engaged as general manager rather than president, although it was clearly intended that he should be top man. At forty, he was out of work and had little money—circumstances that might have depressed and defeated other men. A photograph of him, seated rigidly erect behind a desk, portrays a drawn and strained appearance. But there is also a firm set to the jaw, and the face has small, bright, piercing eyes.

Watson's career needs little embellishment. At eighteen, two years after Hollerith's machines had gone to work in the 1890 Census, he had driven a brightly painted yellow wagon away from his hometown of Painted Post, New York, to sell pianos, organs, and sewing machines in the rough and tumble business world of the '90s. After several jobs, he talked his way into a position as a regular salesman with NCR. The year was 1896—the same year that Hollerith, fourteen years Watson's senior, nailed, down the Russian Census, won the New York Central, and formed his company. During the next decade, while Hollerith was establishing his commercial business, Watson compiled a brilliant record at NCR. He brought the sales of registers to more than 100,000 a year by 1910—twice what they had been a few years before.

NCR Chairman Patterson encouraged bright young men to rise to the top, but once they were there, he would fire them. When a man gets to feel he is indispensable, get rid of him, he would say. And other companies were peopled with many who had threatened his authority. Like others before him, Watson had felt himself immune to the "Chief's" proclivity—until he, too, got the axe.

It was a devastating way to learn. But Watson had learned from Patterson a great deal more than the pain of being fired. For all his flaws, Patterson flooded his factories with sunlight, installed showers for workers, started up company schools, and, as an avid believer in physical fitness, required his executives to turn out for a brisk canter, in formation, before starting their official labors for the day. For the most part, salesmen elsewhere were a motley lot. They often lacked education, hung out in bars, poached sales from each other, and were ragged in appearance. To be effective, and to market a sophisticated product, Patterson believed that salesmen should be trained, motivated, and imbued with the team spirit. Adapting the pitches of his most successful salesmen, Patterson decreed that all salesmen learn scientific methods of selling. He staged sales conventions called "Hundred Point Clubs." He also pioneered such marketing innovations as the quota system and guaranteed territories, along with large commissions and advances. Give a man a taste for the good life, he believed, and he will work all the harder to maintain the standard for himself and his family. At the Chief's behest, the head valet of the Waldorf-Astoria Hotel composed a booklet prescribing the proper attire for NCR salesmen for every occasion.

Patterson was a man so far ahead of his time, Watson astutely recognized, that people laughed at him and said he was crazy. Now, if the well-schooled protégé could not apply at NCR the techniques he had learned so well, he was determined to succeed with them elsewhere. And to the task he brought his own special qualities: an openness and affinity for ordinary people acquired from years on the road; a talent for showmanship that concealed an innate shyness; and an urge to teach and inspire that, combined with more than ordinary ambition, would, it would later be said, make working for his company as much a religion as an ordinary job.

Much has been made of the clash between Watson and Hollerith—men of strong and contrasting personalities. Like many stories that get repeated over the years, the accounts have tended to become overstated and embellished. For one thing, Hollerith was already withdrawing from active involvement in C-T-R, having resigned as a director more than a year before Watson came on board. "It was a great inconvenience," Flint and Metcalf had told the board, "to attend the meetings regularly, as he lived quite a distance from New York," On August 5, 1914, three months after Watson's arrival, Hollerith asked to resign from the Tabulating Machine Company's board, citing his health and the difficulty of travel. C-T-R President Frank N. Kondolf pleaded with the inventor to "hold this matter in abeyance until Mr. Watson or I can have a personal interview with you." The following day, Watson asked the founder of the Tabulating Machine Company to reconsider. He wrote: "I feel that having you as a director of the company is of great value to the business. I know that your suggestions and advice have been of great help to me during the short time I have been connected with the company."

Relations between the two men were correct, even cordial. In a candid conversation, Hollerith warned Watson of the dangers of overselling. "Too many men," he cautioned, "are out for orders in this business . . . regardless of the consequences." Before a customer could use the machines to advantage, he had to put his bookkeeping in order, to systematize his accounts. Otherwise, the machines would be blamed for any deficiencies and thrown out with lasting consequences: "Every order you take that is discontinued is a failure. It is a black eye for you. It is a good deal better never to have the machines put in than to have them fail." Watson ordered a transcription made of the conversation. Politely deferential, he welcomed the advice, although it is also questionable how seriously the record-setting sales manager could take such admonitions as letting customers "kick their heels until they got in line."

But Hollerith had already made up his mind to quit the Tabulating Machine Company's board. "Kindly give me the language of a formal letter of resignation," he inquired of his friend Metcalf. "I should say English, by all means," the attorney quipped in reply. Hollerith's formal resignation was accepted with regret on December 15, 1914, two weeks after the friendly discourse with Watson.

Surprisingly, Watson's keenest instincts, in his early years with C-T-R, were for sensing the importance of development and acting decisively to ensure its pursuit. Surprising because, under Watson's direction, the company would earn an enviable reputation as a marketing organization. He may not have had a deep technical grasp of the working of machines, but he made up for it with an instinctive appreciation of the importance of superior products in the marketplace and an uncanny insight into inventors and what made them tick. The future of C-T-R, Watson sensed, lay as much with its engineers as with its salesmen. In fact, it may have been Watson's fascination with the tabulating machine that drew him to C-T-R in the first place.

While at NCR, he had called upon the Eastman Kodak Company in Rochester, New York, where he had seen some Hollerith machines in action. Impressed, he had gotten NCR to order some on returning to Dayton, but Hollerith, fearful that the company would pirate his invention, had refused to oblige. Later, after NCR did obtain some machines, Watson proudly demonstrated them to his wife. Although they failed to work on that important occasion, his enthusiasm was undiminished. A long-time associate explains that when Watson left NCR and was considering other offers, he chose the one from C-T-R because he felt that the tabulating machine was a product that was going to go, and that it was important to American industry. Of course, as the newly chosen head of C-T-R, Watson was hardly in a position to show outward preference between any of the company's products. He also valued scales, time clocks and other products for another reason. Because they were sold outright, he could discount installment notes from them at the bank and get money to push the tabulating machine business.

Moreover, the outlook for the company's tabulating machines in 1914 was not as bright as it might have been. On June 26 of that year, Gershom Smith wrote to Watson:

Without desiring to be pessimistic, I wish to advise you that there seems considerable to be feared from Royden Peirce machine in connection with life insurance companies and the Powers Printing Tabulator in connection with other insurance companies.

As our rental from insurance companies amounts to about $91,350 per annum and our sales of cards to insurance companies for the six months ending March 31, 1914, amounted to $23,785, . . . we cannot very well afford to lose this business. . . . it is very important that we should, as soon as possible, be able to print the tabulated totals on our machines.

Flint, in fact, had tipped off Hollerith to the competitive threat two years earlier on intercepting a letter to the Secretary of the Treasury. In it, the Auditor of the Post Office, who was considering the installation of Hollerith machines, had reported on a visit to the Peirce Patents Company, at 17 Madison Street in New York, where the Royden System of Perforated Cards was being manufactured. The equipment being developed, he observed, appeared "to contain certain features of distinct advantage over any of the Hollerith machines now on the market." With barely time to get his bearings in a new company, Watson found himself facing a threat to its future.

Contributing to the urgency of the problem, Watson found that he had no one he could rely on completely to close the gap speedily and decisively. Hollerith was holed up in Washington, and Eugene Ford, who had played an important role in developing the key punch and the vertical sorter, worked out of a faraway laboratory at Uxbridge, Massachusetts. While Hollerith and Ford kept in touch through intermittent correspondence, Hollerith stubbornly refused to go to New York and Watson seldom journeyed to Washington. In short, the total engineering force of the Tabulating Machine Company added up to two people, not counting a handful of draftsmen. Communications were tenuous at best. What's more, there was no clear-cut delineation of authority. "The individual," Hollerith had spelled out in his consulting contract, "shall not be subject to the orders of any officer or other person connected to the company."

Watson acted quickly. On August 6, 1914, he wrote to Hollerith:

The matter of . . . an experimental department was taken up at our last C-T-R board meeting and it was suggested that we start up this department in New York City and I was asked to get in touch with Mr. Ford and see what arrangements we could make with him to come here and look after the work. I have . . . made him a proposition of $600 per month to devote his entire time to the Tabulating Machine Company work.

While he was determined to get things moving, the always diplomatic Watson took pains to assuage the older man's feelings. He also wrote:

In taking up the proposition of an experimental department, I naturally would have preferred to talk . . . with you more fully than I have had a chance to, . . . I . . . therefore asked Mr. Braitmeyer to . . . look into the matter. He . . . is returning to Washington tonight . . . [to] . . . see you personally and report on everything that has been done.

Despite Hollerith's ambivalent attitude following the sale of his company, his creative energies were still very much in evidence. From 1911 to 1914, he filed for and was issued patents for numerous improvements. Among them: a new lever-set gang punch put out about 1912; a speck detector that electrically detected flaws in card stock under manufacture—tiny holes or specks of conducting material could cause the machines to register incorrect totals; and the forerunner of the electric key punch, which was later adopted. But by far the most significant developments were Hollerith's advances in printing devices, based upon his earlier work, and a new technique called automatic control. This last patent, filed for in March 1914, was especially important.

For some time, operators of Hollerith machines had been forced to rely on stop cards. These cards signaled the tabulator to stop after processing one group of cards, say, belonging to a customer account, so that totals could be copied from the counters before another group of cards was processed. But putting the stop cards in by hand and taking them out again was a bothersome chore. One competitor, urged on by a customer, was now working on a means of getting around the use of stop cards entirely. Hollerith's automatic control concept turned the machine off automatically after it got through a batch of cards, by means of brushes, that sensed the change in the group designation punched in the card. Later, he would improve the technique further so that the machine turned itself off and resumed operation automatically, while totals for different subgroups were recorded on separate counters.

The automatic control concept, combined with a printing attachment, Watson quickly grasped, could result in a highly versatile machine, one that could answer competition and provide the basis for future development. But how quickly could it be completed? To rush development, Watson rented a top-floor loft in a twelve-story building at 510–512 Sixth Avenue (now Avenue of the Americas) near Pennsylvania Station, only a month after proposing the new experimental department. It was a light and airy place. Watson, decked out in a morning coat, went there to see what was going on soon after the sixty- by ninety-foot room was occupied on Columbus Day, 1914. Ford came down from Uxbridge with several draftsmen to run the small shop. But soon some unfamiliar faces also appeared. Among the first were Fred M. Carroll, who had worked on mechanisms for adding machines and registers at NCR, and Clair D. Lake, a durable Scotsman whose numerous inventions over thirty years with IBM would earn him the nickname of "Mr. Accounting Machine." It was the new company's first attempt at organized development. "In support of the men who are at the head of the engineering division and their expert mechanics," the Tabulating Machine Company's house organ would announce within a few years, "no expense has been spared to furnish the best facilities with which improvements could be studied and worked out."

By 1916, Ford could report to Watson that four printing tabulators were under development and another model, based on ideas submitted by Hollerith and built under Ford's supervision, was completed. The leading contenders were the Carroll machine, identical in principle to Ford's, and the Lake machine. "The Lake machine," Ford told Watson, "is decidedly better than the Ford or Carroll machines both as to the fundamental principle and arrangement." Carrying forward and building on Hollerith's earlier work, Lake hatched the company's first printing tabulator in 1917, but because of the interference of World War I, it was never put on the market. A second Lake printing tabulator, which embodied automatic control, including automatic start-up after operations, was finished in 1921. Toward the end of that year, C-T-R placed on the market twelve of the new printing tabulators that it had struggled so long to develop. The machine, it was said, saved the company from extinction.

Hollerith had supplied a firm base for development. But Watson was seeing to it that others could carry on—with or without "the mastermind of the Doctor." Not only did Watson display a gambler's penchant for betting on the right men, he would also enthusiastically spur them into action. He chased engineers out of the laboratory to customers' offices to see what they wanted. And after the machines were installed, he chased his engineers back again to find out what the problems were. "I want this," he would say, scribbling a few notes for an assistant on a pad. Often, he would give more than one man the same assignment at the same time. There was said to be some pretty stiff competition at the Endicott, New York, laboratory, to which development was moved in 1917. Some years later, the lab was divided into eight parts—four offices in the corners of each of two floors. And the doors of each office were kept locked against everyone else in the building. Sometimes, the engineer in charge of development reportedly had difficulty getting past the barricaded doorways, although he was the one responsible for what occurred inside. Not only was intramural competition fierce at Endicott, but, as late as the 1940s, Watson kept a separate staff of inventors in New York City, seeing if they could outdo the upstate engineering staff.

J. Royden Peirce, a former competitor hired by C-T-R in 1922, struck up an internal rivalry with Lake. Peirce, it was rumored, would always build a wooden model of the machine he was going to make, and drag it into Watson's office. Time and again, the other engineers would shake their heads in dismay because Peirce would run around the end on them and get in there first.

However, aware of the charges of unfair competition leveled at him while at NCR, Watson was careful to treat competition fairly, and on occasion even generously. Shortly after joining C-T-R, he learned that James Powers's basic patents for tabulators and sorters had been judged in conflict with Hollerith's and the latter's given priority. Watson could easily and quite legitimately have put his principal rival out of business. It must have been a tempting step, since some of Powers's machines were said to be both superior to and cheaper than Hollerith's. Instead, Watson quickly granted licenses to Powers, ensuring his main competitor's survival.

As the new company gained a life of its own, relations between Hollerith and Watson became increasingly strained. Hollerith would have resented any man who had taken over "his" company. For over the years the Tabulating Machine Company had become an extension of its founder's personality. It was his life, and he was no more capable of letting go than of giving up life itself. But if Hollerith disliked Watson in a generalized way as a symbol of his replacement, he saved his special wrath for long-time associates who "betrayed" him by transferring their loyalties to the new man. An associate explained:

Although he had decided to sell out, Hollerith was reluctant to sit anywhere but at the head of the table. Most of the people already associated with Hollerith who came into C-T-R maintained their loyalty to Hollerith and were really in opposition to Watson. The two who weren't were Joe Wilson and Otto Braitmeyer. Braitmeyer, especially, was of tremendous value to Watson.

Since Braitmeyer had started with Hollerith at the age of sixteen, the inventor had taken a fatherly interest in the young man. He had stayed on, becoming secretary and office manager while obtaining a law degree at night. He had also become part of the Hollerith household, living with the family while the inventor was away. Later, he brought his own wife and children to Sunday dinner at the Hollerith's. As Watson rightly sensed, Braitmeyer had become Hollerith's alter ego. Matching the inventor's quick stride, Braitmeyer jotted down orders on an ever-present pad and saw that they were faithfully carried out. He ran the business in Hollerith's absence, and he carried every detail of it in his head. Now, when Hollerith proved stubborn or simply inaccessible, Watson discovered he could turn to Braitmeyer. On his part, Braitmeyer welcomed the chance to come into his own. When differences arose, Braitmeyer found himself caught between the two men and also caught between the future, his own future, and the past. He increasingly favored Watson. Hollerith was deeply hurt by the seeming rejection.

Despite differences, Watson continued to value Hollerith's advice. In March 1917, he asked the inventor to go to Endicott. "We would like to have you talk over matters with Messrs. Lake,

Carroll, Knistrom," he wrote, "and, as I have several matters to take up in Endicott, I would like very much to arrange to go up with you as it will give me an opportunity to go into things with you." Hollerith obliged by making the trip and, soon after, Watson wrote again:

I would appreciate . . . very much . . . your opinion regarding the experimental work . . . in Endicott. I was at the factory one day last week and found all of the men greatly encouraged over your visit. . . . I would very much like to have your criticisms and suggestions regarding the work.

Relations between the two men continued to be polite and cordial. On June 14, Hollerith wrote to Watson suggesting an automatically controlled tabulator with a printing attachment and using a smaller card. Watson assigned Carroll to work out the idea and wrote to Hollerith on October 6:

Mr. Carroll will be in a position to go to you within the next 10 days with this suggestion fairly well worked out. He has made plate models of some of the movements. He would like to have your criticisms of the work he has done so far and any suggestions that you have to give.

When, during the year, a Powers patent application relating to automatic control came to Watson's attention, Hollerith advised Lake how to design around it. As he wrote to Watson:

I outlined to Mr. Lake a machine which could be made and be automatically controlled, having only one brush plate (equivalent to a pin box). I, of course did not feel at liberty to give Mr. Lake any instructions, but told him that . . . it would be advisable to put that idea in the shape of patent office drawings and get it on file at an early date.

There is a hint of deference, even of resentment in the tone. For unlike Ford, Lake clearly belonged to the new order of things. But no such reserve was shown by Watson when, two years later, the Commissioner of Patents gave Hollerith priority of invention for automatic control. On April 23, 1919, Watson wrote: "The time has expired for filing appeals from the decision of the Commissioner of Patents on the Powers-Hollerith interference on the automatic control, and you will no doubt be pleased to learn that the Powers Company has not taken an appeal."

Watson never failed to be outwardly generous and courteous toward Hollerith. When the inventor sent him a newspaper clipping describing the use of Hollerith machines in the New York State Census of 1917, Watson promptly replied. "This description might have been considered exaggerated if it had given the machines credit for the ability to talk, but since we claim that they really do read and write, we feel that it is a particularly good portrayal of the impression one receives on seeing them in operation." There were toasts at Tabulating Machine Company banquets "to the man who made it possible for us to be there." Every man, it was pointed out, owed a debt of gratitude "to the man who conceived and established before the business world the ideas which they are now exploiting." There were also the inevitable songs. To the tune of "On the Trail of the Lonesome Pine," one such gathering hailed the founder of the business:

Herman Hollerith is a man of honor
What he has done is beyond compare
To the wide world he has been the donor
Of an invention very rare
His praises we all gladly sing
His results make him outclass a king
Facts from factors he has made a business
May the years good things to him bring.

Watson had a keen sense of history. To build for the future, an organization should also have a sense of its own past. He urged Hollerith to save his letters and papers. "It occurs to me," he wrote, "that if we could get together all of the clippings which you have on hand and letters, etc., and have a good writer go over the proposition with you, that he could write a very interesting story about the tabulating machine and the man who invented it." There is no evidence that Hollerith responded to the request.

Such praise was not enough for Hollerith when he was no longer at the center of events. When Watson telegraphed that his old friend and patent attorney Jonathan Balcan Hayward was visiting Washington, Hollerith apparently did not receive the message in time. Returning from out of town, the inventor thanked the head of C-T-R and added:

I notice that there were 13 words in that telegram. Whenever a telegram doesn't reach me . . . I generally find it a message with 13 words. I will eat at table with 13. I will sleep in room with 13. Ride in Pullman with 13. But I will never send a telegram with 13 words.

Whatever the reply signifies, beyond a fascination with numbers, Hollerith's attitude was hardly helpful and, possibly, hostile. He implied, at least indirectly, that it was Watson's fault that the message did not arrive. The plain fact is that as time went by, and Watson's star rose, Hollerith had less and less to do with the affairs of the Tabulating Machine Company. In 1915, the general books of the company were moved to New York, from where all disbursements were to be made. Two years later, customer records followed. With little to do, Hollerith moved his office to a small suite of rooms on the third floor of the Georgetown plant, where he seemingly cut himself off from the world. Yet he rang his bell as fiercely as ever, demanding immediate attention. "One day he rang for me," recalls Dan Pickrell, "and I wasn't quite as fast on the ball as I usually was because I had other things to do. When I got to the bottom of the steps, he was at the top yelling, 'The king is dead . . . the king is dead!'"

Like Shakespeare's Lear, Hollerith had shed his power, all the while expecting that he would still be accorded the prerogatives of the monarch in full control of his kingdom. It was not to be. And loyal friends were leaving, putting him further out of touch with the life he knew. In July 1918, he heard from Merrill, who had resigned as Cleveland district manager: "It is no fun killing oneself and that is about what I feel I were doing in giving up my job, as the Tabulating Company has pretty nearly been my life for the past 18 years—since I left school one June for a summer vacation with you, Herman." Several months later, he received a letter from Gershom Smith, the man he had chosen to succeed himself. "You will, I know," Smith wrote, "be interested to hear that I am now connected with George Goethals and Co., Inc., consulting engineers in the capacity of consulting accountant." A once familiar world was moving on, and Hollerith was no longer part of the one that was taking its place. By the end of the year, he wrote: "I am entirely out of touch with the Tabulating Machine Company affairs and really do not do anything but putter around with my own little personal affairs."

How far out of touch came out a short time later. When Otto Braitmeyer, Hollerith's one-time office boy, moved to New York as Watson's right-hand man, the inventor learned the news from a friend.

In the meanwhile, the United States entered World War I. "The government, recognizing the importance of our machines in speeding up war production," the *Tabulator* informed salesmen, "has so increased its demands for our equipment that our manufacturing facilities are taxed to the utmost." Other customers would have to wait, the house organ explained, and urged salesmen to so inform those ordering machines. The war was doing what the company's salesmen could not hope to do for many years— it was making the punched card a daily fact of life for thousands of clerks marshaling the nation's food supply and other resources. And unknown to Hollerith, in faraway Germany some of his machines were being used to chart the journeys of U-boats foraging for Allied shipping.

Down on his Virginia farm, Hollerith took to flying American flags. Each morning, he had Nan run the Stars and Stripes up a pole on the front lawn at Brighton and take it down again at night. He did so, a daughter recalls, because someone said that he was German and he deeply resented the remark. Like most other Americans at the time, Hollerith had believed that the United States should keep out of foreign wars. But once his country was involved, the inventor supported the war effort wholeheartedly. Besides trying unsuccessfully to donate his yacht to the Navy, Hollerith sold butter from his pedigreed cows to benefit the American Red Cross. He put so much of himself into his well-intended gestures that he was bound to be disappointed. Describing his not altogether successful efforts at flag flying, he wrote to a friend: "I am commencing to appreciate why there are not more flags flying down here. It is too expensive. I have brought four flags down with me some time ago and two of them are commencing to go to pieces already. We may be shy of many things, but there is an abundance of wind."

War production drained labor from the farm, leaving the inventor's wife and daughters struggling to keep the large place going without a laundress, cook, or housemaid. To make things easier for his family, Hollerith purchased a Laundryette washing machine through his friend Merrill. It is uncertain to what extent General Electric's new appliance relieved the household drudgery, but the inventor's personal confrontation with things mechanical revived his spirits. He wrote to Merrill:

Last Monday William called me into the laundry . . . the motor had gone bad and I believe the trouble was due to defective work on the part of the General Electric Company. . . .

In regard to the matter, because I did not want to lose the use of the Laundryette, I hustled downtown and got a Westinghouse motor and the machine was at once put back into service. It seems quite like old times to be fussing with the General Electric Company about their motors.

It was like old times, poking around with machines. Was there any way of going back? Of getting busy again? At fifty-nine, Hollerith's mind was alert, although the state of his physical health was far less certain. The previous winter, he had taken several falls, serious enough to mention to a friend. And in November 1919, he entered a hospital "for a couple of days."

"There is only one point about my possible death," he had written with a touch of humor. "I would not be able to read what they would publish about me." Whatever his ailment, by the summer, Hollerith felt well enough to think ahead. His consulting agreement with C-T-R, which forbade him from competing with the company, would expire in two years. So, too, would his broad patents, which the company owned. "Now I often think when the patents expire," he wrote to Merrill on August 4, "someone will come out with a compact tabulating machine which can be handled more like an adding machine and sold outright for a fixed amount." It was the kind of machine, Hollerith believed, that might do well in the export trade. And while it might not appeal to the large concerns already employing the Tabulating Company's equipment, there was a still larger market to be explored. "The future business," Hollerith wrote, "lies with the much larger number of smaller concerns that are not equal to the present machine and prices."

By the close of the year, he had pretty well decided to start up again, even if it meant giving up a year or two of his $20,000 annual income from the Tabulating Machine Company. Earlier, he had confided to a friend, "I am trying to arrange with Watson to terminate my relations with C-T-R. That would mean my income would be reduced by $20,000 and, still, I would this year have to pay a tax on my last year's income including the $20,000." A friendly visit set his mind working. "Metcalf was here the last few weeks," he wrote to a friend. "One night at dinner he made the remark that he was getting tired of loafing and wanted to find something to do. I have not said a word to him, but the thought struck my mind. Perhaps I could persuade him to get back into harness."

Maybe it was a pipe dream. Nevertheless, the inventor set up a small drawing table in his office at the farm and another in his bedroom in town, and went to work. When his son Charles visited home for several months in early 1920, he joined in the effort. "My father had some ideas on a new tabulator," the son recalled. "He set up a drawing board and I was doing some drafting on the new design." However, Charles soon left for Michigan to help set up a company for making automobile parts.

Hollerith labored on the machine fitfully over the next several years. On December 14, 1921, he wrote a two-page letter to Metcalf detailing the design of a counter mechanism. He also told of a meeting with Watson: "Watson did ask about you and I told him I thought you had gone to Italy to spend the winter. From his actions, I judge that he thought as long as you were in Italy and I in the U.S., why worry?" In fact, there was not very much for the president of C-T-R to worry about. Although Hollerith continued to refine his ideas, progress was slow. On September 14, 1922, he wrote to a friend.

As you know, I started a short time ago formulating some ideas I had recently conceived regarding a tabulating machine which could be operated with a storage battery and an alternating current. I think I have some novel ideas along this line. I have had preliminary investigation made and it seems clear. However, I have done very little along this line this summer and am awaiting Metcalf's return before considering the matter. All this, you see, is too nebulous to offer any hope at present.

The last mention of the machine is in a letter written in 1923, some four years after Hollerith began thinking about it. "As yet," he reported, "we have done practically nothing on the tabulating machine, principally as a result of my feeling so wretchedly as a result of an attack of grippe." He continued:

My idea would be to make a machine that might reach a field that is not now touched by T.M. It might almost be said to be between a tabulating machine and an adding machine. . . . there is a large field for this sort of machine in many places not big enough for a regular Tab. outfit. Should this matter ever develop, it would be much more a manufacturing and not so much a system proposition.

Nearly 40 years after he had begun working out his ideas for a "census machine", Hollerith's mind was still reaching ahead. Not only steel mills and railroads and insurance companies could use the machines. Even a small business might employ such equipment in the future if the cost were low enough. The tabulating machine, the Italian statistician Luigi Bodio had told him so many years ago, would be as useful to business as the sewing machine is in the home. However, the inventor's poor health, his family said, halted work on the machine.

Surprisingly—because he found little meaning in life beyond his work—Hollerith's remaining years were, for the most part, contented, even pleasurable. He dropped his stricture against being photographed long enough to be pictured with his oldest son, Herman, Jr., and holding Herman III. He appears erect, pleased, and as proud as any grandparent. When Charles was married, he traveled west to Michigan, bringing a Model T with red wire wheels as a present for the bride. Going West, he told the son he would miss, was the smartest thing he had ever done. Besides the techonology he had fostered, he had raised strong-minded, independent sons who would carry on.

He continued to dispatch large quantities of butter, oysters, hams, shad, and other delicacies to friends, with the size of his orders causing some consternation among the purveyors of the produce. "I am afraid that my letter," he informed the Gloucester Fresh Fish Company, "gave you the impression I was a dealer. I simply wanted some haddie for myself and several of my friends." In April 1926, he wrote to Metcalf:

When I get codfish, I get it packed in three pound boxes, 12 boxes packed in a case. Now when you say that you would like to have a box of codfish, do you mean a three pound box or a box with 36 pounds. . . . In case you don't want as much as 36 pounds, I will gladly send you whatever number of three pound boxes you want.

It was not inconceivable to Hollerith that Metcalf, a bachelor, might want thirty-six pounds of codfish.

There were also bound to be sad moments when news reached him that old friends had passed away. In 1921, he learned in a letter from Hyde of the death of Robert P. Porter, the man who had staked his reputation on the tabulating machines as superintendent of the 1890 Census: "Mr Porter was riding in a hired auto driven by a girl chauffeur. Something went wrong with the machine and the girl was out trying to fix it. Mr. Porter then got out and walked around the back of the machine and was struck by another auto coming from the other direction." Hollerith himself had a narrow escape when the car he was driving went out of control and landed on its side in a ditch. His relation to machines—his own or someone else's—remained antithetical. After the accident, in which he got off with minor cuts and bruises, he gave away the offender, a seven-passenger Lincoln, and never drove again. His own death, however, was unexpected.

On November 15, 1929, he became ill, seemingly of a cold. He developed difficulty breathing. Two days later, he died at 4:20 in the morning at his Georgetown home. He was sixty-nine years old. Death was officially ascribed to heart failure. If Hollerith had been curious about what the newspapers would say, he almost certainly would have been disappointed, for public attention was taken up with other matters.

"Prince of Wales Now Knitting with Other British Notables," the *New York Times* proclaimed in a front page headline on the day of his death. Three scarves knitted by the Prince, the writer went on to say, are on display at Queen Mary's London Needle-work Guild. Such trivia helped to obscure the deeper concern that was gripping the country. The same day, the *Washington Post* noted that one of the most interesting features of the forthcoming Census would be the enumeration of the unemployed. "The real need for such an enumeration," the paper said, "is demonstrated by the fact that, during the past two years, estimates of unemployed have varied from 1.5 million persons to as many as eight million." Hollerith might have noted with approval the use of his machines.

On November 18, the local papers noted the fact of Hollerith's death—just barely. In a squib on page 5, the *Post* said that "Herman Hollerith, inventor of the electric tabulating machines now in use by the United States and foreign governments in compiling census reports and widely used by business concerns in the country, died yesterday." Beyond the single sentence, the rest was devoted to funeral details. The *Star* did little better, adding only that Hollerith had sold his invention to the "International Machine Corporation." Picking up the story the following day, the *New York Times*, in a two-inch squib, also misquoted the name of IBM.

The day of the funeral, flags in Washington were flown at half mast, not for Hollerith, but out of respect for James W. Good, the late Secretary of War. The Executive Mansion, where the Secretary's funeral was to be held, was closed to the public. Out in Georgetown, friends gathered at Hollerith's three-story brick home. Among them, to the astonishment of the family, were Thomas J. Watson and Otto Braitmeyer. They were suitably dressed in striped pants and morning coats with gardenias in the lapel. Within ten days, *Business Machines*, the IBM publication, would do better than the public press in recognizing the man who had "contributed vastly to the progress of the business." "Dr. Hollerith's invention," it said, "has lessened drudgery, mental toil, and human error in business and statistical organizations; and both business and human welfare have benefitted through his contributions to the world's progress." Despite any differences, Watson was always generous in his praise.

Following the ceremony at home, family and friends followed the casket the short distance up 29th Street to Oak Hill Cemetery, where Hollerith was buried. The burial ground is bordered on one side by Lover's Lane, the same steep incline up which Hollerith had pulled the painted cart he had brought back from Norway, the time that Herman, Jr., had fallen out and scolded his father, at which Hollerith, seeing a smaller image of himself, had laughed.

After it was over and passing days and weeks had dulled the grief, memories from early years came flooding back. Among them may have been the letter to his wife from a hotel room in Bern forty-four years before, when, deeply discouraged over his prospects, Hollerith had written:

This machine or the principle will be potent factors in Statistical Science long after I am gone. Whether I or someone else will do it, this system is bound to be developed in many ways. It will take many years and perhaps it will be something for the two boys . . . to be able to say their daddy originated it.

The machine, as it exists now, may and probably will appear crude and inefficient, still it is the genesis. This may appear like conceit and vanity on my part but you will understand how I say it, and I have no idea of ever talking like this to anyone else.

According to his family, he never did.

Notes

To the reader: notes are keyed to the text by page number in the left-hand column below. Each page number is then followed by a short quote from the part of the text to which the note refers. The note itself follows the colon at the end of each short quote.

Chapter 1: Discovering the Census Problem

1. Arriving in Washington, D.C., in the fall of 1879: Hollerith was appointed expert special agent on October 17, 1879; F. Walker to C. Schurz, U.S. Census Office Records, National Archives.

1. statistics . . . had often been discreditable and even disgraceful: Report to Secretary of the Interior on the "Temporary Nature of Census Operations," November 15, 1879 (F. A. Walker) (Washington, D.C.: GPO, 1879).

1. lively pulse-taking: *Ibid.*

2. "not only technical knowledge, but high scientific training": *Ibid.* Walker referred specifically to the inquiry into power and machinery of which Hollerith's report forms a part.

2. At nine, he had bolted public school: V. Hollerith, "Biographical Sketch of Herman Hollerith," p. 69. When nearly sixty, Hollerith was assured by a friend, "Please do not worry about any such little things as errors in spelling. . . . I am only too glad to hear from you even if every word is spelled wrong and, after reading your letter, I could find only two errors": G. Smith to H. Hollerith, February 7, 1919, Hollerith papers.

2. At the College of the City of New York: Hollerith's family was unaware that he attended City College. Annual registers of the school show him as a member of the Introductory Class in '72–'73, a freshman in '73–'74, and a sophomore in '74–'75. He evidently transferred to Columbia for the second half of his sophomore year. Although five years younger than his brother George, he was only two classes behind him. The spelling class incident may be exaggerated, since the rules for admission stated that "No student can be admitted unless he . . . has attended the

common schools in the city twelve months and passed a good examination in spelling" as well as other subjects. Since students took the exams in June before attending in the fall, Hollerith was barely thirteen when he passed them. At the time, the college was housed in a handsome Tudor-style building at 23rd Street and Lexington Avenue designed by James Renwick, architect of the Smithsonian "Castle" in Washington, which the building resembled. Students had to be in the chapel on the top floor of the building at precisely 8:45 every morning, when the doors were closed for roll call. Hollerith's home address at the time was 428 East 58th Street.

2.   graduated with distinction from Columbia School of Mines: The curriculum of the School of Mines is from the "Catalogue of Officers and Students of Columbia College, 1876–1877." Hollerith's grades were transcribed from alumni records. The description of the school is partly from Finch, *History of the School of Engineering*, pp. 145–46.

2.   Such training ... seemed to foretell little in Hollerith's future: The tenuous relationship between Hollerith's courses and his later accomplishment is observed by Blodgett in "Herman Hollerith: Data Processing Pioneer," p. 10.

2.   His father ... died in an accident: According to family accounts, Johann George Hollerith owned farmlands in Wisconsin or possibly Illinois, which he rented to farmers. Once school was out for the year, he would travel west from Buffalo, New York, to collect rents from his tenants, often walking twenty-five miles or more a day. On one such trip, he hired a one-horse conveyance to make the rounds. He was severely injured when the horse shied, overturning the carriage. He never fully recovered from his injuries and died three years later on March 9, 1869. From V. Hollerith, "Biographical Sketch," p. 69; also, interviews with Madeline and George Hollerith, January 19, 1972, and May 18, 1970, respectively.

3.   "Paddle your own canoe": Interview with Madeline Hollerith. January 19, 1972.

3.   "Produced many novel designs": *City of Buffalo Illustrated, Commerce, Trades and Industries of Buffalo* (Buffalo: Courier Printing Co., 1890) pp. 162–63.

3.   "A teacher ... affects eternity": Henry Adams, *The Education of Henry Adams*, from John Bartlett, *Familiar Quotations*, 13th ed. (Boston: Little, Brown & Co.), p. 697a.

4.   "Each student ... could rely upon an affectionate personal interest": "In Memoriam, William Petit Trowbridge," *The Quarterly* (School of Mines, Columbia College) 14 (November 1892): 6.

4. Did Schurz recall Hollerith's father: In "Biographical Sketch", p. 69, V. Hollerith says they "became acquainted"; in a letter to V. Hollerith, Erma Hollerith Erbe says that J. G. Hollerith had been "a close friend" of Schurz. Undated. Hollerith Family.

4. the steel industry, in which he was intent on making a career: According to a friend, Hollerith graduated from Columbia "with the intention of going into the steel industry which was just beginning to show signs of great future growth at the time"; from Memorandum of Record by F. S. Blackall, Jr., May 29, 1953, of a conversation with P. P. Merrill, Taft-Peirce Co. Records.

4. an astonishing gain of 336 percent in the application of steam power to steelmaking: "Report on the Statistics of Steam- and Water-Power Used in the Manufacture of Iron and Steel During the Census Year Ending May 31, 1880" (H. Hollerith), Tenth Census, U.S. Census Office, 22: 2. Bureau of the Census, Washington D.C.

5. compute . . . life tables "as an amusement or at least a diversion": H. Hollerith to J. T. Wilson, August 7, 1919, Hollerith Papers.

5. "I am also indebted to Mr. Herman Hollerith": Dr. Billings's letter of transmittal for the 1880 "Report on Mortality and Vital Statistics," U.S. Census, cited by Truesdell, *Development of Punch Card Tabulation*, p. 30.

5. "Chicken salad": V. Hollerith, "Biographical Sketch," p. 70; also, interview with Lucia B. Hollerith, May 6, 1968.

5. "Let's spend the money left on something we might enjoy": Lucia Hollerith, *ibid.*

5. "I have been cleaning up old negatives": H. Hollerith to unknown, December 16, 1919, as transcribed by V. Hollerith, Hollerith Papers.

6. one account places the meeting at Dr. Billings's tea table: For various accounts, see Truesdell, *Development of Punch Card Tabulation*, pp. 30–34.

6. "He said to me there ought to be a machine": H. Hollerith to J. T. Wilson, August 7, 1919. Hollerith Papers.

6. "There ought to be some mechanical way": Dr. Walter F. Willcox, cited in Truesdell, pp. 30–31.

6. "I do not remember . . . Father's remarks": Dr. Walter F. Willcox to H. Hollerith, April 10, 1926, citing Mrs. K. B. Wilson's letter. Hollerith Papers. Truesdell, p. 31, omits the final sentence of the letter, which gives credit to Hollerith.

7. "It is based on my memory": Dr. Walter F. Willcox to H. Hollerith, April 10, 1926, Hollerith Papers.

7. Dr. Billings, at forty, had already earned: Principal sources for Billings's career are Garrison, *John Shaw Billings; Memorial Meeting in Honor of the Late Dr. John Shaw Billings,* April 25, 1913, New York: New York Public Library; and *Dictionary of American Biography* 2:266.

8. "he came to my rooms": Sir William Osler, quoted by Garrison, *John Shaw Billings,* p. 208.

8. "He was a member of the executive profession": Address by Richard R. Bowker, in *Memorial Meeting,* p. 16.

8. "After studying the problem": H. Hollerith to J. T. Wilson. August 7, 1919. Hollerith Papers.

8. "He was not interested any further": *Ibid.* On Dr. Billings's lack of interest in material gain, see also address by Dr. S. Weir Mitchell, in *Memorial Meeting,* p. 4: "[he] lavished on his way through life opportunities for wealth and fame, any one of which would have tempted a man more eager than he for riches or more avid of renown."

8. Hollerith made a nuisance of himself: Truesdell, *Development of Punch Card Tabulation,* p. 31.

9. "It was a wonder . . . that many of the clerks did not go blind or crazy": T. C. Martin, "Counting a Nation by Electricity," *Electrical Engineer* 12, November 11, 1891, p. 521.

9. Walker had "sought promptly to encourage the inventive ability": H. T. Newcomb, "The Development of Mechanical Methods of Statistical Tabulaton in the U.S., with Especial Reference to Population and Mortality Data." Paper delivered to the Fifteenth International Congress on Hygiene and Demography, Washington, D.C., September 23–28, 1912.

9. Hollerith moved to a private desk in Colonel Seaton's private office: Deposition of H. Hollerith, March 6, 1897, before the examiner of interferences, U.S. Patent Office, in Interference No. 17,986, W. F. Roberts, Washington, D. C., p. 22. Hollerith Papers.

10. "with regard to manufacturing and placing the . . . machine on the market": *Ibid.,* p. 23; Dr. Uta Merzbach of the Smithsonian provided a description of the Lanston machine. Interview, Washington, D.C., March 20, 1970.

10. Jeremy Bentham . . . noted that business talent: Quoted from Josephson, *Edison,* p. 64.

10. "The . . . inability of the office": Robert H. Holley, "Machine Tabulation in the Census Office: 1870–1912," unpublished manuscript, Census Records, National Archives.

Chapter 2: Instructor at M.I.T.

11. "to consult you informally": G. F. Swain to H. Hollerith, January 24, 1882, Hollerith Papers.

12. "The amount of salary": W. P. Trowbridge to H. Hollerith, March 8, 1882, Hollerith Papers.

12. "We are very poor": F. A. Walker to H. Hollerith, March 20, 1882, Hollerith Papers.

12. in entire charge of the seniors: *The Tech* (M.I.T.), October 11, 1882, p. 6.

12. The drawing room [a] . . . "black hole": *Ibid.*

12. "beginning his work in an energetic . . . way": *Ibid.*

12. present a formal paper: H. Hollerith, "Two Forms of Dynamometer," *Proceedings of the Society of Arts* (M.I.T.) 1882–83, pp. 56–60.

12–13. "a marked success": Letter of recommendation, F. A. Walker to U.S. Patent Office, April 11, 1883, Hollerith Papers.

13. "While at Boston": H. Hollerith to J. T. Wilson, August 7, 1919, Hollerith Papers.

13. "My idea was": *Ibid.*

13. "Various statistical items": U.S. Patent No. 395,782.

14. Hearing of a puzzle contest: Interview with Charles Hollerith, New York City, January 26, 1969.

14. "The trouble was": H. Hollerith to J. T. Wilson.

15. "I was traveling in the West": *Ibid.*

16. "As the first flow of the developer": H. Hollerith, "An Electric Tabulating System," *The Quarterly* (School of mines, Columbia College), 10 (April 1889): 241. Madeline Hollerith emphasized her father's and uncle's interest in photography in an interview, January 19, 1972.

16. he never claimed it for himself: Blodgett, *Herman Hollerith*, p. 23.

17. "His brother said the Jacquard loom": From materials gathered and transcribed by V. Hollerith for C. Greene for "The Beginnings."

17. "Hollerith has recently made some inventions in looms": T. Talcott to H. Talcott, August 15, 1888.

17. he balked at repeating the course material: V. Hollerith, "Biographical Sketch," p. 70.

18. "he has been admirably trained": C. Seaton to E. M. Marple, May 10, 1883, Hollerith Papers.

Chapter 3: Grounding as a Patent Expert

19. "the advancement of the arts": "Annual Report of the U.S. Commissioner of Patients for 1843," from U.S. Department of Commerce, *The Story of the U.S. Patent Office*, Washington, D.C.: GPO, 1972.

20. he resigned his position: Personnel Files, U.S. Patent Office.

20. "As regards patent rights": H. Hollerith to Albert Meyer, September 19, 1884, Hollerith Papers.

22. "This offer on the part of Mr. Richards": *Ibid.*

22. "You asked how much money I should want": *Ibid.*

22. "This money need not be all invested": *Ibid.*

23. "I Herman Hollerith . . . have invented": Hollerith describes the earliest design of his census system in U.S. Patent No. 395,783.

Chapter 4: Experiments with Air Brakes

24. three patents for . . . railway car brakes: U.S. Patent Nos. 334,020, 334,021, 334,022.

24. no certainty where his main chance might lie: That Hollerith was looking into different areas as a free-lance inventor is illustrated by U.S. Patent No. 349,718 for an apparatus for corrugating metal tubing.

24. creating insatiable demands: On the importance of the railroads in shaping industrial development, see Morison, *Men, Machines and Modern Times*, 170.

25. Before the time of regulation: The Interstate Commerce Commission was set up in 1887.

25. "The radical cause of their neglect": Abbott's quote appears in Holbrook, *The Story of American Railroads*, pp. 292–93.

26–27. The essential advantage that Hollerith grasped: Hollerith's brake designs were described by Charles Hollerith in an interview January 26, 1969.

27. "it is desirable . . . to apply the brakes continuously": U.S. Patent No. 334,020.

27. an epochal event: The importance of the Burlington trials is evidenced by extensive coverage of them in *The Railway Age, Railway Review, Engineering News*, and other publications.

28. "I . . . have perfect confidence in . . . electrical tallying": H. Hollerith to A. Meyer, July 14, 1885, Hollerith Papers.

28.   "Father was newly married": Interview with Madeline Hollerith, January 19, 1972.

29.   a pamphlet, dated 1884: *The Mallinckrodt Brake Company* (St. Louis: Buxton & Skinner Stationery Co., 1884), Hollerith Papers.

29.   Who was Henry Flad?: "Memoir of Henry Flad," *Transactions of the ASCE* 42 (December 1899): 565; also, *Dictionary of American Biography* 3: 445; *Encyclopedia of the History of St. Louis* (St. Louis: Southern History Co., 1899) 1: 789–90; *Engineering News & American Contract Journal* (July 3, 1886): 9–10. The last states that Flad's brakes were being tested on a division of the B & O.

30.   his mother . . . was named Franciska Brunn: *Dictionary of American Biography* 3: 445.

30.   "although he took out numerous patents": "Memoir of Henry Flad," p. 565.

30.   "The morning was hot but clear": *Railway Age*, July 15, 1886, p. 384.

31.   "The results . . . cannot help but be of great value": H. Hollerith, "Burlington Brake Tests," *The Quarterly* (School of Mines, Columbia College) 8 (July 1887): 336.

31.   "H. Holleraith who accompanies Mr. Carpenter": *Railway Age*, May 13, 1887, p. 327.

31.   The Carpenter brake . . . "has an automatic valve": *Railway Age,* May 20, 1887, p. 347.

32.   "When electricity is not used": *Ibid.*

32.   In its preliminary report: The report is cited by Hollerith in "The Burlington Brake Tests," *The Quarterly* (School of Mines, Columbia College) 9 (July 1888): 68.

33.   ". . . it would seem strange": *Ibid.*

33.   "Electricity . . . is a new element": *Ibid.*

33.   "Whether the electrical appliances will remain reliable": *Ibid.*, p. 69.

33.   "thinks the time has come": *Railway Review*, July 16, 1887, p. 414.

33.   Hollerith . . . ignored the offer: Interview with Charles Hollerith, January 26, 1969.

34.   "They threw out Daddy's brakes": Notes by Lucia Hollerith of an undated conversation with Edmund Talcott, Hollerith Papers.

34.   "Still further experiments": *Railway Review,* September 10, 1887, p. 520.

34.   "The journey . . . was a splendid . . . demonstration": H. G. Prout, "Safety in Railroad Travel," in *The American Railway*, p. 201.

34. "It is hard to conceive of a condition": H. Hollerith, "The Burlington Brake Tests," July 1888, p. 58.

35. "that scoundrel": interview with Charles Hollerith, January 26, 1969.

35. "Hollerith is in New York": T. Talcott to H. Talcott, February 23, 1892.

35. George Hollerith . . . thinks they were: Interview with J. G. Hollerith, May 17, 1970.

35. "upon which patent workings are due": Minutes of the Tabulating Machine Co., May 8, 1906, IBM Archives.

35. "The engineer deliberately went by signals": H. Hollerith to G. F. Swain, December 5, 1905, Harvard University, Faculty Archives.

36. "Today, many high-speed passenger trains": The Westinghouse Air Brake Co., *75th Anniversary, 1869–1944*, Westinghouse, Eilmerding, Pa., 1944, p. 23.

36. The sentence could have been taken: H. Hollerith, "The Burlington Brakes Tests," p. 58.

36. a punched card system in which pneumatic pressure: U.S. Patents Nos. 526,129 and 526,130.

37. "The idea is similar to that . . . in railway practice": "Mechanical Tabulation," *Engineering*, August 8, 1902, p. 165.

38. Flora Fergusson: She may have had a connection with St. Louis and relatives named Henry living in Georgetown, according to a letter to the author from V. Hollerith, April 12, 1980. A record of Tabulation Machine Co. shareholders in 1911 lists David Ferguson with 250 shares valued at $112,500. It is not known whether the name was misspelled. Hollerith Papers.

38. "I know how much you will prize": The Bible is in the possession of the Hollerith family. Hollerith's later fears about his family's health were described by his daughters.

Chapter 5: Trials for a Census System

39. "I was at the Office of Registration": H. Hollerith to A. Meyer, July 14, 1885, Hollerith Papers.

39. "I compiled the vital statistics": H. Hollerith to J. T. Wilson, August 7, 1919, Hollerith Papers.

39. "Mr. Hollerith came over from Baltimore": T. Talcott to H. Talcott, January 6, 1889.

41. "The number and diversity of statistical items": U.S. Patent No. 395,781, p. 4.

41.   In a paper written in 1887: J. S. Billings, "On Some Forms of Vital Statistics, with Special Reference to the Needs of the Health Department of a City," *Public Health Papers and Reports* (American Public Health Association) 13:203–21.

41.   The Board of Health . . . "has introduced a machine": *New York Post*, July 6, 1889.

42.   Hollerith would always feel grateful to Baltimore: V. Hollerith, "Biographical Sketch," p. 71. In his August 7, 1919, letter to J. T. Wilson, the inventor States: "Some of the very earliest work I did was for the City of Baltimore." Hollerith Papers. However, the city's Health Department has no record that the machines were used. Letter to author from C. F. Poole, Records management officer, City of Baltimore, January 3, 1969.

42.   The young lady's name was Lucia Talcott: The meeting was described by Lucia Hollerith in an interview May 6, 1968.

42.   she had written of washing her dog: Diary of Lucia Talcott, July 2, 1887, Hollerith Family.

42.   "I hear you are quite worried": L. Talcott to Edmund Talcott, February 23, 1887, Hollerith Family.

43.   "His devotion to me is very funny": T. Talcott to H. Talcott, August 14, 1888.

43.   "fattening the cow to catch the calf": T. Talcott to H. Talcott, February 27, 1888.

43.   "He has a fine education": T. Talcott to H. Talcott, November 19, 1888.

44.   throwing a coffee percolator; interview with V. Hollerith, July 10, 1968.

44.   "She appears to like him": T. Talcott to H. Talcott, August 14, 1888.

44.   "He wants us to come to his office": T. Talcott to H. Talcott, March 5, 1888.

44.   "Hollerith has been . . . cleaning out his office": *Ibid.*

45.   the Surgeon General's Office . . . planned to install one: T. Talcott to H. Talcott, April 14, 1888.

45.   The problem . . . was "determining the number of days sick": To J. T. Wilson, August 7, 1919. For use of the equipment in the Surgeon General's Office, see Love, *et al., Tabulating Equipment and Army Medical Statistics*, pp. 41–42.

45.   A contract . . . was signed September 3, 1888: Love, *et al.*, p. 40.

45.   "to a certain extent still . . . experimental": Endorsement to Captain F.

C. Ainsworth, August 27, 1888, Correspondence, Office of the Surgeon General. U.S. Army, Old Records Division, Adjutant General's Office, National Archives, Washington, D.C.

46.   Hollerith entrained for Boston to visit the Western Electric Shop: As the Williams shop, a decade earlier, it was described as a "paradise for inventors of electrical machinery"; Watson, *Exploring Life*, p. 52.

46.   "He is very busy just now": T. Talcott to H. Talcott, October 23, 1888.

46.   the apparatus . . . was in satisfactory working order: First endorsement, F. C. Ainsworth to H. Hollerith, January 9, 1889, Correspondence, Office of the Surgeon General.

46.   Hollerith had been counting on the appointment of Carroll D. Wright: T. Talcott to H. Talcott, November 19, 1888.

47.   "I am very sorry for his disappointments": T. Talcott to H. Talcott, November 19, 1888.

47.   "some statement, in the nature of a certificate": H. Hollerith to the Secretary of War, April 8, 1889, Correspondence, Office of Surgeon General.

47.   "the machine in question": Capt. Fred C. Ainsworth to the Secretary of War, *ibid.*

47.   "Sir, I am directed . . . inform you": C. R. Greenleaf, Major Surgeon, to H. Hollerith, April 15, 1889, *ibid.*

48.   "some 50,000 cards are already prepared": Memorandum on Renewal of Contract for Electrical Statistical Machine, from John Moore, Surgeon General, to Acting Secretary of War, July 9, 1889, *ibid.* On July 22, a contract was signed for further use of the machine for the fiscal year ending June 30, 1890; *ibid.*

48.   "M. Hollerith de Washington . . . exposait un compteur": Alfred Picard, "Rapport General," *Exposition Universelle Internationale de 1889* (Paris: 1891), 4: 547.

49.   "He did not like Paris at all": T. Talcott to H. Talcott, May 24, 1889.

49.   "He wants to wait until he can make a contract": T. Talcott to H. Talcott, May 24, 1889.

49.   With commendable foresight, Porter wrote . . . urging an immediate test: R. P. Porter to Secretary of the Interior, July 3, 1889, National Archives.

49.   "it is not unlikely that the next census will be tabulated by electricity": Editorial by R. P. Porter, *New York Press*, January 25, 1889.

50.   the Secretary of the Interior soon organized a committee: R. P. Porter, "The Eleventh Census," *Frank Leslie's Illustrated Newspaper*, October 12, 1889, p. 188.

50. "The Hollerith Electric Tabulating System": H. Hollerith to G. Chandler, first assistant secretary, Department of the Interior, December 30, 1889, National Archives.

50. "Mr. Herman Hollerith . . . is willing to put one of them in a room": R. P. Porter to Secretary of the Interior, July 3, 1889, National Archives.

50. Hollerith's electrical system was staked against the "slip system": "Report of a Commission Appointed by the Hon. Superintendent of Census on Different Methods of Tabulating Census Data" (Dr. J. S. Billings to R. P. Porter), November 30, 1889, pp. 7–8.

51. "holes may be punched with any ordinary ticket punch": H. Hollerith, "An Electric Tabulating System," *The Quarterly* (School of Mines, Columbia College) 10 (April 1889): 245.

51. The new device enabled Hollerith to record the test data: "Report of a Commission," p. 9.

51. "While the final report . . . has not yet been made": "Report of the Operations of the Census Office Since June 1, 1889" (R. P. Porter to Secretary of the Interior), November 1, 1889, National Archives.

51. "Already . . . he has given Hollerith an order": T. Talcott to H. Talcott, October 27, 1889. The written contract is dated December 13, 1889. Census Records, National Archives.

52. "Just at this time, the family is in very bad condition": T. Talcott to H. Talcott, December 13, 1889.

52. "render the same more efficient": "Report of the Operations," National Archives.

52. "It will be an advantage . . . to put on a night force": R. P. Porter to Assistant Secretary of the Interior, November 1, 1889, National Archives.

52. The machines could be used "at all times": Lease between H. Hollerith and Secretary of the Interior for six tabulating machines, December 13, 1889, National Archives.

53. "no such forfeit shall be inforced": *Ibid.*

53. "With these machines": R. P. Porter to Secretary on the Interior, December 3, 1889, National Archives.

54. "measure twice and cut once": *The Hawthorne Microphone*, Western Electric Co. Hawthorne Works, Cicero, Ill., October 1936, p. 1. Western Electric Co. Archives.

54. "We are making for Mr. Hollerith twenty-five or thirty thousand dollars worth of apparatus": H. B. Thayer to F. R. Welles, April 7, 1890, Western Electric Co. Archives.

54.   The inventor also took on a 15-year-old office boy: Otto Braitmeyer was described by his daughter, Mrs. Alexander D. Shaw, August 30, 1970; also J. Langley, January 23, 1972; H. Hollerith, Jr., May 4, 1968; and Charles Hollerith, January 26, 1969.

55.   "Now that an account . . . has been published": T. Talcott to H. Talcott, January 20, 1889.

55.   "How our sedate great grandfathers would have opened their eyes": *New York Mail & Express*, March 11, 1890.

55.   he contributed to . . . an Emery testing machine: *The Quarterly Bulletin of Alumni and College News* (Columbia College) January 1890, p. 190.

55.   "it is invaluable": "The Hollerith Electrical Tabulating System," Report of the Committee on Science and the Arts, *Journal of the Franklin Institute*, April 1890.

56.   "A communication was received": Minutes of the Faculty of the School of Mines, April 3, 1890. Subsequent quotations are also from the minutes.

57.   "In 1889, Bell devised a sorting machine": Bruce, *Bell*, p. 415.

57.   "Father did have a good opinion of him": Letter from V. Hollerith, April 15, 1975.

Chapter 6: 1890: Beating the Mills of the Gods

58.   "Within a few weeks": *Philadelphia Ledger*, March 13, 1890.

58.   "Our males of arms-bearing age": *New York Times*, June 5, 1890.

59.   he had already rounded up . . . every square foot of . . . space: Report of Superintendent of the Census to Secretary of the Interior, November 6, 1889, National Archives.

59–60.   Hearing of the accident, Hollerith dropped everything: T. Talcott to H. Talcott, May 18, 1890.

60.   "a very tidy and airy machineshop": *Washington Star*, June, 26, 1890.

60.   "It is curious to . . . watch the delicate flying fingers": *Saginaw* (Michigan) *Weekly*, October 23, 1890.

60.   "Hear the Census with its bells": *Ibid.* A bell rang when a circuit was completed, signifying that the card had been counted.

61.   "With a schedule before her": *Chicago Tribune*, August 8, 1890.

61.   "The machines cannot make mistakes": *Ibid.*

61.   "With the aid of one of these machines": *Ibid.*

62.   "The indolent girls": *Ibid.*

62. "Mr. Porter, I'm going home": *Ibid.*

62. "how to extract the honey from the lion's jaw": T. C. Martin, "Counting a Nation by Electricity," *Electrical Engineer*, November 11, 1891, p. 523.

62. ". . . machines invented by a former employee": *Chicago Tribune*, August 8, 1890.

62. "refinements of torture": Martin, p. 524.

62. "These innocent combinations": *Ibid.* p. 524.

64. "As it would be difficult to construct a machine to *read*": H. Hollerith, "The Electrical Tabulating Machine," *Journal of the Royal Statistical Society*, vol. 57, part 4 (December 1894), p. 678.

64. "By simple use of the . . . electrical relay": *Ibid.*

65. "It would be manifestly impractical": *Scientific American*, August 30, 1890, p. 132.

65. "The work of enumeration goes on night and day": *Chicago Tribune*, August 8, 1890.

66. "Some are law students": Unidentified newspaper clipping from Hollerith's scrapbook, Hollerith Papers.

66. "Newcomers reporting for work": *Ibid.*

66. "notes are exchanged": *Ibid.*

66. "One young fellow": *Ibid.*

67. the results were "not of sufficient advantage": R. P. Porter to Secretary of the Interior, June 22, 1891, National Archives.

67. "The amount of work done": *Ibid.*

68. no less than 1,342,318 families or 6,711,590 people: *New York Sun*, August 17, 1890.

68. "the rush and a great deal of the work . . . is over": *Washington Post,* August 17, 1890.

68. "While I devised the machines": *Rough Count Eleventh United States Census* (A. Mugford Engraver and Printer, Hartford), Washington, D. C., August 1890, p. 7. Hollerith Papers. This pamphlet was printed to commemorate the dinner that Hollerith gave for the chiefs of the Population Division.

68. "An engineer might indeed stop to calculate": *Ibid.,* p. 6.

69. "For the first time in the history of the world": *Ibid.*

69. "Superintendent Porter . . . is to be congratulated": *New York Press*, August 18, 1890.

69. save . . . two years' time . . . and $5 million: in an April 5, 1909 letter to Senator R. M. LaFollette, chairman of the Senate Census Committee, attorneys for Hollerith's company stated that use of the system saved "not less than $5 million." Hollerith Papers. The amount was approximately ten times the saving estimated by the Census Commission before the 1890 Census.

69. "With the machines, the most complicated tables": R. P. Porter, "The Eleventh Census," American Statistical Association New Series No. 15, September 1891, p. 330.

70. "The apparatus works as unerringly as the mills of the Gods": Martin, "Counting a Nation by Electricity," p. 522.

70. "cards . . . can be made of almost any material": *New York Sun*, March 24, 1890; See Greene, *The Beginnings*, p. 15, for effect of faulty cards in British Census of 1911; also Otto Braitmeyer testimony of February 15, 1929, to Senate Committee on Printing on how card defects effect machine performance, IBM Archives.

71. "I feel I have done something for the women": Sholes's quote appears in "The Fabulous Writing Machine," *News Front*, May 1963, p. 43.

71. ". . . of the 43 who counted more than 10,000, 38 were women": *New York Sun*, August 17, 1890.

71. "The field of women's employment": *New York Herald*, August 23, 1890.

71. "It saves the eyes of the tallyist": Frederick H. Wines quoted by R. P. Porter, "The Eleventh Census," p. 340.

72. "Mechanics were there frequently": C. W. Springer to T. J. Watson, Jr., December 21, 1965, IBM Archives.

72. "We . . . pay about $35 million annually": H. Hollerith, "The Electrical Tabulating Machine," p. 678.

73. In due time, along came the census": H. Hollerith to J. T. Wilson, August 7, 1919, Hollerith Papers.

73. "The machine is patented": Unidentified newspaper clipping from Hollerith's scrapbook, Hollerith Papers.

Chapter 7: Taking the Census Abroad

74. "He could not control his temper": T. Talcott to H. Talcott, September 15, 1890.

75–76. "It was a very sweet, solemn and quiet wedding": *Ibid.*

76. "He writes Lu's letters": T. Talcott to H. Talcott, September 21, 1890.

76. "Useless machines": *Boston Herald*, December 20, 1890.

76. "His boon companions": *Washington National Democrat*, October 18, 1890.

77. "The electric machines . . . were chosen by a board": *New York Herald*, October 24, 1890.

77. "The newspapers are pitching into Mr. Porter and . . . Mr. Hollerith": T. Talcott to H. Talcott, October 15, 1890.

77. "go to the poorhouse": T. Talcott to H. Talcott, October 5, 1890.

78. "The inventor introduced his machines abroad": *New York Sun*, March 24, 1890.

79. "to hold his Belgian patent": H. B. Thayer to F. R. Welles, April 7, 1890, Western Electric Archives.

79. "He is not anxious": *Ibid.*

79. "Ned has been very busy": T. Talcott to H. Talcott, November 16, 1890.

79. "I had the unfortunate experience with the Austrians": *New York Sun*, March 23, 1895.

79. "Hollerith has just seen a Vienna paper": T. Talcott to H. Talcott, December 21, 1890.

81. "I tell him it's something in this house": T. Talcott to H. Talcott, February 8, 1891.

81. "The Austrian must give a full account of himself": Untitled publication, Vienna, December 10, 1893 Hollerith Papers. Further detail on the use of the machines in the Austrian Census is given by E. Cheysson, *The Electric Tabulating Machine*, trans. A. W. Fergusson, from *Journal de la Société de Statisique* (Paris) (New York: C. C. Shelley, 1892).

81. "Step by step we advanced": Dr. K. T. von Inama-Sternegg, "The Austrian Census of 1890: The Closing of the Census Bureau," trans. from *Weiner Zeitung*, July 16, 1893.

82. "Whatever interest the Austrians can arouse": H. Hollerith to wife Lucia Hollerith, August 26, 1895, Hollerith Papers. However, according to Cheysson, the Austrians did provide the machines with some improvements.

82. "Hollerith will not stay more than two days": T. Talcott to H. Talcott, March 8, 1891.

83. "Any labor-saving device": *New York Tribune*, April 25, 1890.

83. "A couple of the machines . . . need some attention": T. Talcott to H. Talcott, April 11, 1891.

83. "The ones put up in Newark": *Ibid.* The letter had been held open for further news.

83. Hollerith's interest in his insurance customer: The view that Hollerith saw no commercial potential for his machines until considerably later is reflected in Belden and Belden, *The Lengthening Shadow*, p. 110.

83. ". . . invaluable wherever large numbers": "The Hollerith Electrical Tabulating System," Report of the Committee on Science and the Arts, *Journal of the Franklin Institute*, April 1890. Philadelphia, Pa.

83. "my invention is not limited": U.S. Patent No. 395,781.

84. "The Superintendent of the Canadian Census": T. Talcott to H. Talcott, April 19, 1891.

84. The order . . . "was based": *New York Post*, August 10, 1891.

84. If his machines were properly applied: Interview with Charles Hollerith January 26, 1969, as are subsequent quotations in paragraph.

84. "One of the advantages": Census of Canada, 1891, Department of Agriculture Bulletin No. 9, May 1892.

84. "The only thing American": *New York Times*, February 22, 1891. Hollerith Papers.

85. "Not less than 100,000,000 cards": *New York Sun*, March 23, 1895.

85. "The decades . . . have been ominous ones": R. P. Porter, "The 11th Census," American Statistical Society New Series No. 15, September 1891, p. 321.

85. "The Canadian Parliament": *Ibid.*

86. "It sent into spasms of indignation": T. C. Martin, "Counting a Nation by Electricity," *Electrical Engineer*, p. 522.

86. "They cannot spell": Bancroft, *Speeches, Correspondence, and Political Papers of Carl Schurz* 5:128.

86. "Slipshod Work": *New York Herald*, October 4, 1891.

86. "A complete set": *New York Independent*, December 10, 1891.

87. "Dr. Hollerith has presented a very interesting paper": *New Orleans Times-Democrat*, June 1, 1891. Hollerith also pointed out that the percentage of the population over 40, and therefore beyond what is generally considered child-bearing age, had risen with each census from 1850 through 1880. See H. Hollerith, "Rate of Natural Increase of Population in the United States," American Statistical Association New Series No. 13, March 1891, pp. 174–81.

87. "If the current trend continues": "The Infertile Society," in "Science and the Citizen," *Scientific American* (May 1978), p. 81.

88. "He sits and looks at her": T. Talcott to H. Talcott, July 7, 1891.

88. "The time will come": L. Bodio, *The Inventive Age* 4, no. 114 (December 1893), reprinted in "A Forecast of 1893—and its Fulfillment," *The Tabulator* (The Tabulating Machine Co.), August 1916, p. 3, IBM Archives.

Chapter 8: Setting up Shop in Georgetown

97. an old cooper's shop: The original shop occupied a plot with an 89-foot frontage on Congress Street (now 31st Street) that was 108 feet deep. A narrow alley, Niagara Street, ran between the building and the C & O Canal. H. Hollerith to S. G. Metcalf, June 21, 1900. IBM Archives.

97. IBM's first data processing plant: When Hollerith sold his business in 1911, most of his equipment was being made at Taft-Peirce in Woonsocket, Rhode Island. (Records of Taft-Peirce). However, it went through final assembly and test at 31st Street, which was mainly devoted to card manufacture. The shop was also used for development. M. H. Hathaway to E. Young, August 28, 1907. IBM Archives.

98. "I would respectfully call your attention": *Washington Post*, September 7, 1892.

98. "Inside the structure: The shop, as it appeared about 1905, was described by Charles Hollerith. Interview January 26, 1969.

99. "The men made a big fire": T. Talcott to H. Talcott, January 1, 1893.

99. Precisely punctual: Hollerith's insistance on punctuality was described by Joseph Langley, who went to work for Hollerith in 1902. Interview January 23, 1972.

99. "Don't tell me you think": *Ibid.*

99. "If you're doin' to suit him": Interview with Marion Smith, September 11, 1973.

100. Watching through a peephole: Interview with Charles Hollerith, January 26, 1969.

100. He also advanced considerable sums: Loans are evidenced by Hollerith's records of the Tabulating Machine Co., Hollerith Papers.

100. "Mr. Spicer . . . fainted": T. Talcott to H. Talcott, October 24, 1894.

100. the Census Office wanted more machines: T. Talcott to H. Talcott, April 12, 1893.

101. "He doesn't want to go": T. Talcott to H. Talcott, May 22, 1893.

101. "My what a fortune": T. Talcott to H. Talcott, April 12, 1893.

101. ". . . three Italians to dine": T. Talcott to H. Talcott, October 3, 1893.

101.   "The effete monarchies": Unidentified newspaper clipping dated November 26, 1893, from Hollerith's scrapbook, Hollerith Papers.

101.   Professor Bodio had led the way: Carroll D. Wright, "The Study of Statistics in Italian Universities" (address delivered to the American Statistical Association, New Orleans, May 9, 1890).

102.   "the ugliest thing I ever saw": T. Talcott to H. Talcott, September 19, 1892.

102.   "This is a frightfully slow country": H. Hollerith to Lucia Hollerith, March 14, 1894, Hollerith Papers.

102.   "They are all like cows": H. Hollerith to Lucia, March 13, 1894, Hollerith Papers.

102.   "How I wish I had Jack": *Ibid.*

102.   "I am struggling along slowly": *Ibid.*

102.   "Professor Mangarine . . . is to call": *Ibid.*

103.   ". . . quite a man in the electrical world": H. Hollerith to Lucia, March 14, 1894, Hollerith Papers.

103.   "Mrs. Meyer is a German": *Ibid.*

103.   "Perhaps you think": *Ibid.*

103.   "I have no longer interest for Roman antiquities": H. Hollerith to Lucia, March 18, 1894, Hollerith Papers.

103.   "To go to Vienna, I will have to spend two nights . . . in a sleeping car": *Ibid.*

104.   "Bumpkin": *Ibid.*

104.   "Poor Hollerith": T. Talcott to H. Talcott, April 25, 1894.

104–5.   "embodying the same principles": U.S. Patent No. 17,986.

105.   "Hollerith now has no income": T. Talcott to H. Talcott, August 30, 1894.

105.   "I think she is better": T. Talcott to H. Talcott, July 24, 1894.

105.   "He went off rather suddenly": T. Talcott to H. Talcott, October 28, 1894.

Chapter 9: Railroad Experiments

107.   His friend John Hyde had submitted: Records, Royal Statistical Society, London.

108.   "We all wished": Mrs. R. P. Porter to Mrs. H. Hollerith, December 5, 1894, Hollerith Papers

108. "the most important of its kind": *Ibid.*

108. "he should be happy to exhibit the machine": *Journal of the Royal Statistical Society*, vol. 57, part 4, (December 1884), p. 678.

108. the penalty clause: *Ibid.*

109. "He had been making experiments upon a considerable scale": *Ibid.*

109. "While the census was underway": H. Hollerith to J. T. Wilson, August 7, 1919. Hollerith Papers.

110. "They were . . . wonderful machines": *Ibid.*

110. "Now while I was struggling along": *Ibid.*

110. "I am convinced that the future of statistics lies with the . . . Hollerith machine": L. Bodio to Royal Statistical Society, letter in support of Hollerith's nomination for membership, November 22, 1884, Royal Statistical Society, London.

111. "So far the foreign countries have not paid him very well": T. Talcott to H. Talcott, March 11, 1895.

111. "did not know the first damned thing about railroad accounts": H. Hollerith to J. T. Wilson, August 7, 1919. Hollerith Papers.

111. "brushed aside" the first inquiries: Belden and Belden, *The Lengthening Shadow*, p. 110.

111. "Last Saturday, Hollerith had the auditor of the R & D": T. Talcott to H. Talcott, Febuary 14, 1895.

112. "Ned came home quite enthusiastic": *Ibid.*

112. "Hollerith is very anxious": *Ibid.*

112. "Six of their auditors were over": T. Talcott to H. Talcott, April 3, 1895.

113. "So far he has not met with any success": T. Talcott to H. Talcott, April 10, 1895.

113. "We all hope he won't be obliged to do so": T. Talcott to H. Talcott, March 11, 1895.

Chapter 10: Persuading the Russians

115. "So much depends upon the success of my . . . trip": H. Hollerith to L. Hollerith, August 26, 1895, Hollerith Papers.

116. "I have great faith": Copy of undated letter from J. Puleston to H. Hollerith, Hollerith Papers.

116. "We went out to Richmond": H. Hollerith to L. Hollerith, August 26, 1895, Hollerith Papers.

116. "I am dead tired": *Ibid.*

116. "I have not had a chance to talk . . . with Troinitsky": *Ibid.*

117. "If Hollerith doesn't get the Russian Census": T. Talcott to H. Talcott, October 11, 1891.

117. "I have heard nothing definite . . . from Russia": *New York Sun*, March 23, 1895.

118. the Russians had already reached two conclusions: V. Struve, *On the Application of Electricity to the Tabulation of Statistical Data (Herman Hollerith Electric Tabulating System)*, (St. Petersburg, Russia: Central Statistical Committee, Ministry of Internal Affairs, 1894), IBM Archives.

118. "Convenience, intelligibility . . . exactness": *Ibid.*

118. "The punching of the cards": *Ibid.*

119. "Until the present . . . the major time and labor": *Ibid.*

119. "even the most complex combinations": *Ibid.*

119. "I found . . . I will have competition": H. Hollerith to L. Hollerith, August 26, 1895 (second letter to his wife on that date), Hollerith Papers.

120. James Watt . . . would rather have faced a loaded cannon: Smiles says, "He had neither the patience to endure nor the business tact to conduct a negotiation"; *Lives of Boulton and Watt*, p. 246.

120. "So much depends": H. Hollerith to L. Hollerith, August 29, 1895, Hollerith Papers.

120. "I sometimes wish . . . I could keep a grocery store": H. Hollerith to L. Hollerith (second letter), August 26, 1895, Hollerith Papers.

120. "I have decided they will not get the job": *Ibid.*

120. "this machine or the principles will be potent factors": *ibid..*

120. the Russian suggested that he might get some: H. Hollerith to L. Hollerith, August 29, 1895, Hollerith Papers.

121. "My reply was": *Ibid.*

121. "He called me a 'Statistical Engineer'": H. Hollerith to L. Hollerith (Second letter), August 26, 1895, Hollerith Papers.

121. "Mine looked very well": H. Hollerith to L. Hollerith, August 29, 1895, Hollerith Papers.

121. "a fool may have an insignificant nose": *Ibid.*

121. "Dr. Hollerith made a great hit": Article by R. P. Porter, *Cleveland World*, December 1895, as quoted by V. Hollerith, "Biographical Sketch," p. 74.

122. "I have . . . made a favorable impression on the Russian": H. Hollerith to L. Hollerith, August 30, 1895, Hollerith Papers.

122. "They have a large table": *Ibid.*

122. "This is beautiful mountain scenery": H. Hollerith to L. Hollerith, September 2, 1895, Hollerith Papers.

123. "Englishmen can't do anything in a hurry": H. Hollerith to L. Hollerith, September 12, 1895, Hollerith Papers.

Chapter 11: Taking on the Central

124. "He is at present very hard up for money": T. Talcott to H. Talcott, October 4, 1895.

124. "I made the same proposition": H. Hollerith to J. T. Wilson, August 7, 1919, Hollerith Papers.

124. No other rail system in the country: Moody, *The Railroad Builders*, p. 40.

125. "In the tabulation of statistics": Hollerith described the New York Central application in U.S. Patent No. 677,215.

127. "The Russian Empire next June": Editorial by R. P. Porter, *Cleveland World*, October 2, 1895;

127. "During the past five years": *Ibid.*

128. "who realize that, in coming to the fountainhead for this intricate mechanism": *Ibid.*

128. "Out of this small cup to drink": The cup is in the inventor's home.

128. the New York Central had thrown out his machines: H. Hollerith to J. T. Wilson, August 17, 1919, Hollerith Papers.

129. "Hollerith is in New York": T. Talcott to H. Talcott, January 31, 1896.

130. He would be granted a year's trial: T. Talcott to H. Talcott, May 15, 1896.

130. "Would such a course be either wise or right?": undated editorial by R. P. Porter, *Cleveland World*, from Hollerith scrapbook, Hollerith Papers.

131. "Hollerith asked me if I wanted to do something": T. Talcott to H. Talcott, January 14, 1896.

132. *Electrical Supplies Catalogue:* Hollerith's counters are listed in the *Western Electric Co., Electrical Supplies Catalogue* for 1895, 1896, 1900, and 1901. The listing says, "The tabulator is adapted for use on any machine where an electrical contact can be made to register its capacity or output"; Western Electric Co. Archives.

132. "Hollerith has not yet received a definite reply": T. Talcott to H. Talcott, January 14, 1896.

132. "Hollerith told him that he wants to sell out to . . . Western Electric . . .": T. Talcott to H. Talcott, December 4, 1895.

133. "The French government wrote": T. Talcott to H. Talcott, March 21, 1896.

133. he entered the offices of the Library Bureau: The Bureau's business is described in *Classified Illustrated Catalog of the Library Bureau* (Boston: Library Bureau, 1894).

133. "Among life and fire insurance companies": *Ibid.*, p. 7.

133. It studied "the unproductive side of the expense account": *Ibid.* p. 7.

134. the inventor signed a ten-year agreement: The terms are cited in a later contract of March 25, 1899, terminating the earlier arrangement; IBM Archives.

134. "The Library Bureau has made a contract": From undated report to his directors, possibly about 1898–99, Hollerith Papers.

134. "Hollerith has made a contract": T. Talcott to H. Talcott, April 14, 1896.

135. "we think that such an offer": T. Talcott to H. Talcott, April 6, 1896.

135. "Turn down the offer": T. Talcott to H. Talcott, Easter Sunday, 1896.

135. "The Western Electric Company have a branch": T. Talcott to H. Talcott, April 14, 1896.

136. "It is a move as is a move": T. Talcott to H. Talcott, April 30, 1896.

136. "There was no trouble with the machines": T. Talcott to H. Talcott, May 15, 1896.

137. "Hollerith has had a hard time": T. Talcott to H. Talcott, June 10, 1896.

137. "I have an idea as they have one of Hollerith's machines": T. Talcott to H. Talcott, May 15, 1896.

138. "He said he was willing to contract with me": Hollerith's letter of August 20, 1896 is from a copy of it by T. Talcott in her letter of August 26, 1898 to H. Talcott.

138. on September 28, 1896, Hollerith signed the contract: from a copy of the contract of the same date in the IBM Archives.

138. "Now he will have to manufacture some more machines": T. Talcott to H. Talcott, September 23, 1896.

138. "to supply, erect and maintain": Central contract, September 28, 1896, IBM Archives.

139.   "the sum of Five Thousand Dollars": *Ibid.*

139.   "one dollar per thousand": *Ibid.*

139.   "It shall be a success": T. Talcott to H. Talcott, May 15, 1896.

139.   "The more complicated the tabulation": undated report to Tabulating Machine Co. directors, Hollerith Papers.

140.   "Several of the officers present": *New York Post*, June 9, 1902.

140.   "the Central would put in no objection": *Ibid.*

140.   "There has been a great deal said to me": *Railway World*, June 14, 1902, p. 268.

141.   "The news which has just come out": *New York Post*, June 9, 1902.

141.   "I do not think it is worthwhile wasting any energy": H. Hollerith to G. F. Swain, July 18, 1905, Harvard University, Faculty Archives.

Chapter 12: The Russian Census

142.   "we have met the Russians": T. Talcott to H. Talcott, November 13, 1896.

143.   "I am very delighted": *Ibid.*

143.   "What is the use of living in the country": T. Talcott to H. Talcott, November 20, 1896.

143.   "Hollerith's shop is . . . unroofed": T. Talcott to H. Talcott, October 2, 1896.

144.   "He spent all of Saturday and Monday . . . paying bills": T. Talcott to H. Talcott, November 28, 1896.

144.   "As the whole family is in the same fix": *Ibid.*

144.   "The time in St. Petersburg": H. Hollerith to L. Hollerith, November 25, 1896, Hollerith Papers.

144.   "You will no doubt be surprised": *Ibid.*

145.   "What I will ever do with the coat": *Ibid.*

145.   "Should I ever decide to have a picture taken": H. Hollerith to Mr. Ehret, May 29, 1925, Hollerith Papers.

145.   "On the train . . . from Paris": H. Hollerith to L. Hollerith, November 25, 1886, Hollerith Papers.

146.   "fast women and slow ships": Massie, *Nicholas and Alexandra*, pp. 62–63.

146.   "Just before coming into St. Petersburg": H. Hollerith to L. Hollerith, November 25, 1896, Hollerith Papers.

146.   "to furnish you for the Russian Government": Undated copy of Hollerith's contract with Troinitsky, IBM Archives; subsequent terms are also from this document.

148.   900,000 enumerators, a staff of 2,200 persons: *The First General Census of the Russian Empire in the Year 1897*, Notebook No. 1, "Province of Archangelsk," Central Statistical Committee, N. A. Troinitski, ed., January 28, 1899, IBM Archives.

148.   "The distinguished statistician": Letter from R. P. Porter, *Philadelphia Inquirer*, June 19, 1897.

149.   Some non-Christians . . . feared it was a Czarist plot: "Census in Rural Russia," *New York Times*, July 12, 1897.

149.   St. Petersburg . . . closely rivaled New York: Porter letter, *Inquirer*.

149.   "As her development . . . proceeds": *Ibid.*

149.   "The work of tabulating the census returns": Report of H. Hollerith address at Shoreham Hotel, *Washington Post*, October 23, 1897.

150.   "22 cents per thousand cards counted": Minutes of the Tabulating Machine Co., April 15, 1903, IBM Archives.

150.   "His highness . . . examined the sorting of cards": St. Petersburg *Novoe Nremya*, February 6, 1904. IBM Archives.

150.   "The compensation . . . seems very meager": *Washington Post*, October 23, 1897.

151.   "The name of Hollerith was still well known": E. F. Saber to G. Austrian, December 16, 1971, collection of author.

151.   "It is . . . quite likely I will call you": H. Hollerith to L. Hollerith, December 20, 1896, Hollerith Papers.

151.   "Ned is more than busy": T. Talcott to H. Talcott, January 13, 1897.

Chapter 13: The Tabulating Machine Company

152.   yellow pad before him: Three sheets from the pad are among the Hollerith Papers. On the second sheet, Hollerith wrote the number of shares of stock his associates would subscribe to; on the third, the names of four people (probably the incorporators of his company) who, by law, would receive a single share. He probably made the notes while discussing formation of the company with his attorney.

152.   "to act for me in . . . the formation . . . of a corporation": Power of attorney from H. Hollerith to S. G. Metcalf, November 24, 1896. A declaration of trust turning over his patents and other assets was also given to Metcalf on the same date, as was a note introducing Metcalf to G. M. Bond, who was to subscribe $5,000 in stock. The three documents are in the IBM Archives.

153. "He has formed a stock company": T. Talcott to H. Talcott, January 13, 1897.

153. "relating to counting, adding, sorting": Agreement between H. Hollerith and Tabulating Machine Co., May 25, 1897, Hollerith Papers. In the agreement, Hollerith reserved the right to use his devices for other purposes.

153. he was "a peculiar sort of man": Remarks by Willy Heidinger, general manager, German Hollerith Machines Co., on the German company's twenty-fifth anniversary, Berlin, November 1935. IBM Archives.

153. "He said it would be the best thing to do": T. Talcott to H. Talcott, January 21 and 22, 1897.

153. Chartered December 3, 1896: New York State Certificate of Incorporation.

154. Bond's tie with Hollerith's business: He resigned from the Tabulating Machine Co. Division of IBM on October 31, 1934.

154. the Rogers-Bond Comparator: It is described in Bond, *Standards of Length and Their Practical Application.*

155. Ferdinand W. Roebling: Background is from McCullough, *The Great Bridge*, p. 168; also, *National Cyclopaedia of American Biography*, 35: 386–7.

155. "Their grounds cover fourteen acres": *Ibid.*, p. 350.

155. Henry C. Adams: A letter from Meyer H. Fishbein to Dr. Clifford J. Maloney, dated September 4, 1954, reports that Joseph Dorfman, in connection with research at Columbia University, found that Hollerith offered shares to several members of the Columbia faculty, as well as Adams. Courtesy of M. H. Fishbein, National Archives.

156. Harry Bates Thayer: Background is from Western Electric Co. Archives. See, especially, Thayer, H. B., "The Hardest Years," *Western Electric News*, July 1929; also, biographical sketch, July 31, 1944.

157. "Czar Nicholas' brother . . . had been assassinated": Memorandum by E. W. Rockafellow, Western Electric Co. Archives.

157. Albert Lincoln Salt: Background from Western Electric Co. Archives. See, especially, "Albert L. Salt—40 years," June 18, 1921.

158. "to organize, elect officers": Minutes of the Tabulating Machine Co., December 16, 1896, IBM Archives.

158. "There are no salaried officers": T. Talcott to H. Talcott, June 21 and 22, 1897.

159. He would assign all rights under the contract to the company: Minutes of the Tabulating Machine Co., January 12, 1897, IBM Archives.

159. "compensation at . . . $500 per month": *Ibid.*.

159.   "Mr. Hollerith . . . was authorized to carry out the contract": *Ibid.*

159.   "He is on his feet again": T. Talcott to H. Talcott, January 13, 1897.

160.   "I don't think it is worthwhile to be . . . complaining": T. Talcott to H. Talcott, February 25, 1897.

161.   they had better part company: T. Talcott to H. Talcott, April 13, 1897. V. Hollerith reports that Ned later worked for W. R. Grace & Co. until his retirement.

161.   "Porter went to the Navy Department": T. Talcott to H. Talcott, July 2, 1897.

161.   "it would be for the best interest . . . to employ a reliable man": Minutes of the Tabulating Machine Co., March 12, 1897, IBM Archives.

161.   "The work is not going well": T. Talcott to H. Talcott, April 29, 1897.

162.   "Elles sont toutes prêtes": Institut International de St. Petersbourg 1897, *Bulletin* No. 2 (St. Petersburg, Russia: August 20, 1897), p. 16.

162.   "I have arrived at St. Petersburg": H. Hollerith to L. Hollerith, August 23, 1897, Hollerith Papers.

162.   "The testing of the machines": Undated copy of contract between Hollerith and Troinitsky, IBM Archives.

163.   In 1891 I fixed up an arrangement with Mr. Heisler": "Reminiscences by Francis R. Welles," unpublished manuscript, Western Electric Co. Archives.

163.   "I have just received an invitation": H. Hollerith to L. Hollerith August 30, 1897, Hollerith Papers.

163.   "I was standing pretty well to the rear": H. Hollerith to L. Hollerith, August 31, 1897, Hollerith Papers.

164.   "little pig boiled whole": H. Hollerith to L. Hollerith, September 2, 1897, Hollerith Papers.

164.   "I suppose I ought to take advantage": H. Hollerith to L. Hollerith, August 31, 1897, Hollerith Papers.

164.   "You may rest assured": *Ibid.*

164.   "I just looked on": T. Talcott to H. Talcott, September 25, 1897.

164.   no dividends . . . while "any money loaned . . . remained unpaid": Minutes of the Tabulating Machine Co., December 16, 1896, IBM Archives.

164.   It dispensed a . . . dividend: Minutes of the Tabulating Machine Co., July 13, 1897, IBM Archives.

165.   "It is strong and serviceable": Minutes of the Tabulating Machine Co., March 12, 1897, IBM Archives.

165.   suddenly, he was stopped short by a patent interference: W. S. Gub-
         elmann obtained patent interference No. 17, 986 against the Lanston
         and Hollerith patents on June 12, 1896. Although the Lanston-Hol-
         lerith Patents were issued three years later, it is uncertain whether
         Hollerith ever placed the device on the market. He hoped that his
         improved version of the Lanston machine could compete with the
         Comptometer and the widely employed Autographic Cash Registers;
         Hollerith Papers.

165.   "In regard to the tabulating machine:" G. T. Swarts, Secretary of the
         State Board of Health of Rhode Island, to H. Hollerith, January 19,
         1898, IBM Archives.

165.   "The question now is:" H. Hollerith to S. G. Metcalf, January 22, 1898,
         Hollerith Papers.

166.   "It seems clear that: Memorandum from S. G. Metcalf to S. Gill, January
         24, 1898, Hollerith Papers.

166.   the Tabulating Machine Co. served notice: Minutes of the Tabulating
         Machine Co., May 3, 1898, and the termination agreement, March 25,
         1899; IBM Archives.

166.   "The Electrical Tabulating System . . . is now in successful operation":
         Accounting by Electricity, (Washington, D.C.: The Tabulating Machine
         Co., 1903), p. 16. IBM Archives.

Chapter 14: 1900: Putting Information on the Assembly Line

168.   No census office in the past . . . was equipped: H. T. Newcomb,
         "Mechanical Tabulation of the Statistics of Agriculture in the 12th
         Census of the U.S." (Paper delivered to the American Association for
         the Advancement of Science, Denver, Colorado, August 1901.)

169.   mechanical tabulation is "capable of responding to all demands": Book-
         let, *American Census Taking*, Bureau of the Census, Washington, D.C.,
         p. 20, based on W. R. Merriam, "The Evolution of Modern Census
         Taking," *The Century Magazine* (April 1903).

169.   "in case the Director deems it expedient": Census Act of March 3,
         1899, Section 26.

169.   "to make a practical test": Report of the Commission Appointed by the
         Director of the Census on the Competitive Test of Methods of Tab-
         ulation, U.S. Census Office, July 27, 1899, p. 3.

169.   "There is to be a test": T. Talcott to H. Talcott, June 7, 1899.

169.   Charles F. Pidgin: Background is from *Dictionary of American Biography*
         14: 573–74, and *National Cyclopaedia of American Biography* 13: 479–80
         (New York: J. T. White, 1906). The epithet "Pidgin Coops" is in H.

Hollerith to G. F. Swain, July 18, 1905, Harvard University, Faculty Archives.

170. "The superiority of the Hollerith . . . System": Report of the Commission . . . , U.S. Census Office, July 27, 1899, p. 8.

170. "new and extraordinary instrumentalities": E. W. Byrn, "The Mechanical Work of the 12th Census," *Scientific American*, April 19, 1902, p. 275.

171. "The far greater portion of the labor": Newcomb, "Mechanical Tabulation," p. 8.

171. devices "somewhat similar to those . . . "at the New York Central": *Ibid.*, p. 6.

171. "You should understand that the Hollerith machine": F. H. Wines to W. R. Merriam, August 9, 1900, U.S. Census Bureau Library, Suitland, Maryland.

172. "Now the railroad work reacted on the census work": H. Hollerith to J. T. Wilson, August 7, 1919, Hollerith Papers.

172. "Mr. Hollerith [holds] the opinion": F. H. Wines to W. R. Merriam, June 11, 1900, U.S. Census Bureau Library.

173. had formed the Taft-Peirce Company, "for the sole purpose of performing contract manufacturing": F. Steele Blackall, Jr., "History of Taft-Peirce, 1876-1946," unpublished manuscript, Taft-Peirce Co. Records. Except where otherwise noted, the author has relied on this source for background on the company.

173. "models, tools and parts": *Ibid.*

173. "THE TAFT-PEIRCE MFG. CO.": *Ibid.*

173. "It was during the '90's": Memorandum of a conversation with P. P. Merrill by F. S. Blackall, Jr., May 29, 1953, Taft-Peirce Co. Records.

174. many improvements in his machines originated in the brain of Eugene Ford: *Ibid.* Other background on Ford is from *National Cyclopaedia of American Biography* 38: 113, and obituary, *New York Times*, September 5, 1948.

174. Ford put his facility . . . to good use in . . . Hollerith's key punch: Hollerith's first key punch is described in U.S. Patent No. 682,197, issued September 10, 1901.

175. "My invention . . . comprises a traveling carrier": *Ibid.*

176. the Automatic Tabulating Machine . . . was preceded by a little-known Semi-Automatic: The latter is described in *Accounting by Electricity* (Washington, D.C.: Tabulating Machine Co., 1903), p. 15, IBM Archives. It is also cited in Martin and Coles, *The Story of Electricity*, p. 158.

176. "As the plate recedes": *Accounting by Electricity*, p. 15.

176. "The latest development . . . is the automatic machine": Byrn, "The Mechanical Work of the 12th Census," p. 275.

177. "spring-pressed conductive pins": *Ibid.*

177. "After the cards are placed in position": U.S. Patent No. 685,608.

178. "Sorting or grouping of cards": *Accounting by Electricity*, p. 14.

178. "When we were working on those freight integrating machines": Affidavit of C. W. Spicer, *Tabulating Machine* v. *Durand*, Supreme Ct., Dist. of Columbia, February 24, 1910. Records of the case are at the Federal Records Center, Suitland, Maryland.

178. "At luncheon with Governor Merriam": H. Hollerith to J. T. Wilson, August 7, 1919, Hollerith Papers.

179. "The tabulating machines were made idle": R. H. Holley, "Machine Tabulation in the Census Office: 1870–1912," p. 15, unpublished manuscript, Census Records, National Archives.

179. ". . . the worst mistake I made in a business way": H. Hollerith to J. T. Wilson, August 7, 1919, Hollerith Papers.

179. "[The] machines . . . were installed": Affidavit of H. Momsen, *Tabulating Machine Co.* v. *Durand*, March 3, 1910.

180. Spicer would swear that the machines were ". . . faulty": Affidavit of C. W. Spicer, *Tabulating Machine Co.* v. *Durand*, February 24, 1910.

180. "none of the machines . . . was capable of . . . satisfactory work": Affidavit of K. T. West, *Tabulating Machine Co.* v. *Durand*, February 25, 1910.

180. "automatic electric sorters were also used to great advantage": Booklet, *American Census Taking*, p. 20.

180. "They proved indispensible to our work": Affidavit of W. T. McCullough, *Tabulating Machine Co.* v. *Durand*, January 28, 1910.

180–81. "I then developed . . . some vertical machines": H. Hollerith to J. T. Wilson, August 7, 1919, Hollerith Papers.

181. "The wonder to me": *Ibid.*

181. Hollerith completed the major reports . . . within two and a half years: Booklet, *American Census Taking*, p. 26; also, Report of the Director of the Census, 1903, p. 4. Washington, D.C.: GPO, 1903.

181. The value of farm implements . . . had risen 54 percent . . . "the crop producing area has increased": *12th Census Reports*, vol. 5, part I, p. 19, U.S. Census Office.

182. "The application of mechanical appliances": Report of the Secretary of Commerce and Labor for 1904, p. 24.

182. "Whereas the car evolved from an idea": Sorenson, *My Forty Years With Ford*, p. 115.

Chapter 15: Probing the Commercial Market

197. Hollerith bought a controlling interest in Taft-Peirce: Minutes of the Tabulating Machine Co., August 23, 1901, IBM Archives.

197. "Never mind what the first lot costs": F. Steele Blackall, Jr., "History of Taft-Peirce, 1876–1946," p. 11, unpublished manuscript, Taft-Peirce Co. Records.

198. "The big machine shops": *Providence Journal*, August 31, 1901.

198. "Machinery and tools": Report by R. F. Stevens, in Minutes of the Tabulating Machine Co., August 23, 1901, IBM Archives.

199. "Hollerith potatoes": From menu of Solari's in inventor's scrapbooks, Hollerith Papers. How they were made was described by Charles Hollerith, January 26, 1969. The site of many of the company's meetings is listed as 80 University Place, the address of the restaurant.

199. in May 1889, they formed a separate subsidiary to conduct their railroad business: The Auditing Machine Co. was chartered May 26, 1899, in New Jersey. A copy of the charter is in the IBM Archives.

199. to compile statistics "relating to transportation by rail": *Ibid.*

199. Hollerith received 500 shares: Draft of agreement, IBM Archives.

199. "I hope this will lead to a contract": F. W. Roebling to S. G. Metcalf, February 22, 1902, Hollerith Papers.

200. "At first, I met with a good deal of opposition": H. Hollerith to J. T. Wilson, August 7, 1919, Hollerith Papers.

201. "In the contract manufacture of light machinery": Sidney G. Koon, "Cost Accounting by Machines," *American Machinist*, August 1914, p. 1.

201. "Accounting departments . . . must present the records . . . sufficiently promptly": Gershom Smith, *The Use of the Hollerith Tabulating Equipment by the Pennsylvania Steel Company* (Tabulating Machine Co., reprinted from *Frog Shop Digest* [The Pennsylvania Steel Co.] March 11), p. 1, IBM Archives.

202. "They punch cards in which they have . . . the number of hours": H. Hollerith to P. Bontecou, November 4, 1907, IBM Archives.

202. "Suppose . . . a 100-horsepower engine has been turned out": *The Mechanical Accountant*: Tabulating Machine Co., Washington, D.C., p. 5 (reprinted from *Engineering*, December 26, 1902), IBM Archives.

203. The man was Frederick Winslow Taylor: Background is mainly from Copley, *Frederick W. Taylor*.

203. whose business card read: *Dictionary of American Biography* 9: 324.

203. In Taylor's view, accounting was not something to be grafted onto manufacturing: Copley, p. 371.

203. It took the Civil War to bring about standardized sizes of clothing: Boorstin, *The Americans*, p. 98. For background on Marshall Field, see Mahoney and Sloane, *The Great Merchants*.

204. "This came about in a peculiar way": H. Hollerith to J. T. Wilson, August 7, 1919, Hollerith Papers.

204. "one large industrial enterprise": *Accounting by Electricity* (Washington, D.C.: Tabulating Machine Co., 1903), p. 27.

204. "For each invoice a carbon is made": *Ibid.*

205. "Our experimental work with your system . . . seems to warrant extension of same": C. E. Martin to H. Hollerith, February 17, 1906, Hollerith papers.

206. "The Tabulating Machine Co. does not . . . possess a panacea": *Accounting by Electricity*, p. 31.

206. "In what shape do we want to make such a contract": H. Hollerith to S. G. Metcalf, April 27, 1903, IBM Archives.

207. "on condition that all cards . . . are purchased from this company": The U.S. Supreme Court later ruled such tie-in sales illegal. However, it should be noted that in the early days, Hollerith's machines were often incapacitated when cards of inferior quality were used.

207. "We put the machine in at Woonsocket": H. Hollerith to S. G. Metcalf, April 30, 1903, IBM Archives.

207. "The price paid for the cards includes a free license": H. Hollerith to S. G. Metcalf, May 18, 1903, IBM Archives.

208. In placing orders with the Jones Dairy Farm: Interview with Charles Hollerith, January 26, 1969.

208. "I do not see how you can increase prices . . . to . . . old customers": H. Hollerith to T. J. Watson, June 14, 1917, IBM Archives.

208. "My idea of meeting this increased cost": *Ibid.*

209. "Regarding the general form of contract": H. Hollerith to S. G. Metcalf, June 30, 1903, IBM Archives.

209. "The record on the automatic sorter today": H. Hollerith to S. G. Metcalf, April 21, 1903, Hollerith Papers.

209. "The Paper came in a big ream: Interview with Joseph Langley, January 23, 1972.

209. "Mr. George Swift was here": H. Hollerith to S. G. Metcalf, June 21, 1903, IBM Archives.

210. "I cannot help being . . . amused": H. Hollerith to G. Swift, June 27, 1903, IBM Archives.

210. "Your unfortunate paragraph": H. Hollerith to S. G. Metcalf, June 27, 1903, IBM Archives.

210. "I always like to keep two paper mills 'on the string'": Memorandum of remarks by H. Hollerith to T. J. Watson, December 1, 1914, IBM Archives.

211. "Bill Barnes made boards for them:" Interview with J. Langley, January 23, 1972.

Chapter 16: Getting Started in Britain

212. Robert Percival Porter . . . possessed an extraordinary range of talents: Obituary, London *Times*, March 1, 1917; also *Dictionary of American Biography* 15: 100–1.

212. "that damned cowboy": The American Treasury, ed. Clifton Fadiman (New York: Harper & Brothers, 1955), p. 453.

212. Hollerith asked him to see if something could be started . . . in Great Britain: Greene, *The Beginnings*, p. 3.

213. In search of an office in London . . . he met . . . Ralegh B. Phillpotts: Greene, p. 3.

213. the officers instructed Metcalf "to prepare a . . . contract with Robert P. Porter": Minutes of the Tabulating Machine Co., February 18, 1902. A copy of the contract, dated February 24, is in the IBM Archives.

213. "My idea was that your knowledge": Greene, *The Beginnings*, p. 1.

214. "The first job was taking to pieces and reassembly": Greene, p. 5.

214. "All parts should go together without forcing": IBM engineering manual dated 1913, IBM Archives.

215. "In addition, there was need for studying the planning of system and cards": Greene, *The Beginnings*, p. 4.

215. "The [British] Tabulating Machine Company's staff": Greene, p. 4.

215. the company . . . "was of no great size": Greene, p. 3.

215. "It was arranged that I should go to the New York Central": Greene, p. 6.

215. "nothing was excluded from my attempts": Greene, p. 6.

216. "Gershom Smith . . . had the courage": Greene, p. 7.

216. "It was not unusual for machine operators to find": Greene, p. 17.

216. "the staff whistled the 'Dead March'": Greene, p. 17.

217.   remembering the fate of Hargreaves' spinning jenny: Smiles, *Self-Help*, p. 31.

217.   "The most important reason": Speech delivered by Privy Overstate Councilor Blenck of Prussia to Convention of the Polytechnical Society of Berlin, January 2, 1896, in *Polytechnical Central Paper* No. 11 (Berlin), March 16, 1896.

218.   "It was a big surprise": Greene, *The Beginnings*, p. 9.

218.   "Eventually, it was agreed with Dr. Hollerith": Greene, p. 9.

218.   "the reception at Sheffield was somewhat frigid": Greene, p. 9.

219.   After reading what he considered an unjust criticism of his system: Hollerith's rejoinder citing the critical remarks appears in *Journal of the Royal Statistical Society* 63, Part 1, p. 50.

Chapter 17: "My Row with North"

221.   Later, Edison entered the lists: Interview with Charles Hollerith, January 26, 1969.

221.   A descendant of Simeon North: S.N.D. North's background is from *Dictionary of American Biography* 13: 562–63.

222.   "North must go!" became a war cry: Interview with Charles Hollerith, January 26, 1969.

222.   "The Hollerith system . . . is far better adapted": W. R. Merriam to W. F. Willcox, August 9, 1900, based on a report by LeGrand Powers, chief statistician of the Agriculture Division, letter in U.S. Census Library.

223.   "Mr Hollerith . . . never has had any machine constructed": C. F. Pidgin to F. H. Wines, July 16, 1900, U.S. Census Library.

223.   "Mr. North wrote a letter": H. Hollerith to S. G. Metcalf, September 26, 1904, Hollerith Papers.

224.   "It is my intention . . . to transfer other important work to the Bureau": First Annual Report of the Secretary of Commerce and Labor, appearing as George B. Cortelyou, "Plans for Future Census Work," in "American Census Taking," *The Century Magazine*, April 1903.

224.   "Before we can deal . . . with crime and criminals": T. Roosevelt to S. N. D. North, November 5, 1906, Theodore Roosevelt Collection, Harvard University.

225.   "At the time I executed the contract of Nov. 27": S. N. D. North to W. R. Merriam, July 28, 1904, U.S. Census Library.

225.   "The permanent Census Office introduces entirely new factors": *Ibid.*

225.   "All that I desire to be satisfied of": *Ibid.*

226.   "a surprisingly large portion of the total cost"; *Brooklyn Eagle*, January 11, 1902.

227.   "unlike the majority of inventors, Mr. Hollerith had been richly compensated": S. N. D. North to Secretary of Commerce and Labor Metcalf, October 20, 1905, U.S. Census Library.

227.   "Large sums of money have also been paid the company by railroads and other corporations": *Ibid.*

227.   "I was much embarrassed": *Ibid.*

228.   "While there is considerable work pending": S. N. D. North to W. R. Merriam, July 28, 1904, U.S. Census Library.

228.   Merriam had been hired for a five-year term: Minutes of the Tabulating Machine Co., July 12, 1904, IBM Archives.

228.   "If I could have seen the condition of affairs": H. Hollerith to S. G. Metcalf, August 3, 1904, Hollerith Papers.

229.   "I have had a good deal of trouble with machines": *Ibid.*

229.   "I was indifferently asked to take a seat": H. Hollerith to S. G. Metcalf, August 11, 1904, Hollerith Papers.

229.   "Mr. Hollerith expressed his willingness": S. N. D. North to Secretary of Commerce and Labor Metcalf, October 20, 1904, U.S. Census Library.

230.   "It is important to know at once": S. N. D. North to W. R. Merriam, September 17, 1904, U.S. Census Library.

230.   "I have reached the conclusion that": *Ibid.*

230.   "I will submit such a contract": *Ibid.*

231.   "Governor Merriam informs me that the board . . . instructed him": H. Hollerith to S. G. Metcalf, September 20, 1904., Hollerith Papers.

231.   "We have automatic machines": *Ibid.*

232.   "Would it not be the best thing": H. Hollerith to S. G. Metcalf, September 22, 1904, Hollerith Papers.

232.   "Sometimes a man gets so fagged out": H. B. Thayer to H. Hollerith, September 23, 1904, Hollerith Papers.

234.   "Mr. Hollerith . . . was apparently seeking": S. N. D. North to Secretary of Commerce and Labor Metcalf, October 20, 1905, U.S. Census Library.

234.   he applied to Congress and . . . received a $40,000 appropriation: 33 Stat. 683; also, R. H. Holley, "Machine Tabulation in the Census Office: 1870–1912," unpublished ms., Census Records, National Archives.

234. "I now feel at liberty . . . to submit a draft": North's offer of a contract is cited by Hollerith in his letter of September 29, 1905, to the Census Director.

235. North said it was "because of failure to reach agreement as to the rental": Report of the Director of the Census for 1907–8, p. 20 (Washington D.C., GPO).

235. "The real reason was the reluctance of the Tabulating Machine Company": Newcomb, Churchill, and Frey to Senator R. LaFollette, April 1, 1909, Hollerith Papers. (The date the machines were withdrawn or removed was also the date the Congressional appropriation became available.)

235. ". . . the withdrawal of the Hollerith machines": S. N. D. North to Secretary of Commerce and Labor Metcalf, October 20, 1905, U.S. Census Library.

235. "You may be interested to know": H. Hollerith to G. F. Swain, July 18, 1905, Harvard University, Faculty Archives.

236. "The machines North has fired": H. Hollerith to G. F. Swain, July 22, 1905, Harvard University, Faculty Archives.

236. "Many thanks for your favor": H. Hollerith to unknown, May 9, 1905, Hollerith Papers.

Chapter 18: Commercial Success

238. "You never know what he will do": Interview with J. Langley, January 23, 1972.

238. "my invention is no longer a crude idea": H. Hollerith to A. Meyer, July 14, 1885, Hollerith Papers.

238. "Dr. Hollerith's Work-Shop": Affidavit of K. T. West, *Tabulating Machine Co.* v. *Durand*, February 24, 1910, National Records Center, Suitland, Maryland.

238. "After my row with North": H. Hollerith to J. T. Wilson, August 7, 1919, Hollerith Papers.

238. "I have been working . . . with the Pennsylvania": H. Hollerith to G. F. Swain, July 18, 1905, Harvard University, Faculty Archives.

239. . . . the Long Island Railroad started experimenting: Report of W. F. Warren, auditor of freight traffic, Pennsylvania Railroad, August 15, 1960, IBM Archives.

239. "They are using the machines": H. Hollerith to G. F. Swain, July 18, 1905, Harvard University, Faculty Archives.

239.　"We are experimenting . . . with the Hollerith . . . Machines: M. Riebenack to G. Smith, July 11, 1905; copy enclosed in H. Hollerith letter to Swain, July 18, 1905, Harvard University, Faculty Archives.

239.　"We are making a daily distribution of . . . labor": *Ibid.*

240.　"one customer brought another": H. Hollerith to J. T. Wilson, August 7, 1919, Hollerith Papers.

240.　"If I can interest the firm": P. Bontecou to H. Hollerith, December 23, 1906, Hollerith Papers.

240.　"In their case, they make quite a use of the cards for . . . inventory": H. Hollerith to P. Bontecou, November 4, 1907, Hollerith Papers.

240.　"Oh, he's strong for the system": Unclassified article, IBM Archives.

241.　"If the machines are any good": Interview with Charles Hollerith, January 26, 1969.

241.　"If you could get Mr. Tuttle . . . to write": H. Hollerith to G. F. Swain, July 27, 1905, Harvard University, Faculty Archives.

241.　"I had understood . . . that Pidgin was trying to get into railroad work": *Ibid.*

241.　"If you can . . . get some idea of what Pidgin is driving at": *Ibid.*

241.　"We are developing an entirely new line of tabulating machines": H. Hollerith to G. F. Swain, July 18, 1905, Harvard University, Faculty Archives.

242.　it employed Eugene Ford "as a mechanical engineer": Draft of employment agreement dated May 1905, IBM Archives.

242.　"within 40 miles of Uxbridge, Massachusetts": *Ibid.*

242.　"Regarding your stock": H. Hollerith to G. F. Swain, July 22, 1905, Harvard University, Faculty Archives.

244.　"until some experiments . . . should reach greater perfection": *New York Post*, June 9, 1902.

244.　"I was glad to receive the cut": G. F. Swain to H. Hollerith, June 2, 1905, Harvard University, Faculty Archives.

244.　"I would like to have you advise me": E. Young to H. Hollerith, September 8, 1906, IBM Archives.

245.　"Kindly allow me to postpone replying": H. Hollerith to E. Young, September 11, 1906, IBM Archives.

245.　"It is better to go ahead": H. Thayer to H. Hollerith, December 12, 1906, Western Electric Co. Archives.

245.　approved . . . ordering twenty-five automatic machines: Minutes of the Tabulating Machine Co., April 3, 1906, IBM Archives.

246. "I am glad to hear that the tabulating machine is coming out so satisfactorily": H. Thayer to H. Hollerith, May 24, 1907, Western Electric Co. Archives.

246. "I would like to go to Washington": H. Thayer to H. Hollerith, May 27, 1907, Western Electric Co. Archives.

246. "Do you know in what shape that . . . machine . . . matter is": H. J. Stirling to W. H. Anderson, June 19, 1907 (cited in Anderson's letter of reply, June 24, 1907), IBM Archives.

246. "Our preliminary tests satisfy us": H. Hollerith to H. J. Stirling, August 7, 1907, IBM Archives.

246. "I intend to put the new machines in use": H. Hollerith to G. F. Swain, August 6, 1907, Harvard University, Faculty Archives.

246. "Some two or three years ago, I started work on an improved machine": *Ibid.*

247. Each customer . . . would be asked to pay a standard fee: Minutes of the Tabulating Machine Co., July 3, 1907, IBM Archives.

248. "If we can build these machines in reasonable quantities": H. Hollerith to G. F. Swain, August 6, 1907, Harvard University, Faculty Archives.

248. "In regard to . . . sorting machines": H. Thayer to H. Hollerith, October 7, 1907, Western Electric Co. Archives.

248. the inventor promised "to make all necessary repairs": Contract draft for Union Pacific, August 1907, IBM Archives.

248. "The customer pays all the charges for transportation": H. Hollerith to G. F. Swain, August 6, 1907, Harvard University, Faculty Archives.

248. "Always make a customer know": Transcription of remarks made to T. J. Watson by H. Hollerith, December 1, 1914, IBM Archives.

249. "If it can be arranged to have repairs made . . . at Omaha": W. H. Anderson to H. J. Stirling, December 9, 1907, IBM Archives.

249. "Many . . . installations . . . Mr. Stoddard has supervised": *The Tabulator* (Tabulating Machine Co.), March 1916. p. 5, IBM Archives.

249. ". . . the customer buys all of his cards from us": H. Hollerith to G. F. Swain, August 6, 1907, Harvard University, Faculty Archives.

250. "I have an actual order from the Southern Railway": *Ibid.*

250. "I am also going to make a test": *Ibid.*

250. "I remember the old man getting a new machine": Interview with J. Langley. January 23, 1972.

250. "Around 1909, he bought two big Kidder presses": *Ibid.*

250. "I have urgent requests": H. Hollerith to G. F. Swain, August 6, 1907, Harvard University, Faculty Archives.

251. Perhaps untactfully, he informed the Southern Pacific's auditor: H. Hathaway to E. Young, August 28, 1907, IBM Archives.

251. "I found him quick, alert and . . . eager": *Ibid.*

251. ". . . everyone using the machine . . . is more than satisfied": *Ibid.*

251. ". . . better pleased with the machines than with Hollerith": *Ibid.*

251. "a good-size stock company ought to . . . manage it": *Ibid.*

252. "Hollerith will not listen": *Ibid.*

252. "We are up against a very nasty proposition": B. C. Moise to H. Hollerith, July 31, 1907; copy enclosed in H. Hollerith letter to G. F. Swain, August. 6, 1907, Harvard University, Faculty Archives.

252. ". . . for one Hand Tabulator, one Assorter": F. L. Hewitt to H. Hollerith, August 3, 1907; copy enclosed in Hollerith letter to Swain, August 6, 1907.

252. "We have met with unforeseen . . . delays": H. Hollerith to H. J. Stirling, July 21, 1908, IBM Archives.

253. "After hearing from you . . . I got . . . after the armatures": H. Thayer to H. Hollerith, August 11, 1908, Western Electric Co. Archives.

253. "From what he told me about his equipment": H. Thayer to H. Hollerith, March 29, 1907, Western Electric Co. Archives.

253. "There are a large number of orders awaiting to be filled": A. J. Stirling to E. Young, February 15, 1908, IBM Archives.

253. "It is true we are anxious to install a Hollerith machine": A. H. Bullard to P. Bontecou, May 7, 1908, IBM Archives.

254. "Referring to the General Electric Company": H. Hollerith to P. Bontecou, April 30, 1908, IBM Archives.

254. "In view of this extraordinary demand": H. Hollerith to G. F. Swain, August 6, 1907, Harvard University, Faculty Archives.

254. "So many good stocks and bonds": H. Thayer to H. Hollerith, August 16, 1907, Western Electric Co. Archives.

255. "We do not want any money immediately": *Ibid.*

255. "If you or Eaton . . . have money": *Ibid.*

255. the directors declared a 400 percent stock dividend: Minutes of the Tabulating Machine Co., January 16, 1908, IBM Archives.

256. "I closed a contract for . . . 90 tabulating machines": H. Hollerith to P. Bontecou, April 3, 1908, IBM Archives.

256. "not placing any machines as the new lot are not yet finished": H. Hollerith to P. Bontecou, June 10, 1908, IBM Archives.

256. "if the Southern Pacific . . . is any longer interested": H. Hollerith to W. H. Anderson, December 20, 1909, IBM Archives.

256. "My object in asking": *Ibid.*

257. "I started in to create this demand": H. Hollerith to G. F. Swain, August 6, 1907, Harvard University, Faculty Archives.

Chapter 19: An Unusual Competitor: the Government

258. a striking resemblance to . . . Charles Babbage: See Moseley, *Irascible Genius*, p. 16.

259. ". . . we looked out . . . and there come Teddy Roosevelt": Interview with J. Langley, January 23, 1972.

259. "Your repeated expressions concerning . . . social questions": H. Hollerith to T. Roosevelt, February 4, 1905; cited in H. Hollerith letter to T. Roosevelt, December 11, 1908, Hollerith Papers.

260. "No effort is being made by the . . . head of the Census": *Ibid.*

260. the Chief Executive was "greatly interested": W. Loeb, Jr., to H. Hollerith, February 9, 1905; cited in Holleriths' letter to Roosevelt, December 11, 1908, Hollerith Papers.

260. North . . . agreed that the two sets of figures must go together "to make them both complete": S. N. D. North to W. Loeb, Jr., enclosed in W. Loebs' letter to H. Hollerith. February 9, 1905, Hollerith Papers.

261. "I ask you to advise me as to . . . patents for tabulating apparatus": Memorandum to H. H. Allen from S. N. D. North, September 18, 1905, U.S. Census Library.

261. after January 8, the public would have the right to build . . . "the hand machine": Memorandum to S. N. D. North from H. H. Allen, September 26, 1905, U.S. Census Library.

261. "The way is already clear . . . along which new and improved mechanisms can be devised": S. N. D. North to Secretary of Commerce and Labor Metcalf, October 20, 1905, U.S. Census Library.

261. "he intended to advance the art . . . beyond Mr. Hollerith's mechanisms": *Ibid.* This sentence, crossed out, was probably deleted from the correspondence. But it probably reflects North's thinking at the time.

261. "One of [the Census Bureau's] first acts . . . was to secure the services of Charles W. Spicer": R. H. Holley, "Machine Tabulation in the Census Office: 1870–1912, unpublished ms. Census Records, National Archives, p. 29.

262.   "North's retaliation on me": H. Hollerith to G. F. Swain, January 30, 1906, Harvard University, Faculty Archives.

262.   ". . . a perfect outrage": *Ibid.* However, the Bureau of Standards under Dr. Stratton, established a tradition for computing lasting to the present day; see Goldstine, *The Computer from Pascal to von Neumann*, p. 55.

262.   "Protection of inventors is the settled policy": Printed reply to S. N. D. North, September 29, 1905, following withdrawal of Hollerith's systems from the Census; the words are probably those of Hollerith's attorney; Hollerith Papers.

263.   he wrote to Lucius N. Littauer . . . in an effort to choke off funds: Dated February 27, 1906, this letter was also printed for wider distribution; Hollerith Papers.

263.   Friends and associates were also asked to write: Hollerith circulated the draft of "an argument" written by A. B. Brown, a Washington attorney. A copy of the argument is attached to H. Hollerith's letter to G. F. Swain, February 26, 1905, Harvard University, Faculty Archives.

263.   in respect of the large commercial field: A copy of the Roebling letter is enclosed in the same letter to Swain.

263.   "I have known Mr. Hollerith for nearly 30 years": Untitled and undated letter draft found in Swain's correspondence with Hollerith; it is almost certainly the one he sent to Sullivan and possibly to others; Harvard University, Faculty Archives.

264.   "I voted for the item": J. Sullivan to G. F. Swain, March 17, 1906, found in Swain's correspondence with Hollerith, Harvard University, Faculty Archives.

264.   Hollerith . . . "has received from the Government": Testimony by S. N. D. North, quoted by Sullivan to Swain, *ibid.*

264.   "Meanwhile, the company has received . . . great sums": *Ibid.*

264.   The Census Office . . . "proposes . . . simpler, cheaper and more expeditious machines": *Washington Times*, March 28, 1906.

265.   "Assume . . . that I am a fool": H. Hollerith to G. F. Swain, March 21, 1906, Harvard University, Faculty Archives.

265.   "The best thing to do is to . . . forget that the Census Office ever existed": H. Hollerith to G. F. Swain, April 3, 1906, Harvard University, Faculty Archives.

265.   "If this represents all that has been accomplished by North": H. Thayer to H. Hollerith, March 29, 1906, Western Electric Co. Archives.

265.   Babbage spoke "as if he hated mankind in general": Moseley, *Irascible Genius*, p. 22.

266. "I . . . appreciate what you say about government work": G. F. Swain to H. Hollerith, November 17, 1909, Harvard University, Faculty Archives.

Chapter 20: Enter Mr. Powers

267. "I do not believe it is worthwhile . . . to lose any sleep": H. B. Thayer to H. Hollerith, March 29, 1906, Western Electric Co. Archives.

267. "it is one of the most complete shops": *Report of the Director of the Census to the Secretary of Commerce and Labor Concerning Operations of the Bureau for the Year 1907–8* (Washington, D.C.: GPO, 1908), p. 21.

268. "This indirect method of securing": R. H. Holley, "Machine Tabulation in the Census Office: 1870–1912," p. 40, unpublished manuscript, Census Records, National Archives.

268. ". . . not . . . much chance for advancement"; "I could no longer stand the methods and manner of Mr. Hollerith": Affidavits of Askel Hensen and Eugene LaBoiteaux, respectively, February 24, 1910, *Tabulating Machine Co.* v. *Durand*, National Records Center, Suitland, Maryland.

269. "The Cuban Census has . . . permitted a thorough testing": *Report of the Director of the Census . . . for 1907–8*, p. 20.

270. "I have for many years considered the future tabulating machine": H. Hollerith to S. G. Metcalf, January 4, 1899, Hollerith Papers.

271. the shop's mechanics shook hands with a new expert: Background on James Powers is principally from Census Bureau, Personnel Files, General Services Administration, National Personnel Records Center, St. Louis, Missouri.

272. "The aid of a man of Mr. Powers's remarkable inventive gifts": *Ibid.*

273. "The new machine is built on the plan of a typewriter": "Counting Our People by Machine," *Scientific American*, September 11, 1909, p. 176.

273. "In the old punching machine, a hole was punched": *Ibid.*

273. "The punch shown in my patent": H. Hollerith to S. G. Metcalf, January 27, 1914, Hollerith Papers.

274. he moved his experiments . . . to the laboratory of Francis H. Richards: Census Bureau, Personnel Files; also, unpublished Report of Richard Schallenberg to IBM, Summer 1969. IBM Archives.

274. "There can be no doubt . . . as to the possibility of punching twice as many cards": Memorandum to Director of the Census Bureau from R. L. Lafflin, February 25, 1909, U.S. Census Library.

274. "We have found that the Powers punch is capable of doing . . . three times the daily work": Memorandum to Mr. Earl from H. H. Allen, May 24, 1909, U.S. Census Library.

275.   "The new mechanisms . . . are novel in plan and design": *Report of the Director of the Census . . . for 1907–8,* p. 22.

275.   North also told of some progress "on various other machines": Testimony by Director of the Census to Senate Committee on the Census on H. R. 1033, 61st Congress, First Session.

275.   they . . . authorized the general manager . . . "to employ detectives": Minutes of the Tabulating Machine Co., December 2, 1907, IBM Archives.

275.   "in view of the uncertainty . . . it was decided to take no present action": Minutes of the Tabulating Machine Co., December 11, 1907, IBM Achives.

Chapter 21: The Growing Impasse

277.   Hollerith found strong and immediate . . . support: See *Arguments Before the Committee on Patents of the House of Representatives on H. R. 12368, 18884, 18885, to Revise and Amend the Statutes Relating to Patents, February 23–24, 1910* (Washington, D.C.: GPO, 1910), pp. 45–50. This contains earlier legislation as well as that finally passed in 1910.

277.   "The success of the Northern Securities case": Roosevelt, *Theodore Roosevelt, An Autobiography,* p. 470.

278.   "The United States Government issues patents": *Hearings on Statutes Related to Patents,* p. 50.

278.   "Every civilized government": *Ibid,* p. 50.

278.   Roosevelt failed to sign the measure: *Ibid.,* p. 46.

278.   "This is the investigation which Mr. North assured you": H. Hollerith to T. Roosevelt, December 11, 1908, Hollerith Papers.

279.   in a document that amounts virtually to a legal brief: H. Hollerith to T. Roosevelt, January 9, 1909, Hollerith Papers.

279.   Straus . . . essentially denied every charge: O. S. Straus to T. Roosevelt, January 30, 1909; copy transmitted by W. Loeb, Jr., to H. Hollerith, Hollerith Papers.

280.   Hollerith clipped dozens of copies of the article: Multiple copies of the article, undated and unidentified, are in the Hollerith Papers.

281.   "The letter which I wrote to President Roosevelt": H. T. Newcomb to H. Hollerith, November 26, 1921, Hollerith Papers.

285.   "There is a 'nigger in the woodpile'"; "it is charged that the Hollerith people have . . . been after North's scalp"; "Mr. Hollerith is a very clean upright gentleman": Excerpts from newspaper articles cited by

H. T. Newcomb in letter to R. L. O'Brien, May 6, 1909, Hollerith Papers.

285. "On the face of it the purpose of the director": R. L. O'Brien to H. T. Newcomb, May 8, 1909, Hollerith Papers.

285. "Strong efforts to keep him in office": *Washington Star*, May 26, 1909.

285. "North has a powerful backing in the Senate": *Washington Times*, May 26, 1909.

286. statements from the White House and the Census head: The statements and following quotes are from the *Washington Post*, May 27, 1909.

286. "I really feel that ninety percent of the clerks were sorry": *Washington Star*, June 1, 1909.

286. "Men may come and men may go": *Ibid.*

297. The menu for the formal dinner: From Hollerith's scrapbook, Hollerith Papers.

287. Roosevelt . . . was . . . "resting from the hunt": *Washington Star*, May 26, 1909.

287. "Mr. North's contention": *Washington Post*, May 27, 1909.

287. bids "shall be reasonable": *Washington Star*, May 26, 1909.

287. "If the bids do not come up to expectation": *Ibid.*

288. "I was supposed to be an economic and statistical expert": "Memoirs of Edward Dana Durand," unpublished manuscript, U.S. Census Library, p. 153.

288. ". . . He referred . . . to . . . Hollerith's inventions": A. L. Salt to H. T. Newcomb, October 16, 1909, Hollerith Papers.

288. a contract had already been awarded . . . to . . . Sloan & Chace: *Washington Star*, August 19, 1909.

289. "The Powers sorter is a mechanical sorter": Memorandum from H. H. Allen to Mr. Willoughby, September 25, 1909, U.S. Census Library.

289. "So far as I can discover . . . Mr. Hollerith was the first": *Ibid.*

289. "It might be well . . . to purchase . . . their best type of sorting machine": *Ibid.*

290. "the census experts are now at work on a tabulator": *New York American*, November 21, 1909.

290. The inventor was angered by another article: *Ibid.*

290. "The tabulating machine . . . is the result of the combined efforts of several experts": "Handling the Census Returns for the Whole United States," *American Machinist*, May 5, 1910, p. 811.

290.   "Mr. Powers has been allowed United States letters patent": *Ibid.*

291.   "one could infer that before the machines": Letter from Gershom Smith, Letters column, *American Machinist*, June 9, 1910.

291.   "Mr. Newcomb suggests": Memorandum Regarding Tabulating Machines from Director of the Census, November 6, 1909, U.S. Census Library. (This memorandum to the file was apparently written to make note of the Newcomb proposal.)

291.   "Each of these types of machines . . . needs a sorting apparatus": Memorandum from H. H. Allen to Mr. Willoughby, Sept. 25, 1909, U.S. Census Library.

292.   "We cannot believe . . . it is any less obnoxious": *Krupp* v. *Crozier, Washington Law Reporter*, 36: 640.

293.   Waterman found that the one machine had been "wholly rebuilt or reconstructed": Deposition of F. N. Waterman, *Tabulating Machine Co.* v. *Durand*, January 24, 1910. National Records Center, Suitland, Maryland.

293.   "it was necessary to dismantle and then reconstruct": *Ibid.*

293.   "the recognized leader of the patent bar": S. G. Metcalf to E. D. Durand, December 31, 1909, Hollerith Papers. Fish later became head of AT & T largely as a result of his skill in handling that company's patent matters; see Noble, *America by Design*, p. 9.

293.   "The altered apparatus . . . infringes many claims": F. P. Fish to S. G. Metcalf, December 30, 1909, Hollerith Papers.

293.   the opinion ". . . entirely confirms": S. G. Metcalf to E. D. Durand, December 31, 1909, Hollerith Papers.

294.   "The question now for the Tabulating Machine Company": H. Hollerith to S. G. Metcalf, January 10, 1910, Hollerith Papers.

294.   "Thayer will be unable to attend": S. G. Metcalf to G. M. Bond, January 11, 1910, Hollerith Papers.

294.   on January 14, 1910, the directors voted . . . to commence suit: Minutes of the Tabulating Machine Co., January 14, 1910, IBM Archives.

294.   "I beg to inform you that I have given instructions to resume experiments": E. D. Durand to S. G. Metcalf, January 13, 1910, Federal Records Center.

295.   the Bureau could not tabulate the population without electric tabulating machines: E. D. Durand to Attorney General of the United States, January 6, 1912, Federal Records Center; written at the request of the Attorney General following the termination of *Tabulating Machine Co.* v. *Durand* to state the possible advantages that Hollerith sorters would have provided.

Chapter 22: *Tabulating Machine Co.* v. *Durand*

296. "Court Restrains Census Director": *Washington Times*, January 24, 1910.

296. Hollerith's lawyers had gotten Justice Job Barnard . . . to issue a temporary restraining order: *Ibid.*

297. "President Taft Opens Trust-Busting Campaign": *Washington Herald*, January 25, 1910.

297. Hollerith's company repeated the already familiar technical arguments: Memorandum for Complainant, *Tabulating Machine Co.* v. *Durand.* Records of the case are at the Federal Records Center, Suitland, Md.

297. "The Company had made and leased a large number of sorting machines": Affidavit of H. Hollerith, January 24, 1910, *Tabulating Machine Co.* v. *Durand.*

297. ". . . unless this defendant be restrained": *Ibid.*

298. The original sorters . . . had been so crude and imperfect: Brief for Defendant, *Tabulating Machine Co.* v. *Durand.*

298. "one of the finest pieces of mechanism": L. Powers to H. Hollerith, October 27, 1908, Hollerith Papers.

298. the sorters had not really been necessary: Affidavit of L. Powers, February 25, 1910, *Tabulating Machine Co.* v. *Durand.*

298. He now called the machines "mechanically faulty": Affidavit of C. Spicer, February 25, 1910, *Tabulating Machine Co.* v. *Durand.*

298. "I saw baskets of cards . . . ruined in the sorting machines": Affidavit of E. A. Nelson, Jr., February 19, 1910, *Tabulating Machine Co.* v. *Durand.*

298. "They worked about as nearly perfect as was possible": Affidavit of V. Potter, March 4, 1910, *Tabulating Machine Co.* v. *Durand.*

298. ". . . no question as to the efficiency of the machines": Affidavit of H. Hollerith, March 4, 1910, *Tabulating Machine Co.* v. *Durand.*

299. "automatic electric sorters were also used to great advantage": *Ibid*; the booklet cited by Hollerith is "American Census Taking," Bureau of the Census, Washington, D.C. based on William R. Merriam, "The Evolution of Modern Census Taking," *The Century Magazine*, April 1903. The reference appears on p. 20 of the booklet.

299. ". . . at no time . . . was any report made to him": Affidavit of W. R. Merriam, March 4, 1910, *Tabulating Machine Co.* v. *Durand.*

299. "These machines . . . proved indispensable": Affidavit of W. T. McCullough, January 28, 1910, *Tabulating Machine Co.* v. *Durand.*

300.   "The changes that have been made . . . do not . . . destroy the identity of the machines": Opinion of Court, March 14, 1910, *Tabulating Machine Co.* v. *Durand*; also *Washington Star*, March 15, 1910.

300.   "Court Rules Durand May Alter Machines": *Washington Star*, March 15, 1910.

300.   The Census Machine Shop had already altered a second machine: Affidavit of O. Braitmeyer, March 3, 1910, *Tabulating Machine Co.* v. *Durand*.

300.   the higher court overturned its ruling: On April 15, Equity Court No. Two of the Supreme Court of the District of Columbia reversed the lower court's ruling. Its decision was based on *Krupp* v. *Crozier*, 32 Appeals D.C. 1. Because the government had appealed to the U.S. Supreme Court in the *Krupp* case, which rested on the same issues as *Tabulating Machine Co.* v. *Durand*, proceedings in the latter were suspended by agreement of counsel after the plaintiff had closed its *prima facie* proofs and defendant had examined two witnesses. From the plaintiff's motion to dismiss bill and discontinue cause without prejudice, filed May 23, 1912, *Tabulating Machine Co.* v. *Durand*.

300.   "A . . . census enumerator called at the White House": *Washington Times*, April 15, 1910.

300.   One source says that further hearings were held: R. H. Holley, "Machine Tabulation in the Census Office: 1870–1912." Unpublished manuscript, Census Records, National Archives, p. 37.

301.   the U.S. Supreme Court reversed the decision . . . in the *Krupp* case: *Crozier* v. *Krupp*, 224 U.S. 290.

301.   The legislation that he had . . . fought to push through Congress . . . had become the law of the land: U.S. Statute No. 6423, "An Act to provide for the additional protection for owners of patents of the U.S. and other purposes."

301.   Hollerith's remedy . . . was to sue . . . in the Court of Claims: In a letter to the U.S. Attorney General dated May 23, 1912, C. R. Wilson, U.S. Attorney for the District of Columbia, states, "an order was entered in this cause dismissing the bill of complaint and discontinuing the said case without prejudice to the plaintiff to proceed in the Court of Claims upon payment of the costs . . ." The case was ended on the granting of a plaintiff's motion to dismiss bill and discontinue cause without prejudice, filed May 23, 1912, by Tabulating Machine Co. attorney J. Nota McGill. An order for gratification of costs was satisfied on the same date. *Tabulating Machine Co.* v. *Durand*.

301.   "Court Upholds Durand": *Washington Herald*, May 24, 1912.

301.   The friendship of years . . . was shattered: *Washington Post*, May 23, 1912.

302. campaign . . . of "personal vituperation": The *Daily Telegraph* is quoted in the *Post* article, *ibid.*

302. "The case never came to trial": "Memoirs of Edward Dana Durand," unpublished manuscript, U.S. Census Library, p. 162.

302. "I sincerely hope that we will never . . . [go] into the Court of Claims": H. Hollerith to S. G. Metcalf, January 10, 1910, Hollerith Papers.

302. "In order that my opinion in this matter might be of record": *Ibid.*

302. His real objective . . . was to put the Census Director "in a position where he would be obliged to negotiate": *Ibid.*

303. "To take the census with the old hand machines": *Ibid.*

303. the new devices . . . fell down badly on the job: H. Parker Willis, "The Thirteenth Census," *The Journal of Political Economy* (University of Chicago Press) 21, no. 7, pp. 577–92.

303. the Powers mechanical sorter was only two-thirds as fast: Memorandum from H. H. Allen to Mr. Willoughby, September 25, 1909, U.S. Census Library.

304. "The Census Bureau . . . was the only large establishment": H. T. Newcomb, "The Development of Mechanical Methods of Statistical Tabulation in the U.S.," (Paper delivered to the Fifteenth International Congress on Hygiene and Demography, Washington, D.C. September 23–28, 1912).

304. "The complete data are not available": Willis, "The Thirteenth Census," p. 578.

304. "We are now so far on the road to the Fourteenth Census": Unidentified clipping from Hollerith Papers.

305. James Powers resigned from the Census: Bureau personnel records say that he resigned April 10, 1911, to be engaged by a newly organized company. General Services Administration, National Personnel Records Center, St. Louis, Missouri.

305. Powers had entered the employ of Sloan & Chace: Memorandum from O. Louis Cleven to Director of the Census, September 13, 1911, Census Bureau, Personnel Records.

Chapter 23: Hollerith Sells Out

306. he had been advised . . . to give up working: V. Hollerith, "Biographical Sketch," p. 77; Charles Hollerith described his father's visit to the heart specialist, January 26, 1969.

307. "I've wondered whether you've ever reflected on the peace of mind": H. B. Thayer to H. Hollerith, April 8, 1907, Hollerith Papers.

307.   the board turned down the offer: Minutes of the Tabulating Machine Co., December 2, 1907, IBM Archives.

307.   "Hollerith will not listen": M. H. Hathaway to Erastus Young, August 28, 1907, IBM Archives.

307.   The magnetic third force: Background on Flint is mainly from his autobiography, Flint, *Memories of an Active Life.*

308.   "A combination of labor is a trades union": *Ibid.*, p. 286.

308.   six business deals before breakfast: J. H. Bridge, "Charles Ranlett Flint," *Cosmopolitan*, September 1902, p. 539.

308.   Flint rounded up a fleet of vessels: Flint, *Memories of an Active Life*, pp. 88–101.

309.   "Flint and Company . . . sounds to me like Wall Street": R. L. Loesch to H. Hollerith, July 3, 1911, Hollerith Papers.

309.   ". . . a gentleman . . . [whose] business is putting together industrial consolidations": F. W. Roebling to H. Hollerith, January 13, 1911, Hollerith Papers.

309.   Roebling . . . proposed $750 a share: *Ibid.*

309.   "He knew the amount of our outstanding capital": A. E. Salt to H. Hollerith, January 13, 1911, Hollerith Papers.

309.   "Mr. McCullough . . . says they were greatly impressed": *Ibid.*

309.   "He would like to . . . [get] an option on your stock": *Ibid.*

310.   that "I receive for my stock the same amount": From copies of letter in Hollerith Papers. Hollerith set a minimum price of $400. He got $450 a share for himself and his stockholders.

310.   "Please accept my thanks for procuring me the same price": E. A. Ford to H. Hollerith, July 18, 1911, Hollerith Papers.

310.   "Few men would have been so honorable": G. F. Swain to H. Hollerith, July 1, 1911, Hollerith Papers.

311.   "We have been somewhat embarrassed": W. P. Rice to H. Hollerith, June 9, 1911, Hollerith Papers.

311.   "A subscription from you at once": *Ibid.*

311.   Hollerith received $1,210,500 for his 2,690 shares: From checkbook in Hollerith Papers. His records also show that he subscribed to $100,000 in stock in the new company; Hollerith Papers.

312.   Hollerith later assigned his interest in the subsidiary to his sons and daughters: Interview with Charles Hollerith, January 26, 1969.

312.   The new company . . . began to do business: A well-documented account of C-T-R's establishment is found in Engelbourg, "International

Business Machines: A Business History" (Ph. D. diss., Columbia University 1954); also Flint, *Memories of an Active Life*, pp. 312–13.

312. "It was neither horizontal nor vertical": Engelbourg, p. 59.

313. "only a seer or a madman": Belden and Belden, *The Lengthening Shadow*, p. 107.

313. rentals and sales . . . had averaged an increase of approximately 20 percent: *Commercial & Financial Chronicle*, New York, May 4, 1912.

313. "largely behind on the execution of its orders": Subscription Agreement, Computing-Tabulating-Recording Co., June 7, 1911, IBM Archives.

314. "If I were a stockholder": J. Peabody to H. Hollerith, July 7, 1911, Hollerith Papers.

314. "My only regret": G. Smith to H. Hollerith, July 17, 1911, Hollerith Papers.

314. "I never had such luck before": G. F. Swain to H. Hollerith, May 28, 1911, Hollerith Papers.

Chapter 24: A Life of Leisure

316. "like a factory": Blodgett, *Herman Hollerith*, p. 149.

316. attract the attention of the tax collector: *Washington Post*, July 20, 1968.

316. "not so much the architect's gee-gaws": *Ibid.*

317. whose taut nerves were unstrung by the slightest noise: Charles Babbage was similarly sensitive to noise, often doing battle with organ grinders; Mosely, *Irascible Genius*, p. 21.

317. Hollerith had the house demolished: Interview with Nan and Virginia Hollerith, September 12, 1973.

318. the boys . . . took a sledge hammer: Interview with Herman Hollerith, Jr., May 4, 1968.

319. "He is very much interested" [in livestock]: T. Talcott to H. Talcott, March 13, 1896.

320. "The butter on the market": H. Hollerith to unidentified friend, February 8, 1919, Hollerith Papers.

320. "I think she produced 36 pounds of butterfat": H. Hollerith to S. G. Metcalf, November 16, 1922, Hollerith Papers. Years before the county had electricity, Hollerith had a gas-powered generator installed so that his cows could be milked via electricity.

320. "He done a lot to help the local fishermen": Interview with Henry Owens, September 12, 1973.

321.   "He was always giving us things": Interview with Mrs. Vivian Hugins, September 12, 1973.

321.   "He would buy the Fords . . . then give them away: Interview with Marion Smith, September 12, 1973.

321.   "Why, you are": Interview with Nan and Virginia Hollerith, September 12, 1973.

322.   "I don't see how a boat could be fixed up any nicer": Interview with Alonzo Hugins, September 12, 1973.

Chapter 25: The Rise of IBM

323.   "Well, I sold the business": Interview with Joseph Langley. January 23, 1972.

323.   "Then he came over to me"; "I thought I was a millionaire": "We went on and on": *Ibid.*

324.   Hollerith stepped down as general manager: Minutes of the Tabulating Machine Co., October 24, 1911, IBM Archives. At the same meeting, H. B. Thayer resigned as a director.

324.   "we will probably not come in personel contact with you": D. G. Scott to H. Hollerith, undated, Hollerith Papers.

324.   "I would like to ask you if it is not possible . . . [to have] a mechanical man . . . at Hartford": Unidentified officer of Phoenix Mutual Life Insurance Co. to H. Hollerith, undated, Hollerith Papers.

324-25. His contract . . . as consulting engineer: The agreement, dated July 15, 1911, is reproduced in Minutes of the C-T-R Co. of the same date, IBM Archives.

325.   "The Individual shall not be subject": *Ibid.*

325.   A notable exception was . . . George W. Fairchild: For background, see Belden and Belden, *The Lengthening Shadow*, pp. 99–100; also George W. Fairchild obituary, *Business Machines*, (IBM Corp.), January 1925, A son, Sherman W. Fairchild, would serve as an IBM director for forty-four years.

328.   "to duplicate tools, dies . . . in use by Taft-Peirce": Minutes of the C-T-R Co., November 9, 1911, IBM Archives.

328.   "James O'Brien . . . came over from Woonsocket": Interview with Joseph Langley, January 23, 1972.

328.   "The International Time Recording Division was the clock business": *Ibid.*

329.   "In 1912, we were building 200 sorters for Hollerith": Interview with

F. S. Blackall, III, January 7, 1972; production figures were supplied from Taft-Peirce Co. Records.

329. the British Company would soon slide into default: It was declared in default on May 21, 1912; Minutes of the C-T-R Co., IBM Archives.

329. arrangements in Germany required attention: J. Connolly, *History of Computing in Europe* (IBM World Trade Corp., New York, 1967), p. 11; Minutes of the C-T-R Co. for April 11, 1910, indicate that R. N. Williams had been given authority "to contract with certain parties in Germany" before formation of the German company; IBM Archives.

330. Only after protracted negotiations . . . did the German company . . . renew its contract: Minutes of the Tabulating Machine Co. for May 21, 1912, report the contract calling for exclusive use of Hollerith machines, IBM Archives.

330. the directors awarded this potpourri of countries to . . . Charles Flint: Minutes of the Tabulating Machine Co., May 21, 1912, IBM Archives; for Flint and Berg activities in Europe, see Kelly, *The Wright Brothers*, pp. 194–96.

330. "should take the matter up with a Mr. Nolte": Minutes of the C-T-R Co., September 9, 1913, IBM Archives; for Nolte activities in South America, see Flint, *Memories of an Active Life*, p. 84.

330. "Mr. Hollerith had . . . completed certain improvements": Minutes of the C-T-R Co., December 9, 1913, IBM Archives.

331. hired a new man . . . Thomas John Watson: On April 20, 1914, a letter was read to the C-T-R board stating that Thomas J. Watson would be an excellent man to be connected with the company. He was hired as general manager the same day, effective May 1, 1914, at a salary of $25,000 a year plus an option of 1,220 shares of stock; Minutes of the C-T-R Co., April 20, 1914, IBM Archives. Background on Watson is mainly from Belden and Belden, *The Lengthening Shadow*.

333. Hollerith was already withdrawing from active involvement: He resigned from the C-T-R board on January 11, 1913; Minutes of the C-T-R Co., for date, IBM Archives.

333. "It was a great inconvenience": *Ibid.*

333. "hold this matter in abeyance": F. N. Kondolf to H. Hollerith, August 7, 1914, Hollerith Papers.

333. "I feel that having you as a director . . . is of great value": T. J. Watson to H. Hollerith, August 8, 1914, Hollerith Papers.

333. "Too many men . . . are out for orders": Transcription of remarks made by H. Hollerith to T. J. Watson, December 1, 1914, IBM Archives.

333. "Every order . . . that is discontinued": *Ibid.*

333.   "kick their heels": *Ibid.*

333.   "Kindly give me the language": H. Hollerith to S. G. Metcalf, December 4, 1914, Hollerith Papers.

333.   "I should say English": *Ibid.*, note written on bottom of letter apparently returned to Hollerith.

334.   "Without desiring to be pessimistic": G. Smith to T. J. Watson, June 4, 1914, IBM Archives.

335.   "to contain certain features of distinct advantage": Copy of letter from F. S. Cleveland, chairman of the President's Committee on Economy and Efficiency to the Secretary of the Treasury, sent to Hollerith by C. R. Flint, April 17, 1912, Hollerith Papers.

335.   "The individual . . . shall not be subject to the orders": Minutes of the C-T-R Co., July 15, 1911, IBM Archives.

335.   "The matter of . . . an experimental department": T. J. Watson to H. Hollerith, August 6, 1914, Hollerith Papers.

336.   "In taking up the proposition": *Ibid.*

336.   a new technique called automatic control: U.S. Patent No. 830,699.

337.   Watson rented a top-floor loft: Minutes of the Tabulating Machine Co., September 8, 1914, IBM Archives.

337.   "In support of the men": *The Tabulator* (Tabulating Machine Co.), December 1917, p. 3. IBM Archives.

337.   "The Lake machine . . . is . . . better": E. A. Ford to T. J. Watson, December 16, 1916, from copy in Hollerith papers.

337.   The machine . . . saved the company: Belden and Belden, *The Lengthening Shadow*, p. 114.

338.   Watson quickly granted licenses to Powers: Minutes of the Tabulating Machine Co., July 23, 1914, IBM Archives.

339.   "Although he had decided to sell out": interview with IBM executive who preferred to remain anonymous.

339-40.   "We would like . . . you [to] talk . . . with Messrs. Lake, Carroll, Knistrom": T. J. Watson to H. Hollerith, March 17, 1917, Hollerith Papers.

340.   "I would appreciate . . . your opinion regarding the experimental work": T. J. Watson to H. Hollerith, May 19, 1917, Hollerith Papers.

340.   "Mr. Carroll will be in a position to go to you": T. J. Watson to H. Hollerith, October 6, 1917, Hollerith Papers.

340.   "I outlined to Mr. Lake a machine": H. Hollerith to T. J. Watson, June 14, 1917, Hollerith Papers.

341. "The time has expired for filing appeals": T. J. Watson to H. Hollerith, April 23, 1919, Hollerith Papers.

341. "This description might have been considered exaggerated": T. J. Watson to H. Hollerith, September 21, 1917, Hollerith Papers. The clipping referred to is from the *New York Sun*, September 13, 1917.

341. "to the man who made it possible": *The Tabulator* (Tabulating Machine Co.), December 1916, p. 10, IBM Archives.

341. "Herman Hollerith is a man of honor": *Ibid.*

341. ". . . It occurs to me . . . if we could get together all of the clippings": T. J. Watson to H. Hollerith, February 7, 1918, Hollerith Papers.

342. "I notice that there were 13 words": H. Hollerith to T. J. Watson, December 28, 1917, IBM Archives.

342. "One day he rang for me"; Interview with D. Pickrell for IBM History of Technology, October 13, 1970, IBM Archives.

342. "It is no fun killing oneself": P. P. Merrill to H. Hollerith, July 5, 1918, Hollerith Papers.

342. "You will be interested to hear that I am now connected with George Goethals and Co": G. Smith to H. Hollerith, October 9, 1918, Hollerith Papers.

343. "I am entirely out of touch": H. Hollerith to G. Smith, December 5, 1918, Hollerith Papers.

343. "The government . . . has so increased its demands": *The Tabulator* (Tabulating Machine Co.), February 1918, IBM Archives.

343. "I am commencing to appreciate why there are not more flags": H. Hollerith to H. Gordon, July 1, 1918, Hollerith Papers.

344. "William called me into the laundry": H. Hollerith to P. P. Merrill, March 27, 1919, Hollerith Papers.

344. "There is only one point about my possible death": H. Hollerith to P. P. Merrill, October 18, 1919, Hollerith Papers.

344. "Now I often think when the patents expire": H. Hollerith to P. P. Merrill, August 4, 1919, Hollerith Papers.

344-45. "The future business . . . lies with . . . smaller concerns": *Ibid.*

345. "I am trying to arrange with Watson": H. Hollerith to G. Smith, February 4, 1919, Hollerith Papers.

345. "One night at dinner he made the remark": H. Hollerith to P. P. Merrill, December 8, 1919, Hollerith Papers.

345. "My father had some ideas on a new tabulator": Interview with Charles Hollerith, January 20, 1972.

345. "Watson did ask about you": H. Hollerith to S. G. Metcalf, December 14, 1921, Hollerith Papers.

345. "As you know, I started . . . formulating some ideas . . . regarding a tabulating machine": H. Hollerith to unidentified friend, September 14, 1922, Hollerith Papers.

346. "As yet . . . we have done practically nothing": V. Hollerith, "Biographical Sketch," p. 78. "My idea would be": *Ibid.*

346. "Going West . . . was the smartest thing": *Interview with Charles Hollerith,* January 26, 1979.

347. "I am afraid my letter . . . gave you the impression I was a dealer": *Ibid.*

347. "When I get codfish": H. Hollerith to S. G. Metcalf, April 11, 1926, Hollerith Papers.

347. "Mr. Porter was riding in a hired auto": H. Hollerith to H. T. Newcomb, December 13, 1921, Hollerith Papers.

347. On November 15, 1929, he became ill. . . . Two days later he died: H. Hollerith obituary, *Washington Post,* November 18, 1929; also Blodgett, Herman Hollerith, p. 161, and V. Hollerith, "Biographical Sketch," p. 78.

347. "Prince of Wales Now Knitting": *New York Times,* November 17, 1929.

348. "The real need for such an enumeration": *Washington Post,* November 17, 1929.

348. "Herman Hollerith, inventor of the electric tabulating machines": *Washington Post,* November 18, 1929.

348. to the "International Machine Corporation": *Washington Star,* November 18, 1929.

348. "Dr. Hollerith's invention . . . has lessened drudgery": *Business Machines* (IBM Corp.), November 29, 1929, p. 1, IBM Archives.

349. "this machine or the principle will be potent factors": H. Hollerith to L. Hollerith, August 24, 1895, Hollerith Papers.

Selected Bibliography

Document Collections

Research for this book was completed before the papers of Herman Hollerith were donated by his family to the Library of Congress, Washington, D.C. The papers, comprising some 10,000 items, are listed under the category GN and are available for use in the Manuscript Reading Room. The locations of other documents are:

Harvard University Archives, Harvard University Library, Cambridge, Mass.
IBM Archives, IBM Corporation, Armonk, N.Y.
National Records Center, Suitland, Md.
Taft-Peirce Records, The Taft-Peirce Manufacturing Co., Woonsocket, R.I.
Talcott Letters, V. Hollerith, Washington, D.C.
Theodore Roosevelt Collection, Harvard University, Cambridge, Mass.
U.S. Census Office Records, National Archives, Washington, D.C.
U.S. Census Bureau Library, U.S. Census Bureau, Suitland, Md.
Western Electric Co. Archives, Western Electric Co., New York, N.Y.

Other Sources

American Railway: Its Construction, Development, Management, and Appliances, The. A series of papers in *Scribner's* magazine, in 1888. Reprint. New York: Bramwell House, undated.

Bancroft, Frederic, ed. *Speeches, Correspondence, and Political Papers of Carl Schurz.* 6 vols. New York: Putnam, 1913.

Belden, Thomas G., and Belden, Marva R. *The Lengthening Shadow: The Life of Thomas J. Watson.* Boston: Little, Brown, 1962.

Bernstein, Jeremy. *The Analytical Engine: Computers—Past, Present, and Future.* New York: Random House, 1963.

Blodgett, John H. "Herman Hollerith: Data Processing Pioneer." Master's thesis, Drexell Institute of Technology, 1968.

Bond, George M., ed. *Standards of Length and Their Practical Application.* Hartford: Pratt & Whitney Co., 1887.

Boorstin, Daniel J. *The Americans: The Democratic Experience.* New York: Random House, 1973.

Brown, John Howard, ed. *Textile Industries of the United States.* Boston: James Lamb, 1911.

Bruce, Robert V. *Bell: Alexander Graham Bell and the Conquest of Solitude.* Boston: Little Brown, 1973.

City of Buffalo Illustrated: Commerce, Trades and Industries of Buffalo. Buffalo: Courier Printing Co., 1890.

Clarke, Arthur C. *Profiles of the Future.* New York: Harper & Row, 1962.

Connolly, James. *History of Computing in Europe.* New York: IBM World Trade Corp., 1967.

Copley, Frank B. *Frederick W. Taylor: Father of Scientific Management.* Norwood, Mass.: Plimpton Press, 1923.

Dictionary of American Biography. 20 vols. New York: Charles Scribner's Sons, 1928–1973.

Engelbourg, Saul. "International Business Machines: A Business History." Ph.D. diss., Columbia University, 1954.

Finch, James K. *History of the School of Engineering, Columbia University.* New York: Columbia University Press, 1954.

Flint, Charles R. *Memories of an Active Life: Men, and Ships, and Sealing Wax.* New York: Putnam, 1923.

Garrison, Fielding H. *John Shaw Billings: A Memoir.* New York: Putnam, and London: The Knickerbocker Press, 1915.

Goldstine, Herman H. *The Computer from Pascal to von Neumann.* Princeton, N.J.: Princeton University Press, 1972.

Greene, C. A. Everard. *The Beginnings: Reminiscences of C. A. Everard Greene,* London: The British Tabulating Machine Co., 1936.

Holbrook, Stewart H. *The Story of American Railroads.* New York: Crown, 1947.

Josephson, Matthew. *Edison.* New York: McGraw-Hill, 1959.

Kelly, Fred C. *The Wright Brothers.* New York: Harcourt, 1943.

Lerner, Max. *America as a Civilization: Life and Thought in the United States Today.* New York: Simon & Schuster, 1957.

Lord, Walter. *The Good Years: From 1900 to the First World War.* New York: Harper, 1960.

Love, Albert G.; Hamilton, Eugene L.; and Hellman, Ida L. *Tabulating Equipment and Army Medical Statistics.* Washington, D.C.: Office of the Surgeon General, Department of the Army, 1958.

Lydenberg, Harry Miller. *John Shaw Billings.* Chicago: American Library Association, 1924.

Mahoney, Tom, and Sloane, Leonard. *The Great Merchants.* New York: Harper & Row, 1966.

Martin, T. C., and Coles, S. L. *The Story of Electricity.* New York: The Story of Electricity Co., 1919.

Massie, Robert K. *Nicholas and Alexandra.* Pap. ed. New York: Dell, 1969.

Mazlish, Bruce, ed. *The Railroad and the Space Program: An Exploration in Historical Analogy.* Cambridge, Mass.: M.I.T. Press, 1965.

McCullough, David. *The Great Bridge.* New York: Simon & Schuster, 1972.

Moody, John. *The Railroad Builders.* New York: U.S. Publishers Co., 1919.

Moore, James P. *A Life of Francis Amasa Walker.* New York: Holt, 1923.

Morison, Elting E. *From Know-How to Nowhere: The Development of American Technology.* New York: Basic Books, 1974.

—— *Men, Machines, and Modern Times.* Cambridge, Mass.: M.I.T. Press, 1966.

Moseley, Mabeth. *Irascible Genius: A Life of Charles Babbage, Inventor.* London: Hutchinson, 1964.

Nevins, Allan. *Grover Cleveland: A Study in Courage.* New York: Dodd, Mead, 1932.

Noble, David F. *America by Design: Science, Technology, and the Rise of Corporate Capitalism.* New York: Knopf, 1977.

O'Conner, Richard. *The German-Americans.* Boston: Little, Brown, 1968.

Paine, Albert B. *Theodore N. Vail: A Biography.* New York: Harper, 1921.

Rae, John B. *The American Automobile: A Brief History.* Chicago: University of Chicago Press, 1965.

Roosevelt, Theodore. *Theodore Roosevelt: An Autobiography.* New York: Macmillan, 1913.

Rule, James B. *Private Lives and Public Surveillance: Social Control in the Computer Age.* London: Allen Lance, 1973.

Schurz, Carl. *The Autobiography of Carl Schurz.* Edited by Wayne Andrews. Abridged (1 vol.). New York: Scribner, 1961.

Smiles, Samuel. *Lives of Boulton and Watt.* Philadelphia: Lippincott, 1865.

—— *Self-Help: With Illustrations of Character and Conduct.* London: John Murray, 1862.

Sobel, Robert. *The Entrepreneurs: Explorations Within the American Business Tradition.* New York: Weybright & Talley, 1974.

Sorenson, Charles E. *My Forty Years With Ford.* New York: Norton, 1950.

Truesdell, Leon E. *The Development of Punched Card Tabulation in the Bureau of the Census, 1890–1940.* Washington, D.C.: GPO, 1965.

Watson, Thomas A. *Exploring Life: The Autobiography of Thomas A. Watson.* New York: Appleton, 1926.

Index